MAKING AN AFRICAN CITY

MAKING AN AFRICAN CITY

Technopolitics and the
Infrastructure of Everyday
Life in Colonial Accra

JENNIFER HART

INDIANA UNIVERSITY PRESS

This book is a publication of

Indiana University Press
Office of Scholarly Publishing
Herman B Wells Library 350
1320 East 10th Street
Bloomington, Indiana 47405 USA

iupress.org

© 2024 by Jennifer Hart

All rights reserved
No part of this book may be reproduced or utilized in any form or by any means, electronic or mechanical, including photocopying and recording, or by any information storage and retrieval system, without permission in writing from the publisher. The paper used in this publication meets the minimum requirements of the American National Standard for Information Sciences—Permanence of Paper for Printed Library Materials, ANSI Z39.48-1992.

Manufactured in the United States of America

First Printing 2024

Cataloging information is available from the Library of Congress.

978-0-253-06932-0 (hdbk.)
978-0-253-06933-7 (pbk.)
978-0-253-06934-4 (web PDF)

CONTENTS

Acknowledgments vii

Introduction 1
1. "Fruity" Smells, City Streets, and the Politics of Sanitation 32
2. "Health is the First Wealth" 70
3. African Trade and Expatriate Enterprise in the Colonial City 112
4. Of Pirate Drivers and Honking Horns 148
5. Building Homes in the "New Accra" 176

Conclusion 217

Notes 235

Bibliography 279

Index 291

ACKNOWLEDGMENTS

THIS BOOK WAS INITIALLY IMAGINED very differently. But, like much else over the last several years, plans changed. There were pragmatic realities—the inability to travel due to the quarantine and ongoing health risks that interrupted research, the challenges of my own health and the shifting burdens of work and care that forced a rebalancing of priorities—but there were also changing intellectual commitments. I began writing this book in the midst of the Black Lives Matter protests, which took place every day for weeks just blocks from our house in Detroit, and I am finishing it in the midst of turmoil within two different related professional associations over what our responsibilities should be as historians and as (particularly white) scholars of Africa. This book is, in many ways, both a conscious and unconscious response to these events. My own position on these issues is not a secret and would probably come as no surprise to people reading this book. I came to history out of a curiosity about the *why* behind the *way* of things, and I believe strongly that history can be a powerful tool to inform present debates and craft more just futures. Understanding the historical roots of our assumptions and using the historian's tools and skills to lay bare the production of systemic inequality and structural violence is, I believe, not only possible through historical research but also responsible. Being honest about some of the more craven motivations of historical actors—even as we acknowledge their complexity and resist the temptation to reduce people to either villains or heroes—can be a radical act, but it doesn't have to be. It might have radical implications all the same.

In this book, I seek to responsibly deploy historical methodologies, to ask different kinds of questions through the embrace of what I often refer to as "rigorous interdisciplinarity," and to take seriously what people said and did on their own terms. In doing so, however, I think we come to some conclusions with potentially significant consequences for the way we do our work and the way we live. But rather than being intimidating or negative, I see this as an opportunity, particularly now, to translate historical research for new audiences of practitioners and policymakers who could meaningfully disrupt patterns of inequality and violence and imagine new alternatives. It is also an opportunity to stand with communities as they fight for access and opportunity and to transform the ways we teach in order to empower our students to ask questions rather than make assumptions about the world they live in.

I am in this place at this time because of many people. My grandparents taught me to always respect the dignity of others. I learned from amazing and committed scholars at Denison University who challenged me and gave me the tools to look at the world in new, interdisciplinary ways; to never be content with received wisdom; and to think more carefully about what it means to "do good" and "be good." At Indiana University I witnessed John Hanson's excellent example of what it means to be a principled scholar and administrator and was fortunate to learn alongside colleagues who also embraced those lessons and who continue to inspire me. At Goshen College I worked with colleagues and students who showed me what it could mean to be active scholars in and for the world, not just of it. At Wayne State I met a number of scholars (faculty, staff, and students) who sought to use their knowledge, skill, and privilege in service of the communities around them as part of movements that sought equity and justice. In Detroit I learned from extraordinary community organizers, entrepreneurs, practitioners, and social movement leaders who understood that passion for and connection to their community was a strength rather than a liability in achieving transformational change; they were never afraid to challenge the status quo and understood that the world's problems (and possible solutions to these problems) were complicated. They showed me what hard work looked like and generously embraced opportunities for collaboration. In Accra, I was inspired by the many entrepreneurs, activists, artists, educators, and creatives who are imagining an alternative world for themselves and their communities, and for my friends in the La Drivers Union who continue to remind people of the history, dignity, and creativity of this kind of work. And in the broader scholarly community, a huge network of dedicated teachers and scholars across a wide range of fields showed me what it meant to be an ethical, engaged, compassionate, and responsible teacher-scholar. I am particularly grateful to my friend T. J. Tallie who always challenges me to be better in every way and who has taught me so much about what it means to stand up and stand out (but also, sometimes, stand back or stand aside).

In many ways, this book has grown out of the work I did in *Ghana on the Go*. That book—and the work of other scholars in the rapidly growing fields of African technology studies, infrastructure studies, and mobility studies—created opportunities I could never have imagined and put me in conversation with a dynamic group of scholars around the world—but particularly on the continent. I am constantly inspired by the work of young researchers in Ghana, Nigeria, Tanzania, South Africa, and elsewhere who are transforming their fields, and I look forward to following their lead. I am grateful to my colleagues at the *Journal of Transport History*, and to colleagues like Baz Lecocq, Dmitri van den Berselaar, Samuel Ntewusu, Andreas Greiner, Njogu Morgan, and Ruth Oldenziel who have organized workshops that brought together these diverse groups of scholars in new ways. I am honored that you invited me to join you in that work. It has been extremely gratifying to see this field grow and challenge long-held scholarly assumptions about the role of technology, infrastructure, and mobility in the world. Josh Grace has long been my intellectual partner-in-crime. We'll probably never be done talking about cars. I have learned so much being in conversation with him and am grateful for the warm welcome and friendship that he, Bre, Si, and Benny always provide.

Making an African City, however, stands on its own and has been profoundly influenced by the work of our interdisciplinary, internationally collaborative research group on DIY Urbanism in African Cities. Steve Marr and I met many, many years ago on a small panel at the ASA where he presented an extraordinary paper on Detroit and Lagos, and we struck up a collaboration that has grown in totally unexpected ways. Thanks to support from STINT and FORMAS, our research group has run workshops in Sweden, Nigeria, and Malawi that brought together highly diverse groups of scholars, community members, practitioners, and policymakers to think about what we learn when we place the actions and innovations of communities labeled as "informal" at the center of policy debates and development plans. Those conversations and the opportunity to work with students in Malawi, Ghana, and Detroit have been hugely influential on my thinking in this book, and I am grateful for everyone in these workshops who have been willing to think through this work with us. I am also grateful to Patience Mususa, Jonathan Makuwire, Martin Murray, Christina Rodrigues, Marwa Dabieh, and other members of the group for taking the lead in making these events possible.

In the pre-pandemic times, Laura Fair, Nate Plageman, Caleb Owen, Josh Grace, and Waseem Bin-Kasim agreed to stir up some good trouble with me at the Urban History Association Conference. Ellen Bassett graciously created a forum in which to think about the book's arguments about urban planning and infrastructure at the University of Virginia along with Josh Grace and Brad Weiss. Dmitri van den Berselaar, Baz Lecocq, and Andreas Eckert welcomed me to Berlin to present at re:Work even though my connection to labor history was increasingly tenuous. Numerous invited talks at SOAS, Indiana University, University of Witwatersrand's African Center for the Study of the United States, University of Basel, University of Leipzig, University of Michigan, University of Bremen, and Yale University have helped me crystallize the arguments of this book in important ways. Deborah Pellow invited me to contribute to a new *Africa and Urban Anthropology* volume that gave me an opportunity to think about the broader story I was trying to tell in this book and what it meant to do an ethnography of the colonial state as a historian. Steve Marr and Patience Mususa invited me to give a talk and edited a special issue of *Urban Forum* and a book on DIY Urbanism in Africa that helped me think about sanitation. Lauren Morris Maclean gave me an opportunity to think about how the pandemic had changed this work. Tony Yeboah and Nate Plageman helped me write about these issues for public audiences in the midst of the pandemic. Victoria Okoye and Joseph Frimpong helped me think about doing work "in conversation" and push the boundaries of what traditional journal publishing looks like. Carly Goodman invited me to think about the implications of this in light of the real and ongoing challenges of the pandemic in a very public way. Juliet Sakyi-Ansah invited me to participate in her extraordinary TAP Narratives project and do an Instagram takeover that expanded the audience of this work to engage with practitioners in new ways. Norman Aselmeyer and Avner Ofrath convened a fantastic conference on urban conflict and space in Bremen. Kim Yi Dionne and Enoch Osei Koduah invited me to participate in podcast conversations. Steve Marr and I worked with Carl Nightingale to convene a "Dream Conversation," jointly hosted by our African Urban Dynamics Collaborative Research Group (AEGIS) and the Global Urban History Project, about urban theory from the Global South, and I continue to be inspired by the work presented by participants Prince Guma, Anwesha Ghosh, Wangui Kimari, Rafael Soares Gonçalves, and Abdou Maliq Simone. Michelle Moyd and Ebony Coletu were virtual writing group partners who helped me over the crucial hurdle of the first chapter. Gabrielle Hecht, Bianca Murillo, T. J. Tallie, and Richard Rathbone read sections of the book toward the end and provided encouragement and advice. All of these opportunities to think and write and receive feedback (and many other conference presentations) helped me along the journey to this final product.

This book brings together much of this work over the last six years. A portion of chapter 1 was published in a special issue on climate change adaptability in *Urban Forum*, edited by Steve Marr and Patience Mususa. Small sections of chapter 3 were published in the edited volume *Africa and Urban Anthropology*, edited by Deborah Pellow and Suzanne Scheld. A version of chapter 4 was published in a special issue of *Technology and Culture*, edited by Laura Ann Twagira. A portion of the conclusion will be published in the edited volume *DIY Urbanism in Africa:*

Politics and Practice, edited by Steve Marr and Patience Mususa. I am grateful for the opportunity to revise and re-present them here as part of the whole they were always intended to be. I am also endlessly grateful for the kind and supportive reports from two anonymous readers who so enthusiastically endorsed this project and clearly saw what it was trying to do.

This book has also been inextricably bound up with the development of the *Accra Wala* digital humanities project (www.accrawala.com), and I am grateful to Kwabena Agyare at the Nubuke Foundation, Ato Annan and colleagues at the Foundation of Contemporary Arts Ghana, Will Senyo at the Impact Hub Accra, Joey Chase of Accra We Dey, and colleagues at the Meltwater Entrepreneurial School of Technology for creating space for conversations about the issues that connect these two projects. I'm incredibly grateful to Adam Perkins for his work on this project. I also appreciate the archival staff at the National Archives of Ghana and the Photographic Archive at Information Services in Accra and the Public Records Office in London for their warm welcome, and I am grateful to Yijie Zou for helping arrange permissions for many of the photographs used in this book. I continue to mourn the loss of my friend Nana Osei Kwadwo, and I hope that I can realize some of the visions we had to creatively engage the public with information about the past.

I am always grateful for the support of friends like T. J. Tallie, Jill Kelly, Emily Burrill, Liz McMahon, Nate Plageman, Jeff Ahlman, Bianca Murillo, Jeanne Marie-Awotwi, Victoria Smith-Madjoub, Joseph Frimpong, Victoria Okoye, Jackie Mougoue, Steve Feld, Martin Murray, Laura Fair, Timothy Burke, Misty Bastian, Naaborko Sackeyfio, Ebony Coletu, Lacy Ferrell, Alice Wiemers, Jonathan Roberts, Jonathan Reynolds, Trevor Getz, Wendy Urban-Mead, Saheed Aderinto, Beth Buggenhagen, Girish Daswani, Corrie Decker, Steven Fabian, Tony Yeboah, Ablie Yabang, Brad Weiss, John Aerni-Flessner, Miles Larmer, Julie Cummiskey, James Yeku, Kuukuwa Manful, Elizabeth Perrill, Tavy Aherne, Alex Lichtenstein, Laura Ann Twagira, Michael Stasik, Dagna Rams, and many, many others who have encouraged and supported me over the last six years and connected me to a broader community at a time when I often felt particularly isolated. I continue to be inspired by Garth Myers, and I'm grateful for his work and his generosity. John Parker's *Making the Town* inspired this book in so many ways, and, when I first met John as I was embarking on dissertation research many years ago, he generously encouraged me to explore these issues. He's been a kind and supportive colleague in the years since then, and his comments and critiques have made many parts of this book better. Richard Rathbone is a dear friend and a wise (despite his own protestations) mentor who has always generously offered both a kind word and counsel when I needed it most. I am a better person and a better scholar for knowing him.

At the height of writing this book, I had the honor to serve as the leadership director for WSU's Young African Leaders Institute. In the process, I got to know twenty-six extraordinary fellows from across the African continent: Ahmad Abdulsamad, Frieda Abilba, Alaa Abusufian Dafallah, Beza Aseffa, Collins Chepkwony, Daniel Demissie, Dinga-Nyoh Mbekuveh, Josian Darwatoye, Anyse Essoh, Florence Fundi, Innocent Grant, Nozuko Hlwatika, Ange Iliza, Onyekachi Kanu, Hend Kheiralla, Joel Kouadio, Stan Maphosa, Selvana Mootien, Muchinga Mutambo, Aphiwe Nkosimbini, Chidiogo Odunukwe, Mildred Okwako, Sophy Phohleli, Fanta Secka, and Cedric Bationo. They helped me think a great deal more about the implications of this book beyond the academic realm and challenged me to join them in advocating for systemic change and thinking carefully about both the value and limits of technocracy. They were also incredibly inspiring and became dear friends. Supporting them on their leadership journeys also, selfishly, helped me rediscover myself. I'm so grateful for them. Lia Paradis created a Historians' Happy Hour Zoom during the pandemic, which was often my only social outlet during the long quarantine period, and through whom I have met so many lovely friends, including Brian Crim, Susie Steinbach, Jennifer McNabb, Marjorie Levine-Clark, Gary Darden, and Phil Harling. They all helped keep me sane through the long quarantine and continue to be a support system in person. I also gained new friends through HERS who continue to inspire me to advocate for myself and work to make a better future.

Outside of work, Jacob Krause, Steven Davis, David Fluck, Charles Miller, Jeremy David Tarrant, Sam Schaefer, Norm Weber, Katie Else, Mike Shalast, Adam Geffen, Phil Jessel, Elaine Belz, Paula Styer, Jim and Chris Hooker, Nicole Keller, and Scott and Tina Hunter have provided a rich network of friendship and fun over more than a decade. They make Detroit feel like home. Sylvan Geffen supported the writing of the chapter on sanitation with his potty-training insights about the way that poop and toilets and sewer systems work. I was particularly challenged by his question about "real" versus "imaginary" toilets—it was far more apt than he anticipated. I can trust David and Charles to always have my back and cheer me on. Jacob is my adventure friend—sometimes you need to take a writing break to shop the four-hundred-mile yard sale—but he also sees exactly how hard I work and reminds me to be proud of myself. Katie connected me to some great people and was always game to help imagine and achieve structural change. Scott and Tina always see the best in me and helped me remember home. When I was in graduate school, Sita Ranchod Nilsson told me to keep singing because I needed to have an outlet and an identity outside of work. She was so right. Singing in the choirs of the Cathedral Church of St. Paul has been one of the most important and meaningful experiences of my life. I love being able to watch kids grow up through music and to be part of a kind of beauty that can be life-changing. And I love the family I've gained in the process. I appreciate Ashley Flintoff for helping me explore pottery as a new outlet and opportunity for growth, and I love that Ashley, Tim Flintoff, and Sarah Brownlee are always up for a good meal and some time on the water. I am grateful to Cathy Barrette, Elaine Carey, Laurie Lauzon Clabo, Annmarie Caño, Kate McConnell, Meg Mulroney, Bridget Trogden, Sara Kacin, Tonya Whitehead, Fareed Shalhout, Jeff Potoff, Christine Jackson, Loraleigh Keashly, and Jeff Stoltman for their mentorship, friendship, support, and encouragement.

My parents always encourage me, even if they don't always understand me. They also provided a place to escape in the middle of the pandemic where we could breathe and spend time outside, and they came to save our basement so that I could get back to work. I appreciate that they brag about me, even if I act like it's embarrassing. Lucy and Ella—my beagles—are probably better known and more widely beloved than I am. They are sometimes annoying and inconvenient but also often sweet. They might not read or speak or even know what's happening most of the time (because they're normally sleeping), but they have provided the best kind of distraction in the process of writing this.

The period during which I wrote and edited this book was, without exaggeration, the most difficult of my life. The pandemic certainly didn't help, but it was so much more than that. Being on the other side of it now puts in sharp relief all the people who believed in me, supported me while I struggled, helped me celebrate small wins, and kept telling me I could do it. I look forward to my own new chapter at Virginia Tech with colleagues who have already been so supportive of this project and my broader body of work.

MAKING AN AFRICAN CITY

INTRODUCTION

A FIRE BROKE OUT ON MARCH 31, 1894, in Accra. Burning through the night and into the following day, a large section of the town's oldest and most heavily populated quarters was destroyed, and several lives were lost. George Robinson, the marquess of Ripon and secretary of state for the colonies, wrote from Downing Street noting "the ready and valuable assistance given by the various public officers mentioned, by the Police, the Hausas, the Volunteer, and the other sections of the Community."[1] While Ripon expressed "special admiration" for Mr. Stuart, the assistant inspector of the Civil Police, he also recognized that the Native Police Sergeant who saved Mr. Stuart and the Hausa Regimental Sergeant Major who were involved in relief efforts "deserve great praise."[2] The diverse community in the new colonial capital came together, it seemed, to ward off further disaster at mutual risk. And yet, in dealing with "the settlement of the various questions arising in connection with the fire," British officials saw an opening to rebuild the city according to new logics.

In October of that same year the Legislative Council of the Gold Coast passed an ordinance "to provide for the establishment of Town Councils in the towns of the Colony."[3] Popularly known as the "Town Councils Ordinance," these new rules called for the establishment of town councils with equal numbers of "official" (appointed) and "unofficial" (elected) members. As the colonial capital, Accra was an early adopter of the town council model. Appraisers assessed the annual value of houses in the town and created a series of rates (or taxes) that property owners would pay to support the work of the Council. Those same ratepayers voted in elections to determine who would represent the interests of their quarter on the Council.

While in theory these actions gestured toward the advancement of mutual self-interest and democratic principles, in practice the interventions of 1894 marked the beginning of a new phase of colonial urban governance in Accra, defined by the power of regulation, the interests of capital, and modernist conceptions of order. In physically altering and remaking the built space of the city—not at its margins but at its core—British officials saw the possibility and power of planning and regulation firsthand. Empowered by the new Town Councils Ordinance, the expanding regulations that governed urban life in Accra reshaped the organization of space and the social, cultural, political, and economic practices of daily life for residents.

In many ways, these actions—and the values and goals underpinning them—were not new. British colonial officials had attempted to assert control over spatial order and governance in Accra before 1894, and the implementation of these new plans was far from smooth or self-evident. Officials were unable to translate their rebuilding efforts beyond the fire-damaged areas, and local residents vehemently protested the imposition of new taxes. To some degree the failures and inconsistencies of colonial strategy were a reflection of the underlying contradictions of the colonial project itself. But importantly that resistance was also part of a much longer and more complex history of interaction between Indigenous Ga people and the various "strangers" who had come to settle and trade in their midst over the course of several centuries. Accra, as John Parker argues, was a Ga town long before it became a colonial capital.[4] Even as the economic and political power of the Ga waned in the late nineteenth century, the political, economic, social, and cultural patterns of urban settlement and urban life in Accra proved difficult to alter. But even if colonial officials were unable to radically remake the city, the regulatory power of new institutions like the Accra Town Council (ATC) and the technocratic and bureaucratic offices of new urban governance did fundamentally shift the power dynamics of the town. New colonial order was inscribed not necessarily in the physical organization or form of the city but rather in the systems, infrastructures, and practices of everyday life—from sanitation and health to trade, mobility, and housing.

This book traces the history of that regulatory expansion and technopolitical contestation in Accra from the early years of colonial consolidation: the late nineteenth century through the beginnings of independence in the 1950s and 1960s. Far from mere words on paper, technocratic rules and regulations—backed by the power of the police and the judicial system—defined the boundaries of colonial order that had real consequences for the daily lives of city residents.[5] In defining a wide range of perceived "nuisances" as illegal acts and setting out new parameters for acceptable urban living, members of the ATC, and the technocrats and bureaucrats who alternately reinforced and supported their work, sought to enshrine a new order on the growing city. "Order" certainly meant physical planning, as officials struggled to build infrastructure and housing in ways that would serve the needs of a rapidly expanding population. But "order" also implied a new way of living, defined by emerging technocratic fields like engineering, public health, social work, and development inspired by new advances in science and technology. In using regulation and infrastructural development to implement and enforce these new expectations of urban life, ATC members and employees fundamentally reshaped the town, marginalizing long-standing African practices by marking them as "illegal" and targeting development and investment in sectors that aligned with the interests of (often white) expatriate capital. The history of technology and regulation, in other words, is a history of informalization, reinforced by the power of the colonial state and the theories and practices of emerging technocratic fields. But the form and function of this technocratic colonialism was rarely straightforward. Diverse constituencies debated what urban life should look like in Accra. "Official" British representatives sought to balance local demands with policy prescriptives from London. Technocrats sought to reconcile the certainty of formula and theory with on-the-ground realities. African elected representatives sought to balance their own aspirations with the needs and demands of their constituencies. Accra citizens sought to embrace technological advancement and economic opportunity while protecting their own social, cultural, and economic autonomy. These contestations and negotiations constituted a form of "making" that shaped the foundation for a new kind of African city and a new model for technocratic urban governance that continues to resonate today.

GA TOWN

The shifting dynamics of the late nineteenth and early twentieth centuries were simultaneously new and yet another manifestation of Accra's "long history of urbanism," which was characterized by centuries of cultural exchange, interaction, and adaptation.[6] Archaeological evidence suggests that the area around contemporary Accra has been inhabited since at least the fourth millennium AD. Guan speakers and Ga-Dangme speakers migrated to the region in the fourteenth and fifteenth centuries; the Guan likely arrived first, absorbing indigenous Kpeshi populations.[7] Oral traditions suggest that the Ga-Dangme peoples migrated from the north and east to present-day Accra.[8] Though archaeologists have not found enough evidence to support an exact point of origin, Ga origin stories point to Yoruba and Dahomey.[9] Rather than one single migration, it seems more likely that various groups of Ga-speaking immigrants migrated from the eastern interior down the coast and settled among Indigenous Kpeshi peoples beginning in the fifteenth century.[10] The descendants of these original migrants are known as *Ga mashie*, or "true" Ga (*Ganyo kron*), as distinguished from other Indigenous peoples and later settlers.[11]

As early as 1557, the Ga Mashie had established an extensive commercial network, which connected coastal and interior trade. Scattered in decentralized communities across the plains that extend from the Akwapim Hills to the coast, Ga leaders increasingly sought to consolidate their political and economic might to compete with their Guan neighbors for control over trade with Europeans, who arrived at the coast near Accra in the mid-sixteenth century. This consolidation culminated in King Ayite's founding of the Ga state—Great Accra—on the Ayawaso Hill in the late sixteenth century. The smaller settlement at the coast (at Aprang) was known as "Little Accra."[12] While the Ga were early and enthusiastic traders, they were less interested in allowing Europeans to build structures in Ga territory. Individual European traders had engaged with the Ga as early as 1557, but the Portuguese did not build a fort in Accra until several years later, and that fort was quickly destroyed in 1576.[13]

Ga traders took advantage of the economic possibilities that Great Accra and the new European trading interest provided. *Ga Mashie* built on their strengths in farming, fishing, and salt making as well as their new connections with European traders at the coast to expand their control over long-distance trade. As Parker notes, "Salt, preserved fish, and European trade goods from the Ga coastal outposts were exchanged for gold and ivory from the north, while slaves moved in both directions."[14] While the Portuguese had controlled most of the trade on the Gold Coast from the fifteenth century, European mercantile expansion increased considerably during the seventeenth century. In Accra, European trading companies sought to build forts. After a long negotiation, Ga leadership allowed the Dutch West India Company to build Fort Crèvecoeur (later Ussher Fort) at Little Accra in 1649. King Okaikoi granted the Danish permission to build Fort Christiansborg at Osu, two miles east of Little Accra, in 1661. The Royal Africa Company built James Fort in 1672–73, only a half mile from Fort Crèvecoeur.[15]

The settlements around these forts grew alongside the expansion of trade. The area around Fort Crèvecoeur was called Kinka (later Usshertown). James Fort was associated with Nleshi (sometimes Jamestown). Fort Christiansborg was connected to Osu. These three *nshonamajii* or seaside towns formed the core of the coastal Ga settlements, which also included Teshie, Nungua, Tema, and La,[16] and their residents became powerful middlemen, "mediating a variety of transactions across geographical, political, and cultural frontiers"[17] and providing important connections between the forest and the sea.[18] While European goods played an important role in the economic power and wealth of Accra, it is clear even as late as the 1730s that the Ga maintained tight control over trade at the coast.[19] John Barbot wrote in 1732 that, while the three villages were each "under the cannon of a European fort" that were "reckoned among the best on the coast," Europeans held little power:

> The three European forts have but little authority over the blacks, and serve only to secure the trade, the blacks here being of a temper not to suffer any thing to be imposed on them by Europeans; which, if they should but attempt it, it would certainly prove their own ruin. On the other hand, considering the boldness and warlike disposition of those blacks, it is strange they ever permitted Europeans to build three such good forts so close together: but so great is the power of money, as well in that golden country, as in all other parts of the world, that the late king of Accra, about forty years since, being gained by considerable presents the Danes and Dutch made him, for each of them to build a stone house, to settle a factor in, under the obligation of seven marks of gold yearly for each house.[20]

While Barbot's accusations of greed are unconfirmed, Accra's power was tied directly to its commercial position, which required its leaders to maintain good relations with European traders even while maintaining careful distance. The success of these relationships also attracted the interest of other ambitious states in the region. Beginning in the 1680s and extending through the 1820s, Accra found itself under the control of a succession of Akan states.[21] The Akwamu attacked the Great Accra settlement and destroyed the centralized Ga state at Ayawaso in 1677.[22] The survivors fled to the seven *nshonamajii* at the coast, where, protected by the canons of the European forts, they continued the resistance until the final conquest in 1680–81. While some Ga leaders fled the region, others remained under the rule of the Akwamu. In 1730, the Akwamu themselves were overthrown by the Akyem and pushed east toward the Volta.[23]

Even outside observers like Barbot could see that the conflict and control from outsiders hampered trade in Accra.[24] And yet, the skill of Ga traders and politicians, who were adept negotiators, preserved the city's commercial dominance and relative autonomy against these competing forces. Santi, an African intermediary described by Barbot, was said to "manage the commerce by the king of Nungwa's appointment": "He settled the prices of slaves according to their sex and age, as also of the European goods; then hostages being given on both sides, he sends the slaves aboard the ships by degrees, as they are brought down from the inland country to the town, and receives goods from the Europeans in proportion to the number of blacks shipp'd off at each time, and thus a ship is often furnish'd with four or five hundred blacks in a fortnight or three weeks."[25] More than a hundred years later, Nathaniel Hawthorne and Sir Henry Huntley wrote with a similar reverence for James Bannerman, an Afro-European merchant and politician. Bannerman, who Hawthorne described as "the principal merchant here," transacted "a large business with the natives, who come from two or three hundred miles in the interior, and constantly crowd his yard."[26] Huntley described twenty or thirty people entering into trade with Bannerman at a time, enduring long negotiations marked by patience and what Huntley perceived as an indifference to wasting time.[27] While there were significant similarities between the intermediary roles that both Santi and Bannerman played, there were also significant differences that in many ways symbolize the dramatic changes in the social, cultural, economic, and political life of Accra between 1732 and 1845. If Santi, an African, represented the king of Nungua (one of the secondary *nshonamajii*) in trade negotiations in 1732, by 1845, much of the trade was headquartered in Accra. This mercantilism was controlled by independent African or Afro-European merchants like Bannerman who were connected to Europeans both through their participation in government—Bannerman helped created the Legislative Council, served as a member, and later served as the Lieutenant Governor of the Colony from 1850–1851—and because they were the descendants of early European traders.[28] By the mid-nineteenth century, travelers noted several stone houses in Accra and remarked on the educational status and residential grandeur of the city's merchant class.[29] That wealth—fueled by the trade in palm oil, gold, and slaves—enabled merchant families to send their children abroad for education. The merchant class grew to include Sierra Leonean and Brazilian families who migrated to the Gold Coast beginning in the 1830s.[30] It also allowed Ga elites to invest in agricultural enterprises, including coffee and cocoa plantations.

Chiefs, too, were often traders—or employed traders—in order to directly benefit from the wealth of Accra's networks.[31] But chiefs also benefited from the taxes and fees generated through trade and the various disputes that resulted from it. As early as the eighteenth century, the three townships that constituted coastal Accra "were the political, economic, and sacral epicenter of Ga state and society."[32] Each township, developed around one of the three European forts, was organized into quarters or *akutsei* and headed by a *mantse* ("father of the town" or chief). Ushertown (or Kinka) grew up around the Dutch Fort Crèvecoeur (later renamed Ussher Fort) and was divided into four *akutsei*: Abola, Gbese, Asere, and Otublohum. Jamestown (or Nleshi) was connected to the British James Fort and was divided into three *akutsei*: Akan-Maji, Sempe, and Alata. Osu had only one *akutsei* and was connected to Christiansborg Castle.[33] The development of the *akutsei* reflected what Ato Quayson describes as "the tensions between ethnicity, multiculturalism, and hybridity."[34] Whereas indirect rule and the concomitant invention of tradition, tribalism, and custom (and early ethnographic studies) often reduced ethnic identification to a single origin story, the incorporation of outsiders or strangers played an important role in Ga social and political development and the development of Accra as a "multi-ethnic polity."[35] The prominence of Afro-Europeans in Accra—often with European surnames and foreign connections and, at least before 1857, through their active role in colonial government[36]—were perhaps the most obvious example of that multiculturalism. However, the Ga also readily incorporated other outsiders—Akwamu and Akan settlers, slaves from Allada, returnees from Brazil, traders from Sierra Leone. Unlike the *zongos* of Akan communities, these *akutsei* were readily incorporated into the core of Ga social and political life, and their leaders often quickly took on prominent roles in the Ga state.[37]

Power in the town was shared among members of three institutions: the *mantse* (or chiefs), the *asafo* (or sociomilitary groups[38]), and the *wulomei* (or priests). In addition to these three "official" institutions was the *oblempon* or "big men, who exercised power not through an established office but through the authority conferred through wealth and influence."[39] These different groups constituted a system of checks and balances that governed the social, political, economic, and spiritual life of the town, and their symbols of power—borrowed from both Akan and European sources—highlighted the city's multicultural roots.[40] Power, and particularly judicial authority and responsibility for law and order, was further complicated by the presence of European forts and the various Akan overlords who controlled Accra for much of its history. Accra residents navigated complex and often contradictory systems of regulation and authority, paying fees and fines, negotiating access to resources and opportunities, and participating actively in the responsibilities of the town through public court proceedings and other "benchmark[s] of civic status"[41] like the asafo.[42]

These leaders exercised their power within an increasingly complex urban milieu. While wealthy traders are more prominent in the archival record, their trade was impossible without the agricultural products, smoked fish, and salt produced by the farmers and fishermen who constituted the vast majority of Accra's population. However, with the establishment of the Basel Mission Society's industrial schools and factories in the 1850s, Accra residents increasingly took on new kinds of occupations. Engineering/mechanic work, carpentry, brick-laying, shoemaking, and sewing joined petty trade, transport, goldsmithing, and other older artisanal work to form the core of an emergent modern working class in Accra.[43] As Parker notes, "In 1891 only 814 people in Accra—about 5 percent of the total population of 20,000—were classified as farmers, compared to the 1,190 'mechanics' and 2,103 engaged in commerce."[44]

While the authority of the Ga state extended into the countryside and the welfare of the city increasingly depended on close connections with inland traders and farmers, Accra residents clearly saw themselves as "townsmen"[45] or "children of the town" (*manbii*)[46]—a status that indicated full civic rights and was contrasted with *kosebii* ("bush people").[47] The Ga word for town (*man.*, pl. *majii*) can also mean people, nation, or state, suggesting a degree to which the urban nature of settlement pervades both the culture of the people and their political system.[48] Indeed, while Accra itself was quite cosmopolitan, the social relations of Accra residents were almost entirely contained in the town, eclectic though they may have been.[49] This distinction between *man* (town) and *kose* (bush) highlights not only the importance of urbanity and urban culture for Accra residents but also a vested interest in urban order and management—a set of values and practices that defined "urban civility" (in contrast to the wildness of the "bush"), which contrasted sharply with European perceptions of the town that were published in traveler's accounts, circulated in colonial correspondence, and reported in newspapers: all of which constitute much of Accra's written history.[50]

The dynamism of the city was in many ways a function of its origins. Parker argues that Accra leaders' incorporation of outsiders reflected the desire to rebuild and grow the Ga polity after its destruction at Ayawaso.[51] But as trade grew, so did the power of Accra's political, spiritual, and economic leaders. As Kilson argues, urbanization in Accra was "dependent upon its commercial and administrative functions."[52] As a site of cosmopolitanism and opportunity, urban coastal centers like Accra provided attractive opportunities for refugees, freed slaves, artisans, and traders who circulated along the West African coast.[53] Of course, Accra's history is not one of constant growth. But in many ways Accra was significantly different at the end of the nineteenth century than it was at the beginning. The decline of the slave trade and the shift to legitimate trade reshaped Accra's commercial and political landscape in significant ways.[54] The expansion of British authority over the Gold Coast and the declaration of Accra as the new colonial capital had significant implications for Accra's political leaders, who found their authority over land, labor, law, and wealth severely circumscribed as colonial officials established new institutions of order in the city.[55] Merchants similarly found themselves marginalized in Atlantic commercial networks as European trading houses sought to consolidate control and maximize profits through the import-export trade.[56] Fires, earthquakes, and disease also hampered urban growth in significant ways from the second half of the nineteenth century through the early twentieth century, and colonial officials often seized these opportunities—as with the fire in 1894—to assert greater control over the town.[57] However, as Sackeyfio-Lenoch and Parker have argued, these changes marked a shift in, rather than a destruction of, power in Accra. Residents who engaged with the new systems and institutions of order in the British colonial state did so not to replace existing power relations but to renegotiate their place in the shifting landscape in ways that would preserve their autonomy and protect the interests of themselves and the town.

In *Making the Town*, John Parker argues that Accra was "an indigenous core community for which colonial rule was but one—albeit important—thread in the fabric of urban life."[58] He rightly notes that the expansion of colonial authority in Accra was "characterized by subtle continuities and discontinuities, rather than an abrupt rupture."[59] The protests, contests, negotiations, and failures detailed in this book serve as testimony that this process of continuity and discontinuity persisted even at the height of colonial power in the late nineteenth and early twentieth centuries. And yet, 1894 (not 1877) seems to mark a significant shift in the nature of colonial governance in Accra, implemented through the new Town Council and the courts and marked on the landscape through new kinds of infrastructural interventions and built/planned spaces that embody new visions of urban life. Regulation was, in other words, the backbone of a new form of power and authority in Accra, which substantively reshaped the possibilities of urban life for Accra residents. Many residents continued to live in the same kinds of houses, organized in the same neighborhoods, and engaged in the same kinds of economic activities and patterns of mobility and sociality that they had before. But the balance of power seemed to have shifted; the impact of residents' actions and the relative freedom they had to live in and profit from urban life were significantly circumscribed. The cosmopolitanism that had defined the city in the sixteenth through eighteenth centuries had transformed by the late nineteenth and early twentieth centuries. Accra was still a Ga town, but it was also, increasingly, a colonial capital in a way that felt more consequential in the daily lives of residents at the beginning of the twentieth century than it did at the beginning of the nineteenth.

COLONIAL SPACES

This introduction and the chapters that follow explore what it meant to create colonial spaces that simultaneously embraced and disrupted the past and fostered competing visions of an urban future in Accra. The city has long been a site of interrogation through which scholars of Africa sought to better understand the limits of colonial authority and the power of African agency and autonomy— what constitutes a "colonial space" and to what degree is that "colonialism" consequential for the people living there? For early scholars, these questions were intimately connected to the imperatives of colonial governance and economic development. Anthropological and sociological studies, both from organizations like the Rhodes-Livingstone Institute in Zambia and through the work of individual scholars, sought to better understand local societies and urban dynamics in order to better control land and labor and counteract the corrupting influences of urban life.[60] Underlying this scholarship was a belief that African agency and autonomy, in the context of colonialism, was something to be controlled in order to advance the aims of the colonial state. "Modernity"—a vision of a liberal, ordered, and technological future, which the British were so eager to bring to cities like Accra—also came with the risk of corruption and degeneration if African engagement was not carefully monitored and controlled.

In the Gold Coast, fears about the possible corruption of city life informed the development of social welfare programs, urban planning schemes, public health campaigns, and educational enterprises. But coastal cities like Accra—the product of four centuries of dynamic development, which incorporated but was not defined by European influence—differed significantly from the urban colonial constructions of eastern and southern Africa.[61] If the goal in cities constructed in settler colonies like Nairobi or Johannesburg was to control African access to mobility and urban life—so as to preserve the city as a zone of European power and authority—in cities like Accra that was impossible.[62] In Accra, colonial officials grappled with how to alter, rather than restrict, African urban life. Cities like Accra challenged the assumed structures of "decentralized despotism" that characterized practices of colonial governance in many parts of the continent. Lugard's strategy of indirect rule, taken up in various forms across the continent, assumed the rurality of African states.[63] Cities, Mamdani argues, were the province of the colonizer, subject to direct rule and direct investment and dominated by colonial officials and settlers, while rural areas were left to Africans under the leadership of "traditional chiefs" or "native authorities."[64]

As a Ga town, Accra blurred these distinctions, which often frustrated colonial officials who were convinced of the power of scientific classification and social order, and necessitated innovations in the structure and practice of governance. The ATC and the technocratic and regulatory structures deployed through the ATC represented an urban application of indirect rule thinly disguised as proto-self-government. Earlier efforts to establish a municipal council in 1858 had been withdrawn after only a few years when townspeople refused to pay taxes or participate in elections for a body that they believed would undermine their own autonomy, while placing the financial burden for the development and maintenance of the town on local residents. By the 1890s, however, conditions had clearly changed. As we shall see in chapter 1, a series of lands bills and towns ordinances redefined the legal jurisdiction and responsibility of the colonial state in cities like Accra. While these lands bills may not have ultimately been effective in establishing public lands, they did generate new kinds of "publics."[65] The Aborigines Rights Protection Society and other proto-nationalist organizations were founded to protest the new laws and generated a new form of political consciousness around colonial urban governance. It was against this backdrop that the new ATC was formed in 1898. Despite persistent complaints about taxation—and an initial unwillingness on the part of property owners to pay taxes—the institution did hold the promise of at least limited self-government, allowing elected African representatives to have a direct say in the governance of the city.

As the debates of the Town Council make clear, however, the promise of elected representation and self-government was rarely realized in practice. The "official" or government-appointed members of the Town Council constituted a majority, which they regularly used to push through legislation that advanced the interests of the colonial state or shut down proposals from elected African representatives. This imbalance came to the fore when, in 1936, the Accra town clerk, Mr. J. W. Blankson Mills, was arrested for falsification of accounts and dismissed from his office, and the ATC president appointed Mr. Duncan MacDougall (formerly of the Basel Mission) as the town clerk. African representatives and Accra's rate-paying class protested. In a petition sent to the governor, rate payers argued that "to take away from the African at this time of great economic distress in the country the only highly paid post occupied by him in an institution designed to educate him in the art of self-government and maintained by revenue contributed by him will generate in him the bitterest of feelings and create in him such a sense of unfairness as would eventually end to undermine that confidence which he has always reposed in the wisdom and justice of the British Administration."[66] While this protest, which went on for months, was undoubtedly fueled by the growing anticolonial sentiments of the interwar years, African representatives and rate payers had been complaining about similar action from the earliest years of the ATC's founding. The colonial state—as represented by the British-dominated Town Council—frequently mobilized the regulatory and technocratic power of the state to target development, planning, and investment in ways that advanced colonial priorities, undermined the power and autonomy of African communities, and attempted to reshape the daily life of urban residents to better fit the "urban imaginary" of colonial officials.[67]

In navigating this tension between the demands for autonomy and opportunity in daily life and the realities of colonial regulatory power, African residents in Accra participated in a form of dynamic urban politics found in cities across the continent. For at least the last forty years, historians of leisure and African urban social and cultural history have used popular culture, oral history, material culture, newspapers, and other sources to detail the powerful ways that men and women asserted their "rights to the city," creatively fashioning lives that embraced new opportunities and possibilities emergent in the late nineteenth and early twentieth centuries.[68] As these scholars have made clear, African urban residents shaped the physical space, economic networks, and sociocultural practices of the urban environment, within, against, and outside of the asserted power and control of colonial states. Leisure activities, fashion, trade, entrepreneurship, and mobility formed the foundation of a powerful form of grassroots urban politics and asserted alternative visions of city life.

Residents of Accra, informed by their long history of urbanism, were no exception. Over the course of the twentieth century, Accra residents used the strength of their urbanity to protest colonial legislation, reshape physical space, appropriate and redeploy infrastructure technologies, and craft dynamic and cosmopolitan urban cultures. The creative agency, insistent ambivalence, and outright defiance of African residents provided a powerful challenge to a colonial state that, even in the best of times, was "marked again and again by incoherence, incapacity, and incompleteness."[69] The failed colonial visions of urban modernity, in other words, were often a testament to the resilience of Indigenous urbanity. This book explores the persistence and creativity of urban residents across the twentieth century, articulated through debates about sanitation, health, economy, mobility, and housing. As the following chapters describe in greater detail, colonial plans were rarely fully realized. Lack of funding, capacity, understanding, and popular support frequently hampered colonial visions for Accra in practice. On the ground, in other words, the "modern city," as described and envisioned by colonial officials, never fully materialized. Rather, I argue that the real impact of colonialism was felt less in the built form and infrastructure of the city than in the systems of regulation that reinforced broader structures of inequality through the policing of everyday life. These regulations shaped Accra as a colonial space in ways that had profound impacts for African residents on both a local and global scale.[70] Colonial space, in other words, was less about the *built form* of the city and more about the *access and opportunities* of its residents. In creating and enforcing regulations, backed by the power of the courts and the police, colonial officials marginalized African values and practices within both local and global networks. Colonial officials, technocratic experts, and African representatives on the ATC utilized regulation to advance the interests of expatriate capital and advance new visions of institutionalized, systematized "modernity" in Accra. In the process, regulation—and the Eurocentric forms of order and industry that it sought to engender—effectively informalized African urban cultures and advanced a new understanding of the "African city" within emerging structures of global governance and technocratic expertise.

TECHNOCRATIC COLONIALISM

This new colonial "urban imaginary" was informed by a modernist faith in technological progress and a commitment to the expansion of capitalism. Colonization was, in the words of Timothy Mitchell, "not simply . . . the establishing of a European presence but also . . . the spread of a political order that inscribes in the social world a new conception of space, new forms of personhood, and a new means of manufacturing the experience of the real."[71] British explorers and colonial officials' observations about the state of cities and towns in Africa were marked by a profound ethnocentrism. Accra and other cities in the Gold Coast were certainly no exception. Henry Morton Stanley's 1873 description of Accra as "a town of native and European buildings jammed" between the port and the lighthouse is perhaps the most infamous.[72] However, just a few years before the Sierra Leonean physician and scientist James Africanus Horton wrote in his famous call for African self-government that Gold Coast "towns contain a few large houses, but the majority of the native huts are so completely jumbled together that they present a confused mass. There are no properly laid-out streets, but the towns are intersected with crooked lanes."[73] Here, Horton draws on language frequently found in Western accounts of cities that predated European influence. Similar to the kinds of complaints from Euro-American observers that Bissell documents in Zanzibar, these writers frequently objected to irregularity and "haphazard" development in cities and insisted on the universal superiority of regularity and geometric order without any particularly power supporting evidence of its effects on health, society, or living standards.[74] These differences in temporal and spatial perception were often explained by observers steeped in the values of Western science and technology as a symptom of the "general disregard on the part of Africans and Asians for the accuracy and precision that had come to be valued so highly in western culture."[75] As Adas notes, many of these observers interpreted the differences in human settlement patterns as "chaotic."[76] British complaints about Africans as "hopeless when it came to measuring a distance or drawing a straight line" were part of a broader set of stereotypes about Africans as "sloppy, prone to exaggeration, inattentive to details, devoid of uniform standards, and incapable of quantification beyond (and sometimes including) elementary counting."[77] These critiques also often took on moralizing tones that justified a kind of politics in which "deficient" spatial layouts were evidence of Africans' general inability to rule themselves "properly."

European expectations of technology in the late nineteenth and early twentieth centuries were tied to notions of progress and a faith in the importance of measurement as a tool of regulation, order, and rationality.[78] Measurement made it possible for scientists and members of emerging technological fields like engineering and architecture to "control" the natural and social worlds, "containing" and thus rendering them legible and malleable.[79] Surveying, mapping, and planning utilized the tools of measurement, combined with assessment of social and spatial form to organize the present and plan for the future.[80] As a space of perceived disorder and degeneracy, the modern city—and emerging European notions of it—were defined by a concern with the measurement, planning, regulation, and ordering of built space, the infrastructure and buildings within it and the way individuals interacted with it. These concerns both grew out of earlier (seventeenth- and eighteenth century) forms of colonialism in North America, the Atlantic, and India and were uniquely constituted by the emergent metropolis and modernity of nineteenth-century Europe.[81] Emerging fields of architecture, engineering, public health, social work, and town planning sought to bring order to the perceived chaos of rapidly growing cities and address "social ills" and environmental contaminants that offended the sensibilities of the bourgeois classes and injured the social, economic, and cultural health of the nation.[82] Science and technology were seen as both a testament to the superiority of Western civilization and a tool in achieving civilization, both at home and abroad.

Colonial policy toward cities like Accra, then, were unsurprisingly imbued with these notions of technology and progress. Early explorers, traders, and government officials often viewed colonial territories as "empty land" where they could finally realize their visions for ordered modernity, which were too difficult to achieve in the midst of social and material chaos of the built environment of the metropole.[83] Government officials and experts often viewed colonies—and particularly colonial cities—as "laboratories of modernity" or "experimental terrains."[84] Accra both reinforced and challenged these systems of urban governance. Colonial projects to reimagine the physical space and systems of governance in Accra in the wake of the fire in 1894 coincided with major shifts in British approaches to the administration, development, and maintenance of their colonies.[85] As secretary of state for the colonies, Joseph Chamberlain integrated science and technology into decision-making and strategy at every level of the Colonial Office in the late nineteenth century, recruiting scientific and technical experts and expanding the bureaucratic power of the CO. In the interwar period technocratic methods were further consolidated and professionalized. Town planning, in particular, took on new importance in colonial strategy under the leadership of Lord Passfield (Sidney Webb) as colonial secretary (1929–1931). Passfield sent a circular to colonial leaders recommending planning "as an orderly and scientific method of controlling work already in progress or inevitable in future, in a manner which secures the best and most far reaching economic results from current expenditures as it takes place."[86] This new era of technocratic colonialism was rooted in notions of civilizational superiority and committed to the advancement of global trade and expansion of industrial capitalism through "development," both at home and abroad.[87]

This book recognizes the power of technocratic colonialism in shaping African urban spaces and experiences in twentieth-century cities. As Carlos Silva notes, across the continent there was "a clear lineage from colonial-military engineering to civil service architects and urban planners in the first decades of the 20th century."[88] In Accra, technocratic colonialism was implemented through the ATC and the bevy of advisers, consultants, technical officers, and inspectors who identified, implemented, and reinforced technological solutions to address perceived urban disorder and advance colonial visions of urban development. The power of the ATC was, at least in theory, rooted in the Town Councils Ordinance, which granted the Council authority over a wide range of issues related to sanitation, infrastructural development, and spatial order. That power was backed by the colonial government, the courts, and the police, as evidenced by extensive inspections and prosecutions for even the most minor infractions. But the very act of building and maintaining infrastructure was, in itself, an exercise of power. Monumental buildings, roads, railways, harbors, markets, and residential neighborhoods were often designed to convey authority and organize urban space, mobility, sociality, and economic activity in ways that advanced colonial priorities.[89] As the "built forms around which publics thicken,"[90] infrastructure was an important means of interaction between citizens and the state, a point of contact and access through which standards and ideas were made concrete in the world.[91] In establishing, reinforcing, and reproducing the rules governing the "space of everyday life," Keller Easterling argues that infrastructure constitutes a form of "extrastatecraft"—"accidental, covert, or stubborn forms of power... hiding in the folds of infrastructure space."[92]

In Accra infrastructural projects certainly reinforced various forms of social and economic privilege. The ATC was never successfully able to replan or rebuild the city center to conform with colonial expectations, but they were able to strategically use infrastructural investments and policy prescriptions to legitimize new visions of urbanity and modernity in Accra. Backed by regulation and the power of the state, infrastructural investments created new forms of social, economic, and spatial inequality in the city and created new structures that urban residents had to navigate in order to access resources and opportunity. This "colonial dualism" was, on some level, a representation of the tendencies toward segregation embodied in the Dual Mandate and reinforced by early scientific theories of town planning and sanitary health—what Garth Myers describes as the "intrinsic racism of urban space."[93] However, William Bissell argues that the actualization of this intended dualism was marked by "incompleteness and inconsistency"; colonial officials never could fully segregate cities across the continent.[94] Particularly in Accra, where long histories of cosmopolitanism were central to the development of urban forms and the everyday realities of urban life, that level of social, economic, and spatial segregation was impossible and even undesirable. In Accra, rather, infrastructural development was often marred by intentional underinvestment, which directly contradicted the British claims to superiority through reason. British officials increasingly insisted that the ATC and Accra residents fund the development and maintenance of the city themselves, gradually withdrawing grants-in-aid in the decades after the Council's founding and refusing to invest in major infrastructure projects at a level that would provide equal access to all residents in the growing city.[95]

In tracing the rising power of the "rule of experts" in shaping modern development practice and urban governance, scholars of technology and empire have often highlighted the frequent gap between rhetoric and reality, or "distinctions between what was real and the forms of its representation."[96] As James Scott notes, "Designed or planned social order is necessarily schematic; it always ignores essential features of any real, functioning social order."[97] The universalizing assumptions of technological theories and forms and the technological arrogance and ethnocentrism of many technocrats, even in the face of contradictory evidence or popular protest, meant that infrastructures, development initiatives, and town plans frequently failed to achieve their goals. Colonial development policy was shaped by the interaction of various levels of colonial administration who had different understandings of and solutions for the challenges they faced—a "complex and dialectical intersection of ideas, expertise, and bureaucratic power" that, Hodge argues, was "torn by inconsistency, indecisiveness, and objectives falling in divergent and often conflicting directions," a symptom of the "friction and paralysis of late colonialism."[98] The increasing segmentation of colonial bureaucracy and its regulatory regime created a system in which the purportedly more "professional" and "modernized" system produced its opposite—an unwieldy structure full of cracks that allowed both large and small issues to remain unaddressed or ineffective.

Even in these gaps, technocratic practice often aligned all too easily with the stated and unstated aims of colonial governance.[99] If colonies were "laboratories of modernity," the technocratic practices they engendered took on new forms in the professionalized societies, fields of study, and professions of practice that emerged over the course of the twentieth century, sitting at the core of the new field of "development" as the operationalized arms of emerging theories of modernization. On the ground in Accra, however, the daily practice and lived realities of colonialism often diverged from these lofty goals. Technology broke down, infrastructure was unbuilt or allowed to decay, plans were undermined, and regulations were avoided. For many, the incompleteness and inefficiency of the colonial state simultaneously created space for continuity and opportunities for innovation. But, in focusing almost exclusively on technological failure and colonial incompetence, scholars of colonial planning and urban development have often failed to recognize both the structural consequences of classification and regulation and the power of Indigenous technological systems.

As Clapperton Mavhunga argues for Science and Technology Studies (STS) scholarship broadly:

> The task of doing STS in nonwestern contexts need not be one of simply tracing the mobility of Western artifacts and practitioners, situating them in the Global South, and commenting on their behavior in different environments, but taking seriously what technology means from the perspective of people of the South. It requires not merely looking at how people respond to incoming things, but placing the latter's arrival, meanings, knowledges, and materialities within the locals' technological longue durée. The arbitrary restriction of what constitutes technology to measurable things and experiments in the built laboratory performed only by those with mastery over them constitutes not just an epistemological exclusion, but also an ontological and sociological one.[100]

In Accra, the organization of neighborhoods, construction of houses, production of food, conduct of trade, movement of goods and people, and other critical practices of urban life reflected long histories of interaction and adaptation with dynamic natural, social, and economic environments. These forms of knowledge, skill, and practice were more than the "practical knowledge, informal processes, and improvisation in the face of uncertainty" championed by scholars like Scott.[101] They constituted local technologies that formed the foundation of a resilient urban civilization. Accra residents who embraced new technological introductions—from streetlights to piped water to motor vehicles—did so within the context of these broader systems of technological knowledge and practice. But Indigenous technological knowledge just as often informed protest, criticism, and resistance as Accra residents balked at the failure of imported technologies and technicians to account for local realities and rebelled against forms of infrastructural development or regulation that unnecessarily infringed on local autonomy—a form of technopolitics at the foundation of what Frederick Cooper called the "struggle for the city."[102]

The lines within this broader contestation, however, were often blurred. African technopolitics was complex—a reflection of the high degree of socioeconomic diversity within Accra's Ga population. Individual self-interest and class solidarity often inspired opposition to proposed plans or infrastructural interventions, suspicious of colonial plans given persistent evidence of inadequacy, incompetence, failure, or planned obsolescence and the expanding range of regulations, categorizations, and classifications associated with colonial technological interventions that often pathologized African bodies and practices. Residents in some Accra neighborhoods demanded electric lights while others destroyed them in protest. Traders demanded improved market structures but often refused to relocate or change their practices. Drivers wanted vehicles and passengers but did not want to obey traffic laws. While Western-educated elites sought to embrace what they saw as "development" and "civilization," even they had their limits and pushed back against plans that infringed on their autonomy, undermined their right to property, or questioned their ability to participate actively in processes of governance.

Blinded by ethnocentrism, colonial officials and ATC members, who often interpreted these protests as further examples of "backwardness" and renewed calls for education and acculturation, fundamentally misunderstood the issues at hand. This book argues that, far from the thoughtless, irrational acts condemned by colonial officials, local response to technology and planning constituted a vernacular culture of technology.[103] In adapting the objects, forms, and ideas of modern technology to meet local needs and values and pushing back against imposed agendas in the face of colonial failure, residents highlighted the inherent ethnocentrism of colonial technocratic practice and British expertise and challenged the projected superiority of Western "modernity." If machines were the "measure of men," the British were found wanting in tropical regions like the Gold Coast. More importantly, however, in pushing back against the inadequacies of colonial development, residents also highlighted the systemic or structural inequalities that lay at the core of modernist, technocratic principles and practices, articulated often in Accra through the lens of race, class, and gender.[104]

Contemporary scholars of technology, urban development, and colonial governance who point to examples of urban resilience as evidence of the ingenuity of local residents in the midst of dramatic change have done a great deal to refocus urban history on the agency of African urban residents. But the actions of African urban residents were much more than mere reactions or responses to imported technological systems and colonial logics.[105] This book follows Mavhunga's lead by "locating Africans between their locally generated and inbound ideas, instruments, and practices."[106] In doing so, it seeks to resituate twentieth-century African urban politics as a form of technopolitical contestation, which recognizes both the power of technocratic colonialism and the historicity and resilience of Indigenous urban technologies. It also raises questions about the constructed universality of technological models, standards, and practices by exploring the history and politics that shaped their development through the lens of Accra's unique urban history and advances alternative interpretations of African urban development rooted in much deeper histories of the values and practices of local residents.

INFORMALIZATION AND THE MAKING OF AN "AFRICAN CITY"

Colonial obsession with order required a construction of its opposite—disorder. As Mitchell notes, "The identity of the modern city is created by what it keeps out.

Its modernity is something contingent upon the exclusion of its own opposite. In order to determine itself as the place of order, reason, propriety, cleanliness, civilization and power, it must represent outside itself what is irrational, disordered, dirty, libidinous, barbarian and cowed."[107] To some degree, colonial officials sought to implement order through interventions in the built environment. As the chapters of this book document, colonial officials and their technocratic allies proved generally incapable of fundamentally altering the built form of the old Ga town beyond the opportunities afforded by natural disasters like fire and earthquake. Preexisting forms of spatial organization were deeply rooted in locally meaningful urban histories, social networks, economic activities, and cultural practices that not only helped define what it meant to be urban (vs. the "bush" or *kose*), but also what it meant to be Ga—an identity and form of urbanity that had already adapted in many ways to the dynamic, cosmopolitan realities of coastal life. Accra, then, posed challenges similar to those faced in metropolitan cities in Britain itself: How to create the city of *colonial* urban imaginaries in the middle of a preexisting urban settlement?

In some cases the "othering" described by Mitchell took the form of alternative settlements, built outside of the old town to model European visions of ordered urban life and provide "safe" and suitable spaces for British officials.[108] As we will see in chapters 1 and 2, these new urban spaces were influenced by misguided and often racialized concerns about sanitation and health, which often pathologized African bodies and practices as not only "filthy" but also dangerous.[109] However, new settlements also served as sites of imagination where colonial officials could implement ideal technocratic urban plans and provide alternatives to the model of the old town. These very physical and material forms of intervention in the built environment were perhaps the most obvious examples of urban planning in Accra, marked by new kinds of infrastructure, housing, and municipal services. But, as the chapters of this book demonstrate, the built environment was only one component of a much larger technopolitical strategy, rooted in the emergence of a new culture of regulation, articulated through ordinances and backed by a series of inspections and trials, fines and prison sentences that sought to reinforce order in the city.

In tracing the unfolding regulatory framework of governance in Accra, regulation, as Janet Roitman argues, operated as "political technologies that serve to constitute 'that which is to be governed' or . . . a field of regulatory interventions based on a set of suppositions about the nature of economic life and economic objects."[110] The economic regulation that Roitman describes is part of a broader system of "political technologies . . . that render aspects of social life both intelligible and governable."[111] In Accra, ordinances turned urban life (and thus urban residents) into "problems" that required "solutions." As such, regulations were "not simply instrumental methods for obtaining or assuming power; they [were], rather, the very material form of power itself."[112] In regulating the way that people disposed of garbage, used the bathroom, stored water, organized their compounds, built their houses and neighborhoods, moved along city streets, and engaged in trade and other economic activities, these ordinances marginalized long-standing African urban cultures in favor of the models and theories developed and implemented by a newly emergent class of technocratic "experts" who shaped the field of modern urban planning.

As Robert Home notes, the term "town planning" did not appear until the late nineteenth and early twentieth centuries, but the underlying goals of town planning practice had long played a prominent role in colonial governance. Rules devised to control enslaved peoples on Caribbean plantations, Benthamite principles of utilitarianism and the panopticon as a way to organize local government in England and the colonies, the cantonments of India and Africa, trusteeship and indirect rule from Burke and Lugard, and Locke's philosophy of private property and land tenure all served as important legal and philosophical underpinnings to the emerging legal and regulatory systems of colonial governance.[113] But spatial interventions in the context of global capitalism and the industrial age also required new forms of expertise: forms wrapped in technocratic assumptions about the universality of technological and scientific laws and bureaucratic values of "order" and empowered through the growth of interconnected but competing imperial networks.[114] As early as the 1890s, a wide range of increasingly transnational technocratic experts moved throughout and between empires, including "colonial administrators (the British career officials of the Indian civil service and later the colonial service); lawyers, judges, and magistrates; doctors specializing in sanitation and public health; engineers both civil and military; land surveyors; and (relatively late in the colonial period) architects and urban planners."[115]

Ideas and practices moved throughout the empire via the central supervision and coordination of the CO, which transferred experts and consultants regularly between colonies and operated regional administrative units.[116] However, knowledge was also shared through the networks and associations of newly expanding professions like engineering, architecture, planning, and public health. International conferences, initially in the field of tropical medicine and engineering, allowed British imperial consultants to interact with experts from French, German, Portuguese, and Italian colonial territories. The result was a consolidation of material and building techniques, housing structures, and infrastructural development and policy strategies across the boundaries of empire and colony, giving the appearance of universality and abstract neutrality. The ordered, regulated technocratic systems seen and constructed in the context of British colonial rule was characterized by what Mitchell describes as "a remarkable claim to certainty or truth: the apparent certainty with which everything seems ordered and organized, calculated and rendered unambiguous—ultimately, what seems its political decidedness."[117] It was, in other words, a world reduced to binaries, around and through which both local and global systems were ordered and interpreted: order versus disorder, tradition versus modernity, and formal versus informal.[118] These plans rendered cities like Accra "picture-like and legible, rendered available to political and economic calculation," enframing and ordering the city while not necessarily capturing its reality.[119]

This book argues that, in using ordinances, regulations, theories, models, and plans to problematize and reform African urban practices in Accra, colonial-era technocrats and government officials established systems and structures that privileged the interests of expatriate capital and advanced colonial visions of urban modernity. The process of categorization and classification implicit in technocratic systems reframed African practices as "disorder"—alternatively labeled "illegitimate," "illegal," "unsuitable," "nuisance," "pirate," "filthy," and "unsanitary"—in order to justify policy interventions that reshaped the parameters of urban life in Accra. Even in the midst of colonial incompetence I argue that colonial regulation represented a violence of categorization, which had significant consequences for African urban residents. In particular, I argue that debates over the mundane forms, infrastructures, and practices of everyday life represent early incarnations of a process of informalization—not in name, but in practice—through which both European and African members of the Town Council sought to redefine the boundaries of legality, legitimacy, and morality in the city. Invoking the notion of a "nuisance," town councillors effectively criminalized long-standing indigenous social, cultural, economic, and spatial practices and reshaped public discourse about city life through the lens of regulation.[120] This process was inspired by the desire to protect and promote "expatriate enterprise" and "ordered modernity," as Parker notes.[121] Regulations privileged expatriate capital and sought to marginalize African practices that challenged European expectations of city life. As the British colonial state sought to decentralize financial responsibility for urban governance, the Town Council took on increasing responsibility for the development and maintenance of infrastructure in the growing city. Categorization and regulation became important means of generating revenue for the operation of the city. The regulation of African urban life, in other words, became embedded in both the logics and finances of governance—the "capitalist city" and the "colonial city" intertwined.[122]

These acts of regulation and categorization initiated a process of informalization that effectively marginalized and criminalized long-standing African economic and spatial practice. In discussing the process of informalization, scholars of the contemporary city seek to understand the ways that urban citizens adapt to changing economic systems in order to "access opportunities and, at the same time, maintain social coherence."[123] This structuralist approach highlights the processes of social, economic, and cultural construction that generate the "reserve army of urban unemployed and underemployed" and shape their economic activities.[124] Keith Hart and the many scholars that followed him employed "informal economy" as an analytic that helpfully captured the labor and practices who operated outside or on the margins of the wage economy and, thus, "escape enumeration by surveys."[125] Much of the work on informal economic activities in Africa and elsewhere expands on this notion, tracing the origins of economic activities like market trading and exploring their significance as a means of both survival and accumulation in the context of persistent precarity and economic uncertainty.[126]

Here I invoke the concept of "informal economy" not as an analytical tool but as the subject of study itself. Informalization is a *historical* process, with roots in modernist rhetoric about the urban poor. In particular, the process of informalization, I argue, was a by-product of what Alan Mayne calls "slum deceits."[127] Mayne argues that nineteenth- and early twentieth- century social reformers and politicians adopted words like *slum* to "describe diverse social conditions in terms that were comprehensible to the new ruling culture."[128] Slum, he argues, was central to an emerging discursive and political strategy, which used stereotypes of urban poverty to shift blame for structural inequalities onto the most vulnerable local communities—"characterized ... as what the dominant culture regards as being the deficient 'Other,' or 'the other half of society'"—while justifying interventions and investments that privileged the capitalist class and further entrenched the structural disadvantages of poor communities.[129] This form of bourgeois ethnocentrism obscured complex forms of spatial, social, commercial, and financial organization that shaped urban communities and economies—what Perera calls "the city that is out there."[130] While colonial officials and Town Council members did not use the term "informal economy" itself, their actions and policies shaped a process through which African practices were increasingly marginalized within the institutions and systems of social, economic, and political power.

These terms—and the policies and interventions they inspired—were certainly central to the way that British planners and policymakers understood the politics of space in the metropole. Urban reform in British cities targeted low-income neighborhoods and vulnerable communities in public health and social welfare campaigns that highlighted the contradictory dangers and desires of city life. However, the rhetoric around spatial order and social reform took on a particular form in colonies, informed by persistent theories of racism and the demands of industrial capitalism. As Bissell argues, in order to understand these processes, we must engage the realities and legacies of colonial governance, "treating the colonial state as an arena for ethnographic inquiry in its own right [...] by regarding colonial rule itself as a form of cultural practice and process" (Bissell 2010, 71). Bissell notes that "by focusing on the inchoate nature of colonial rule, we can begin to rethink the state as an unfolding practice or process of becoming" (2010, 73). In tracing the history of informalization in Accra, I argue that we clarify the historic roots of "informality" as a category of colonial governance that reshaped and relegislated the categories of belonging in cities like Accra and limited global political imaginations about economic possibility in African cities more broadly.[131]

Scholarship on and political rhetoric about informality has often interpreted the persistence of African social, economic, political, and cultural practices as a form of resistance—a protest against the exclusionary practices of the formal sector and the misguided or unpopular priorities of government. This is certainly more palatable than early colonial assessments that viewed these practices as evidence of African "backwardness" and did, in some cases, reflect the underlying motivations of residents. Yet, at least in Accra—though almost certainly in many instances across the continent and throughout the Global South—the actions residents took outside of the state-sanctioned structures of social and economic life also often represented a continued investment in long-standing systems of social and economic reproduction in the absence of accessible and meaningful alternatives. Residents embraced infrastructure when it advanced their interests and conformed to their values. They were not antiscience or antitechnology, and they were not incapable of understanding the possible benefits that new forms of sanitation and housing might have for themselves and their communities. They did, however, question the legitimacy and efficacy of new regulations and highlighted the unevenness of investment and seeming double standards in enforcement among African and European sections of the town. Many of the activities targeted by Town Council regulations predated European arrival or, at least, the consolidation of British colonial power in the Gold Coast. Before the new kinds of regulatory action that emerged in the late nineteenth century, market trading, corn milling, and other activities were not part of an "informal economy"; they were *the* economy. Indigenous housing and residential settlement patterns were not examples of "informal settlement"; they were *the* settlement. Informality, in other words, is an invention of colonialism, rooted in an assumption that "certain historical experiences of the West [are] the template for a universal knowledge" and backed by the power of capitalism and the "rule of experts."[132] But it was also produced through contestation as local residents sought to assert their own rights to the city and tried to shape its future.

While the historical process of informalization certainly has its roots in the colonial period, the binary thinking of technocratic colonialism quickly became entrenched in global systems, fueled by the emergence of new kinds of international intellectual, economic, and political institutions. In the mid-twentieth century, technocratic ideas and practices were further systematized through colonial development and welfare initiatives, which funded massive planning and infrastructure projects across the continent and legitimized new professions of practice. The consolidation of colonial practices into new professional fields in architecture, planning, engineering, and development coincided with the creation of new international professional organizations and fields of academic practice that transformed colonial practices into universal "theories" in social and applied sciences. These new fields were further legitimized by emerging institutions of "international governance," which embraced theories of modernization and development as universal models for the advancement of well-being for peoples around the world.[133] As chapter 5 demonstrates, modernization theories embraced by postindependence leaders and technical experts sought to advance national development and secure economic independence, both inspiring and restricting imagination about the future in cities like Accra.

Rooted in modernist assumptions about the forms and theories of city life, urban history and urban studies are similarly plagued by binaries—formal versus informal, failure versus success, problem versus solution. The persistence of these categories in scholarly analysis highlights the degree to which the technocratic models and frameworks of planners, public health officials, and other policymakers, who sought to simplify the city for the purposes of governance and marginalize the power of residents in shaping its form, have become "naturalized" both within and outside of scholarship.[134] If, however, these categories were constructed as a tool of colonial governmentality that was never intended to capture the complexity of urban politics and the dynamism of city life, we must rethink our fundamental assumptions and seek alternative ways of understanding the city that are derived not from the perspectives of planners but from the experiences of residents.[135] This book seeks to begin that work in Accra, tracing the history of informalization through the politics of regulation, planning, and development. This history is, in many ways, profoundly local. Accra's own unique history of urbanity helps to highlight some of the fundamental contradictions and assumptions of technocratic approaches to the city, making clear the politics and contestations that shaped these emergent systems. In Accra, informality manifested both through the persistence of African urban systems in the face of capitalist expansion and the pursuit of opportunity in the midst of the incompleteness of colonial urban development. We can more plainly see the unfolding of informalization in Accra because it required regulating and marginalizing preexisting systems of social, economic, political, and cultural organization and practice. The "Ga town" described by Parker provided a foundation from which

Accra residents could contest plans and advocate for their own interests. The long history of cosmopolitan urban development in Accra meant that Ga Mashie had different kinds of tools and skills at their disposal in navigating this new phase of technocratic colonialism. Even in the face of regulation, Accra residents often used these new systems and technologies for their own purposes.

But this history of informalization in Accra also has implications for the way that we think about cities, broadly—in Africa and around the world—and raises a number of important questions that are beyond the scope of this book but have profound consequences for how we think about both the academic study of cities and the past and present practices of urban development and governance. While cities like Accra are often cast as exceptions to global models of urban development that require additional planning intervention to "formalize the informal city," this book argues that Accra's exceptionalism should instead push us to think about the assumptions that inform prevailing theories and normative models of city life. As Steve Marr has argued for Lagos and Detroit, cities that are too often now associated with the detritus of global capitalism and thus excluded from conversations about urban formation have important lessons to teach us about the violence of the past, the systemic inequalities of the present, and the path toward more just futures.[136] "The history of the present," the Comaroffs argue, "reveals itself more starkly in the antipodes."[137] This book argues that, in tracing the profoundly local contestations over the shape of development and governance in Accra, we can more clearly trace the roots of systemic inequalities and begin to rethink the ways that we imagine and understand city life.

ARCHIVES AND ETHNOGRAPHIES

The ideas that inform this book and the history it tells were inspired by a circular from the Colonial Office about "pirate passenger lorries" (which can be found in chapter 4). The language of piracy that colonial officials evoked in that document led me to delve deeper into the minutes of the ATC and down an archival rabbit hole, tracing policies related to spatial regulation and ordinances related to urban governance and planning in Accra. But it was the minutes of the ATC and the petitions and letters that accompanied those minutes that gave the ordinances and policy documents meaning. There, transcribed directly from the meeting, were the debates and disagreements of British and African Council members who, from their various positions of appointment or election, sought to represent the interests of their respective constituencies and advance a vision for the city's future. Passed by an "official" majority, the ordinances and policy documents that laid out the legal framework of urban governance in Accra seemed to carry weight and a kind of finality. Revisions to the ordinances were often focused on what seemed like relatively mundane details. But, as the minutes of the ATC made clear, these expectations were far from straightforward in their implementation. Elected African representatives often argued with appointed British officers over inadequate investment, undemocratic actions, and concerning precedent. They also raised petitions from community members who were protesting Town Council action. And yet, ordinances often passed anyway, backed by the weight of the "official" British majority.

At first glance, these minutes seem to tell a story of colonial oppression even in the context of purported self-government. In raising objections and sending petitions, African residents and their elected representatives appeared to be engaging in a futile form of resistance. As African representatives repeatedly complained, British officers would almost always band together to vote in the interest of the state against the wishes of local residents. These policies carried power, both in the attempted policing of the most intimate details of everyday life and in the violence of categorization. But as Stoler and others note, colonial "words on paper" were just as often "affections and attachments" that sought to project authority in its absence.[138] In invoking language like "piracy" and in complaining about the ineffectiveness of policy and strategy in remaking Accra, British officers conveyed an underlying anxiety about colonial authority in the city.

This book is not a "history from below" in a conventional sense. It relies heavily on colonial archives, but, following Stoler, I turn my attention to the colonial archive itself, not merely as a set of cultural facts to be mined for content but rather as a site of historical production in itself.[139] As this book argues, it is in the debates, protests, contestations, and failures that we can most clearly see colonialism (and connected concepts like informalization and regulation) in practice, as part of an unfolding process, not a historical fact.[140] In exploring the detailed notes, maps, and plans scattered throughout the colonial archive, we can trace the emergence and consolidation of a particular definition of and approach to Accra as an "African city."[141] The minutes of the ATC allow us to trace the politics of colonial urban regulation as they unfolded in real time, through the words of competing but also often strangely allied agents of power and authority. Importantly, however, the petitions and protests that are often referenced in those documents also evidence alternative visions of urbanity in Accra, rooted in the long history of social, economic, political, and cultural practice in the city. In following their echoes in related files throughout the colonial archive, I seek to advance a more layered and nuanced approach to the complexities of colonialism, assembling an archive through fragments and traces threaded throughout the historical record. Because ultimately, I argue, in its fragments and forms the archive highlights the dynamic technopolitics of urban governance.

If the government documents of the colonial archive often require us to read between the lines, meeting minutes, petitions, and newspapers allow us to hear directly from at least some of the African residents in Accra. The Gold Coast was noted for its high literacy rates and eager embrace of Western education. Afro-European families and other wealthy traders and farmers regularly sent their children abroad to pursue higher education, and students from a wide range of economic backgrounds attended government- and mission-sponsored schools in the twentieth century.[142] As Newell notes, however, like other systems of imported knowledge and technology, Anglo-Western practices of literacy were interpreted within preexisting local practices, and highly literate populations in coastal towns used literary culture and techniques to "play the game of life" and generated new forms of self-fashioning that often challenged the colonial state.[143] For many, petitions provided an important means of participating in and speaking directly to political leaders. A range of petitioners—from individual residents and business owners to organized groups of ratepayers and Ga political leaders—wrote to both the governor's office and their elected African representatives to demand access to infrastructure, protest a lack of representation and investment, appeal taxation and fines, and push back against the emerging culture of urban governance in Accra.[144] Petitions also ranged in style from "simple pleas in simple language" to elaborate, highly formal documents in florid language.[145] The latter were often written by professional petition writers employed by local residents who added their "marks" at the end of the petition but who valued the power of formal language to add weight and sophistication to their appeals.[146] Some of these petitions can still be found in the archives, but many others are referred to indirectly or quoted within government files. As a body of sources, Korieh argues, "petitions paint a vivid picture of daily life, of the practical realities of living under colonial control, and of how people dealt with these situations."[147]

Newspapers, likewise, provided an important outlet for residents in coastal cities to express their concerns and mobilize public opinion. The first newspaper was published in the Gold Coast in Accra in 1857. By the twentieth century there were a number of African-owned newspapers in towns along the Gold Coast. As Plageman and Newell note, the owners and readers of these newspapers were members of a fairly elite group based in coastal towns, and they used these publications as a space to debate and critique British colonial policy and organize and advance new kinds of publics dedicated to the cause of self-government and nationalist mobilization.[148] Some prominent intellectuals and politicians used newspapers to expand their reach beyond the Gold Coast and achieve prominence in pan-African or imperial circles. But for many, newspapers provided an important space where contributors could debate highly local concerns about the impact of expanding colonial authority in daily life.[149] The majority of the people who either owned or wrote into newspapers were elite businessmen, politicians, and traders who were highly educated and visible. Their writing, both in terms of subject and content, often betrayed their class status. However, editors frequently showed themselves open to feedback, willingly changing editorial positions on policies related to urban colonial governance when they realized "the masses" were displeased and incorporating anecdotes from family, friends, and neighbors. But, as a relatively democratic space, the editorial pages of the newspaper also sometimes welcomed middle-class and working-class people who could and did write into the newspaper, expressing their opinions and detailing their lived experience in relation to ongoing debates of public concern.[150]

Taken together, these sources provide us with an extensive, if still incomplete, window into the politics of urban governance in twentieth-century Accra. In reading the archive closely, we're better able to disaggregate the different groups claiming a stake in shaping the city—technocrats, colonial government officials, ATC members, African representatives, ratepayers, nonratepaying residents, and urban migrants.[151] While existing sources do not allow a detailed accounting of the daily life of any of these groups, in thinking about how they overlap and interact, we are able to better understand the complicated and multilayered nature of politics in the city. More importantly for the purposes of this book, we are able to see how the city was, at least in the abstract, formed and reformed through the technopolitics of space. Far from simple opposition, these various groups often reinforced similar assumptions connected to investment in a particular notion of global capitalism, economic development, and civilizational "progress" and "order," even if they often differed over who and how those aims should be achieved. Colonial politics, in other words, was something more than mere resistance.

To understand the technopolitics of colonial Accra we must acknowledge an interconnectedness between technocratic fields and the social sciences. History and anthropology often justified or reinforced colonial strategy, eased colonial consciences, and enabled the process of colonization.[152] This book argues that in order to understand the past we have to explore the history of our own analytical concepts: not just to explore the usefulness or salience of those concepts but to interrogate the various ways in which they have become normative.[153] Methodology, sources, and concepts, then, can just as often become sites of interrogation as the engines of analysis. By contextualizing and historicizing concepts and models that have come to dominate the way we think and talk about cities like Accra, we are better able to highlight the systemic violence and structural inequalities underlying supposedly "universal" and "natural" principles. As this book argues, regulation had a "social life" and informalization was a historical process that was constructed and produced just as much as the forms of technocratic colonialism and expertise that have been more widely studied by scholars.[154] Understanding how that happened, however, requires that we think about Accra simultaneously on multiple scales and consider the numerous people living in and shaping the city interacting in a way that was both profoundly local, continental, imperial, and global.

THE PLAN

The chapters that follow explore the unfolding politics of regulation and trace the process of informalization both chronologically and thematically. The first three chapters focus on the core pillars of twentieth-century colonial urban governance: sanitation, health, and trade. Driven by the desires and imperatives of an emerging system of global—or at least imperial—capitalism and new theories in the field of medicine, government officials sought to reshape cities to better control land and resources, make urban spaces healthier for European residents, and reorder space to advance the interests of expatriate capital—debates over sanitation, health, and trade were moments "in which the particular targets of regulation [were] circumscribed as such."[155] The ordinances, policies, regulations, and plans championed by technocratic experts and government officials were inspired by new research in Britain and around the empire. However, these processes were also driven by very local concerns, organized through the new ATC, which was tasked with overseeing the physical and economic health of the town.

The first chapter explores the politics of sanitation, which provided early justification for ordinances that extended government authority over land and space in cities along the Gold Coast. Accra served as an early site of experimentation for these emerging forms of urban sanitary governance. The declaration of Accra as the new capital of the Gold Coast Colony and the formation of the ATC created new kinds of energy and attention around infrastructural issues. Far more than mere "words on paper," Town Council ordinances created a new structure of urban governance, funded through a new system of taxation that was justified by imperial concerns over sanitation. Taxation and representative government generated new kinds of debates in the public sphere over the purpose and practice of colonial order. In contesting sanitary regulations, residents raised important questions about the state of urban governance and development in Accra and throughout the Gold Coast.

Chapter 2 traces the ways that concerns about health and disease informed urban governance. In particular, the chapter looks at the way government officials responded to epidemic disease and malaria in the twentieth century. Guided by imperial medicine consultants like Dr. William Simpson and other experts in the emerging field of tropical medicine, the ATC and other government agencies sought to decongest the old Ga town and resettle residents into newly planned neighborhoods. While Simpson and other metropolitan experts were vocal advocates of residential segregation, local leaders and residents alike resisted plans that would explicitly segregate the city along racial lines. Unequal patterns of infrastructural investment and targeted regulation and policing, however, effectively reclassified old neighborhoods as inferior to new developments, even if the Town Council was never able to fully realize its goals to decongest the city. Importantly, however, this policing of the intimate details of everyday life, exemplified by malaria inspectors who issued fines for improperly stored water or dirty compounds, criminalized the most mundane aspects of urban life in new ways. If sanitation was a public problem, concerns about health looked inside the private sphere of the home itself.

Chapter 3 explores the politics of trade, tracing the consolidation of new forms of economic activity under European control in Accra over the course of the twentieth century. Whereas African intermediaries had long been important conduits to both coastal and interior trade in Accra, by the late nineteenth-century European mercantile firms increasingly sought to assert more direct control over various aspects of trade. In Accra, new regulations to reorganize and move markets were certainly part of ongoing concerns over health and sanitation, but they were also informed by the economic interests of European companies. In moving and rebuilding markets, city officials were pushing out local traders' market stalls in favor of new company shops selling imported goods. At least in principle, officials argued that these actions were part of a broader reordering of the city to better organize its activities and improve the health and safety of all residents. In practice, however, these policies were riven with contradictions, and local residents actively protested double standards that privileged European firms and marginalized or criminalized long-standing African practices.

The last two chapters trace transformations in late-colonial governance as residents sought out new forms of opportunity in the city. Chapter 4 explores the ways in which new forms of African mobility subverted authority and challenged underlying assumptions about infrastructural order. Entrepreneurial drivers seized the opportunity to expand their business in the city, meeting the demand of local residents by picking them up along the roadside. In the process, however, they provided direct competition with the city's municipal bus system, which constituted an important form of revenue for the ATC and represented a new form of urban spatial awareness and interaction in the city. Labeled by officials as "pirate passenger lorries," these vehicles transgressed the official boundaries of city life and, in the process, highlighted the arbitrariness of those boundaries. Organizing their work in response to the practices and values of local residents, drivers shaped a vibrant alternative infrastructure that laid the foundations for entrepreneurial urban transport systems that would emerge in full force after independence.

Chapter 5 traces debates over housing in Accra. Because property taxes constituted the primary source of revenue for the ATC, the condition and quality of property had long been a concern for city officials. To some degree, these concerns were shaped by the theories of health and disease discussed in chapter 2. However, housing also constituted its own sphere of technocratic regulation. Specific ordinances governing the organization, construction, and maintenance of houses served as an important point of contestation between residents and the ATC, and the Council constructed a number of new neighborhoods for both European and African residents in the early twentieth century that served as both tools of decongestion and models of urban living. However, the widespread devastation wrought by the 1939 earthquake created an unprecedented opportunity to remake large portions of the town and create new construction cultures, particularly as increasing numbers of urban migrants sought opportunity in Accra. This chapter explores the development of housing models and ideal homes through new forms of town planning in the second half of the twentieth century and traces fundamental continuities in the policy and practice of Kwame Nkrumah's newly independent government in the 1950s and 1960s. The brief conclusion considers the implications for these histories within contemporary planning and policy debates and highlights the possibilities of grassroots models of development in light of contemporary concerns about sustainability, systemic inequality, and structural violence in Ghana and around the world.

ONE

"FRUITY" SMELLS, CITY STREETS, AND THE POLITICS OF SANITATION

IN 1902 THE EDITORS OF the *Gold Coast Leader* published an editorial voicing widespread frustration with the politics of sanitation in Accra and other towns in the Gold Coast:

> Whoever places about these [refuse] boxes always takes fine care to do so near the houses of the natives, keeping them yards from European Houses, which in itself shows clearly that he is conscious of the fact, he is creating nuisance and offensiveness, and of course for the native anything will do; for a government so solicitous about the sanitation of our Towns, to put such boxes in prominent streets, and actually encourage the people to create nuisance and render the Town unhealthy, really smashes us to smithereens. It may not be so, but it would seem, as if it is a principle with the local Authorities to make provisions of some sort for the necessities of the people either to justify what is said it reports, or to be able to claim some justifiable ground to dole out heavy fines to the people. They think the towns ought to be lighted and street lamps we must have though they may be "miles" apart: the necessity of latrines arises and latrines of some sort are provided, where no decency is taken into account, male and female almost mixing up together (!) a provision must be made for the refuse of the people, and look at their boxes offensively staring at you in the streets. Whether all this is the fault of the Health Inspector or the D.C. or the Authorities at Accra, we are at a loss to say. But there the scavengers are, actually vying with each other in the number of people they may pounce upon for the D.C.'s Court for nuisance—and heavy fines too. But we must keep crying, Sanitation! Sanitation. Then be on the war-path after mosquitoes, then talk of segregation, and a thousand things more![1]

For these prominent African intellectuals, government rhetoric about the importance of sanitation rang hollow when confronted with the realities, inadequacies, and contradictions of sanitary reform. Investment was limited and unequally distributed in ways that privileged European neighborhoods, and African residents disproportionately shouldered the more insalubrious by-products of inadequate sanitary infrastructures. The smells and health consequences of poorly maintained refuse boxes and latrines, which overwhelmed the compounds of many residents living in the African quarters of town, were compounded by the sociocultural indignities and constant prosecutions for sanitary violations to which African residents were regularly subject. Sanitary regulations that blamed residents for the town's perceived problems failed to acknowledge the degree to which the state—through a combination of both inadequate investment and inappropriate implementation—often created the very conditions they were supposed to regulate. As the editors noted, "It would seem, as if it is a principle with the local Authorities to make provisions of some sort for the necessities of the people either to justify what is said it reports, or to be able to claim some justifiable ground to dole out heavy fines to the people."[2] Sanitation, they argued, was a means through which the state justified its existence through a combination of intentional underinvestment and regulation. The "public interest" advanced through sanitary reform, it seemed, was about the well-being of the state rather than the townspeople.

The editors' suspicion was a reflection of widespread debate about the purpose and implementation of sanitary reforms on the Gold Coast. Accra was, in many ways, ground zero for these debates, and its residents felt the full force of sanitary regulation, reform, and disinvestment. Sanitation was at the center of new forms of colonial urban governance in the late nineteenth and early twentieth centuries, anchored by a series of regulations that expanded government authority over land and created new institutions of urban governance, taxation, and planning that justified unprecedented intervention into the lives of African residents. As the new colonial capital, Accra received the greatest attention and investment, as colonial officials sought to reshape the city's landscape of power and authority. The formation of the Accra Town Council (ATC) and the introduction of a new system of rates sought to decentralize financial responsibility for urban development and maintenance while creating new opportunities for representative government. However, as elected African town councillors, journalists, and urban residents complained, these new structures of governance were merely an illusion of representation and democratization. In practice, sanitary regulation, taxation, and Town Council politics placed the responsibility for implementing colonial visions on townspeople who could not afford it. In their repeated complaints to the Town Council, petitions to the governor, and editorials in the newspapers, residents asked: Who benefits from sanitation? In whose interest are sanitary regulations advanced? At whose cost? By whose definition or standards?

These questions were more than mere public health debates. They were fundamental questions about the state of urban governance and development in Accra and throughout the Gold Coast. The ATC and its system of ratepaying was a test case, and other towns were slated to undergo similar political and regulatory reform in the early twentieth century. As such, Accra and other Gold Coast towns were drawn into broader colonial infrastructural politics that dominated the first half of the twentieth century. As John Parker notes, by the early twentieth century, "'sanitation' and 'order' became linked by an emerging imperial ideology in which the new concern with tropical medicine contained a variety of encoded messages about wider social control."[3] Issues surrounding epidemic disease were of immediate and obvious concern to everyone, even if the methods deployed in response were politicized and contested. As a public health concern, however, sanitation was more slippery. Informed by new understandings of public health and disease, government officials sought to remove sources of contagion through careful urban planning and improve hygiene through education and decongestion. In the process, Black bodies, which were often associated with disease, were pathologized in new ways through public health reforms, and sanitation shaped the way that colonial officials and elite African representatives experienced the city and interpreted the values and practices of its residents. Colonial sanitation schemes, like other forms of urban sanitation and public health in the metropole, transformed physical and cultural practice into a "technological problem,"[4] which was interpreted through both the racial politics of the "civilizing mission" and the political economy of extractive capitalism and indirect rule.

What appears on the surface to be a relatively straightforward conversation about public health and urban infrastructure obscured more fundamental cultural fissures over both the relatively mundane details of daily life and the long-term plans for urban development. Questions of drainage and sewerage connected a diverse set of public works projects: from the provision of water, removal of trash, and building of latrines to the layout of new urban neighborhoods and the construction of new roads, railways, and ports. Beyond considerations of health, then, sanitation often indexed more expansive visions of urban development and urban form. Colonial officials sought to shape the built environment of the city and the practices of its residents through new forms of spatial organization and regulation; these officials would use sanitation as an excuse to "rid the town of activities deemed unsuitable for the seat of imperial power."[5] In Accra, this project was particularly urgent as British officials sought to establish authority over the Ga town and transform it into the "envisaged urban showcase of expatriate enterprise and ordered modernity" as the new capital of the Gold Coast colony.⁶ The process of implementing these sanitary visions, however, was far from straightforward. Accra's sanitary regime produced and was produced by debates over the categorization of space, the ability of the colonial government to control land, and the responsibilities of various colonial and Ga institutions to provide and maintain infrastructure for residents. In the process, it generated questions about belonging, authority, and responsibility in the city: Who belonged in the city? To what degree should they have a say over its form and function? What rights did they have to make demands on the state?

Between the 1870s and the 1940s, the answers to these questions—about sanitation, regulation, and infrastructure and about belonging, authority, and responsibility—shaped a new political reality marked by a contradiction and seeming arbitrariness that united African residents across class, gender, and ethnic lines. Formed in 1894, the ATC played a central role in colonial imaginaries about Accra's development. Tasked with implementing government sanitary mandates and engendering a democratic culture of engagement and ownership among the citizens of Accra, members of the ATC played a simultaneously powerful and liminal role in the development of the town. Sanitation, in particular, was at the center of this new form of urban governance, creating a powerful connection between the macro-level questions of infrastructure and planning and the much more intimate issues of hygiene and conduct in both the private and public spheres. The Town Council was the result of the devolution of responsibility and authority in colonial Ghana that effectively extended the logics of indirect rule into urban areas and, in the process, created new forms of electoral politics and representative democracy in the town. The ATC and its sanitary debates epitomized an emergent form of urban indirect rule in Accra, organized around seemingly straightforward colonial visions of decentralized authority, representative government, and taxation but struggling in reality under the weight of "considerable internal hybridity."⁷

Robust infrastructural politics in the first half of the twentieth century transformed the Town Council into both a beacon and a lightning rod in the midst of ongoing contestations over responsibility and authority in the Ga town. Decentralization created new forms of opportunity, but it also presented challenges of responsibility within a complex web of authority that limited the ability of African residents to shape the town's development. The frustration expressed by the editors of the *Gold Coast Leader* echoed not only within the elite spheres of journalism and politics but also on the streets and in the markets of the Ga town. Overlapping bureaucracies, fiscal austerity, and regulatory uncertainty shaped a form of urban governance marked by contradictions, inconsistencies, and incompleteness—a "dual colonial city [that] was formed through the complex interplay of material realities and ideological forms, fixity and fantasy."⁸ For

Bissell and others, the inconsistency and incompleteness that marred colonial urban development was an inevitable by-product of indirect rule, both as a political structure and a pattern of investment.[9] British colonial officials who envisioned "hegemony on a shoestring" underestimated the complexity of African urban realities, particularly in cities like Accra, which had a long history of urban settlement and trade that predated its position as the colonial capital.[10] As the editors of the *Gold Coast Leader* suggested, however, these inefficiencies were just as often a product of design.

This chapter traces the politics of regulation and taxation, construction and maintenance, responsibility and authority, representation and oppression through debates about the practice and infrastructure of sanitation in colonial Accra. While much of this debate focused on the activities of the ATC, multiple constituencies vied for influence over the city's sanitary affairs. Elected town councillors, local political leaders, colonial officers, merchants, market women, and family members alike shared an understanding of how important sanitation was to the city's development. The reality of how that vision would be implemented and who would benefit, however, was much more complicated. The illusion of democracy and local authority, embodied in the urban extension of indirect rule through the Town Council, created new tensions between the colonial government and Accra residents in ways that both flattened and magnified differences among the town's diverse African populations. British officials often utilized failed or incomplete infrastructure projects, coupled with rigorous regulatory enforcement, to criminalize or pathologize large portions of the city's residents and justify increasingly intrusive colonial authority over both public and private space. Ratepayers and their elected representatives quickly realized that decentralization was no guarantee of democratization; the "official" majority in the Town Council, buoyed by other colonial officials, used disorder to limit investment, marginalize African residents, and protect colonial financial interests. This chapter places two subjects of vibrant public debate and contestation—sewage and drainage—in the broader context of the political economy of sanitation in twentieth-century Accra. In a tropical port city, water—its provision, flow, treatment, and disposal—was a central sanitary concern, and colonial technopolitics sought to reshape both the form and practice of urban life to correspond with the prevailing sanitary wisdom of technical experts in public health, engineering, and urban planning.

SANITARY RESPONSIBILITY

The obsession with water and sewerage in Accra was part of a broader transformation in sanitary policy, spatial politics, and municipal governance in the colony. The British captured Accra in 1874 and quickly set about laying the groundwork to move the colonial capital from Cape Coast to Accra. The transformation of Accra from a relatively decentralized trading town under the leadership of the Ga Manche to the capital of the Gold Coast Colony required legislative reform that would reorder the political and spatial landscape of the city and establish the authority of the new British administration. Land was central to this urban reimagining, and British officials quickly introduced legislation that would give them unprecedented control over urban lands in the name of a newly defined "public interest." The 1876 Public Lands Ordinance gave government the power to seize lands "required for the service of the Colony."[11] These powers were extended further by the 1892 Towns Ordinance, which clarified responsibility and expanded authority for the development and maintenance of towns in the Gold Coast. The director of works was placed in charge of streets and granted the authority to "from time to time cause any street to be levelled, drained, altered, and repaired as occasion may require."[12] The colonial governor was granted the power to seize land (with compensation) "for the purpose of widening, opening, enlarging, draining, or otherwise improving any street, or of making any new street" and the director of works was empowered to take materials without compensation from private land to complete public works and to regulate the construction and condition of buildings in Gold Coast towns.[13]

The ordinance marked a dramatic expansion of the government's power to control land in the colony and also marked a significant departure from what the Aborigines' Rights Protection Society (ARPS) described as "one of the main principles guiding the administration of the Gold Coast." In a petition protesting the implementation of the Towns Ordinance in Sekondi, the ARPS argued that in seizing and later reselling land that belonged to residents, the government overturned decades of community-government relations rooted in "the protection of the rights of the people to their ancestral lands."[14] In expanding authority over the naming of streets and numbering of houses, abatement of fires, regulation of slaughterhouses and markets, colonial officials sought to seize control over the shape of the town.

Importantly, however, the Towns Ordinance—which was formally named the "Towns and Public Health Ordinance"—also sought to reshape the colony's sanitary policy by "devolv[ing] responsibility for sanitation to local town councils" and "declaring open spaces by the Government with a view to the promotion of the public health."[15] Sanitary policy was backed up by a new understanding of "public nuisances," an expansive list that included:

1. Any street, house or premises in such a state as to be a nuisance or injurious to health;
2. Any pool, ditch, gutter, watercourse, privy, urinal, cesspool, drain, or ashpit so foul or in such a state as to be a nuisance or injurious to health;

3. Any animal so kept as to be a nuisance or injurious to health;
4. Any work, manufactory, trade or business, injurious to the health of the neighbours, or dangerous, or so conducted as to be dangerous or injurious to health;
5. Any growth of weeds, prickly pear, long grass, or wild bush of any sort;
6. Any hole or excavation, well, pond or quarry, in or near any street, which in the opinion of the Director of Works is or is likely to becoming dangerous to the safety of the public;
7. Any well, pond or tank, the water of which is so tainted with impurities or otherwise unwholesome as to be injurious to the health of persons using it;
8. Any house or part of a house so overcrowded as to be dangerous or injurious to the health of the inmates; and
9. Swine.[16]

As we will explore further in chapter 3, the implications for this new category of "public nuisance" touched many areas of daily life in cities like Accra. In marking off these spaces or practices as "nuisances" it also allowed the state, through its newly appointed sanitary inspectors and backed by law and the power of the courts, to intervene in private African spaces and prosecute offenders. As representatives of the government, the ordinance granted unspecified numbers of new sanitary inspectors unprecedented authority over both the public spaces of shops, warehouses, manufacturing sites, and workshops as well as the private spaces of households and compounds: "Any inspector of nuisances, health officer or Director of Works, or any person or persons authorized in writing by any health officer or Director of Works, together with any assistant or assistants bearing any official badge or token, may enter and inspect any premises at any time between six in the morning and six in the evening, for the purpose of examining as to the existence or continuance of any nuisance therein, or of abating any nuisance."[17] These powers were backed by the threat of prosecution and fines for anyone who refused entry to inspectors.[18]

If the Public Lands Ordinance gave the government the right to shape the physical space of the town, and the Towns Ordinance created new systems of sanitation and oversight in residents' public and private spaces, the 1894 Town Councils Ordinance created new political structures that devolved responsibility for the implementation of sanitary guidelines. In creating a new institution of local government that had at least some elected representatives chosen by newly designated ratepayers, the ordinance sidestepped chiefs who, under indirect rule, were responsible for local governance and empowered a new class of urban residents who were identified solely on the basis of property ownership. Town councillors—half "official" (i.e., appointed by the governor) and the other half "unofficial" (i.e., elected)—and an appointed president (the district commissioner) and his town clerk were responsible for overseeing the improvement and maintenance of the town and collecting property taxes (or rates). While expectations of improvement were left undefined and subject to revision over time, the Council's sanitary responsibilities were explicitly laid out in the ordinance:

> In any town to which this ordinance is extended the Council shall have the power
>
> a) To provide for the removal of night soil and refuse from every house.
> b) To provide public latrines and bathing places.
> c) To make wells and otherwise to provide a good and sufficient supply of water for the use of persons in the town and to keep in good repair all public drains, aqueducts and tanks and to preserve the same from contamination.
> d) To perform any duties for the time being lawfully performed by any officer of the Colonial Government which the Governor may from time to time declare by notice in the Gazette to be transferred to the Council.
> e) Generally to do such acts as may be necessary for the conservancy of the town and the preservation of the public health therein.[19]

The president also appointed "Inspectors of Nuisance, Health Officers, and Surveyors" who were responsible for duties laid out in the 1892 Towns Ordinance.[20] Ultimately, however, the system of rates also placed sanitary responsibility on property owners, who were expected to maintain their properties under threat of prosecution and fine.

Colonial officials often heralded the new Town Council structure and the introduction of taxation as an important step toward local government. Rates, they argued, encouraged city residents to take responsibility for the financial, political, and social welfare of the town. For many residents, however, the rate system was an example of the colonial state's deep hypocrisy. The editors of the *Gold Coast Chronicle* noted the following amid public protest over the new system of taxation in 1896:

> Once more this horrible nightmare looms before us, with its iniquitous taxation, self-contradicting offers of self-government, one-sided provisions, impossible promises, and the oppressive and destructive grinding of the poor, for the simple purpose of putting more money into the coffers of the Government which according to the provisions of the Ordinance is practically to represent itself first, and then the people whilst as many salaries of officials as can on one pretence or other he conveniently saddled on the new fund is to be clapped on, leaving just a sufficient margin as an excuse for fresh imposition

of taxes. Water works, Roads, Sanitary measures, Drains, Latrines and what not are to be laid on the shoulders of the luckless Municipality. Of course it will be division of labour, the Government as usual draws the money and the people are now to have the privilege of attending to their own wants. The people pay the taxes and the exempted officials enjoy the honour, salaries, fees and the casting vote to boot. Though this Ordinance purports to allow the people some measure of self government as in other Colonies and the term "Town Councils" is applied to it, the voice of the Town is studiously forced into the background. As in the Legislative Council the three or four unofficial members are to be dummies to all intents and purposes. One cannot understand why this institution is not named "Official Council" as it is in point of fact, with mock representations of a voiceless people.[21]

The rate system created new burdens on the city's property owners, which included not only the merchant and professional classes but also chiefs and family heads. Appraisers surveyed the town annually and assessed rates based on estimated property value. This new system of taxation sought to elevate the status of private property owners in the city and undermine the control that chiefs had over town lands. But it also created new financial burdens on residents, sparking widespread protest, particularly since taxpayers would still be in the minority on the Town Council. As one resident complained:

> This Ordinance imposes fresh taxation of the most objectionable character in as much as it is far from being equitable. The Community is to pay a certain percentage on such annual value of each house as the owner would derive from rentage, whether the house in question is under rent or not. Business houses are placed on the same footing as dwelling houses, whilst the dwellings of the class which is to form the majority of the Council being Government property would be free of taxation. We would not consider it fair that this class in whose interests, alone we might almost say—sanitation at least is to be rigidly attended to, should be free from taxation. But whilst they are exempted as a class they are made the majority on the Council to disburse Funds to which they have not contributed a farthing.[22]

Editorial complaints in newspapers were backed up by more direct forms of popular protest.[23] The "kings, chiefs, and people of Accra" sent petitions to the governor protesting the Town Councils Ordinance in 1895 and 1898.[24] When Ga leadership failed to speak out strongly enough against the notion of taxation, asafoatsemei organized more public protests that put pressure on both the Ga Manche and the governor and forced a meeting to resolve the dispute.[25] In embracing more popular forms of protest, urban residents argued that property taxes (or rates), licensing fees, and other forms of municipal taxation created an undue burden on urban residents who, by the late nineteenth century, were suffering from an economic depression. As European firms sought to exert more direct influence on the coast in the late nineteenth and early twentieth centuries, even wealthier merchants and traders who owned grand houses in the city found themselves unable to pay taxes.[26] The financial burdens of taxation were compounded by new sanitary requirements. Residents whose properties ran afoul of sanitary inspectors faced fines and demands for building improvements; the Town Council seized or demolished property that violated regulations.

Town councillors also struggled to balance the physical and financial requirements of town maintenance and sanitary regulation. Within the context of indirect rule, the Town Council was supposed to use collected taxes to pay for town maintenance, reducing the financial burden on the colonial state and creating new forms of local investment. In some ways, this mirrored models of colonial governance in rural areas, where local chiefs collected taxes and maintained law and order as a representative of the governor (via the district commissioner). In Accra, however, the demands of a colonial capital city, the costs of modern infrastructure, and the rapid growth of the city beginning in the twentieth century placed increased financial burdens on the Town Council's relatively meager resources. In the first several decades of its existence, as town residents protested taxation, the Town Council relied heavily on government grants to fund infrastructural and sanitation initiatives. By the 1920s, however, residents had largely accepted the idea of taxation, which meant that the Town Council had more regular revenue.

This shift, which might seem abrupt and contradictory given the fierce resistance of the 1890s, evidences a persistent underlying strategy in British colonial governance in cities like Accra. While proposed changes often provoked resistance, those changes were rarely dramatic enough—fundamentally undermining the welfare or well-being of residents or abruptly subverting the power of their leaders—to provoke widespread outrage or prolonged resistance. As with the Public Lands Ordinance and the Town Councils Ordinance, British colonial leadership often played the long game, courting local elites and building coalitions of support until proposals were more tenable. In other cases, however, they simply waited out the initial outrage and ignored objections, which they often viewed as further evidence of "backwardness" or conservatism among Ga people. The persistence of the day-to-day implementation of a new "order of things" through inspection and enforcement was—more than grand construction projects or spatial interventions—the real power of colonial governance, expanding piecemeal over time through regulation. Expanding regulation, however, was also accompanied by expanding bureaucracy. This bureaucratic expansion took place via specialized offices and new categories of professional experts who oversaw regulatory implementation and enforcement and created increasingly complicated and expensive systems of governance, which added to the Town Council's fiscal and organizational burdens.

Acquiescence to the political reality of the Town Council structure and its attendant taxation, however, did not mean that Ga people passively accepted the new regime's mandates. Residents frequently used their position as taxpayers to pressure government to invest more heavily in the growing city. In the 1920s when Governor Guggisberg sought to reform the Town Council and make it more self-sustaining, Accra residents took to the streets again to protest excessive taxation and limited development.[27] Meanwhile, the ATC constantly negotiated with the governor and the director of public works to determine who held financial responsibility for town development. Town councillors sought to balance the demands for infrastructure and planning with the long-term financial costs. Councillors were concerned about "setting a precedent" that would leave the Town Council in an impossible financial position.[28] African members of the Town Council, in particular, worried that assistance in infrastructure provision during periods of general economic crisis would "sanction a broader decentralization of government responsibility over infrastructural development in cities."[29] But they were arguing against a broader colonial bureaucracy that saw Accra as merely one point within a larger imperial scheme, which simultaneously required efficient management in the march toward "civilization" as well as sacrifices "for now" in light of economic forces at play across the empire and around the world. As town councillors' frustrations made clear, these calls for "economy" and "efficiency" rarely impacted the salaries of British officials or metropolitan government expenditures and did little to enforce accountability when expenditures were wasted through inefficiency or incompetence.

As the ARPS petition regarding public lands in Sekondi suggests, these legislative and regulatory changes upended long-held understandings over who controls land and who defines how people live on it.[30] For elite residents who were more likely to hold property, new regulations increased the responsibility they held for the maintenance of their properties. But regulations also generated new kinds of conversations about sanitation as an infrastructural and social right/obligation. Residents, Town Council members, and colonial officials alike debated how the new regulations would be enacted and what they might mean for the city's future. Residents who engaged in the politics of placemaking did not reject colonial infrastructural and sanitary improvements outright. In fact, resident complaints and petitions often demanded *more* access to urban infrastructure and technology—a demand for equity in urban development. While colonial officials and town councillors often pointed to finances as the source of their struggles over uneven development, scholars have also highlighted the inefficiency, incapacity, and incompetence of colonial governance.[31] However, as residents' petitions, protests, and obstructions made clear, the "unruliness of urban life"[32] was more an organized assertion of control over the future vision of the city as a social, economic, political, and cultural space that had its own history and logic.

THE POLITICS OF WASTE

Water sat at the center of these debates. Community leaders in Accra and other major urban centers had long complained about the lack of water and its adverse effects on the health and welfare of residents. As one resident, writing under the name Vortigern,[33] complained in 1894,

> About 4 years ago, we commenced advocating in the columns of this paper for a water supply for each of the principal towns of this Colony; and when we come to consider that Accra is the Headquarters of the Government, the question, why there are no water works here, forcibly presents itself to us. But it could be answered, "That to bring water to Accra would cost £40,000, and that the matter was still under consideration of the Secretary of State." Since return to the Colony from leave of absence of the surveyor, who some time last year was sent to Beulah, the source of the intended water supply, we have been anxiously waiting to hear what has to be done, but until now we have heard nothing more on the subject. If hope is the anchor of expectation, our anchor has neither dragged, fouled, or parted chain, our sea is however exhausted and our ship is left on dry land, while scarcity of water is staring us in the face; and unless we make our voice heard at this critical juncture, and sometimes is done to aver the impending calamity, the blame will lie at our own door. We have lived and thrived under most fascinating promises heretofore, and is it possible without any assurance at this stage, to rely any longer on such promises and which are never intended to be fulfilled! Our duty now is to demand water, and it is but just and fair that we should do so, because the authorities have not the courage to speak their mind.[34]

For this commentator and many others who wrote to the newspapers that proliferated in Gold Coast towns throughout the late nineteenth and early twentieth centuries, demands for water were more than elite calls for Westernized infrastructure like piped water and indoor toilets. Gold Coast towns like Accra faced increasing water shortages that endangered the lives of inhabitants, particularly in the dry season. In Accra, proximity to the sea meant that well water was brackish and largely undrinkable; even wealthy residents could not dig their own wells to compensate for infrastructural inadequacies. With the growing population of the town, existing reservoirs were quickly depleted, and open reservoirs were easily contaminated by livestock and waste. In one extreme circumstance, Ga residents continued to use water from Opoohu even after a corpse was left floating in the water for several days.[35] Residents who regularly used contaminated water may have been unaware of the deleterious health effects. But in the absence of water locally, households were forced to expend significant time and labor walking to fresh water sources farther inland—a luxury that many could not afford. Even the colonial state, which at one point experimented with hiring carriers to transport water from fresh springs, could not afford such a luxury.[36] Colonial officials and African residents of all classes made strategic choices in adapting to scarcity, "for want of something better."[37]

The deep frustration expressed by journalistic commentators and echoed throughout Gold Coast towns was exacerbated by a seeming hypocrisy in both the rhetoric and practice of colonial policy. Despite the governor's repeated recognition that "effective sanitation including a good water supply ... is still the most urgent need of the Gold Coast,"[38] the provision of water was repeatedly postponed because of cost, even as construction of new government buildings in Accra continued throughout the 1880s and 1890s. Delays in state investment in a water system coincided with new demands from colonial officials for urban residents to shoulder the financial burden of urban development, claiming that the colonial administration could not afford to continue providing infrastructure and maintenance for the growing town. Responding to the new Municipal Ordinance in 1896, one resident echoed the complaints of many in the pages of the *Gold Coast Chronicle*:

> Whether the policy persued [sic] is sound or otherwise, it is not for me to say, but how long have we been paying an ad valorem duty of 10 o/o and specifics as 6d on the wine gallon, and yet our thirst is unbearable. I am far from grudging the Government the levy of duties, but what I say is this, as we pay the taxes willingly you must give us water—the most important need which should have been considered first before Bungalows and what not. If the Colony were poor, one might excuse this blind economy, if economy it can be called of those in power; but with the Revenue of this Colony at their command need there be any excuse for this ... policy?"[39]

The hypocrisy of the colonial officials, who prompted growth by appointing Accra as a new colonial capital and encouraged further growth through at least some limited investments in economic development (while blaming African residents for the increased population resulting from that growth), rankled Accra's taxpaying residents and highlighted many of the inconsistencies in urban colonial governance.

As Accra residents began paying house rates more regularly in the early twentieth century, these complaints were redeployed as a critique of the Town Council

Figure 1.1. Street Scenes, 1955. Source: Photographic Archive, Information Services Office, Ministry of Information, Accra R/2200/5.

structure. Residents pointed to the "foul water into which all sorts of refuse has been, and is being thrown, the awful stench of which is, from its situation wafted, over almost the whole Town."[40] As Quashie, an Accra resident, pointedly questioned: "Are these the great benefits we were to receive from the Government Town Council and for the rates of which the poorest of the Town are being driven to all sorts of subterfuges to meet?"[41] These demands for accounting were part of a broader critique of power in Gold Coast cities like Accra, rooted in the economic contributions of residents who viewed taxation as a form of investment in the state that was expected to produce tangible returns in their community. In critiquing colonial administration at both the colony and municipal level, residents laid bare the blatant profiteering and uneven investment that sat at the core of the British colonial project and raised important questions about governance in the city—Who belonged in the city? To what degree should they have a say over its form and function? What rights did they have to make demands on the state?

These questions were directed just as much at British colonial officials as they were at the increasingly diverse African population of the town.

After more than a decade of "costly experiments including experts at nothing,"[42] Governor John Rodger announced that "the Accra Water Supply has been definitely settled and the whole scheme is expected to be completed including a connected scheme for draining Accra within the next three years."[43] Debates about cost continued, however, as colonial officials weighed the difficulties of implementing the scheme and the implications that investment in Accra would have for future infrastructural development in other parts of the colony.[44] Work commenced in March 1910, including the construction of support infrastructure like a light rail to bring equipment to the site and the development of new harbor works. Plans continued to change even in the midst of construction, as engineers debated whether the dam could include turbines for electricity generation—a proposal that was ultimately abandoned.[45] This lack of clear planning and leadership from the Public Works Department led to delays in the project and undermined public confidence, having "failed to give satisfaction to the public with respect to the ability of their officers to discharge well and efficiently their public duties."[46] A combination of poor construction quality, delays, and waste of funds led the editors of *Gold Coast Leader* to declare the Accra Water and Harbour Works "practically failures."[47] Residents' annoyance with the slow speed of construction was amplified due to persistent water shortages. By the end of 1912, there was "a great scarcity of water in town and those who are fortunate in having tanks are reaping a rich harvest."[48] Patience wore thin as residents relied on the rains for renewed fresh water supply.[49] Finally inaugurated in 1914, the Accra Water Works directed raw water from the Densu River through a series of filters to a large reservoir. Town residents drew on that water over the course of a day, with pumps driving more water from the Densu into the reservoirs as needed, connected by cast iron pipes, twelve inches in diameter, to the distribution mains in Accra. In 1918, the government began to treat water with lime to remove impurities and, coupled with the filters, produced water "of a very high standard of purity."[50] Town water lines serviced all of the "important buildings"[51] in Accra, including colonial bungalows, government buildings, commercial spaces, and the homes of the town's merchant and educated classes, as well as supplying public stand pipes placed around the city.

Water usage expanded with the growth of the city. The town had 20,000 residents in 1913; by 1932 the population had tripled to an estimated 60,000.[52] By 1924, daily demand exceeded 500,000 gallons of water per day. In response, colonial officials doubled the capacity of the water works. Government again took advantage of the Colonial Development Fund to lay a second line of pipes in 1932 to improve the water pressure, and they replaced pumps in 1935. Few of these investments reflected African patterns of building and demand, however. By the time officials proposed an extension of the Water Works in 1936, they noted that "building activity in the environs of Accra is proceeding rapidly and it therefore becomes necessary to extend the system of distribution mains in conjunction with extensions at the headworks."[53] Korle Bu, Abbosey Okai, Adabraka, North and East Christiansborg, Labadie and Teshie—all areas that had witnessed significant (often government-sponsored) growth over the first decades of the twentieth century—remained without reliable access to water.

THE POLITICS OF WASTE

While colonial officials sought to provide and protect the flow of water in the city, they were often obsessed with waste. Within the water system itself, officials acknowledged that some changes in the behaviors of individual residents—like the introduction of private water carriage sewage systems on their premises or the increase in gardening activity using hose pipes—could account for the dramatic increase in domestic consumption among "unofficial" (i.e., private/nongovernmental) consumers. In the abstract, these activities represented new forms of African investment in sanitary domestic spaces, which officials encouraged. Private water carriage sewage systems, in particular, were "a development worthy of encouragement because it will be some years hence before it will be possible to extend a general water carriage system to the residential areas of the town."[54] However, this autonomy also posed the risk of waste. As one official report noted, "Gardening activity . . . is most desirable when it is reasonably developed, but waste water inspections have disclosed the fact that the unintelligent use of hose pipes is a very considerable source of water. A hose pipe used with care is of great convenience, but consumers generally leave the use of them to illiterate labourers who have very little idea of what they are doing."[55]

If using natural resources and infrastructure required a particular form of intelligence and education, many colonial officials saw regulation as an important form of public protection against waste. The Accra Water Works opened their doors to the general public, provided lectures to school children, and utilized the broadcasting system as part of a broad-based public education project. However, one official argued, these educational measures "rely purely on the good-will of the people to render them effective."[56] The majority of waste, they noted, occurred at stand pipes used by the general community and only loosely controlled by either the Water Works or the Town Council. Other egregious examples motivated more deeply rooted concern about African capacity to appreciate and operate new forms of public infrastructure. In justifying the adoption of the Water Works Ordinance in 1936, for example, officials pointed to a 1933 report from the District Foreman in Accra of an African laborer watering the lawn of an official compound during a heavy rain: "The labourer had been instructed by his employer to put plenty of water on the grass and appeared to consider either that this order was to be obeyed slavishly or that pipe water possessed virtues superior to those of rain water."[57] These extreme instances of waste generated cynicism among many government leaders and justified the extension of legal powers that would authorize police intervention. "Such appeals," one official noted, "have no meaning for a large proportion of the community but when the Water Works Ordinance is brought into operation will be possible to exercise control over wastage generally."[58]

Colonial narratives about wasted water, however, often ignored or minimized the impact of waste and water on urban communities. While the Water Works received sustained investment and attention from the government, sanitary inspectors, medical officers, town councilors, and residents alike complained about the government's persistent failure to construct an adequate waterborne sewage system in the town. As Governor Sir Hugh Clifford noted to Secretary of State for the Colonies Harcourt in 1913, even in colonial bungalows that were early recipients of pipe-borne water "the sanitary benefits to be derived from a pipe-borne water supply will be only partially reaped until such time as water can be laid on to these houses in the ordinary way, and carried off by a proper system of drains and sewers."[59] Even if, as Clifford argued, the provision of pipe-borne water and adequate drainage facilities was "the most important sanitary measure which can be taken for the improvement of the Public health of any town of this Colony," the large expenditure on the Water Works and town drainage would be wasted if not accompanied by "an efficient drainage and sewerage scheme for Accra."[60]

The importance of a sewerage system, then, was not in doubt in early twentieth-century Accra; by 1913 it was, as Clifford noted, "no longer a question of expediency, but one of sheer necessity."[61] Colonial officials' interest in sewage may have cited theories of sanitation and public health in justifying the sewerage scheme, but in their debates about its urgent necessity, it was more often the sensations associated with waste rather than the outbreak of disease that provoked the most urgent conversations. The 1913 drainage and sewerage scheme was never implemented, and in the absence of a proper sewerage system, waste was discharged into the Korle Lagoon from the main surface drains. The water was "purified" during heavy rains when the lagoon overflowed the sand bar separating it from the sea, bringing in fresh salt water. By 1929, however, it was clear that these measures were insufficient. As J. E. W. Flood noted:

> Sixteen years ago I was getting into the position of knowing something about the drainage of Accra, which was then considered to be a very urgent

matter in view of the introduction of the pipe borne water supply. Since then many things, including the Great War, happened and such money has been spent; but Accra is still without its drains and the Korle Bu Lagoon has been becoming more of a nuisance than ever. The position is that the surface drains of Accra empty into the lagoon at its north end. In the wet season when there is a lot of water about this does not matter much, but in the dry season surface drains really carry nothing but sewerage and as the lagoon is not very deep and the sun is very hot, the result is getting too much even for an African nose.[62]

Located between the town's most densely settled area and the Korle Bu Hospital, the concentration of sewage in the lagoon was both an olfactory discomfort and a public health hazard. The politics of waste and debates about what to do about the Korle Lagoon was further complicated by the lagoon's status as a sacred site among Ga people, tended by a priest and his followers.

African town councillors also evoked smell in calling for reform of the town's sanitary policies. Councillor Kitson Mills argued that "owing to the prevailing financial stringency it had not been possible to carry on the sewerage system contemplated some years ago, and asked whether it could not be possible to carry out the removal of night soil in the evenings instead of in the day."[63] Kitson Mills's appeal in 1932 was not the first—the president of the ATC noted that the question had been brought up before for discussion—and it would not be the last. Throughout the 1930s, African councillors noted the offensive smell associated with the pan latrine system that had been adopted in the absence of a water carriage sewage system. Waste removal by night-soil workers required removing, cleaning, and replacing galvanized iron buckets that collected refuse in public latrines. Doing so in the middle of the day aggravated the already strong smells associated with the latrine. But scheduling that was more sensitive to the daily life of African residents entailed costs that exceeded the Council's financial and logistical capacity. Reporting on their investigation of the matter in 1935, the acting municipal engineer and the medical officer of health reported that the scheme was "impracticable for the following reasons":

a) Absence of lighting both in public latrines to ensure effective cleansing, and in certain of the streets through which the conservancy lorries would have to pass.
b) Disturbances to the general public owing to the noise of lorries being unloaded of their clean pans, and also from the passage of lorries through the streets of the town when the inhabitants are asleep.
c) Additional cost of maintenance and supervision, European and African involved, since Health Officers, Health Inspectors, Engineers, Fitters and Drivers would have to be paid at special rates or overtime for being

on duty between 6 p.m. and 6 a.m. (breakdowns, petrol filling, cleansing, etc.).

d) Additional cost of lighting required in latrines and streets.[64]

For Kitson Mills and many others, the impossibility of the current system created renewed urgency for investment in a proper sewerage system: "One had only to be near any of these latrines when the pans were removed, and one would understand the situation," he argued.[65] Others noted that the conditions of latrines rendered their surroundings unsanitary. Councillor de Graft Johnson noted the "terrible stench in the vicinity" of the latrine on Horse Road.[66] In some cases, the stench of public space caused discomfort, which, though significant, was a by-product of living in crowded urban quarters. The Adabraka Market, Councillor Odamtten complained, "was bounded by latrines on one side, [and] the stench from them when the pans were being removed in the morning was too much for the people."[67] With an incinerator blowing "foul smoke when in action" on the other side of the market, patrons were inundated and inconvenienced by the odors of urban waste.[68] In other cases, however, inadequate waste disposal had real health consequences for urban residents. In calling for the construction of more public latrines, the medical officer of health noted that in 1933, twenty-five cases of typhoid were traced to houses that had no private latrines.[69]

As residents of the town, African town councillors were undoubtedly drawing on their own experiences in complaining about smells and other sensations that arose from inadequate sewerage infrastructure. In calling for more consideration of sanitary sensation, however, town councillors also echoed the complaints of their constituents who lodged complaints directly with their representatives and through the pages of coastal newspapers. As "Pexbroke Playfair" wrote to the editors of the *Gold Coast Independent* in 1922,

> Our principal towns are extremely filled with bad odour, and Accra ranks first in this. The stench arising from the latrine buildings is appalling and I should like the Governor to prove this statement by going round the town once at a slow drive. Here in Akuse the latrine pans are removed by prisoners who do this work without applying any Jeye's Fluid or any other disinfectant fluid whatever except where the European latrines in the bungalows are concerned, and surely one cannot expect these poor prisoners to clean these latrine pans under this condition; and so it happens that these pans are only emptied of their contents and put back again willy-nilly, and flies and bad smell that arise into the air beggars description. From this you will realize how annoying it is to a sensitive citizen of the country to witness a poor old woman being sent to the Court—if I were to call it a Court—to answer a charge of having allowed water to stand in an old cigarette tin in which the Sanitary Inspector has discovered two or three mosquito larvae wriggling merrily about.[70]

In writing under the pseudonym "Playfair," this resident's thoughts exemplified a broader public discourse that connected the indignities of sanitary smell and the condition of latrines with questions about the Town Council's legitimacy and effectiveness. Throughout the first several decades of the twentieth century, African politicians and residents regularly pointed to the Town Council's sanitary failures—evidenced by the physical and sensational experiences of the city—as justification for abolishing the Town Council altogether.[71] If the Council did not have sufficient funds to fulfill their primary responsibility—sanitation for the town—then why were they paying taxes? Where was that money going? Critics frequently pointed to the large number of highly paid European employees and sanitary inspectors who spent most of their time conducting home inspections and dragging residents to court for minor violations of sanitary laws. These fines generated yet more revenue for the Town Council. In the absence of significant infrastructural improvements and education, sanitary regulations appeared to be nothing more than yet another mechanism to extract revenue from residents. These inspections particularly targeted women who generally did not pay taxes as property owners.[72] In questioning the fiscal responsibility of the Council and the effectiveness of its regulations, residents directly challenged colonial constructions of the "public good." As Playfair noted,

> It is a disgraceful sight, apart from being gross inconvenience, that in the morning especially, to witness the long queue of our male community ranging from boys of five up to the bearded and grey haired men at one entrance of a latrine room, and at the other entrance opposite, our female folks ranging from blooming girlhood up to withered old womanhood waiting the 'tide' because of insufficient latrine pans. And our doctors advise us that it is dangerous to health to linger about after one has felt to go to latrine—we should attend to nature's call as soon as we felt it.[73]

This persistent lack of investment in town infrastructure—forcing men and women, often of the same household, to use the same latrine building with inadequate partitions (often nothing more than a partial swish wall or a piece of corrugated iron)—was an indignity that violated both Ga social and cultural norms as well as European expectations of gendered propriety. This sort of construction-driven social indignity was a more subtle form of much older infrastructural danger, produced through active disinvestment in African sanitary infrastructure that dated back to 1896:

> Another distressing accident occurred on the 23rd ult [sic] when a man attending the call of nature was overtaken with a fainting fit and dropped into a latrine on the beach; before help could be afforded. Coming into contact with the rocks beneath the skull was fractured to such an extent that he died

on the spot. This is not the first latrine accident. An old infirm woman fell into one of those dug outside the Town and there being none on the spot to lend a helping hand came to an untimely end, by the horrible process of drowning in the latrine. Since then another woman met with a similar accident but was fortunate enough to escape with a bleaching of many parts of the body which has made her a hideous object to behold presenting as she does, the speckled appearance of yellow and black more like the colour of a cat than of a human being. One would suppose after these two terrible accidents that the 'Powers that be' would have taken steps to prevent any further occurrences but our parsimonious Government—parsimonious in every thing concerning the tax-paying could only afford the masses the squatting surface of a three inch beam with sufficient space behind, which one losing his or her balance may easily fall through—in the first instance; and now holds the lives and limbs of the Governed so cheap as to allow this state of things to continue to exist. May we ask who is responsible for the lives thus lost, and how much longer this sort of thing is to last?[74]

Sanitary investment (or disinvestment), at the expense of human life and general well-being, seemed to contradict the espoused goals of sanitary regulation. The smells and dangers of latrines were compounded by that of dustbins, placed around town for the disposal of rubbish, which "aside from their evil effect on the public health, they are unsightly."[75] A commentator in the *Gold Coast Nation* echoed the complaints of many: "The Town Council should justify their establishment in this country by giving better attention to the *real* needs of the municipalities than appears to be the case at present."[76]

Public complaints about sanitary regulations, malicious prosecution, and underinvestment did little to change state practice. As one commentator noted, "After the outbreak of Plague at Accra in 1901 and the great outcry of inefficiency of the Town Council as a Sanitary authority, it was thought that the Government would take off the mask, put a stop to the pretext of teaching the people self-government, take matters into their own hands, and abolish the Town Council. But this was not done. The same old jugglery goes on, and with the trump cards in the hands of the Government, the game of fooling and bamboozling the native continues as merrily as ever."[77] Particularly in the cramped quarters of the old town, demand clearly exceeded the infrastructural capacity of the city's sanitation system. In 1933, the most populous parts of the city, including James Town and Asere, had as many as 67 people/pan; other areas had 37 people/pan.[78] Newly developed parts of the town were disadvantaged in different ways. Councillor Kojo Thompson noted in 1934 that there were only two public latrines to serve the entire community of Adabraka.[79] If the latrine system needed to be doubled in 1912 "in order to secure any approach to efficiency,"[80] the lack of sustained investment in expanding the city's waste removal system over the decades that followed meant that by 1942 the town's 78,000 residents used public latrines that were "thronged with ever-increasing crowds of people" and the Council maintained a fleet of conservancy lorries that were "continuously employed in emptying the pans."[81] The daily influx of people from surrounding districts into Accra—particularly around commercial districts and markets—meant that some latrines were emptied two or more times per day, a practice that would have to continue until more public latrines were constructed or the sewage system was otherwise improved.[82] These same densely settled communities, however, afforded little space for the construction of additional public facilities.[83]

SANITARY DEMOCRACY

In their complaints, African councillors certainly sought to represent the constituencies who elected them, often in protest against the misrepresentations of colonial sanitary and medical officers who constituted the bulk of the "official" membership of the ATC. The more politically radical councillors like Akilagpa Sawyerr regularly questioned the neglect and mismanagement of colonial officers and European officials, and all of the African councillors pushed at various times for the extension of major infrastructure in their communities and demanded that the central government take African concerns seriously through repeated funding requests, petitions, and protests. Particularly in relation to the town's sewage system, councillors used their positions to advocate both for a comprehensive sewerage scheme and for funding to expand the number of latrines in the town.[84] These complaints evidenced a limited form of representative democracy.

The "constituencies" that African councillors represented were, in many ways, members of their same socioeconomic class of ratepayers and property owners. Their class position and cosmopolitan aesthetics often complicated questions of representation. Councillors repeatedly called for various forms of public education, which when combined with free access, would help Accra residents learn how best to use "up-to-date and sanitary" public services.[85] In doing so, they often sought to forestall ATC action against residents and support the success of Council projects. As a barrister himself who sometimes defended residents against the actions of the ATC, Councillor Kitson Mills regularly pushed the medical officer of health and his sanitary inspectors to embrace the possibilities of education rather than "take out summonses indiscriminately against offenders."[86] Councillor Kojo Thompson, likewise, argued that "money was scarce, and people had to be educated that it was to their own interest" to listen to the advice of the Council's technical and medical staff.[87]

To some degree, calls for education were rooted in a desire to make regulatory systems more just. As early as 1894, coastal elites complained that

> There is no system of Ethics in any civilized country which would justify in these days punishment for an offence where there was admitted or demonstrated ignorance of the law. A man, in plain words, should not be punished for the breach of law where there is ignorance—involuntary ignorance—of it. Now, without giving into an investigation as to the merits or demerits of this or that principle of morality, or of this or that system of evolutional ethics, it is sufficient for our purpose simply to say that as the Laws of this Colony are not known by all the people in it, those who don't know then should not be punished for any involuntary breach of them. Look at the thousand and one ordinances of the Colony! Are they known by all the illiterate kings and chiefs? Are they thoroughly understood by the illiterate people of the colony? To say that each of these questions can be answered in the affirmative is to place on record what we know to be false. As a matter of fact, the majority—say without exaggeration 90%—of the people on the Gold Coast have not the slightest conception of the nature of nine tenths of the laws that the authorities pass. And when we look at the Calendar in the Supreme Court, and occasionally at the lists of cases in the District Commissioners Courts, we may well express surprise where the offenders are illiterate and the offence is virtually an infringement of some Ordinance that perhaps was never known.[88]

For these elite critics, education transformed oppressive impositions into a comprehensive set of regulations that generated new publics and a new civic consciousness. Educating the public about new regulations would decrease pressures on the courts. The sanitary regulations that were inscribed in towns, police, and public health ordinance generated "constantly recurring nuisance cases."[89] How would people know to obey the law if they did not even know the law existed? Yet the numerous cases in front of the Magistrate's Court in the 1930s suggested that little had changed in the intervening forty years. Limited representative government—complicated by class politics in coastal towns like Accra—was unable to significantly democratize governance in the town.

Education also often highlighted some of the gaps between Town Council representation and the values and practices of urban residents. In 1934, members of the local press condemned "Health Day"—an educational program that worked with schools to teach children about sanitation—for endangering the health and safety of children. The ensuing debate among ATC members highlighted fundamental differences among the African councillors. Kitson Mills, who had served as a schoolmaster and teacher for over twenty-five years, argued that "there was no better way [than Health Day] in teaching sanitation to the children."[90] In siding with the president of the ATC, he set himself apart from both the local press

"FRUITY" SMELLS, CITY STREETS, AND SANITATION   55

Figure 1.2. Scenes in Accra, 1955. Source: Photographic Archive, Information Services Office, Ministry of Information, Accra R/2342/8.

and other elected African councillors. De Graft Johnson argued, however, that "not every parent wished his child to be a 'scavenger,' and suggested that the views expressed by Councillor Kitson Mills should not be taken as the opinion of all the people in the country."[91] In asking children to pick up trash, Kojo Thompson said, "There was the danger of children coming in contact with some infectious disease, and it should not be done."[92] These kinds of concerns reflected a flattening of African community interests in ATC policy and action. Councillors themselves expressed concern about how they themselves would fare under the watchful eye of sanitary and building inspectors.[93] No one, it appears, was immune.

The regulatory pressures faced by African councillors and the debates over the relationship between education and governance highlighted the limits of their political power within the Council. Even if they voted as a bloc, elected African councillors remained in the minority and had to convince the "official" members to join them. In the relatively low-stakes Health Day debate, the ATC president demonstrated a willingness to listen to the concerns of African councillors. In matters of personnel, finances, and regulatory policy, however, the "official" members often banded together and used their slight majority against the protests of African members.[94] The efforts of African councillors were supported by members of social organizations like the Korle Gonno Improvement Society, who petitioned councillors to expand access to public services and agitate for the development of the town.[95] However, the broader "urban mob," which included market women and fishermen, asafoatse, and renters had long expressed skepticism about the leadership and priorities of African councillors. As Parker notes, "Notions of urban improvement shared by the government and indigenous intelligentsia were not necessarily endorsed by the townspeople of Accra."[96] Just weeks before the Municipal Councils Ordinance (MCO) was announced by Governor Gordon Guggisberg at the opening of the capital's new Selwyn Market in 1923—a symbol of the new system of municipal governance—a large group of angry market women marched on Christiansborg Castle (the seat of British colonial government) to protest their forced removal from the old Salaga Market. "Youngmen" (asafoatsemei) also mobilized to protest the 1923–1924 Municipal Councils Ordinance. New forms of taxation introduced by the ordinance, the asafoatsemei argued, were an excessive burden on town residents who could not afford to pay more to the ATC. In the absence of more concrete improvements in the development of the town and its public infrastructure, the MCO seemed like a money grab orchestrated by elite leaders in collusion with Governor Guggisberg's administration.[97]

Their actions were also constrained by the financial realities of the Town Council. Ratepayers, African councillors agreed, deserved to see improvements to the town based on their contribution to the purse. However, those rates proved insufficient in the face of the high cost of major infrastructure works and other maintenance and public services. The creation of the Town Council had been motivated by a desire to decentralize responsibility for sanitation and infrastructural development and create new cultures of investment and democratic governance in the towns of the colony. The extension of a sewer system would dramatically expand the financial burdens on the Town Council, which would be expected to cover the cost of caretaking, upkeep, lighting, toilet paper, and disinfectants.[98] These additional expenses seemed impossible, given that in 1913, the Town Council could not even afford to pay water rates for existing buildings. Even Governor Clifford noted, "As regards the fixing of meters, and payments by the Town Council . . . I may point out that the revenues of the Town Council of Accra, even at the present time, are insufficient to defray the cost of more than a small part of the duties which should properly be assigned to it, although they are annually supplemented by a substantial grant-in-aid from Government. Any payment for water by the Town Council, therefore, will be a purely fictitious disbursement, and Government will really be paying itself for that which it is ostensibly selling."[99] Impossible financial realities aside, consulting engineers who helped craft the initial plans for the sewerage scheme argued that "it is essential for the economical administration of the Water Works that water used for flushing purposes must be charged against the Department using it."[100] In balancing the technical requirements and financial obligations for public infrastructure with models of responsible local governance and sustainability, government leaders often relegated public interest to the background. Well into the 1940s, the Council was negotiating with the governor's office and other central government institutions like the Public Works Department over who should pay for the infrastructure and maintenance of the town. Even as protesters argued that rates placed an unreasonable financial burden on town residents, the ATC found itself without sufficient funds to execute even minor projects like latrine construction, which could alleviate some of the most pressing sanitary concerns, without appealing for funds from the governor's office or negotiating with the director of public works for shared responsibility. Despite their legally mandated responsibilities for sanitation in the town, expenditures on sanitation in the 1930s accounted for 20–24 percent of the total Town Council budget.[101] That amount, however, was paltry considering the costs of necessary construction and maintenance. The construction of five new pan latrines in 1933 cost £2,385—the equivalent of nearly 25 percent of the ATC's sanitation budget for the 1932–1933 fiscal year.[102] As the finances of the colony grew tighter, the colonial officials proved increasingly resistant to extend these grants and loans. In reconsidering the sewerage scheme in 1942, government officials argued that "we can agree with the Governor that the Accra Town Council should accept responsibility for the scheme. The proposed loan of £8,000 from Govt with interest at 2 1/2% is to be repaid by annuities over 15 years. The Council will presumably recover this from the rates."[103] By 1942, however, the rates were used to fund an increasingly wide range of public infrastructural needs: from markets and roads to bus systems and public lighting. Many larger and more essential projects—like the sewerage scheme—simply languished for want of funds, while the ATC focused its resources on more feasible projects like markets and bus routes.

The position of African members was complicated by both the Town Council's sanitary responsibilities—laid out in the Town Councils Ordinance of 1894 and updated multiple times in the decades that followed[104]—and the persistent failure of government to fund and execute a water carriage sewage system. Despite regular pleas about the urgency of a sewerage scheme and complaints about the state of the Korle Lagoon from all levels, including multiple governors, government plans to build sewage infrastructure were repeatedly adopted and abandoned throughout the 1920s, 1930s, and 1940s as officials cited the depressions and World Wars I and II, which limited available funds. And yet major infrastructure works, including a major road and rail building project, the extension of the water works, and the construction of Takoradi Harbor continued throughout the 1920s and 1930s, funded by loans that were repaid out of the colony's annual surplus. Phased projects like the sewerage scheme fell by the wayside: the subject of reoccurring hopes and cynical fears about the colony's future and evidence of the failures of African residents to adjust to the demands of modern urban life. "Good enough for now" proved to be an inefficient planning strategy in light of the financial difficulties soon facing both the colony and the rapidly growing city.

As Grace notes, the incompleteness of colonial infrastructural systems and this "make do" attitude had enormous consequences for Africans, even when they did embrace new infrastructural systems like sewerage and sanitation. In the absence of "parallel investments in centralized (or bundled) sanitation infrastructure to move and process excrement, the latrine systems adopted throughout the system created a 'subterranean shitscape' that produced 'seepage and toxicity.'"[105] This simultaneous fetishization of waste and unwillingness to invest in waste removal was a symptom of much more deeply rooted colonial expectations for African cities like Accra as timeless and inherently diseased and decaying. As Flood noted in 1929, the proposals for a sewerage system accepted in 1913 were "in principle as suitable for application to modern Accra as they were sixteen years ago."[106] Official debates about whether Africans could responsibly operate flushing latrines without waste and calls for water regulators and official latrine operators highlighted the degree to which these assumptions were not just spatial but mapped onto the bodies of town residents.[107] Public health officials often blamed this toxicity on "misuse or a pathological form of African urbanization" when it reality it was "an austere colonial technology working as designed."[108]

As William Bissell notes, "Colonial designs on the city, rather than successfully reworking space, repeatedly failed to rationalize the urban sphere. These schemes, sponsored by an overextended and disjunctive state apparatus, foundered precisely in the gap between intention and implementation, hindered by internal disarray as well as the incapacity of legal and bureaucratic instruments to reorder to totality of the everyday."[109] Bissell rightly argues that this bureaucratic disarray had profound consequences for African residents in the colonial city.[110] Sanitation was political, social, and profoundly personal, and the failed struggles in implementing effective sanitations policies or building new infrastructural systems served as a legal justification for colonial regulatory intervention into the private spaces of everyday life among African residents. Sanitation, in other words, was a "racializing technology that affixed growing amounts of shit to African residences."[111]

SANITARY MOBILITY

In technocratic and governance circles, debates about sewage often went hand-in-hand with conversations about roads. The same drains that would ultimately carry waterborne sewage for waste disposal also played a central role in the maintenance of streets and the mitigation of flooding. Proper road drainage, however, also protected investments in road construction. Heavy rains on poorly drained roads destroyed road surfaces and generated constant complaints. Responsibility for the construction and maintenance of roads, however, was the product of ongoing negotiation between British colonial officials like the director of public works and the members of the ATC. While early roads were heavily subsidized by the governor's office, that began to change in the 1930s. In 1931, the president of the ATC reported to members that the grant-in-aid they received from the government had been reduced by £1,000 and the Council's annual contribution to the government for the maintenance of town roads would be increased by £200.[112] If the Public Works Department was responsible for constructing roads, the cost of maintenance increasingly fell on the ATC, particularly as the Council expanded into new forms revenue generation like the Municipal Bus Service.[113] Revenue from public services supplemented the rates collected from property owners and increased the resources available for public works in the town.

In urging the Town Council to take greater responsibility for the construction and maintenance of town roads in the 1930s, the colonial government evidenced a clear shift in the financial prospects of the Gold Coast. The economic boom of the late 1910s produced excess revenue that was redirected to infrastructural development across the colony. Roads had occupied a prominent place in Governor Gordon Guggisberg's Ten-Year Development Plan, inaugurated in 1919. By the end of his term in 1927, Guggisberg had tripled the road mileage in the colony.[114] Accra clearly benefited from these investments. Between 1913 and 1930, the government engaged in a consistent program of constructing main and subsidiary surface drains and making up new roads in Accra.[115] Roads connected the town to other centers of trade, particularly in the cocoa-growing regions that lay to the north and east. But road construction also played a central role in the modernization of the town as a colonial capital and commercial hub. While much of the early investment was made in areas of concentrated European settlement or governmental and commercial activity, road construction was also part of broader plans to decongest the city center and lay out new neighborhoods for African residents across the socioeconomic spectrum. In the early 1920s, the Public Works Department introduced tarmac road construction to Accra, which produced more durable road surfaces, along with extensive road drainage systems. These new investments simultaneously created more reliable infrastructure and greater responsibility for maintenance and upkeep. "If the sealing coat [on tarmac roads] is allowed to break up," the director of public works argued, "the road is doomed and entire reconstruction is the only remedy."[116]

With the global depression in 1929, however, revenue-fueled infrastructural development collapsed just as quickly as it had grown. The regular program of road construction, drainage, and maintenance was shut down in 1930 due to a shortage of funds.[117] In the estimates for 1932–1933, the director of public works acknowledged that increased traffic and delayed maintenance meant that "the entire reconstruction of some of the most highly trafficked streets must be undertaken an early date."[118] However, decreased revenue meant that large-scale reconstruction was now impossible. He focused instead on a small section of road in the elite neighborhood of Christiansborg. Austerity also extended to town planning. When the governor's attempt to cut expenses from the 1932–1933 budget led to the complete elimination of all funding for the layout of townships, the director of public works argued that "the cutting out of this item will preclude practically all work on Town Planning, as no funds will be available for necessary survey labour and demarcation."[119]

While the Town Council was not directly responsible for road construction, these financial decisions had implications for the Council's work. As early as 1930, Councillor de Graft Johnson noted "the deplorable condition of some of the main streets and roads in Accra" and called for the redirection of funds from the "less important" Labadi-Teshi Road to the roads in Accra itself.[120] The acting senior public health engineer noted that the construction of roads and drains was the responsibility of the government, but he suggested that the Council should forward proposals and suggestions for town roads for consideration.[121] Early Town Council action focused on areas in middle-class African neighborhoods where councillors had direct experience and investment. In 1931, a yearlong campaign began to pressure the government to complete Boundary Road, which had been completed at either end but was left with a big gap in the middle that often proved dangerous. Councillor Dr. Reindorf had provided land for the road free of charge and had funded its construction himself, and Councillor Kojo Thompson was also building a house along the road and would give the government the land it needed without being compensated.[122] Councillor Akilagpa Sawyerr echoed the sentiments of other African councillors when he condemned the state of Boundary Road as "disgraceful" and argued that the Council "should raise a protest."[123] Similar protests were raised regarding nearby Castle Road.

The dedication and persistence with which town councillors pursued improvements for Boundary and Castle Roads were certainly influenced by their personal connections to the dangers and inconveniences of undrained, unfinished roads. As elite and powerful property owners, African councillors could afford to give up land for road development, and they had access to power that allowed them to agitate for action. While their privilege directed more attention to the condition of Boundary Road, it did not necessarily produce results. In 1931, the director of public works expressed his sympathies for the Council's position but reported that all financial provision for surface water drainage had been cut out of the estimates as part of austerity measures.[124] The situation did not improve in the following year. There was no provision made for roads in the estimates. Between 1931 and 1933, the municipal engineer proposed improvements to Boundary and Castle Roads three times, only to find his proposals denied.[125]

Motivated in part by petitions and protests from constituents and emboldened by public pressure on the governor's office, the Town Council did ultimately expand its efforts and attention related to road construction and drainage. Both official and unofficial members of the Council raised concerns about the condition of town roads. The medical officer of health (MOH) reported in 1934 that "many of the streets in Accra were in very shocking state of disrepair." Road conditions worsened significantly in heavy rains when "some of these streets were little less than quagmires" and "there were many depressions full of liquid mud which was splashed on pedestrians by motor vehicles."[126] The MOH named twenty-four individual streets in addition to all of the streets in Adabraka. Councillor Kitson Mills insisted on adding all of the streets of Korle Gonno to the list. It seemed like the entire town was suffering from deteriorating roads and untamed water.

Motivated to act, the ATC formed a subcommittee in 1934 that sought to "investigate the condition of certain roads in Accra."[127] In intensifying their action, members of the ATC were responding to both their legislative responsibilities to provide for the sanitation of the town, their own interests in the welfare and infrastructure of the town, and increasing pressure from town residents to see meaningful development of town infrastructure in exchange for their taxes. This sort of public pressure was far from unusual; residents regularly consulted with their ATC representatives, encouraging them to intervene in disputes, clarify policy, advocate for legal rights, and complain about a lack of infrastructural investment. The decline in government funding, evidenced throughout the 1930s, brought renewed protests about the pace of urban development. The depression that inspired austerity in government budgets also impacted the incomes of Accra residents who saw taxes as an extraordinary burden during a time of financial

Figure 1.3. Images captured decades later in the Old Town illustrate the same kinds of underdevelopment and uneven development debated by Accra residents and officials in the colonial period. Various Places in Accra, 1975. Photograph by Ben Kwakye. Source: Photographic Archive, Information Services Office, Ministry of Information, Accra PS/1834/5.

hardship. Residents were indignant about the government's piecemeal approach to development in the city.

Residents also complained about sewage, as well as the insalubrious effect it had on their daily life and work. Roads, however, generated new forms of protest, particularly as poor drainage put homes at risk and made physical mobility difficult in the city. Some of those complaints appear in the archives as generalized appeals from African councillors like Kitson Mills who pointed out that people living in areas like Korle Gono, which had suffered particular infrastructural neglect, "were taxpayers also, and they should have the same degree of attention as paid to other parts of the town."[128] Other residents, however, took their complaints directly to the government, demanding immediate improvements. When residents of Kofi Oku Road in Jamestown found themselves left out of neighborhood improvements in 1932, they wrote to the director of public works (DPW):

> We the undersigned, owners and occupiers of houses in Kofi Oku Road in James Town, beg to invite your attention to the condition of this road which has apparently escaped the notice of those responsible for its maintenance. The importance of the Road can be appreciated from the fact that it runs from the Horse Road near the Palladium to the London Market; but for a number of years no repairs whatever have been done to it and at every rainy season old cavities are deepened while new ones are cut and the road has consequently become dangerous not only to pedestrians but also to vehicles especially at night. The Road also boasts of a number of modern buildings and a few motor vehicle owners but the approaches to some of the houses, particularly those on the West of the Road are rendered increasingly dangerous year by year by surface rain water owing to the absence of proper drainage and it is feared that the safety of the houses themselves is likely to be affected. We respectfully ask therefore that this road be now given the attention it deserves; if it cannot this year be made a tarmetted street with side gutters, it should *at least* be made safe for those who use it. A year or two ago we were glad to notice the improvement to the neighboring Adedenkpo Road and we expected that a similar improvement would be extended to Kofi Oku Road but we were disappointed. We hope however that this our petition will receive favorable consideration for which we would assure you of our deep gratitude in advance. We respectfully invite inspection by a representative of your Department and, if you would let us know the time of his visit, two or three of us would be glad to meet him on the spot to explain the matter more clearly.[129]

In passing off the petition to the acting colonial secretary, the DPW noted that Kofi Oku Road had fallen between the cracks of responsibility and authority in colonial governance. The road had been laid out as part of urban redevelopment plans, and individuals had built homes, encouraged by government officials who were eager to decongest the older districts of Jamestown and encourage residents to relocate to new, planned neighborhoods. Plans, however, did not guarantee funding. The road had never been properly constructed or drained, and Public Works Office estimates for the year only accounted for the maintenance of already constructed town roads. As a result, no one seemed to be responsible for Kofi Oku Road. Expressing frustration over both the financial limitations of his office and the protest of town residents, the DPW argued that "having laid out a system of town roads, and allowed people to build on these roads, I suggest that it is not unreasonable for the people who build to expect the Government to maintain the road surfaces in passable condition, even though the roads have not been properly made up and drained."[130] Kofi Oku Road, described by the executive engineer in 1932 as "badly scoured and cut up by water courses" was still on a list of deteriorated roads in 1935, noted as "not drained or carriage-way formed."[131]

While the petitioners from Kofi Oku Road did not include Town Council members, the language of their petition and their representation by Mr. James Godfrey Tetteh O'Baka Torto, MBE, a recognized public servant who had connections across British West Africa, suggest that they were well-positioned and well-resourced residents of Accra. If their relative class position got them a hearing with the governor, it did not ultimately change the outcome. Merchants, likewise, sought to use their position within the colony to agitate for infrastructural investment. In 1935, the Rumball Street Trading Company wrote to the municipal engineer of the ATC highlighting the absurdity of prevailing maintenance policy:

> Passing along High Street today, the undersigned saw a squad of PWD [Public Works Department] repairers getting ready to do further work on a road surface which is already in almost perfect condition. Such very shallow declivities as they are apparently leveling off would contain little or no water after the heaviest rain. Orgle Street, as you already know, is a long expanse of humps and hollows which becomes an area of stinking quagmires after rainfall. In the Minutes of the Town Council Meeting held 14th May last, the MOH stressed the danger to public health arising from street pools in the rainy season, and whilst private individuals can be prosecuted for harbouring mosquito larvae on their premises, the authorities responsible for road maintenance are outside the law. Such a situation could be considered Gilbertian were it not such a serious matter. We have today had a conversation with Mr. Sutherland, and have his assurance that he is doing everything possible to direct early attention to the needs of Orgle Street.[132]

The proprietors of the Rumball Trading Company sought to leverage their position as business leaders to agitate for more immediate action. They wrote to the municipal engineer and spoke to the ATC president numerous times over the course of several months. In doing so, they argued that "quite apart from considerations of health, the residents of Orgle Street have equal rights with those more fortunate rate-payers who have houses and stores in those thoroughfares which are blessed with constant attention by levelling and tar-spraying squads."[133] Orgle Street was, indeed, added to the long list of town roads and was reported to the governor as needing critical attention. Despite having unanimous support from Accra officials, the government took no action. The Rumball Trading Company took their complaints a step further, writing directly to the governor that "the rights of ratepayers are secondary to the considerations of health, and we do assure you that in the rainy season, Orgle Street is a menace to the entire town, being a vast area of breeding pools for mosquito larvae."[134] Much like Kofi Oku

Road, Orgle Street seemed to slip between the policies and plans of government infrastructural development. Not yet "made up," the street was not eligible for maintenance.

Given the persistent difficulties posed by the Depression, colonial officials saw complaints from both Accra residents and Town Council members as both frustrating and annoying. Viewed within the broader system of indirect rule, the requests of the Town Council seemed presumptuous to some. "Accra characteristically asks for more money for a purely local service," wrote one official, "while the unfortunate up-country chiefs nowadays maintain long stretches of trade-road and consider themselves lucky if they get 5/- per mile dues for doing so."[135] Others complained that "Accra is very lucky to have had so much money spent on it, and the Town Council should be reminded of what they have authority do if they so wish. Until the country is better off financially people must be content to be splashed occasionally by passing lorries!"[136] These comments seemed to reverse a discourse of improvement, modernization, and sanitation that had been the norm in Accra for decades. At the very least, colonial officials used technicalities of categorization to pass off responsibility to the Town Council. As the DPW noted, because Orgle Street had not yet been constructed, the government could not be accused of neglecting maintenance. If the ATC wanted to see improvements, they had to arrange for residents to give property free of charge for the widening of the street. In the meantime, he argued, "If this street is so full of holes which holds storm water and breed mosquitoes, I suggest the ATC might dump ashes from their incinerator to level up the ground."[137]

The DPW's dismissive suggestions in response to the situation in Orgle Street suggest that this particular case had become a significant annoyance to central government officials. Only a few years earlier, the DPW had characterized the decreased investment in roads as a temporary setback in light of economic challenges. "It must be realized," he argued in 1931, "that a yearly programme of reconstruction, in future, will have to be provided for."[138] In response to many other ATC proposals for road maintenance or construction, he regularly offered to construct the road if the ATC would construct the drains[139]—a compromise that allowed the road program to continue, even if the pace remained slow. For town residents, like those on Kofi Oku and Orgle Streets, however, these delays were "disgraceful."[140] Residents could not reach their homes or use their motor vehicles, their houses flooded in heavy rains, and they risked illness and injury on the streets of the town.

Targeted investment meant that, while some would be frustrated by a lack of progress, other residents would see their protests and petitions finally paying off. Throughout the mid-1930s the Public Works Department did continue to work on a pared-down program of road construction. Most of the resources for the reconstruction of roads were focused on Christiansborg, but the government also dedicated significant energy and investment to constructing a road to the new cemetery, opened in 1920, that would connect Hansen Road to the Ring Road. Introduced as early as 1933, the question of a new cemetery road was of pressing interest to all residents in Accra.[141] The long distances mourners had to walk to reach the new cemetery constituted a "hardship and inconvenience."[142] "Looking at it from the African point of view," Councillor Akilagpa Sawyerr argued, "it seemed to him that African feeling regarding their dead should be considered. He had known of cases where many of the people got sick after walking to the Cemetery and back."[143] While not strictly a question of drainage, African councillors and residents alike considered the road a safety issue, both due to the dangers of flooding on the existing path and the danger that mourners would have to face as they passed on more congested town roads to reach the cemetery.[144] Sawyerr's comments also suggested that the circuitous routes also posed spiritual danger to mourners. European councillors, however, struggled to understand why the cemetery road was so important. The president of the ATC noted that the estimated £6,000 cost could supply Labadi with electric light, fund the construction of a moderately sized town hall, or contribute to decongestion efforts in the old quarters of the town.[145] But, with African councillors insisting on urgency of the matter and residents relaying "many complaints and much dissatisfaction"[146] to their representatives, government agreed to support the construction of the road (i.e., providing culverts and gravel) as long as the Town Council would use ashes from the incinerator to form banks to keep the road above the lagoon flood level.[147] While the new road was ultimately celebrated, the long process of negotiation took a toll on everyone. As Akilagpa Sawyerr noted as construction on the new road was negotiated, "The feeling of the community on the matter was very strong indeed. European members of the Council could not know how much elected members were worried by the people with this question."[148] The Town Council, as both the representatives of colonial power in the town and the mouthpiece of its residents, found itself forced to compromise—as with the sewage system—in fulfilling their responsibilities. They were both agents and impediments in the town's development.

CONCLUSION

The politics of water and waste—and the sanitary infrastructures, both physical and regulatory—that shaped politics in twentieth-century Accra were marked by highly contested processes, both within and outside of colonial governance structures. As "the built forms around which publics thicken,"[149] sanitary infrastructures certainly generated new debate about the purpose and responsibility of the state, the meaning of representation and self-governance, and the visions for urban governance and city life in Accra. This was in part by design; urban governance was, in the minds of British colonial officials, both a means to achieve sanitary goals and a way to decentralize or devolve responsibility for the construction and maintenance of the town onto African residents. Accra municipal government was formed as (and remained) a sanitary state throughout the first half of the twentieth century. Municipal revenue funded the salaries of sanitary inspectors, engineers, and other public health officials. As we shall see, urban development and colonial administration was in many ways driven by sanitary priorities—from the planning of the town to the organization of the economy. However, sanitary politics also highlighted the persistent ambiguities of colonial rule.

In creating and maintaining incoherent, inconsistent, unreliable, and often overlapping structures of authority in the town, colonial officials often blurred boundaries of responsibility and complicated the organization of town affairs. In part, as many town residents argued, this confusion evidenced a broad-based incompetence within the colonial administration, exacerbated by constantly changing personnel. For African contemporaries and present-day scholars alike, this incompetence highlighted the failure of a colonial state that never could realize its grandiose visions of "civilization" in model towns like Accra. As one (possibly sarcastic) writer argued

> Four or Five Hundred Years' contact with the Continent of Europe ought to give us at the present day, at least, one model Town, one Mecca, to which Fantis, Twis and Gas may go to for inspiration, instruction and improvement in the materialities of life. In this respect, the Government has been an egregious failure; the Authorities have come sadly short of the glories of civilization. With all their big talk of Sanitary Inspection and Mosquito expeditions, with all the fat emoluments connected with these high-sounding terms, with all the rigorous Sanitary precautions vigorously applied and carried out by an army of inspectors of all grades and colour, even Accra, the modern capital of the Colony is still full of filth and caked with dirt such as may not be found in other places away from the natural centre of light and progress. The whole system pursued in administering the Government of this Colony requires overhauling; the policy in vogue is too extravagant for a backward country like the Gold Coast and we look up confidently to His Excellency with his fine sense of proportion and moral fitness of things generally to put matters right for all concerned.[150]

For some, this was a question of responsibility. Having extracted taxes and other forms of wealth from the colony for many years, these residents argued that the British administration should be financially responsible for constructing infrastructure in the town before it attempted to hand over maintenance and governance to local authorities.[151] For still others, inadequate sanitary infrastructure and persistent underinvestment in African quarters of the town evinced an underlying infrastructural segregation, driven by underdevelopment, through which European residents were the primary beneficiaries of investment drawn from African taxation.[152]

African leaders in Accra and other Gold Coast towns, however, questioned whether all people in the town did or should share that burden equally. If British administrators insisted on maintaining a majority of "official" members—and thus ultimate authority—in town governance, many residents argued that they and they alone were responsible for the mismanagement of sanitation in the town, having "failed to discharge efficiently."[153] Town councillors, members of the Legislative Council, and journalists who complained about the hypocrisy of colonial urban governance and the inadequacies of indirect rule recognized what many scholars have not. The seeming "failure" of regulation and implementation was not the result of mismanagement; it was written into the very structures of urban governance. Writing and protesting actively in front of British officials, African residents made clear the consequences of urban underinvestment and oppressive, capricious regulation. In refusing to productively and proactively respond to public complaints, Town Council leaders and British officials transformed infrastructural questions into a debate about African rights to the city and its resources, in which the use of infrastructure itself was a potential violation that required regulation, policing, and punishment.

As the local arm of colonial bureaucracy in the city, the ATC implemented and enforced the regulatory visions of the British colonial state, and its "official" majority ensured that state interests would remain at the center of urban governance. However, the Town Council also created important new spheres of political debate and contestation. Through their elected town councillors, in the pages of newspapers, in petitions to government officials, and on the streets in protest, African residents helped shape this infrastructural politics in important ways. In some cases, that meant resisting government plans altogether, including protests against excessive prosecution, taxation, and fines. More often, however, residents protested to increase access to infrastructure and more evenly distribute investment in the colonial capital. As one resident complained in 1900:

> To send scavengers at five in the mornings to lurk about for the apprehension of people who may be throwing nuisance at places where prisoners also may be seen ditto-ing, or at the dusk of the evening for the "capturing" of poor strangers who may not even be committing any nuisance, to huddle poor innocent boys, girls, men and women before His Worship's Magisterial bench for throwing water here and there as the scavengers somewhere allege, or for

not sweeping their gates, when they will be muleted in fines ranging from five shillings to thirty shillings and more, to bury at times the seasoned fish of some poor women at the beach, may be considered fair means of giving us a clean, healthy Town, whereas in our humble opinion, to give us a clean, well-swept and watered streets, with clean drains and gutters, to have the outskirts of the Town well cleaned, and not made reservoirs of, for what dirt the Scavengers may collect from the Town, and from certain firms, to give us decent latrines far away from the Town and not nearly in the Town, to give us good water to drink, and not the wretched wells we see about, with other good things, and the kind of attention such a subject demands at the hands of the Authorities of which they are very well acquainted, may go some way to improve the sanitation of this place, which is one of the needs of the hour.[154]

Colonial officials who invoked "public health" as a justification for these changes were increasingly met with alternative questions of public interest—whose health was being protected? Why? Who was paying for it? Who was deciding? These issues were fundamental questions of the meaning and practice of governance in the colonial capital. Asking them did not guarantee an answer, however. Even as the state began to increase investments in the 1930s and 1940s, it was increasingly clear that state power lay not in big infrastructural projects or in their ability to physically remake the town but rather in the power and willingness to regulate and prosecute. In policing and prosecuting African behavior in both public and private spaces, the Town Council and other regulatory bodies consistently placed responsibility for the unsanitary state of the town on African residents. Backed by the power of the police and the courts, the regulation and enforcement of sanitary measures marginalized and criminalized African behaviors and bodies in new ways and enshrined new forms of state authority over both public and private space.

TWO

"HEALTH IS THE FIRST WEALTH"

IN THE FEBRUARY 17, 1912, issue of the *Gold Coast Leader*, the newspaper's editors publicized instructions compiled by Sir Ronald Ross of the Liverpool School of Tropical Medicine. Reprinted from *African Mail*, a Liverpool publication founded by Edmund Morel, the instructions detailed European understandings and expectations of the necessary conditions for health "out in Africa." The list, which was targeted primarily at European traders, missionaries, and colonial officials, detailed a range of recommendations from food safety and diet to clothing choices and exercises. The mosquito, however, reoccurred throughout the list, influencing recommendations for the storing of water, the use of fans and mosquito nets, and the planting of gardens. This focus on the mosquito was unsurprising given the author. Ross had discovered that malaria was a parasite transmitted through the bite of the *Anopheles* mosquito in 1898 and had spent years advocating for various forms of prevention and treatment to decrease death rates and improve overall health in tropical zones. While much of the advice presented focused on the actions that Europeans could take to protect themselves, including alteration to the environmental and living conditions of everyday life, the last line embodied a colonial approach to health that had become entrenched by the early twentieth century: "It is usually very dangerous, often deadly, for Europeans to live or sleep in houses occupied, or recently occupied by natives."[1]

In warning of the perceived danger of cohabitation, Ross echoed a persistent sentiment among tropical disease and colonial medicine specialists in which Africans were viewed as "causative agents" or "reservoirs" of disease.[2] To some degree, these views were connected to Victorian sensibilities about cleanliness and sanitation. As an observer from the Liverpool School of Tropical Medicine argued on a tour of Britain's West African colonial capitals in 1900, the "native town" of Accra was "a standing menace to the health of the community at large."[3] Among the general organization of the street, the presence of animals, and the nakedness of children, these observers were fixated on the environmental conditions that were thought to foster disease. In addition to the presence of garbage and the absence of latrines, which preoccupied sanitation officials, these public health observers were often obsessed with mosquitoes. "Mosquitoes abound, and the odor is often frightful," the Liverpool observer noted:

> Every now and then one comes across a butt or other receptacle filled with stinking water, infested with mosquitoes, and infected with bacteria ... a complete absence of any system of drainage completes what to a European eye is nothing but a noisome and pestilential district. The dangers of such neighbors to the white population is obvious, and some of the commercial community, as I have said, live very close indeed to those parts of the town. This danger is, I think, increased by the fact that the prevailing wind sweeps over and through these native dens before reaching the houses of the white inhabitants.[4]

This description echoes dominant imperial narratives about the Gold Coast—and Africa broadly—as a "repository of death, disease, and degeneration" that represented distinct forms of mortal danger for European traders, missionaries, and administrators.[5] To a large extent, this obsession with health and the regulation of the body in West Africa was a reflection of the very real risk of death for Europeans traveling to the tropics. Even in India, where disease risk had been mitigated significantly by the late nineteenth century, British officials' experience was "intensely physical ... written on the Anglo-Indian physique, from the boils, mosquito bites and the altered composition of the fibres and tissues of the body, to the colonists' characteristic clothing and confident demeanor."[6] If, as Collingwood argues, "Britishness in the colonial context was ... conceptualized through a dialogue with difference," that difference also reshaped the body itself.[7] What's notable in the description above, however, is its focus on the "neighbors" rather than the environment alone as the source of disease. Imperial "myths and beliefs about the supposedly dirty tastes, habits, and practices of Africans" often influenced the "practical application of scientific discoveries" in West African colonies.[8] By the late nineteenth century, British physicians and sanitary engineers used new discoveries in the medical sciences to justify increasingly aggressive forms of regulation that transformed African bodies into "living laboratories" that could be studied and through which diseases could be isolated, mapped, and controlled.[9] But, similar to what we've seen in debates over sanitation infrastructure, narratives of "dirty natives" and "diseased bodies" also often justified an expansion of cultural and economic regulation into the daily lives of African urban residents. These were new boundaries that defined what was acceptable and unacceptable, legitimate and illegitimate: all realized through the practices and policies of Accra Town Council officials and backed by the police, the courts, medical experts, and many members of the African elite, including lawyers and doctors.[10]

These new practices of regulation and residential segregation in the late nineteenth and early twentieth centuries marked a shift in the spatial politics of the city. Like other cities along the West African coast, European and African residents had long lived side by side in Accra.[11] Traders wanted to stay near their shops and customers, missionaries wanted to be close to their parishioners, and the relative itinerancy of Europeans on the coast meant that nearly everyone needed to stay near the coastal castles, which were closely connected to the Ga neighborhoods. And yet, even though Western medicine could offer little protection against tropical diseases before the twentieth century and European visitors regularly visited local healers when they were ill, this association of disease with African environments and bodies was far from new. Writing about Sierra Leone, Festus Cole argues that "since the establishment of the colony, when miasmatic theories attributed the origins of disease to the climate and noxious exhalations from putrid organic matter, up to the evolution of the germ theory and elucidation of the aetiology of malaria, West Africa's environment and its inhabitants have been portrayed as inherently pathological."[12] Nineteenth- and early twentieth-century medical theories about tropical disease were simultaneously part of an unfolding scientific revolution and a continuation of centuries-old practices that were often utilized to reinforce racism and imperialism. Public health experts reasoned that even if individual African residents were healthy—a baffling phenomenon for many in light of high European death rates—their way of living must be unhealthy.[13] Medical theories that blamed "tropical miasmas" and "tropical fevers" for poor health in colonies like the Gold Coast were no longer supported within professional scientific circles or prevailing medical opinion. Yet the racial discourses of early twentieth-century colonial public health often merely repackaged these theories and attached them to a new human source—African urban residents.[14] If scientific advances had increasingly helped establish distinctions between hygiene and health, sanitation and medicine, practitioners themselves were often slow to make the shift, insisting on a vision of public health that just as often actively undermined the public welfare and ignored obvious evidence drawn from experience.[15]

Widely known and feared as the "white man's grave," West African colonies were a particular target of these medicalizing, pathologizing discourses.[16] The robust concentration of trade and capital investment in the Gold Coast made it a particular target of medical anxieties and public health interventions in British West Africa.[17] In moving the colonial capital to Accra in the late nineteenth century, British officials cast Accra as "a colonial capital founded on the promise of health."[18] Accra's drier climate and higher elevation promised a healthier environment for European residents. The city's new status also brought more concentrated investment in Western medicine and a new kind of intensity of the clinical gaze imposed on African residents. Driven by an assumption in the universality of science and the promise of medical triumph, British officials believed that science could vanquish diseases that impeded "civilization," paving the way for colonial economic and territorial expansion and, at least by the 1920s, creating a healthier African labor force that would support socioeconomic development in the colony. But the spatial and social organization of the city and the daily lives of its residents challenged many of the prevailing medical theories and practices of emerging fields of public health.

This chapter explores shifting regulations and policies related to health in Accra during this period of scientific transformation, tracing their development through the lens of diseases like bubonic plague, yellow fever, and malaria. Taken together, these policies constituted an emerging practice and profession of public health—what Roberts describes as a "unified vision of the bodily and spatial relations of illness in the tropics," rooted in colonial anxieties about tropical disease and imperial profits and informed by a persistent racism and classism that obscured official understandings of health.[19] As with sanitation and other spheres of colonial regulation, the increased public health scrutiny that urban residents faced from colonial technocrats was certainly consequential. The enactment and enforcement of regulation reshaped the organization of space and the realities of daily life among Accra residents in significant ways, from residential segregation plans to mosquito inspections. And yet, as Roberts and others have argued in relation to therapeutic practice in Accra, state regulation fell short of the kind of biopower described by Foucault. Realities on the ground contradicted Western assertions of the presumed superiority of Western science and medicine even as some members of the African elite supported the expansion and implementation of Western medical and public health regimes. These contradictions and the protests and petitions of urban residents and their representatives made clear that the power and efficacy of the medical department and the perception of colonial public health initiatives was far from certain and that alternative understandings of health and healing continued to circulate in Accra in ways that were central to the daily lives of its residents.[20]

"UNHEALTHINESS OF THE COAST": MEDICAL ENCOUNTERS IN THE GOLD COAST

Colonial narratives of unhealthiness, disease, and danger in coastal cities like Accra belied the rich cultural understandings of health and practices of healing in African communities. Among the various ethnolinguistic groups in southern

Ghana, "medicine is understood to be material devices that not only directly heal bodily ailments but also fight off the malicious spirits that cause illness."[21] For the Ga these dual material and spiritual dimensions were captured in the words associated with health and healing practice: *tsofa* (medicine), *tsofatse* (healer), and *won/woji* (spirit).[22] In the absence of more efficacious alternatives from ship's surgeons, early European explorers and traders on the Gold Coast often participated in African healing traditions, even if their understanding of health and healing was less spiritual and more environmental: according to Curtin, "Temperature, humidity, and emanations from the soil were the sources of danger."[23] Transformations in the late nineteenth century, however, soon redrew these relationships and understandings regarding health. As Jonathan Roberts has argued for African histories of medicine in Accra, the fervor of religion, the emergence of a medicalized colonial state, and the desire for social distinction underlay transformations in the history of healing in the city.[24] European understandings of healing also changed radically in the late nineteenth century, driven by the development of germ theory, which made prevention and cure of diseases increasingly viable, and new forms of colonial investment in colonies like the Gold Coast. These transformations—just like the early medical encounters—were interconnected even as new forms of colonial policy and practice sought to reinforce difference and separation. New understandings of health and medicine were also intimately connected to the past; transformation was not marked by a sudden rupture but, as Curtin argues for new European theories of disease, "It was not assimilated immediately by the public mind or even by the medical profession."[25] Change took time, and many practitioners continued to cling to older theories and practices, thus incorporating them into emerging public health strategies at home and abroad. Backed by the power of the state, British colonial policies were in many ways more obviously consequential. But Africans also integrated new changes into dynamic practices of "therapeutic pluralism" that shaped colonial medicine in both direct and indirect ways.[26]

These transformations were, in many ways, essential for British officials who sought to consolidate their authority over the Gold Coast and expand their control into the interior. West Africa's notorious reputation as the "white man's grave" made service in the colonies a highly risky endeavor, and the missionary societies, merchant houses, and government offices operating in the Gold Coast struggled to recruit qualified officers given the low salaries and high mortality rates.[27] Between 1881 and 1897, the average annual death rate for European officials in the Gold Coast was 75.6 per 1,000. For missionaries, traders, and miners, the mortality rates were even worse—an average of 81.48 per 1,000 every year between 1879 and 1888.[28] As Roberts notes, "Most Europeans who visited the coast were struck with fever within a few weeks. On average, half were dead within the first year. Those who survived a bout with malaria gained a temporary respite from the illness but they were still vulnerable to yellow fever, typhoid, guinea worm, and gastrointestinal illnesses."[29] Long leaves for rest and recovery—the "short leave system"—provided some degree of protection for those who did sign up, but the constant cycling of staff made it impossible to build any sort of institutional knowledge or continuity of administration for colonial governments.[30] In 1896 alone, out of 176 officers stationed in the Gold Coast, 89 took a leave of absence, 26 were invalided, and 15 died.[31] Trading companies and merchant houses also complained regularly to the Colonial Office, citing "polluted ponds and wells, refuse-strewn streets and yards, and open sewage pits, which stood as obvious sources of contagion."[32]

Elite African coastal residents, demanding the same kinds of development efforts that were being undertaken in British cities, often backed these calls for improved sanitary regulations and infrastructural investments. In 1895 even the editors of the *Gold Coast Chronicle* acknowledged the dangers that tropical diseases posed for Europeans, arguing that "something will have to be done in the matter of the present death rate among the Europeans, as it does not require a special pair of spectacles to see that the white men in the western province are passing away one after the other in a most extraordinary manner, and unless the question of improved sanitary arrangements—particularly in Cape Coast and Elmina where the greatest number of deaths must have to be recorded during the past three months—is seriously discussed, we cannot say what will be in store for us."[33] The eastern districts, including Accra, appeared to be healthier, confirming the government's decision to move the colonial capital farther east. But African coastal residents suffered from many of the same diseases as their European counterparts, and the arrival of European ships often brought new dangers, from smallpox to plague, which African Town Council (ATC) representatives and other public figures often complained were being ignored by British officers. In the realm of colonial policy, poor African health was recognized as a barrier to long-term social and economic progress by incapacitating large portions of the population.[34] Colonial and commercial development needed healthy workers, and Western medicine was expected to improve overall health and aid in the economic, social, and cultural transformation of the region—a manifestation of the "civilizing mission."[35] However, the resulting solutions tended to privilege economic interests over general public health. Those results would be achieved with only the least possible investment. The "visible decimation" of the relatively small British population in coastal towns like Accra generated more urgent responses and concentrated investment.[36] Colonial officials obsessed over European death and invaliding rates, but there were no reliably comparable statistics for African health. British health officers argued that Africans were less likely to report births and deaths, fearing quarantine or other kinds of health interventions, and fewer Africans addressed their health needs through colonial hospitals. But leading African representatives also regularly critiqued the colonial administration for not investing sufficiently in health education, and the inequalities in resource allocation were often thrown into stark relief in the context of major health campaigns to fight epidemic diseases and malaria. Africans, it was clear, were seen as a source of disease and a health threat in colonial public health logics.[37] They were not the "public" that technocrats had in mind.

Colonial officials, who saw economic potential in the Gold Coast, sought to tackle the health problem, at least for Europeans, with "prophylactic action."[38] Until Ross's discovery of the mosquito vector for diseases like malaria, much of this early strategy was based on older notions of "noxious vapors." In attempting to control odors and smells as a central public health strategy, early colonial officials often blurred the lines between sanitation, health, and social policy—a form of "sanitary salvation."[39] Practices like segregation and swamp or lagoon drainage were often inspired as much by the bourgeois sensibilities of colonial officials as actual scientific research.[40] Smell was another way to mark African bodies and bodily practices as diseased. Practices like racial segregation protected European officials from diseases associated with the urban poor and with colonial subjects—health being used to justify various forms of racism and classism in the context of colonial governance.[41] Colonial officers often used "health" as an excuse to intervene in various areas of daily life in order to better align urban living with Victorian/Edwardian sensibilities; these interventions for "health" came with assumptions about what constituted "well-being" and what the conditions for health actually were—an issue of contestation by various constituencies in the Gold Coast throughout much of the late nineteenth and twentieth centuries.

While some early colonial governors, including J. F. Rodgers, J. J. Thorburn, Hugh Clifford, and F. G. Guggisberg opposed policies like segregation on practical and financial grounds—it was seen as unnecessarily expensive, ineffectual, and likely to meet with opposition from African residents—leading medical officers continued to recommend it well into the 1930s.[42] But even if particular policies struggled to take root, health did serve as a primary motivator or lever in shifting the nature of European presence in the colony. Western medicine was not particularly effective in the tropics until much later, and there was little evidence on the ground to back British assertions of their superiority besides smallpox inoculations. Public health interventions—and the responses of African residents—existed in this space in between ideological coercion and practical efficacy. British medical superiority was often expressed—the "power to govern" was often presented as the "power to heal"—but rarely demonstrated in practice, a fact that even Colonial Office officials and the Colonial Secretary Lord

Chamberlain himself acknowledged.[43] Despite extensive efforts to count, report, and review health statistics and invest in new scientific research, compromise was more characteristic of colonial medicine than control, and Western medical knowledge did not displace or erase African healing traditions, even if they clearly ignored them in constructing new "public health mandates."[44]

"TROPICAL MEDICINE" AND THE BUREAUCRATIZATION OF PUBLIC HEALTH

The various interests and anxieties related to tropical disease were consolidated at the turn of the century through the development of new kinds of bureaucratic institutions that sought to professionalize the study and deployment of tropical medicine using new scientific theories and research methods. The Liverpool School of Tropical Medicine was founded in 1898 through a donation from Sir Arthur Lewis Jones, a prominent ship owner with trading interests in West Africa. The London School of Tropical Medicine was opened a year later by Sir Patrick Manson, medical adviser to the Colonial Office and funded through a donation from the Indian philanthropist B. D. Pettit. These new institutions were dedicated to the study of tropical diseases, which Manson, who was a pioneer in malaria research, described as "a natural division of diseases, a division which, in the case of the tropics at all events, has to be recognized in practice, and which, if we are to do full justice to the claims of diseases, of those who suffer from them, and of our national interest, we have to meet by special educational arrangement."[45] Epidemic diseases like cholera, plague, and yellow fever existed alongside endemic diseases including, most prominently, malaria. While the epidemics often attracted more attention and intervention, endemic diseases like malaria provided the most serious threat. "When we describe a tropical country as 'unhealthy,'" Manson argued, "we really mean that it is malarious. West Africa is unhealthy."[46]

The London and Liverpool schools targeted tropical disease as an existential threat. Manson's dual invocation of individual suffering and national interest captured the conflicting motivations that informed emerging fields of tropical medicine and public health.[47] Thanks in part to Manson's relationship with the Colonial Office, the London School quickly became a training ground for departing colonial officers. These new schools were part of an emerging understanding of empire advanced by Joseph Chamberlain, who advocated for a more directly interventionist approach to colonial governance during his time as colonial secretary from 1895 to 1903.[48] Having been founded by commercial interests, the Liverpool School was initially independent of the government, but within a few years it too had taken on a role as a training ground for colonial officers. Importantly, however, the study of tropical medicine also aimed to make imperial government more cost effective.⁴⁹ As Manson argued, "unhealthy" countries doubled the cost of colonial administration in places like the Gold Coast:

> What with death and invaliding and the necessity for frequent leave of absence to Europe in order to avert disease, in these Colonies two men have to be employed to do the work of one, and that to induce them to accept employment these men have each to get double pay. It means that continuity of work and accumulation of personal experience which are so necessary for successful government and administration are almost impossible. It means that Government is robbed of many of its best servants just as they are becoming valuable. It means an enormous financial drain on a sorely handicapped community. In the face of these figures it is difficult to see how such Colonies can get along at all.⁵⁰

And yet, Manson says, tropical medicine promises to reverse these conditions: "Malaria is a rope round their necks, and the fact that they continue to exist, some of them to prosper even in spite of it, is testimony to their economic value and eloquent testimony as to what might be made of them and what they would blossom into were this ever-floating cloud of malaria that hangs over them dispelled. Can this cloud by any practicable means be dissipated? My answer to this question and to the same question as regards all the other diseases I have enumerated is emphatically, 'Yes.'"⁵¹ Manson's confidence was rooted in a growing faith in modern medicine and its ability to redress both physical and social ills. Hygiene, Bashford argues, "came to be a personal and political imperative and mission" in late nineteenth- and early twentieth-century Britain—"a noun which spawned ever more adjectives which connected the bodily and the personal to larger governmental projects."⁵²

Both of these institutions combined medical research with public health training. This was a reflection of older public health practices that targeted the urban poor in both London and Liverpool several decades earlier, imported into a colonial context with new forms of unknown disease to more effectively "administer" colonized peoples and territories and render them "intelligible to colonizers."⁵³ In a meeting with Chamberlain in 1901, a deputation from the London, Liverpool, and Manchester Chambers of Commerce and the Liverpool School of Tropical Medicine advocated for a diverse range of policies to address both the political/economic and moral consequences of health policy including "a) the removal and disposal of refuse, b) surface drainage of the soil and removal of bush and undergrowth in and near towns, c) removal of native huts when their presence is a menace to European residents, d) installation of sanitary regulations for observance in the coastal settlements."⁵⁴ Investment in the health of the colonies, Chamberlain acknowledged, was essential to the success of colonial economic development programs in West Africa.⁵⁵ The research conducted in the new schools informed and justified the expansion of investments in health infrastructure in colonies like the Gold Coast while also training officers to fill those positions.⁵⁶ Ronald Ross and Patrick Manson's research on the mosquito vector for malaria fueled the British government's investment in research and training on tropical medicine.⁵⁷ In the first year after its opening in 1899, the London School of Tropical Medicine had already trained fifty students in the study of tropical diseases.⁵⁸ By the early twentieth century, all newly appointed medical officers were required to take the course in tropical medicine at either London or Liverpool.⁵⁹

Medicine often brought Africans "into tighter relations with governance" and constituted both a representation and tool of government power in colonies.⁶⁰ "The power to govern," some scholars have argued, "is often presented as the power to heal,"⁶¹ allowing Europeans to live anywhere on the globe.⁶² Cities in both the colonies and the metropole became sites of experimentation, connecting medical research and public health practice with new fields of urban planning, design, and development as a part of a bureaucratization of health and healing.⁶³ These new bureaucratic and technocratic practices fused early genealogies of public health—the philanthropic-missionary and the governmental/political—in new ways that simultaneously sought to advance and restrict freedom.⁶⁴

In the colonies, the professionalization of medicine corresponded to a progressive alienation of Africans from the medical service. The Gold Coast Medical Department was founded in the 1880s, led by a physician who held the position of "principal medical officer."⁶⁵ Between 1892 and 1897 that officer was Sierra Leonean Dr. J. F. Easmon. But British officials pushed Easmon out in 1897, and they passed over qualified African physician Dr. B. W. Quartey-Papafio in favor of a white candidate with training in "tropical medicine." By 1902 applications were formally restricted to Europeans.⁶⁶ The high salaries and political clout of medical officers ensured that these conditions remained in place well into the 1920s. The conservatism and racism of the medical establishment was well known even among European officials. As one European (and unofficial) member of the Legislative Council complained in 1914, "Medical officers are not renowned for being broad minded."⁶⁷ Conservatism and racism also informed more general complacency among the medical staff toward African health—a condition that left even Governor Hugh Clifford (served 1912–1919) appalled.⁶⁸

The medical service expanded through the 1920s. In 1923 the position of principal medical officer was redesignated director of medical and sanitary services (and later director of medical services), reporting directly to the governor through the colonial secretary and often serving as an official representative on the Accra Town Council. In 1919 the government created a new Sanitary (Health) Branch, which was responsible for sanitation, vaccinations, and preventive measures, and a Medical Research Institute (Laboratory) Branch, which pursued scientific investigations as well as conducted tests and postmortems. These new units complemented the work of the Medical Branch, which was responsible for all hospitals and clinics.[69] If Chamberlain had resisted early calls for substantive investment in health interventions in West African colonies, that attitude had clearly changed by the 1920s, buoyed by several decades of statistics and reporting.[70]

COLONIAL SCIENCE

Tropical medicine, then, sat at the intersection of colonialism and science, which, Tilley argues, was characterized by a "complicated web of relations."[71] The need for tropical medicine specialists and the general importance of the medical sciences in the colonies justified government funding, increased the size and stature of scientific societies, the number of academic posts, and the significance of training programs.[72] Beginning in the late nineteenth century through the Second World War, hygiene and health were increasingly seen as both personal and political imperatives.[73] Colonial officials, medical experts, and African elites alike argued that "health is the first wealth" and advocated for increased investment in medical services.[74] This belief was most obviously exhibited in support for public health and medicine for Europeans in Accra. Moving the colonial capital to Accra motivated increased investment in Western medicine in the city. Even if nineteenth-century medicines and medical strategies were poorly suited to dealing with tropical disease, new forms of colonial investment introduced an increasingly intense clinical gaze on African residents—a form of "sanitation syndrome" discussed by Swanson in which Black residents were thought to embody infection and disease.[75]

Undoubtedly, some elite African residents welcomed the new developments. The editors of the *Gold Coast Aborigines* argued that the district commissioner, the health officer, and the inspector of nuisance, who were directly responsible for the town's health, could not be entirely blamed for persistently poor health in Accra and other coastal cities "because they can only move as redtapeism directs."[76] While the officials in charge of the colony's health were neglecting their duties in Accra, native merchants and traders were contributing thousands of pounds of revenue to the colony, and the European population was growing. "If the building of new houses can be a criterion to judge the growth of a town by, then this town is growing in the hands of those directly responsible for this work, should be strengthened to enable them to discharge their work faithfully," the newspaper's editors argued.[77] However, new public health measures, introduced in the name of sanitation, were widely considered by Accra residents as both "an instrument of oppression and a tool of tyranny." As many commentators noted, positions like "inspector of nuisances" often failed to correct behavior (accompanied by education) but rather represented yet another way to collect taxes or fees from Africans and further enrich the colonial coffers. In medicalizing life and death, the colonial state sought to justify a more intense form of surveillance of the daily life and private spaces of African residents.[78] Officials passed laws banning house burials and enforcing cemetery burial, transforming the ways that Ga communities understood spirits, the afterlife, and property.[79] Inspectors of nuisance "sent scavengers out at five in the mornings to lurk about for the apprehension of people who may be throwing nuisance at places where prisoners may also be seeing *ditto*-ing, or at the desk of the evening for the 'capturing' of poor strangers who may not even be committing any nuisance, to huddle up poor innocent boys, girls, men and women before his worship's magisterial bench for throwing water here and there as the scavenger sometimes alleged, or for not sweeping their gates, when they will be mulleted in fines ranging from 5 shillings to 30 shillings and more, to bury at times the seasoned fish of some poor women at the beach."[80] Meanwhile, the editors of the *Gold Coast Chronicle* complained in 1897 that the town was at risk of an epidemic of smallpox because the government refused to take necessary steps to vaccinate inhabitants.[81]

The contradictions were in many ways unsurprising in the context of an emerging practice of scientific research that saw Africa as a "living laboratory."[82] For colonial administrators, scientific knowledge provided "reliable information" they could use to do their work effectively, for technical officers to facilitate socioeconomic development and other Europeans to advance their own interests, and for some Africans who sought to effectively position themselves within this new form of pluralistic society.[83] African realities often challenged scientific "certainties" and raised questions about British imperial supremacy, but that often did little to change colonial rhetoric or policy.[84] On the contrary, these contradictions often justified further interventions in the private spaces and daily lives of African urban residents.[85] As the former assistant colonial secretary, Mr. T. H. Hatton Richards, described Accra in 1897, the city was a place of danger, yet "the first thing which strikes one arriving at Accra is the apparent absence of anything to make the place so unhealthy, and, perhaps, a casual observer might think the place could not be as bad as is generally reported."[86] Hatton Richards argued that it was the condition of the "native town" that was at issue. The town itself and individuals within it might be healthy, but their way of living was not—both in form and practice. The 1894 fires that destroyed large portions of the town "turned out to be a blessing in disguise, so far as the native quarter of Accra was concerned."[87] In drawing Europeans into African neighborhoods, the fires created a new form of awareness about the living conditions of the town and raised increasing awareness about the need for public health through spatial intervention.

THEORY AND PRACTICE

In seeking to make direct interventions into the daily lives and spaces of Accra residents, health policy and inspections "could produce collisions between ruler and ruler."[88] These collisions were, on the one hand, a consequence of the delicate balance between the professionalized, technocratic practice that advocated centralized control and the local knowledge and priorities that shaped the daily lives of many residents. British officials themselves struggled to balance these demands as part of the "decentralized improvisation" of indirect rule.[89] Even as the Colonial Office issued health directives to West African governments from London, the ways in which officials within individual colonies sought to implement the directives were dictated by local political, economic, social, and cultural factors. Even Chamberlain, who eagerly wielded his power as colonial secretary, allowed governors to use their discretion in creating and enforcing policy. The Colonial Office did not create a centralized sanitary authority, but it did create an Advisory Board that administered the Tropical Diseases Research Fund in 1904 and an Advisory Medical and Sanitary Committee for Tropical Africa to oversee the selection and organization of West African medical staff in 1909. But these bodies remained well removed from the day-to-day practicalities of enforcing and implementing plans, policies, and regulations.[90]

These structures reflected broader imperial approaches to scientific research. As Helen Tilley argues, emerging scientific knowledge was simultaneously "situated" in particular locations and highly mobile within, across, and between metropole and colony.[91] There was, in other words, no such thing as a homogenous "colonial science" in practice. Certainly colonial officials and British technocrats aspired to create a "system of medicine that attempts to reorder the lives of subject people employing medical discourses that affirm the colonizer's own medical, cultural, and racial superiority."[92] Colonial states used advances in Western medical research and practice as a "tool of empire"[93] that would enable them "both to conquer and to live in the tropics," but Echenberg argues that the kinds of political, military, and economic transformations wrought through "new imperialism" also facilitated the spread of a range of diseases, including cholera, malaria, yellow fever, trypanosomiasis, and bubonic plague.[94] British scientists and colonial officials often pointed to these changes as testament to the triumph of Western medicine. However, as recent scholarship on the history of medicine has shown, "indigenous knowledge" as a theoretically distinctive body of knowledge was not "disrupted or destroyed by colonialism."[95] Rather, Roberts argues, African residents in Accra embraced multiple forms of healing as part of a practice of "therapeutic pluralism" or "therapeutic diversity"—a direct challenge to assumptions about the universality of science and narratives of Western medical triumph.[96]

As Roberts notes, scholars struggle to historicize therapeutic pluralism, hampered by the lack of indigenous sources, the impossibility of proving curative efficacy of Western versus non-Western therapeutics, and the potential to negate the agency of African patients who often creatively combined treatment regimens in search of health.[97] However, the policies—and responses to those policies—related to health and the body, centralized control and local knowledge, help us to understand to some degree the parameters of the debate. In criticizing the "inadequacy of the health laws and the unwillingness of chiefs or political officers to enforce them or to levy substantial fines on those found guilty of violations," Dr. P. S. Selwyn-Clarke, both lauded and maligned as medical officer of health, highlighted some of the contradictions and challenges at the core of colonial health policy.[98] Europeans and Africans alike often resented the work of the medical officer of health and his staff of inspectors who seemed not to care about the impact their work had on residents' daily lives.[99] Governors were wary of medical interventions because of their cost and the risk of local rebellion; public health officials often chose to do things "on the cheap" by focusing on the city's white population.[100] But this restrained action generated its own form of critique. By both criticizing African practices as "unhealthy" within emerging conceptions of international technocratic standards while also refusing to invest in urban development or medical education, colonial officials created an impossible double bind for Accra residents. This dilemma highlighted the inconsistencies and inefficiencies of a segmented colonial bureaucracy and generated public complaint and condemnation, both in the pages of the newspaper and in the debates of the Accra Town Council.

At the root of this contestation lay a persistent racism that infected Western medical research and practice. Like other technocratic fields, practitioners and scholars alike have long assumed that the biomedical revolution that gave rise to modern conceptions of medicine and public health was scientifically "neutral" and disconnected from social and racial ideologies that dominated the nineteenth and early twentieth centuries. However, as Echenberg argues, "Even though bacteriology in the wake of Robert Cox's model of the germ theory clearly adopted a 'civilizing mission' to root out diseases, its vocabulary could also incorporate nonwhites as causative agents of disease and as the contributors to the spread of infections."[101] In evaluating practices and applying rules governing medicine and public health, medical officers and inspectors exercised significant class and racial prejudice.[102] British officers were "quick to list the African domestic behaviors responsible for incubating contagious diseases, encouraging vermin, and harboring malarial mosquito larvae," Newell notes, often pointing to their inability to pay for imported commodities like soap as a sign of their danger to public health.[103] These attitudes were embedded in the rhetoric and practice of medicine and public health and, consequently, in the urban planning models that they inspired. As Vaughan and many others have noted, tropical medicine spawned a new way of thinking about African cities and their inhabitants, helping to translate British ideas about town planning into new colonial and imperial realities and inspiring new obsessions with "proximity" in physical and social space.[104]

And yet, medical interventions in Accra could not fully separate African and European residents and did not fundamentally transform the town's health.[105] As Patterson notes,

> The MOH and his African inspectors did not erect impressive hospitals or provide injections to heal the sick; instead, they poked around people's compounds, looking for mosquito larvae, unauthorized buildings, excess lodgers, or the sick; they issued a steady stream of summonses and fines for those who relieve themselves in a place other than the filthy public latrines, sold food on the streets without an expensive cover, or dumped garbage in a handy gutter rather than a distant and already overflowing dustbin. In short, the MOH and his men badgered people in many ways without any obvious benefit to anyone except those who collected the fines or got jobs as inspectors.[106]

Regardless of the rhetoric, these realities highlighted struggles over more than just health. Chiefs, sanitary inspectors, traders, medical officers—not to mention African political representatives, lawyers, doctors, and newspaper editors—and other colonial officials all struggled over power, land, and resources through debates about the meaning of "public health" in the town.[107]

HEALTH INFRASTRUCTURE IN THE GOLD COAST

Patterns of investment in health infrastructure generally reflected the rhetoric from the Colonial Office, even as local conditions shaped the realities of daily practice. When observers from the Liverpool School of Tropical Medicine visited Accra in 1900, they noted that investment was only noticeable in the European community of Christiansborg.[108] Four years later, little had changed. Francis Hart noted that "apart from a hundred pounds or so a year for Accra absolutely no financial provision is made for the protection and preservation of the public health, the Government doctors, who are nominally the health officers of the towns in which they are stationed, not being provided with the funds, which will enable them to keep the communities entrusted to their care sweet and clean."[109]

Hart noted that the medical service, and its principal medical officer, Dr. Henderson, CMG, were "exceptionally efficient." Government doctors, however, seemed to spend much of their time and energy in private practice where they charge exorbitant prices that prevent individuals from seeking care.[110] And yet, these observations reflect a growth from early hospitals established in 1882 and 1883 in abandoned bungalows with limited staff. As Dr. J. Desmond McCarthy noted, any moderately ill European preferred to be sent back to Britain rather than pursue treatment at the colonial hospital.[111] Despite this underfunding, the number of African patients seeking treatment did increase steadily through the late nineteenth century and justified an expansion. Jonathan Roberts argues that the increases likely represented the increasing authority of the colonial state over the health of African residents—Africans employed in the colonial service sought treatment at the hospital in order to document illness, merchants and elites sought treatment as a way to signal status and wealth, and individuals who were injured in accidents or were in custody may have been taken to the hospital by the police. However, Roberts argues, Accra residents also likely saw the hospital as yet another addition to the plurality of therapeutics available in the city, particularly for more serious trauma cases.[112] The presence of early African doctors like Dr. J. F. Easmon and Dr. Benjamin William Quartey-Papafio also likely increased the willingness of African residents to trust the colonial hospital as a source of treatment and undercut the possible spread of rumors about nefarious activities associated with colonial medicine, which did circulate in other parts of the continent in which medical systems were dominated by white medical professionals.[113]

The establishment of professional centers of training in London and Liverpool, however, marked a shift in colonial patterns of investment. By 1904 there were six government hospitals in Axim, Elmina, Cape Coast, Accra, Ada, Keta, and Kumasi, as well as dispensaries at Sekondi, Tarkwa, Saltpond, and Akuse. At three hospitals—Axim, Cape Coast, and Accra—there were special services for Europeans as well as dedicated nurses. In Accra there was a dedicated building for contagious diseases as well as a lunatic asylum. In all, 1,305 patients were treated at various hospitals in 1902; 2,109 patients were treated in 1900.[114] Medical services continued to expand through the early twentieth century—in 1916 a new European hospital was built at Ridge—and yet, government officials continued to complain about the colony's inadequate medical care. Doctors complained about sanitary conditions, overcrowding, and poor maintenance. The construction of the new Gold Coast Hospital at Korle Bu in 1923, however, marked a major new form of investment. The hospital became the major medical and surgical center for the entire country. In 1927, Korle Bu served 206 inpatients and 11,283 outpatients. By 1938, they were serving 292 inpatients and 17,903 outpatients. These more general medical services were complimented by a new venereal disease clinic (1920) and maternity and children's hospitals like the Princess Marie Louise (1926), which were widely popular in the city and made a significant impact on high infant mortality rates in the city. In 1925, infant and maternity clinics of various sorts were serving 13,438 patients. By 1937 the number had risen to 21,253.[115] Expenditures for health constituted a quarter or more of the total Town Council budget through at least the 1930s.[116]

These increases in investment, however, also reflected an increasing European control over the health of the town and subjected doctors and government officials alike to public criticisms. Critics, like the physician writing into the *Gold Coast Independent* as CER, acknowledged that "all the business of the physician is more especially the care of the sick with reference to the cure of disease or where that is beyond his power as is too frequently the case."[117] The challenges of diagnosis and treatment led physicians to focus on medical questions related to disease, reducing the patient to an object of scientific curiosity. And yet, they argued, the physician also had responsibilities to the general public health:

> These duties become more numerous and important as the density of population increases, so that in a large town as Accra he finds himself "nolens volens,"[118] in almost daily contact with legally constituted authorities in the shape of 'a mock municipality,' sanitary department, road department and whatnot, and is not infrequently summoned before the courts. Moreover, the physician who has been placed at the head of these institutions invariably forgets that he becomes an adviser to the government as well as to the public at large; consequently his responsibility so far as it affects the public, corresponds to a degree, the position which she takes and the advice which he gives in regard to public health matters; this is true whether his attitude on these subjects be active or passive; for his silence will be taken to mean that there is no necessity for action or change.[119]

Whereas doctors were focused on the physical health of their patients, these commentators argued that an improvement in mortality rates required direct investments in the development of the entire community. Instead, investment seemed to have resulted in a number of conflicting and overlapping institutions of authority with no clear and coordinated plan of action—"a practitioner finds it difficult to know who is actually responsible."[120] As this physician noted, the broader group of professionals supporting public health included a range of practitioners including local healers. Coordination and cooperation, rather than bureaucratic expansion, seemed like a more effective path forward—a sentiment that was echoed in the calls for education and community engagement by ATC members around issues of sanitation.

CULTURAL CONCEPTIONS OF
HEALTH AND DISEASE

European narratives about the "unhealthiness of the coast" oversimplified the competing definitions and understandings of health within Accra's diverse population. Despite long histories of interaction along the coast, there was little hybridity in Accra's health cultures. Roberts argues that the difference between Western and African approaches were "largely incommensurable."[121] Among African residents, illness was largely understood as "the struggle between the body, society, and the supernatural forces that surrounded them."[122] A "sick" person was one who could not fulfill the responsibilities of their social role and, as a result, African patients often put off treatment until their illness was significantly advanced or they were disabled in some way.[123] Europeans, however, arrived at the coast with an understanding of health as the result of miasmas, and later bacteria, which could be treated with medicine and privileged early intervention—a position that was further strengthened with advances in medical research that inspired a new form of confidence in the efficacy of Western medicine in the tropics that often defied lived realities.[124]

Individual patients often combined multiple forms of treatment or chose between a range of possible treatment options as part of what Roberts calls "therapeutic pluralism."[125] Patients were often cautious and pragmatic, but African healing cultures were also highly adaptable and responsive, and local healers often served as an "interpreter of shared values."[126] The healers that Kilson interviewed in the 1960s and 1970s were "enterprising older Ga men" who would have been born, come of age, and trained during this period. Kilson was struck by their "diverse social background and experiences": "Some spoke only Ga; others spoke and wrote English fluently. Some were members of Christian churches; others adhered to traditional religious cults, and one was a Muslim. Earlier in their lives they had pursued various occupations including those of school teacher, cloth designer, soldier, Christian evangelist, and fisherman."[127] While these healers experienced different degrees of socioeconomic success, they all eagerly embraced the opportunity to learn and apply new information and treatments that might aid their patients. Despite stereotypes of the "fetish" priest, these Ga healers were often keen observers who recommended social, psychological, or physical interventions that effectively addressed underlying problems, even if patients ascribed their issues to supernatural causes.[128] African-born physicians also complicated overgeneralized and racialized assumptions British officials had about African understandings of health, embracing the efficacy of Western medical practices and theories and often being openly critical of African healing traditions.[129] Boundaries, in other words, were often not as simple as either discourses at the time or scholarly interpretations made it seem, and Africans were much more responsive to the introduction of new scientific knowledge.[130]

These different approaches to health were complicated by obviously uneven investment in health infrastructure and health standards within European and African communities in Accra.[131] Early commentators highlighted inequalities that were exacerbated and laid bare during outbreaks of smallpox and influenza in the early twentieth century.[132] As late as 1935, Councillor Akilagpa Sawyerr noted that lepers were found begging in public markets on a regular basis and that regulations were not adequately enforced to protect the public.[133] Colonial officials regularly disputed accusations about double standards and disinvestment, driven in part by a belief that African health would inevitably improve through an investment in European health.[134] But there were also more tangible investments in health infrastructure, education, and research.[135] The new hospitals represented distinctly new kinds of experiences that removed patients from the network of family and friends who formed their therapeutic management group and put themselves in the exclusive care of Western medical experts. The physical and social conditions of the hospital—its construction and organization, the process of patient intake and treatment—reduced individuals to autonomous patients and "abstracted, medicalized bodies" who were transformed "from a colonial subject into a medical subject."[136] This never amounted to the kind of "biopower" described by Foucault, but colonial health interventions were consequential in their intrusion into the daily lives of residents. Rules and regulations did result in various kinds of punishment but did not necessarily change practice and weren't necessarily rooted in reality. But these rules did change the ways in which African bodies and health practices were classified within emerging technocratic fields, which had both immediate and long-term effects for local communities.

RATS AND DISEASE: THE BUBONIC PLAGUE

The plague outbreak in 1908 was arguably the first major test of new colonial and public health strategies in the Gold Coast. In early twentieth-century Accra, medical officers of health like Mrs. M. S. Deacon (1901–1904) pursued numerous public health initiatives that included the preparation of educational materials for schools and the operation of a thirty-man "scavenging crew" that sought to eliminate various forms of "nuisance" in the city.[137] But, as complaints from townspeople, visitors, and British officials alike attest, these programs had done little to change the shape of the city or the practices of its residents. The kinds of significant interventions that health reformers envisioned were deemed largely impossible in Accra, where local populations and political leaders fiercely resisted changes to the spatial layout of the city and maintained a significant degree of autonomy in its social, economic, and cultural spheres. As we shall see, justifications and strategies for plague prevention overlapped in significant ways with antimalaria campaigns, but the epidemic nature of the disease generated new kinds of urgency both in terms of intervention and investment. When rats and livestock began dying and individuals began falling sick in late 1907, rumors quickly spread among residents that the illness was the result of a "poisoning."[138] British officials, however, recognized the signs of plague and requested "expert" assistance from Dr. William John Ritchie Simpson. Simpson was a professional adviser to the government, a professor of hygiene at King's College London, and a cofounder (with Sir Patrick Manson) of the London School of Tropical Medicine. But Simpson was also a self-made expert on plague control, having worked on India's plague outbreak in 1896 and followed the disease as it spread throughout the British Empire in the late nineteenth and early twentieth centuries.[139]

Simpson represented an interesting bridge between older miasma theories and new breakthroughs in bacteriology and immunology. Medical research offered few insights into the prevention, treatment, and cure for plague in the early twentieth century, and Echenberg argues that "public health officials trying to cope with outbreaks between 1894 and 1901 were hardly better equipped than their pre-germ theory predecessors had been either to establish causation, or more important, to treat plague patients."[140] Simpson's own *Treatise on Plague*, originally published in 1905, reinforced statements by the British India Plague Commission (of which Simpson was a leading member) that identified the source of plague as "unsanitary conditions of overcrowded human habitations" and pointing to highly unpopular strategies like demolition and construction of overcrowded and infected neighborhoods as the primary effective strategy for halting the spread of the disease.[141] By the time plague arrived in the Gold Coast in 1907–1908, however, researchers had recently identified the flea as the primary transmission vector for the bacteria *Yersinia pestis*. Simpson thus arrived in the Gold Coast armed with the most recent medical knowledge, older models of European public health measures, and racist and colonialist stereotypes about non-Western peoples. Like many other medical practitioners, Simpson continued to evoke the dangers of human-to-human transmission and miasma explanations of causation through his plague control measures. Despite being widely embraced as a field manual for the colonial service, the strategies outlined in his *Treatise on Plague*, which focused on cost savings and expediency, largely ignored the sociocultural issues that such measures would undoubtedly provoke in communities like Accra.[142] Importantly, however, Simpson saw plague measures as an important means through which officials could achieve larger planning goals. Whereas the manual began with "how to" suggestions for plague mitigation—rat kills, fumigation, inoculation clinics—it quickly transitions to more comprehensive strategies for surveying new towns and constructing buildings with appropriate sanitary infrastructure.[143]

And yet, given the dangers that plague posed to both European and African residents and the "serious inconvenience" that quarantine had caused for trade in the colony,[144] Simpson's arrival was initially welcomed by many who hoped to limit the spread of the disease. Rumors abounded about the origins of the disease and the cause of its spread. The *Gold Coast Leader* published a detailed summary of some of the public discussions and concerns circulating in the early days of the outbreak:

> The Accras, as is well known, are great travellers, most of whom find employment down the coast; and some are known to have been engaged on Railway lines being laid in the Portuguese Colony, where we understand coolies also are employed, and it is probable these have brought the disease from India or China from whom the Accra workmen may have caught it, and that is has thus found its way to Accra. This disease is also said to have visited the French Colony not long ago, but whether German Kratchi, the French Colony, or Benguela is responsible for the introduction of the plague to Accra, it has visited the place and raised the mortality of Accra—ever greater than that of any other town in the Colony—to an alarming proportion, and done much havoc for days before the authorities were aware of its presence. Anyone who knows Accra is aware of two facts namely that funerals are there, a matter of every day occurrence, ranging from two at the lowest to as many as twelve in a day and averaging 6 or 7 a day in Accra town alone, exclusive of Christiansborg; and that as a rule the Accras have more confidence in fetishmen, native medicines, and charms than in European practice, as they never go near the Hospital if they can help it, and only do so as a last resort, seldom appearing to the European Practitioner til native medicines and the fetishmen have signally failed after having been well fleeced by them. We have no information as to the date of the first appearance in Accra, but it was already prevalent and doing its fell work as reported by passengers from Accra by the 'Burutu' when they left Accra on the 9th instant.[145]

In drawing connections between the relative mobility and cosmopolitanism of Accra residents and the appearance of plague elsewhere in the world, the Fante editors of the *Leader* were simultaneously expressing an outsider's assessment of Accra life and connecting the city to networks of imperial labor and trade. Accra's connection to other parts of the world, both through its role as a port city and trade hub and through its residents' migration to other parts of the continent, put its people—and, as a result, the rest of the Gold Coast—at risk. However, the newspaper's editors also argued that the city's social and cultural practices might help to spread plague. Large crowds gathered at funerals and suspicion of Western medicine could make it difficult to control the epidemic. Danger, it seemed, came from both home and abroad.

Accra was undoubtedly the epicenter of this particular outbreak. However, on arrival Simpson quickly began a tour of the colony to assess the conditions and evaluate the extent of the spread. As he traveled, he spoke to public assemblies, sharing knowledge about the disease, including detailed descriptions of the high mortality rate and the suffering of victims. Containment of the disease required careful quarantine that limited the active connection between rural and urban areas that defined economic, social, and cultural life throughout southern Ghana. Speaking to community leaders in Cape Coast, Simpson stressed the importance of inoculating foreign traders and limiting the movement of carriers and kola buyers coming from infected regions. Individual actions also mattered. Upon the prompting of J. Mensah Sarbah, Simpson recommended a number of key actions that could prevent the spread:

1) Every room, yard and surroundings of a house must be swept daily.
2) All rat holes must be filled up; white wash the inside of houses instead of the outside.
3) All house refuse, and town or village sweepings must be collected outside the town or village, and there burnt daily. Pigs ought not to be allowed to roam about.
4) Rats propagate plague by their leavings, urine, or spittal getting into uncovered food; people must therefore cover up all food. Fleas from rats also spread the plague, a relentless war must be waged against rats, and the more they are killed the lesser the risk of an outbreak.
5) The outskirts of town or village must be kept clean; windows of rooms should be opened for free ventilation.
6) Strict isolation, away from town or village of any one attacked.

Since the smell of fish attracted rats, Professor Simpson recommended that smoking, curing, and keeping of herrings and highly seasoned fish should be in reserved spots outside the town.[146]

Many of the recommendations echoed a broader sentiment that the plague was at least partly the result of poor sanitation—namely, the "bad air" and poor water supply in cities like Accra and Cape Coast—which reflected the persistence of older understandings of disease and contagion.[147] But even in relation to rats, these recommendations seemed to misread scientific research about the flea vector and emphasize cleanliness rather than rapid and widespread inoculation.[148] Importantly, however, community leaders also used these sessions as opportunities to make claims to better resources and infrastructural investments. The Tufuhene called for the erection of "public urinals suitable for the tropics" and invited Simpson to return to Cape Coast to inspect the town and make

Figure 2.1. Street Scenes, 1955. Source: Photographic Archive, Information Services Office, Ministry of Information, Accra R/2200/8.

recommendations to government and commercial leaders.[149] As one commentator wrote in the *Leader*, "What matter, if men, women and children die, not of the plague, but from exposure and hunger. 'The man on the spot' has spoken and his word is enough; if any one dare remonstrate, he is put down as an interfering semi-educated nuisance, and he who seeks to serve the public by using the knowledge he received in school is branded a usurper."[150] In focusing so much energy, attention, and investment on plague cases and deaths, colonial strategies seem to validate "the official on the spot" while simultaneously putting into sharper relief the lack of support for broader community health in non-emergency times and generating new forms of public critique in cities along the coast.

Intervention was particularly intense in Accra as a site of widespread outbreak. Before Simpson's arrival, acting governor Major H. Bryan called on Dr.

Quartey-Papafio to help coordinate a campaign to fight the disease, marshaling Ga leaders to collaborate and support government efforts to fight the disease. Despite having been excluded from the colonial medical service on racial grounds, Quartey-Papafio largely agreed with government strategies centered on Western medical research and established public health practices.[151] Ga leaders, however, were more skeptical of the possible strategies deployed in fighting the plague, even if they were in general agreement about the urgency of intervention. In January 1908 Bryan formed a Sanitary Committee, which was empowered to "inspect any dwelling suspected to harbor plague, to demolish any house deemed infected, and to quarantine anyone who had contact with the disease."[152] These new measures effectively sidelined the chiefs in planning or implementing public health measures and created new punishments (jail or fines) for anyone who obstructed or interfered with the work of the committee or its representatives: this created an unprecedented centralization of authority under the guise of protecting the public health from imminent danger.[153] The Sanitary Committee immediately began work fumigating infected houses and attempting to demolish abandoned or dilapidated structures but were immediately threatened with legal action by property owners—a form of resistance that echoed ongoing challenges around urban planning and sanitation reform in Accra.[154] Unable to make direct interventions in the physical space and structures of the city, the Sanitary Committee quickly changed strategies, isolating patients and transporting them out of heavily populated areas via armed guard. Held in leg irons with mentally ill patients in the asylum in Victoriaborg, patients and their families were unsurprisingly outraged by the treatment they received. Kojo Ababio, the chief of James Town, gave the Sanitary Committee a piece of open land at Korle Gonno, which served as a quarantine site for those who had been in contact with sick patients. Ababio's actions, however, reflected more than a mere desire to support public health. Chiefs in Ussher Town protested that Ababio had used the situation to make a claim for the land at Korle Gonno—a contestation that continued to reverberate throughout the epidemic and beyond.[155]

Simpson arrived in February armed with a two-pronged approach: widespread vaccination and demolition. Simpson's plan to demolish the old quarters of the city was met with immediate resistance, despite Quartey-Papafio's support as a son of Ussher Town. The Sanitary Committee agreed that a portion of Ussher Town should be evacuated, and the committee held a meeting with the Ga Manche in which the chiefs and people exhibited "unfriendly distrust."[156] As Roberts recounts, "When Quartey-Papafio led the Sanitary Committee into the neighborhood to destroy infected houses, the residents stoned him and forced his team to retreat."[157] Colonial officials' theories about the role of "fetish priests" in the uprising seemed to ignore other forms of discontent connected to the public health initiatives, including the ongoing contestation over land at Korle Gonno.[158] While Simpson backed off from some of his most aggressive plans, the committee made clear that "what was then being asked of them might afterwards have to be forcibly carried out, if the disease any more got worse."[159] When residents who were asked to aid in the construction of temporary housing were slow to provide assistance, the Ga Manche himself had to threaten to charge the chiefs and people for the cost of using prison labor.[160]

The mass vaccination campaign found a much more receptive audience in Accra. British and Ga leaders alike, including the governor and his wife, the colonial secretary, and the Ga chiefs, received their vaccines at a public event to highlight their safety and encourage public participation.[161] By the end of the campaign, nearly all of Accra's population had received a dose of Haffkine's prophylactic. While Simpson and other colonial leaders viewed the successful vaccination as a triumph of Western medicine, Ga residents likely embraced vaccination because of its similarities to ritual scarification, which sought to protect the body from spiritual forces, or variolation, a long-standing practice among local healers that introduced small amounts of contagion directly into the skin of patients in order to generate immune response and protect against infection.[162] Importantly, however, vaccination also cost residents little in comparison to the demolition exercises.

In the tightly knit Ga community, residents who witnessed their neighbors' houses marked for demolition or their belongings burned would have been understandably skeptical of the plague-fighting strategies. Their concerns were also rooted in a much deeper suspicion about Simpson's plans to use demolition to pave the way for a new reordering of city space through segregation.[163] In advocating for quarantine and segregation as a strategy for plague prevention, Simpson was drawing on strategies that predated germ theory by centuries.[164] Segregation was a familiar concept in Accra. In 1901, Governor Matthew Nathan had declared his intention to segregate white populations from their Ga neighbors due to concerns over sanitation and health: inspired, in part, by new studies about the mosquito vector for malaria that viewed African neighborhoods as "native reservoirs" of disease.[165] Nathan built new colonial offices and bungalows near the Danish fort of Christiansborg and the new European community of Victoriaborg, a significant distance from the old Ga town, surrounded by open land and scenic vistas, free of perceived contagion and separated by a buffer or cordon sanitaire. Importantly, this move also redirected investments in sanitary infrastructure and public works away from the old Ga quarters of Kinka, Nleshi, and Osu and toward new European communities.[166] In doing so, Nathan and others were inspired by changes in the medical understandings of disease that had accelerated by the end of the nineteenth century.[167] These strategies sought to avoid disease, but they also sought to "segregate the governors from the governed" and to secure more amenable vistas to support the morale of European officers.[168] Buffer zones constituted a "line of hygiene" that was one of the "boundaries of rule" in colonies like the Gold Coast, which reinforced the ways that emerging practices of public health were deployed as a "special form of governance" that could regulate the circulation of objects and people that were considered different and, thus increasingly, dangerous.[169] But distance could not completely eliminate interaction and movement. European officials, merchants, and missionaries challenged rigid residential segregation models and continued to live in and engage African communities to fulfill their responsibilities, and African residents regularly moved between these different areas for work and trade.[170] The experience of the segregated city in Accra, in other words, more closely followed the model of many West African cities, which had distinct areas for foreigners who settled for trade or other activities but still engaged in the life of the town.[171] When Simpson arrived in Accra, he was impressed by Nathan's work to segregate the city and pushed Governor Rodger to further reinforce the distance between European communities and African quarters that he judged to be congested and unsanitary.[172]

By the time the plague was contained in December 1908, the Gold Coast had recorded 344 cases with 300 deaths; in Accra, 250 Africans died, and no Europeans were infected.[173] Despite the varied success of these strategies, Simpson leveraged his experience and professional credentials to push for further reforms to the town's infrastructure, spatial organization, and sanitation. Simpson's report described Accra as an "exceptionally healthy site" that was in "deplorable sanitary condition." Congestion, poor housing, narrow streets, and disordered neighborhoods created opportunities for rats to hide and were breeding places for mosquitoes. Drainage was terrible, markets were filthy, and the water supply was deficient. Importantly, Simpson noted that the Accra Town Council had failed in its sanitary responsibilities—there was insufficient staff and the medical officer of health and other councillors were too busy to properly attend to sanitary matters.[174]

Even in the aftermath of the plague, memories of the sickness and death it caused continued to motivate officials to reform sanitation and health services, guided by Simpson's report. In the years immediately following the epidemic, the British government made new investments in water, sewage, housing, mosquito control, and infrastructural development and increased funding for the Public Works Department.[175] The process of reconstruction began in 1908 with compensation for landowners and a surveying of the town. And then a plan for the reconstruction of the port area of James Town and Ussher Town was drafted that called for wider boulevards and roads.[176] The government formed the Accra

Improvement Committee in 1908 to consult with the governor on strategies to improve the town.[177] The government constructed new streets, hospitals, and permanent housing projects in Korle Gonno and Adabraka. The health branch was established in 1909 as a direct result of the plague epidemic, which institutionalized public health as a key component of governance.[178] But this energy and investment was short-lived. As a result of the costs associated with the plague, the Accra Town Council faced increasing pressure to collect revenue.[179] Ten years later, British observers noted that the towns between Accra and Winneba "are now in a much worse condition than they were before Professor Simpson visited them in 1908," and the Accra Town Council was regularly criticized for its perceived failures in providing for the sanitation of the town.[180] Segregation and slum clearance activities, which were accelerated during the plague further reinforced inequalities in sanitary investment, made congestion and squalor worse, and reinforced government calls for even more demolition.[181] While Simpson's specific recommendations for Accra may not have been implemented with a great deal of lasting success, his broader strategies influenced policy within the Gold Coast and across the British Empire as a new model for town planning, motivated by fears of contagion and rooted in the principles of segregation.[182]

WHITE MAN'S HUMBUG: MOSQUITOES

While the urgency of the plague epidemic prompted prompt action and concentrated intervention, plague mitigation strategies and public health policy in Accra emerged in conversation with much older attempts to address the threat of endemic tropical diseases. The "fevers" that had long decimated European populations in the "white man's grave" presented significant challenges to British officials seeking to consolidate and extend colonial authority in the Gold Coast. In the 1890s new tropical disease experts like Patrick Manson and Ronald Ross established the importance of the mosquito vector in propagating a wide range of tropical diseases, from elephantiasis and dengue fever to malaria and yellow fever. Like the plague, these fevers presented enormous health risks for European residents and, being conveyed through an insect, it presented similar kinds of challenges for those seeking to eliminate the threat. In attempting to prevent the disease, public health officials drew on emerging theories and models of urban planning that flourished in the late nineteenth century: if you could not cure the disease, you could mitigate the threat by attacking it at the source—waging a war on mosquitoes through the reconfiguration of city space and urban living. Importantly, however, mortality rates for African residents with mosquito-borne diseases like yellow fever and malaria were significantly lower. Individuals were often infected in infancy and, while this did contribute to a high infant mortality rate in Accra and throughout the southern Gold Coast, those who did survive maintained some form of immunity that, in most cases, protected them from death or serious illness.

These differential disease experiences undermined the kind of social solidarity that characterized much of the public health concern associated with the plague. This obsession with mosquitoes, many Africans argued, was a "white man's humbug," even as they acknowledged the high death rates among Europeans resident on the coast.[183] Even more than the interventions associated with the plague, these tensions over spatial practice and disease through the war on mosquitoes shaped emerging forms, theories, and practices of urban life that cast African bodies as inherently diseased and justified new forms of intervention into urban residents' daily lives. In doing so, colonial officials often blurred the boundaries between "sanitation"—often a highly cultural matter—and "medicine" under the broad umbrella of "public health." By the early twentieth century, sanitary officials, medical officers, and town councillors focused extraordinary amounts of energy and resources on the elimination of mosquitoes and the mitigation of mosquito-borne diseases. These efforts were organized around three major approaches: residential segregation, larva inspections to prevent breeding in domestic water supplies, and interventions in the built and natural environment to prevent breeding in ponds, drains, puddles, and the Korle Lagoon.[184]

Segregation was first proposed by Sierra Leonean physician and medical officer, Dr. J. F. Easmon, in 1893.[185] Particularly after the discovery of the mosquito vector, a wide range of medical experts advocated segregation as a way to protect Europeans from *Aedes Aegypti* (which spread yellow fever) and *Anopheles* (which spread malaria). Governors Maxwell (1895–1897) and Hodgson (1898–1900) refused to implement segregation strategies in Accra out of concern that it would provoke strong resistance among African residents. However, in 1901 Governor Matthew Nathan embraced segregation as an official government policy, building bungalows in newly developed European residential areas in Victoriaborg and Ridge, separated by a buffer zone a half mile east of the African sections of town.[186] Nathan argued that African bodies and homes were "native reservoirs" of disease that must be separated from that of European officials, who did not have the same kinds of immunities that resulted from adaptation to tropical climates. As he noted to Ronald Ross, "There are many times as many Europeans here as in any other West African colony, and that, though I don't undervalue sanitation for natives, I fear they themselves do. Improvement in the health of Europeans is absolutely the first desideration for general improvement in these colonies."[187] Public health, it seems, was actually about protecting European health.

While Nathan waited for construction to begin on the new European neighborhoods, he also sought to clean up the city, reactivating dormant portions of the

Towns Police and Health Ordinances of 1878 and 1892, which "compelled house owners to clean unsightly premises and provided the government with direct authority to appropriate private property for street widening and drainage." He also expanded the powers of the governor further through the Towns Amendment Ordinance of 1901, which "allowed the governor wide powers to expropriate private property where needed for any public purpose."[188] Nathan and his successor, John Rodger (1904–1910), used these new powers to condemn and demolish buildings in African neighborhoods, paving way for a sanitary cordon or buffer zone that would surround European residential districts.[189]

These policies provoked resistance from a number of quarters. Officials initially refused to compensate householders who were evicted, prompting protest from both individual residents and African organizations like the Aborigines Rights Protection Society. For elite Africans, segregation seemed to exacerbate racial tensions that had been growing throughout the late nineteenth and early twentieth centuries, undermine the class and social solidarity they often expected from European officers, and limit their access to the benefits and opportunities associated with colonial development.[190] But European residents also bristled under the new segregation scheme, which created false separations between European officials who were allowed to work in the city during the day but were expected to return to their homes the newly constructed residential districts at night.[191] In practice, many merchants, missionaries, and officials continued to live in the old town, continuing centuries of social and spatial culture, while Africans moved back and forth to the new official districts for work. Complete separation was impossible. When Hugh Clifford became governor of the Gold Coast in 1912 he quickly eliminated the formal practice of segregation and actively resisted the formal imposition of a "quarter-mile rule" for residential segregation in British West African cities; he argued that "even if complete segregation of European habitations on the Gold Coast could be affected at moderate cost, the European dwelling in them would not thereby be rendered immune even from mosquito borne disease. No European in this country can exist without his staff of native servants, who cannot live at a distance of at least a quarter mile from his house. Europeans are required by the exigencies of their public duty to come into daily contact with natives of all ages, and most Europeans have from time to time to make tours through the country, during which anything resembling segregation from the native population is a sheer impossibility."[192] But, importantly, he asserted that the policies also provoked active resistance from African residents who were being asked to fund public works from which they would receive no obvious benefit. Instead, segregation seemed to further exacerbate the imbalance in investment and enforcement through policies that were informed more by racial stereotypes than actual scientific evidence.

Mosquitoes and mosquito-borne diseases, however, remained a persistent problem. In 1913, the *Gold Coast Nation* reported that a "Wesleyan Sister" had died from fever in coastal towns and used this death to renew calls for addressing mosquito problems in Cape Coast and Accra. The city's leadership was disgraced by "unsatisfactory drainage of the capital" and the "drains, pools, and swamps of Accra and its swarms of mosquito."[193] In publicly calling for greater intervention through these cases, African newspaper editors and other African elites contributed to a growing conversation about the public threat of mosquitoes, even if that threat was primarily seen as one centered on European residents. The threat of endemic disease and the failures of other health interventions to significantly alleviate the risk associated with mosquito-borne diseases justified increasing levels of intrusion by government into the private spaces of African residents in Accra. As early as 1901, sanitary inspectors organized through the Health Department were empowered to check compounds for larvae. Amendments to the Towns Ordinance in 1904 further empowered the ATC to "carry on the war to death against the noxious mosquito" and again in the 1911 Destruction of Mosquitoes Bill.[194] This 1911 bill crystallized long-standing practices and expanded the authority of the inspectors over an unprecedented swath of public and private spaces. The medical officer of health or their appointees were granted the authority to enter any property between 6 a.m. and 6 p.m. to inspect for larvae, and owners and occupiers of "premises" were subject to prosecution and fine if inspectors found larvae or otherwise unprotected water sources on their property.[195] Vague guidelines in the bill, however, led to arbitrary and capricious enforcement. Sanitary officers were "known to rudely invade the privacy of people and search about among their belongings as if they were suspected of having done something wrong," causing offense to householders.[196] Community members questioned the respectability and qualifications of individuals appointed to positions as sanitary inspectors and other public health positions by the MOH as "scavenger[s] or ... common laborer[s]," particularly when their authority was backed by the sympathy and power of the courts.[197]

These inspections constituted "one of the most frequent contacts between rulers and ruled in Accra," and African larvae inspectors were extremely unpopular.[198] Residents questioned whether the inspections were even effective, particularly as puddles and drains in public spaces remained, and rules were rarely enforced in European residential areas until the ordinance was extended to cover those areas in 1930.[199] As Newell notes, the materials found in typical African compounds were less likely to collect water in significant quantities compared to the garbage produced by imported European goods.[200] And yet, over one hundred thousand inspections were conducted every year in Kinka, Nleshi, and Osu. Every year, sanitary authorities reported detailed numbers—how much brush was cleared, how many bottles were collected, how many puddles or drains were filled or treated.²⁰¹ It's unclear whether the inspections were effective, particularly given the lack of enforcement in European quarters and, as we'll see, the government's inability to address the Korle Lagoon. Rumors circulated that the monies collected through fines were used to pay the inspectors' salaries or contribute to the upkeep of the Town Council, encouraging additional prosecutions.²⁰²

These rumors were rooted in Accra residents' deep suspicion about the effectiveness of inspectors, viewing sanitation as "nothing but an instrument of oppression and device for affording opportunity for a number of Government officials to lord it as tyrants over them."²⁰³ The constant flux of policies and plans raised questions about the efficacy of colonial strategies and the science behind their claims. "Nuisances," it seemed, were a particularly "urban" phenomenon, and commentators wondered whether this was a real concern for the broader public or a particular investment in European health.²⁰⁴ In the 1920s, the Town Council hired special "mosquito brigades," a new class of sanitary inspectors who operated like a quasi-police force responsible for monitoring the habits of residents and whose work was rewarded with relatively lucrative salaries and opportunities for advancement within the colonial service.²⁰⁵ These brigades were reviled for intruding into "women's spaces," destroying personal property unnecessarily, and violating sacred objects.²⁰⁶ Inspectors contaminated water used for cooking and drinking by using ladles in multiple vessels without proper cleaning.²⁰⁷

African town councillors brought their constituencies' concerns to ATC meetings, noting that "in many instances the officers did not understand the language of the people and consequently their instructions could not be intelligently followed, with the inevitable results that [women in the house] were often committed for nuisances or such like offences."²⁰⁸ Summonses, Kitson Mills argued, seemed to be issued "indiscriminately" against offenders.²⁰⁹ Akilagpa Sawyerr asked "whether some steps should not be taken to ameliorate the condition of the people brought before the District Magistrate every week for sanitary offenses."²¹⁰ In response, the medical officer of health insisted that he had received no such complaints. But the constant stream of prosecutions and the various derogatory nicknames that residents gave inspectors and the courts in Accra and other districts reinforced these complaints. The district magistrate in Accra saw so many residents brought up for sanitary offences related to mosquito larvae that women in the city called in the loloi court. These realities were certainly not unique to Accra—techniques and strategies related to mosquito mitigation and public health expanded throughout the colony and across British West Africa. The chief commissioner of the Northern Territories noted that people in Tamale referred to the MOH and his staff as "summa summa" ("summons summons").²¹¹

In Lagos, African sanitary inspectors were called *wolé wolé* in Yoruba and were greatly feared.[212]

As observers noted, high rates of crime in urban areas were often less the result of actual crime and more the consequence of ineffective sanitary inspection strategies.[213] Town councillors and newspaper editors alike called for more extensive public education—punishment served only to criminalize the practices of African residents and did little to actually change behavior. As Akilagpa Sawyerr noted, "Sanitary Inspectors should make health suggestions to the people so as to dispel their ignorance instead of dragging them before the district magistrate every time."[214] The goal, it seemed, was not actually to correct unsanitary habits but to maintain the constant stream of prosecutions and fines.[215] In resisting these calls to critically reflect on their practices, medical experts highlighted that the point was not really to "improve the situation" after all.[216] By 1926, an Accra editorialist noted that "education may have been lacking, but coercion was not; thousands of householders were fined every year."[217] Nearly twenty years later, "Buyer" wrote to the editor of the *Gold Coast Leader* described the one hundred people being prosecuted for having larvae in their compounds at district commissioner's court on June 15, 1942: "The worse of it was that the poor people who can scarcely earn one-penny for their living were all fined on the average one pound each. These poor women had each, one empty kerosene tin for water every morning, but as soon as they bring the water into their houses there appeared the Sanitary Inspectors who at once issued summonses against them."[218] These prosecutions were not advancing public health, these commentators argued.[219] They were criminalizing the most mundane and essential details of everyday life, transforming women (and men) cooking and cleaning in the compound into criminals who violated the safety and security of the public.

YELLOW JACK: "THE YELLOW FEVER BOGEY" AND EUROPEAN DEATH

While malaria arguably received outsized attention from medical researchers, yellow fever provoked fear among colonial officials. The *Ae. Aegypti* mosquito, which carried yellow fever, caused a disproportionate number of deaths among Europeans in the Gold Coast and prompted what Patterson describes as "draconian measures" to mitigate its threat.[220] Health officials regularly reported the clinical details of all documented yellow fever cases back to the Colonial Office, individual British officers were instructed to put screens on their windows and sleep under mosquito nets, and various levels of government imposed segregation and larval control measures as part of broader mosquito control strategies.

When a yellow fever outbreak (twenty-four reported cases) was discovered in Sekondi and Accra, as well as in other West African colonies, in 1910–1911, the Colonial Office quickly dispatched a Yellow Fever Commission led by Sir Rupert Boyce to West Africa. Boyce, a pathologist and one of the founders of the Liverpool School of Tropical Medicine, had become a yellow fever specialist, having led government investigations in the West Indies in 1909. Boyce quickly established rigid quarantines, evacuated Europeans from infected areas, and waged a vigorous campaign against the *Ae. Aegypti* larvae by fumigating official buildings and European bungalows with sulfur. Of the twenty-four reported cases, seventeen were European. Sixteen Europeans and three Africans died from the disease.[221]

Recurrent yellow fever outbreaks in 1913 and 1915 highlighted that conditions had not significantly improved since Simpson's visit—widely viewed by British officials and leading African figures alike as a watershed moment in the history of public health in the Gold Coast.[222] For Accra residents, however, the government's approach to yellow fever also further highlighted the inequalities of access and resources related to public health and raised questions about the true intent of these initiatives and the legitimacy of the science that informed them. Some cases of yellow fever resulted in quite mild symptoms that could be difficult to identify, so the Yellow Fever Commission advocated "all cases of fever should be carefully observed and classified in order that so far as possible, such mild cases of yellow fever may not pass unrecognized."[223] In the absence of an effective clinical test that would allow researchers to identify yellow fever cases, yellow fever remained a threat and "an offense to the comity of nations."[224]

These realities, however, also presented alternative possible responses. In 1911, prominent African physicians F. V. Nanka-Bruce and C. E. Reindorf published a series of articles in the *Gold Coast Leader* arguing that official positions that excluded African physicians further endangered the public: "As medical men, although not officially entrusted with prophylactic duties much good may be done by us in the promotion of hygiene, because all sections of the [community] can approach us and do approach us in such times of distress for the obvious reason that we are black. Up to the time of writing we have not as yet received any official notification of the above mentioned outbreak excepting of course the yellow jack at James Fort."[225] The physicians argued that involving private African practitioners would allow them to better support public health initiatives, care for their patients, and learn from the latest scientific and medical research. But these articles also provided important perspectives on African reception to healthcare. As they noted, the Dispensary "offers better opportunity of discovering low forms of infection amongst natives than the absurd practice of sticking thermometers in the mouths of the apparently healthy... especially when rejected cases are not

followed up or isolated."[226] These practices violated African understandings of health and raised suspicions among women and children who "began to make fun of the 'whiteman's juju.'"[227] But it also actively undermined the professional qualifications of these trained physicians. Sending out inspectors of nuisance with limited training to oversee vaccination clinics was an affront when qualified physicians were available in the same town and who later had to treat vaccinated patients who developed infections from improper vaccination. The insistence of "official" control undermined the health of everyone when underqualified individuals confused symptoms or provided improper treatment. A lack of clear authority and organization within the medical and sanitary departments further complicated matters. Things had not improved significantly by 1913, when a misdiagnosis of Mr. J. E. Acquah led to what editors of the *Gold Coast Nation* called "yellow fever panic." Lack of clear guidelines led to a waste of funds and enormous inconvenience; medical officers, they argued, should "hold themselves in check when tempted to go to undesirable lengths in reporting cases that come under official notice." Moreover, these "professional errors" appeared to follow a pattern of overreaction, which was dangerous to African residents who were "sacrificed" due to medical mistakes and fear-informed judgment.[228] What the governor applauded as "prompt measures adopted by the Sanitary Department [that] has caused the disease to be stamped out before it has succeeded in claiming more than a very few isolated victims" was interpreted very differently by those who were less susceptible to the disease but aggressively targeted by prevention efforts.[229]

Larval control measures were extremely unpopular among Africans. Some of those complaints about "mosquito propaganda" echoed the broader concern about the unequal standards, overreach of sanitary officials, excessive prosecution of poor residents, and the effectiveness of mosquito control measures like segregation—a "policy of coercion evidently founded upon a plague bogey in which the people have no faith."[230] In 1913 African Legislative Council representative Hutton-Mills voiced the frustration of a wide range of his constituents when he argued that "the recurrence of yellow fever evidently shows that there is fault somewhere and clearly the fault lies on some body or person and is not due to lack of funds. With the increase of the European Medical Staff—I emphasize the word 'European'—Accra, as the capital of the Colony should not be allowed to remain in its present disgraceful condition any longer, nor should the Europeans be taken away from the town and new quarters provided for them elsewhere from the revenue obtained from the natives."[231] Quarantines for yellow fever certainly disincentivized Africans to report the disease, but popular African opposition was also rooted in a skepticism about the dangers of yellow fever.[232] In the midst of the 1913 outbreak the *Gold Coast Nation* published an article calling for reverse segregation—removing the remaining Europeans from the African town "on the grounds that they were carriers of the disease."[233]

Even as general health improved, investment in health and medicine continued to increase in the interwar period, inspired in part by both the growth of the European population and ongoing fears of yellow fever.[234] Yellow fever outbreaks garnered interventional attention. The Rockefeller Foundation sent a team to visit West Africa in 1920 and followed with a larger group five years later. But it was new vaccine developments that finally ended the threat of the endemic disease. In 1930 the discovery of a vaccine for yellow fever made it possible for researchers to conduct their work. By the late 1930s, mass vaccination was possible, ending the "yellow fever menace."[235]

"THE LAGOON IS A MOSQUITO PROBLEM": MALARIA AS A UNIVERSAL DISEASE

If yellow fever only really presented a serious risk to European residents, malaria was considered a more universal disease that called for a universal remedy. As the homeopathic doctor John William Hayward noted in an address to the Africa Trade Section of the Liverpool Chamber of Commerce, "Malaria and malarial fevers are of the same nature and require much the same treatment wherever they occur, whether in Africa, India or America. In each region they own the same cause: put on the same general characters of intermittent, remittent, or continued, run the same general course, and require much the same remedial measures."[236] For Hayward, this reinforced the importance of training for physicians who would treat malaria, but it also pointed to a broader attitude in scientific communities about the treatment of diseases deemed to be "universal"—universal treatments did not require local knowledge. Hayward, who had never been to the Gold Coast, felt just as qualified to speak on the conditions there as anyone else.[237]

While yellow fever and plague generated hysteria among public health officials, Patterson argues that "malaria is, and has been for centuries, Ghana's most devastating disease."[238] Transmitted by the female *anopheles* mosquito, malaria is the result of infection from one of four types of protozoa, all of which are present in Ghana. Because treatment was similar for all four, however, physicians and clinicians rarely tested for type. Many infants in the Gold Coast were infected soon after birth due to the prevalence of mosquitoes: as a result, there were high infant death rates in cities like Accra. However, children who did survive into adulthood would have some degree of resistance which largely protected them from death or extreme illness.

Europeans who had not built up the same kind of resistance were not similarly protected. British doctors had been using quinine to treat malaria by the mid-nineteenth century, but it was not widely used as a prophylactic. Nineteenth-century tropical service understood malarial fevers as the product of "poisonous vapors" that resulted when strong sunlight or heavy rains reached "decaying vegetable matter."[239] Ronald Ross's 1898 discovery of the mosquito vector "not only revolutionized the study of tropical diseases, but endowed 'tropical sanitation' with scientific status as a means of malaria prevention."[240] Colonial officials were required to screen their houses and sleep under mosquito nets, but Ross argued that the government should adopt a more comprehensive strategy: (1) treatment, (2) prophylaxis, (3) control of mosquito larvae, and (4) control of adult anophelines.[241] Inspired in large part by the work of Dr. Walter Reed and Dr. W. C. Gorgas in Cuba, Ross argued that effective management of malaria required extensive investment in drainage and larvicide. But colonial officials, who were reluctant to spend too much money in West African colonies adopted the more cautious approach advocated by Patrick Manson, which emphasized individual hygienic precautions like mosquito proofing and preventive quinine treatments. Officials were certainly correct that it would be nearly impossible to destroy all mosquito breeding places in tropical areas; but, as Ross pointed out, the more cautious approach of the Colonial Office would provide protection for Europeans but leave the masses completely unprotected.[242] Segregation and uneven investment, instead, followed a broader pattern within public health strategies that defined the twentieth century.[243]

Malaria, like plague, defined the careers of tropical medicine specialists. Patrick Manson became the medical adviser to the Colonial Office in 1897 and became the head of the new London School for Tropical Medicine in 1899.[244] Ross launched a major medical expedition to West Africa in 1899, which raised his profile throughout the region as the "distinguished and gallant Major."[245] Liverpool and London merchants likewise invested heavily in research to prevent and treat malaria in the late nineteenth and early twentieth centuries. But this new research on "blood-based diseases" often reinforced British stereotypes about a "homogenous and bad-blooded 'native,'" justifying segregation and other spurious public health policies on racial grounds and directly shaping the politics and practice of town planning in West Africa[246]—what Newell calls the "haemopolitical turn in imperialist rhetoric," in which epidemiological evidence seemed to justify racial discrimination in colonial policy.[247] These new forms of scientific research transformed African bodies and nearly every part of the daily life of residents in cities like Accra—cooking, cleaning, bathing, going to the toilet, disposing of waste—into a threat that required regulation and mitigation.[248]

Ross and other tropical medicine specialists like Dr. M. Logan Taylor consulted with colonial officials and provided "proper" training for sanitary officials on how best to drain or fill puddles and potholes that might provide breeding spaces for *anopheles* mosquitoes. Government living quarters were mosquito-proofed and the Accra Town Council hired a thirty-man scavenging crew supervised by Mrs. Deacon, one of Ross's protégés. The Town Improvement Committee sought to advance "proper methods of individual hygienic protection" in the name of public health.[249] The new strategies that Nathan advocated, however, were almost immediately criticized by African political leaders in towns throughout the Gold Coast as an attempt to introduce new forms of racialization and transform the colony into "the Land of Fines."[250] Colonial officials and medical researchers were also disheartened by early efforts, which had limited success in eliminating mosquitoes and thus required constant treatment.[251] New strategies—the introduction of "millions" (cyprinodont) fish, and new medications and treatments, such as homeopathy—began appearing in Gold Coast newspapers.[252] And yet, as early as 1901, the death rate among Europeans had already begun to fall. In 1903 Governor Rodger attributed the 50 percent reduction in European death rates to the public health efforts of his predecessor Nathan. However, Roberts and others argue that it was unlikely any of the public health strategies associated with mosquito control were responsible for these improvements. Rather, the widespread availability and use of quinine as both a treatment and a prophylactic and the standardization of quinine doses was more likely responsible for the improved mortality rates.[253]

Uneven results from malaria prevention efforts often did little to dissuade colonial officials as to the effectiveness of "professional" recommendations. A visitor to Accra in 1913 "came to Accra to experience much trouble from mosquitoes. During my stay . . . I never enjoyed a sound sleep." The visitor's experience highlighted through first hand experience the contradictions of colonial policy. As he argued, "Those posts seem to have increased tremendously in spite of all the action of the famous Mosquito Brigade. A fruitless expenditure of energy, eh? And of money too, eh?"[254] Other African residents readily critiqued the "liberties" that Town Council officers took with such mundane objects as swish collected for building, and they protested the seemingly constant expansion of the category of "nuisance," through which town councillors sought to regulate daily life in the city.[255]

Accra residents did not protest the elimination of mosquitoes per se, but they did readily recognize that the methods and justifications for antimalarial and antilarval strategies often did not line up in obvious ways. For Accra residents and Gold Coast intellectuals, mosquito campaigns raised questions about just governance, taxation, and representation. As we saw in chapter 1, colonial officials often readily dismissed African residents' and town councillors' petitions and proposals for infrastructure that called for modern public services. They were, however, much more responsive to a "mosquito point of view."[256] Effectively eliminating mosquitoes required the reconfiguring of public spaces and the maintenance of infrastructure—responsibilities that produced their own politics and required negotiations between the colonial government, the Town Council, and Ga spiritual and political leaders. But colonial officials and town councillors alike also used the "mosquito problem"[257] to justify regulations that allowed sanitary inspectors and other Town Council representatives increasing authority to intervene in private, domestic spaces of all town residents, backed by the power of the courts.

These tensions and contradictions were perhaps best embodied by the ongoing struggle to address the "mosquito problem" in the Korle Lagoon. Colonial officials had long been suspicious of the lagoon as a "reservoir of miasmatic gases" that caused the deadly tropical fevers that killed so many European officials. As early as 1877 colonial medical reports blamed contamination in the lagoon on local Ga residents. Ross's discovery of the mosquito vector transformed discourses about the lagoon; while it was now reviled as a mosquito breeding ground, Accra residents continued to be blamed for the condition of the site.[258] For Ga people in Jamestown and Ussher Town, the Korle Lagoon, which bisected the city, was not only a source of fresh water and food but also a site of spiritual significance.[259] Colonial technocrats, however, saw an opportunity. As Accra grew in importance as a port city during the cocoa boom, colonial officials launched a plan in 1919 to dredge the lagoon and transform it into a deep-water harbor. However, the project quickly ran into problems as the rights to the land and its proceeds were contested—a fight that dated back to Kojo Ababio's "donation" of land in Korle Gonno in the midst of the plague epidemic. The case was tied up in colonial courts for years as subchiefs in Ussher Town and the priests of Korle fought over who had rights to land and fees in the lagoon. The contractor ultimately abandoned the project.[260]

Despite these failures, medical officers continued to push the government to address problems with mosquito breeding in the lagoon throughout the 1920s. The marshy shores of the lagoon provided a particular threat to antimalarial efforts. Government engineers and public health officials implemented a number of different solutions to improve conditions in the lagoon, building channels and gates and oiling the lagoon waters; however, the channels soon silted up, the gates washed away, and the oil could not quite reach the marshy edges of the lagoon.[261] In large part due to the persistent advocacy of Principal Medical Officer Selwyn-Clarke, who viewed the lagoon as the source of a "plague of mosquitoes,"[262] the Gold Coast government finally secured funding from the

Colonial Office to begin work on the lagoon in 1929. "There can be no question of the lagoon being completely filled in," Selwyn-Clarke noted, acknowledging the importance of the waterway to the surrounding Ga community. But at the same time Selwyn-Clarke felt that "there can be no doubt that a proportion of the ill-health of the town of Accra results from the presence of marshes chiefly along the eastern margins of the lagoon from the bund on the south of Agbogbloshie, Adabraka, and Kokomlemle to the north."[263]

In preparing the estimates for the project, the acting director of public works argued that reengineering the lagoon was "essentially a mosquito problem" but that engineers would need to also consider how to balance concerns about the smells emanating from the sewage that was discharged into the lagoon from the city's main water drains. Straightening the banks and deepening the bed of the lagoon would require a delicate balance between health and sanitation, disease and sensibility, sickness and smell.[264] In "reclaiming" the lagoon, British officials sought to address both of these challenges simultaneously, taming the dangers of the lagoon through technical and mechanical intervention and the application of engineering and scientific research, turning it into an "artificial lake with level or gently sloping banks free from pools and pot holes and not subject to erosion."[265] Secretary of State for the Colonies Sidney Webb granted the Gold Coast government £195,000 to remediate this "serious menace to the health of Accra" and asked for regular updates on the project.[266] Work began, and engineers built a causeway over the sandbar, but—as with the engineering works installed in 1919, these quickly filled with sand and could not be maintained. As colonial officials struggled to manage the financial challenges of the global depression, the reclamation project was eventually abandoned. Looking back ten years later, government officials acknowledged the futility of their efforts.[267]

By the 1940s Korle Lagoon was once again considered an infamous mosquito breeding ground.[268] The construction of a major Anglo-American air base in Accra during World War II once again renewed interest in Korle's mosquito problem. The British and American scientists who constituted the Inter-Allied Malaria Control Group considered Africans living in the city as a "reservoir of disease that could be cleansed with the help of chemical pesticides."[269] These scientists used Ga residents as experiment subjects, housed in test cabins overnight to attract mosquitoes, as they compiled the Accra Anopheline Index and tested new strategies for addressing the city's mosquito problem.[270] Military authorities were highly critical of previous civilian efforts, arguing that, by the 1940s "malaria control in any sense of the word simply did not exist. Oiling was haphazard, larva inspection had become perfunctory, and there was profuse breeding in the Korle Bu Lagoon, the Klotey Lagoon near Christiansborg, and in small bodies of water all over the city. The colonial medical department cannot even give intelligent advice."²⁷¹ In response, these new scientists doused the lagoon with larvacides and engaged in a widespread spraying campaign throughout the city—a first in Accra. American reports on the campaign noted that "the application of larvicide ... was strongly resented by the local native population who associated a high religious significance to these lagoons ... [but the] natives [were] placated through negotiation by British authorities with the African chiefs."²⁷² Roberts argues that the reports highlight both the residents' resistance to the use of chemicals and concern about colonial encroachment on sacred spaces; the report also describes how government officials used indirect rule to curry favor with local chiefs to disenfranchise religious authorities and undermine local politics in the city.²⁷³ Importantly, however, the reports also highlight a shift in public health strategy. If the government had resisted the deployment of larvacides for decades out of fear of local discontent, by the 1940s scientific research trumped any local concerns as long as funding and manpower were available.

CONCLUSION

Despite lofty rhetoric, the reality of public health interventions in Accra rarely lived up to the hype from colonial officers. Concentrated efforts at intervention, as seen in the plague epidemic of 1908 were rare—more like parenthetical moments than sustained processes of hegemony.²⁷⁴ As Roberts argues, "The governors to come would show little interest in massive sanitary projects so long as the white population was relatively free of disease, and there were men like Simpson to put out brush fires like the plague of 1908."²⁷⁵ But we must also be careful not to take for granted the power of the British colonial state or the predominance of Western medicine in the health and healing of Africans. As recent studies of indigenous medicine and therapeutic pluralism have shown, biopower was always incomplete. That would have been plainly obvious to townspeople who lived with and suffered from the consequences of inadequate infrastructure and incomplete projects.²⁷⁶ These failures were widely debated in newspapers throughout the first half of the twentieth century, and the reports of African town councillors about complaints from their constituents suggest they were also widely discussed and debated in the streets of Accra.

Public health and medical departments largely remained in the "partial paralysis" that Governor Hugh Clifford observed in the 1910s, caught between ever-proliferating public health regulations, the demands and protests of the public, and the realities of insufficient resources.²⁷⁷ In 1915 the editors of the *Eastern Star* published an indictment condemning the condition of the town and the failure of its Town Council.²⁷⁸ In 1922 African observers noted the "mess at the dispensary" of the acting director of medical and sanitary services and the "conditions obtaining at present at the lunatic asylum," which were "anything but satisfactory."[279] While the arrival of development-minded Governor Gordon Guggisberg led to more investment in hospitals and a greater focus on African health, these developments did not necessarily translate into more substantive changes in the structures of investment or the prejudices that underlay policy.[280] Under Guggisberg, Roberts notes, "The health branch intervened more and more in the daily life of the inhabitants of Accra"[281] through infrastructure, inspections, and fines. Controlled by British colonial government and the "official" representatives of the Accra Town Council, public health strategies often exacerbated inequalities and justified greater racial segregation without appreciable benefits in actual public health.[282] Health and hygiene were not "just metaphors and rhetoric... for cleansing and purifying, but were the actual modes and tools of management for colonialism and nationalism."[283] Investments in African health were an investment in the future development and wealth of the colony, not an inherent good.[284]

As Roberts has argued, even if the memories of mosquito inspectors, loloi courts, and segregation have faded, the impact of all this is marked on the landscape of a city in which high levels of inequality are embedded in both spatial organization and infrastructural provision. But importantly, these early encounters also shaped the prevailing practices, theories, and models of public health and the role of Africans within them. Colonial public health strategies often reclassified African relationships to urban space and transformed African bodies and spaces into sites of disease and contagion that must be regulated and managed. As Vaughan argues, biomedical interventions created subjects and objects simultaneously, producing a concept of "the African" that made sense to colonial administrators and erased class differences in the minds of Europeans.[285] These new constructions of "otherness" were embedded in emerging national, imperial, and international scientific infrastructures.[286] The consolidation of colonial rule in places like the Gold Coast coincided with radical changes across scientific disciplines. As Helen Tilley argues, organizations like the Rockefeller Foundation and the League of Nations shaped medical developments in colonies like the Gold Coast in the interwar period, and international scientific congresses connected British colonial officers with other scientists around the world in ways that gave weight to their belief in the universality of their scientific research, despite obvious contradictions and challenges on the ground.[287] Scientific concepts often reinforced the priorities and goals of colonial governance and economics, even if said concepts did not lead to actual improvements in public health.[288]

As numerous scholars of medicine and health in colonial Africa have now demonstrated, Africans were certainly "active agents in the production, application, and appropriation of scientific knowledge," using medical and scientific research to advance their own agendas and advocate for their own health.[289] However, the increasing professionalization and standardization of scientific practice within imperial and international circles had significant consequences for individuals in cities like Accra. Certainly, British technocrats who created and implemented these policies failed to fully understand the dynamism of African cities. And they were never able to successfully control residents' daily lives in a way that would fully appease European racial ecologies and racialized medicine. And many Africans embraced these policies and the ideologies that underlay them. Even Dr. P. S. Selwyn-Clarke, the once-derided medical officer of health who was criticized for his aggressive approach to public health, was praised upon his departure from the Gold Coast. Newspaper reports argued, "At one time, we did not see eye to eye with Dr. Selwyn-Clarke but eventually what was considered by an ultra-conservative people to be a ruthless and inconsiderate overthrow of their accepted order of things was nothing but an overzealousness on his part for the work for which he came out."[290] But in reducing African practices to "dirt" and "disease," set in opposition to the "cleanliness" and "health" of Western medical and hygiene practices, public health officials, medical doctors, and other technocrats and officials reduced complex African cultural realities and criminalized long-standing practices, often based on prejudice.[291]

While the archives are not full of reports of open rebellion, the consistent failure of public health strategies is a testimony, in part, to the quiet resistance of Accra's population: they ignored rules and laws when they were deemed impractical or expensive, thus "playing the game" only when they were forced to.[292] While British officials and elite Africans often interpreted this as a disregard for public health, it might just as well been seen as opposition to ineffective or incoherent policies. This was not resistance for its own sake. It was a response by residents to the realities facing their communities. Biomedical interventions failed because they failed to consider the social, political, and cultural context of health. But they were consequential all the same. Per the mandate of the Accra Town Council, sanitation and health remained at the center of everything, foundational to the categorization and regulation of urban life and urban space. Public health increasingly justified town planning, from segregation and slum clearance to suburban development and infrastructure provision.

THREE

AFRICAN TRADE AND EXPATRIATE ENTERPRISE IN THE COLONIAL CITY

AT A MEETING OF THE Accra Town Council (ATC) on January 8, 1940, councillors engaged in a long discussion about an unauthorized corn mill that had been erected at the house of Mr. K. Armah Kwantreng. The medical officer of health—a British colonial officer—"expressed the opinion that the corn-mill in question was situated in the corner of a very dirty compound which was full of shacks and old lorry parts and other filth and was therefore injurious to health."[1] The conversation that followed reflected fissures within the town's governing body, as the "African Unofficial Members objected to the opinion expressed by the Medical Officer of Health that corn-mills in general were a nuisance"[2] and protested the inequitable ways these categories were applied across the city.

The debate over Mr. Kwantreng's corn mill consumed the Town Council for months. Championed by African members of the ATC, Kwantreng's experience stands out because of the debate it generated. It is one example in a long list of actions on individuals and groups that remain otherwise anonymous or ignored in the colonial record. However, the corn mill raised important questions about the relevance and meaning of boundaries between public and private, social and economic, residential and commercial, clean and dirty, convenience and nuisance, which resonated across a wide spectrum of economic activities in the colonial city. These boundaries or categories, and the tensions that they engendered, reflect the politics of the town and the profound conflicts between two competing visions of economic opportunity in and ownership of the city. Those conflicts flared up repeatedly in debates about the siting and management of markets and cattle kraals, the construction of stores and slaughterhouses, the collection of fees for advertising, the sale of palm wine and food, and the curing of fish, in

Figure 3.1. Corn Mill installed in front of a private residence in Jamestown, Accra, 2018. Photograph by the author.

which colonial officials frequently cited "nuisance" as a justification to regulate or eliminate long-standing African economic practices. However, this politics of categorization also manifest in ongoing debates about the employment opportunities available to Africans and the challenging "financial condition of the inhabitants of the town."[3] African residents petitioned the governor, protested in the streets, and complained to their Town Council representatives about the financial hardships they faced in the new colonial economy. These conditions were certainly exacerbated by global financial depressions, but as many residents witnessed, constricting economic opportunities were also the direct result of colonial policies that sought to privilege "expatriate enterprise" and undermine the control that Ga people had over trade in the town.

I argue that debates over things like corn mills and distilleries represent early incarnations of the process of informalization—not in name, but in practice—through which both European and African members of the town council sought to redefine the boundaries of legality, legitimacy, and morality in the city. "Nuisance" was a nebulous term that could be deployed by zealous inspectors to target a wide range of practices with little distinction between those practices that merely offended the sensibilities versus those that endangered health. Town councillors took advantage of this term's ambiguity to assert broad authority over the lives of Accra residents and effectively criminalize long-standing Indigenous socioeconomic practices and reshaped public discourse about city life through the lens of regulation.[4] This process was inspired by the desire to protect and promote "expatriate enterprise" and "ordered modernity," as Parker notes.[5] Regulations privileged expatriate capital and sought to marginalize African practices that challenged European expectations of city life. As the British colonial state sought to decentralize financial responsibility for urban governance, the Town Council took on increasing responsibility for the development and maintenance of infrastructure in the growing city. Influenced by both prevailing public health rhetoric and the economic motivations of colonial expansion, categorization and regulation became important means of generating revenue for the operation of the city. The regulation of African urban life, in other words, became embedded in both the logics and finances of governance—the "capitalist city" and the "colonial city" intertwined.[6]

This chapter explores informalization through debates over economic activity in colonial Accra. These debates—and the regulations and patterns of dis/investment that inspired them—reshaped the ways that African economic practices were understood in Accra. As colonial control expanded and British officials sought to exert more direct influence on the flow of trade both into and out of the country, African merchants and entrepreneurs who had once been so central to life on the coast found themselves increasingly marginalized and their practices criminalized in favor of "expatriate enterprise." Town councillors and British technocratic officials often invoked the language of nuisance in justifying their interventions, but as African protests made clear, these regulatory actions often evinced a clear double standard that created resentment and frustration. That collective frustration boiled over into public protest numerous times—most notably in opposition to the 1924 Municipal Corporations Ordinance and, ultimately, in the boycotts and riots of the late 1940s—and inspired new forms of anticolonial resistance. Far from a "natural" or self-evident phenomena, the creation of an "informal economy" in Accra was highly contested as both an infringement on the economic opportunities and an expression of the "right to the city" by African residents.

FINANCIAL CONDITIONS

Despite initial resistance, town residents eventually did begin paying their rates and, at least begrudgingly, recognized the authority of the ATC as a new form of municipal governance. However, the underlying critiques of the town council system and the new taxes that would fund its operations continued to simmer under the surface, particularly as African residents saw municipal funds used to develop infrastructure and services in elite neighborhoods. Despite initial promises of self-government and autonomous local development, it was not clear what benefit this new system and its attendant costs had brought to local residents. A new Municipal Corporations Ordinance, proposed by the government in 1924, resurrected these old fears and criticisms. While the growth of new commodity markets, like cocoa, provided new forms of economic opportunity for some in the Gold Coast, Fortescue argues that change "proved much less dramatic" for those whom he describes as "Accra's crowd": laborers, artisans, farmers, fishermen, clerks, unemployed, and a mass of female petty traders.[7] Merchants on the Gold Coast also increasingly struggled to maintain their previous level of wealth and success as expatriate firms like the United Africa Company and the United Trading Company consolidated control over the sale of goods, limited the possibilities for sale on consignment, and eliminated roles for African intermediaries.[8] These economic woes, which were cited repeatedly by African leaders on and off the Town Council, were reflected in the revenues of the ATC. As Fortescue notes, license fees and rates raised £53,679 between 1914 and 1921, but government still had to provide significant grants-in-aid (£34,000) to cover the costs of urban governance and infrastructural development.[9]

Noting these ongoing challenges, Governor Gordon Guggisberg convened a committee, chaired by John Maxwell, to investigate the operations and challenges of urban governance in the Gold Coast. Maxwell's report, published in 1923, called for both greater representation and greater taxation. Majority rule, the British hoped, would offset the discontent of increasing taxes, satisfy demands for self-government, and rid the colonial government of financial responsibility for the development and maintenance of the town.[10] Central to the proposal was a commitment to substantially increase annual rates from 5 percent to 20 percent as a basic rate and expand license fees for activities that were central to the social, cultural, and economic life of the town, from drumming to hawking and market trading.[11] Maxwell and other British leaders felt confident in their proposal, believing that the population had increasingly accepted the idea of direct taxation and would be more willing to do so if they had full control of the institutions of urban governance and could directly shape the way those taxes were spent.

Local elites, many of whom were able to successfully weather the trade depression by investing in new cash crops like cocoa, supported the new ordinance, and it passed easily through the Legislative Council. However, as word about the new ordinance spread, local leaders quickly organized to protest. Just weeks before the Municipal Corporations Ordinance was announced by Governor Gordon Guggisberg at the opening of the capital's new Selwyn Market in 1923—a symbol of the new system of municipal governance—a large group of angry market women marched on Christiansborg Castle (the seat of British colonial government) to protest their forced removal from the old Salaga Market.[12] "Youngmen," led by the *asafoatse*, also organized protests specifically targeting the MCO. After an initial meeting at Amiguina on August 30, 1924, the wulomei and asafoatsemei of Accra and Christiansborg publicly pressured and shamed Ga Manche Tackie Yaoboi to convene a meeting of all of the leaders and ratepayers of Accra on September 12, 1924. At this meeting they decided to immediately send a telegram to the secretary of state for the colonies in London noting that "aboriginal inhabitants and other rate-payers including wulomei and asafoatsemei of Accra and Christiansborg strongly protest against Municipal Corporations Ordinance No. 29 of 1924 just passed by the Legislative Council" and alerting him that they would be sending a petition in due course.[13] Chris Nettey, Captain of the Gbese Asafoatse, forwarded a copy of the telegram to the governor, arguing that "the above course" of appealing direction to the secretary of state "is adopted owing to the urgency and importance of the matter."[14]

Among the various issues cited by Ga leaders in Asafoatse Nettey's petition, the most prominent was the "financial condition of the inhabitants of the town" who, they argued, were unable to bear the "fresh burdens" or "hardships" of the new ordinance. Osu Manche Dowuona III argued that trade in Christiansborg had been undercut by European merchants who had cut out African middlemen in the cocoa trade in order to deal more directly with farmers. Companies like Elders Road Transport Company, which used new motor vehicles to transport cocoa, had rendered unnecessary local services that carted cocoa from the railway station. By training prisoners at Ussher Fort as carpenters, tailors, and blacksmiths, British officials had created competition for craftsmen. The Prison Department stopped purchasing kenkey from the market, cutting into the sales of food sellers. Meanwhile, hundreds of boys left school every year and struggled to find work in government offices and commercial firms, and the prices of everything in the city surged. Ratepayers were in arrears, private houses were heavily mortgaged, business at Salaga Market declined, and the number of building permits decreased.[15] African residents had to pay license fees for vehicles, goldsmiths and cloth sellers had to take licenses, alcohol and kenkey sales were taxed, gun owners needed to pay for licenses, and the fees for dog licenses increased.

Playing music and drums required a license, as did the slaughtering of sheep for traditional ceremonies related to the stool. The Osu Manche noted the impact of economic depression on the housing conditions, including his own:

> I built my own house but the iron roof is now 'turned up' and I haven't got sufficient money to repair it. It is my own house and I keep the stool in it. Many other people's houses are in the same condition. WE have to pay rates, and one who can't pay they come and sell his house. There is no trade in the town to enable one to raise money for one's living and rates. The houses are spoilt and if they are not repaired within a fixed time, they are pulled down. In the past there was a misunderstanding about these rates and that caused the bombardment. At present there is no trade. Many of those present have not paid the rate now due, neither have I. You will see the case is a pitiful one.[16]

As the Osu Manche noted, "We could not live comfortably under the old law, now they bring a new one. What would you do? Go and leave the town."[17] Too many people, he argued, were being arrested and these new changes would mean that "we would die more than as before."[18] The people of Accra refused. As Gbese Asafo Captain J. D. Garshong noted, "This is sufficient to say that the Government have taken all the work in Accra."

In their protests, the asafoatse and their allies marked a clear division in the town. C. W. Welman, secretary for native affairs, spent an hour with the Gbese Manche and Asafoatse Nettey trying to convince them to postpone the mass meeting because "the Ga Mantse anticipated that it would be misused by his enemies to make him appear responsible in the eyes of the people for the Municipal Corporations Ordinance and all the enormities that rumour had informed the common people were involved in that measure, and because it did not seem to me that it could serve any good purpose, but would unnecessarily disturb and excited the populace."[19] Having failed, he noted to other government officials that there now appeared to be two factions in the town. The first comprised the people of Accra—"the masses, the Third Estate"—organized largely under the asafoatsemei, who were strictly opposed to the new law. The second, who had supported and even advocated for the law through the various governance structures in the Gold Coast, was a decidedly more elite group, including African members of the Town Council, the Aborigines Rights Protection Society [ARPS], the unofficial members of the Legislative Council, some of the more progressive Manchemei, and other "thought-leaders."[20] There were undoubtedly numerous issues at play in these protests, including questions about government transparency and the relative independence of the manche in Accra. However, as the testimonies made clear, economic issues were at the center of this split. As one Alata witness noted, "Taxes are never pleasant to contemplate and when Mr. Garshong and others inflame the passions of market-women by telling them that they must come out and help them against the Government in imposing taxes upon them... one can understand the commotion which has been aroused."[21] The self-government elites aspired to was seen as a privilege by many if it came at such tremendous financial costs, and the "crowd" clearly no longer trusted elite organizations like the Aborigines' Rights Protection Society (ARPS)—or increasingly the Ga Manche himself who had increasingly allied with the ARPS and the government—to properly represent their interests.[22] The new governance systems and economic structures of the town had eroded the economic prospects of so many individuals that true self-government and financial independence seemed impossible. As Welman noted after an extensive investigation, "Political stability in Accra [was] badly shaken."[23] Guggisberg ultimately relented, realizing that opposition to the ordinance was "widespread and nearly unanimous," rather than the rabble-rousing of a few discontented individuals, and abandoned the new scheme.[24]

NUISANCE

Popular protest was rooted in very real frustrations about recent changes in the structural condition of the economy in Accra. While the global depression undoubtedly restricted economic possibilities in the city, many of these changes were also structural—the result of very real and intentional changes in colonial economy designed to advance the interest of expatriate enterprise in the name of "development." As those organizing in opposition to the MCO noted, African traders were increasingly reliant on European firms, which cut into their profits, and local producers found themselves pushed out of their work as government increasingly asserted control over local production.[25] Mechanization also had a profound impact on the mobilization of labor and the acquisition of profit in the early twentieth century as motor vehicles and railways usurped the role previously played by head carriers and other local transport workers. As Claire Robertson notes, women were disproportionately impacted by these changes. While many individuals did eventually shift their economic activities to take advantage of new opportunities brought by technological and economic change, women were often prevented from pursuing formal education (beyond training in domestic work) and, within Victorian mores, were discouraged from pursuing employment. Coupled with preexisting restrictions on land ownership and access to labor, it is unsurprising that women comprised a large proportion of the protesters. Pushed out of the most lucrative parts of the trading economy, where they had previously dominated, many traders resorted to hawking staples like kenkey, even as women carried a disproportionate amount of the financial responsibility for the care of their families.[26] As Fortescue argues, the dramatic increases in licenses and fees in the MCO "threatened not only the negligible profits made by the majority of Accra women but also the livelihood of large numbers of dependents" and hawkers constituted the majority of the protesters.[27] However, as the protests made clear, their demands were often much more conservative than that of the elite class, rooted in concerns about economic survival rather than radical demands for self-government and reform. Protests over rates and fees continued throughout the 1920s, rooted in economic concerns.

These contestations over urban politics were reflected in the realms of policy. Even the development-minded Governor Gordon Guggisberg, understood economic development as the advancement of an economy based on raw materials and the importation of European manufactured goods. While these approaches clearly shaped the massive building and infrastructure projects central to Guggisberg's Ten Year Plan for the development of the colony writ large, they had a particular impact on Accra as an international trading port and commercial hub.[28] Institutions of urban governance, led by majority "official" members and empowered by European technocratic consultants, passed a series of regulations and pieces of legislation that sought to "reform" African economic practices. While some of these concerns—like fish-smoking and bread-baking ovens operating in the congested districts of the city—were connected to issues of health, others sought to create both literal and metaphorical space for European firms and their economic interests.

The vague language of "nuisance" invoked in the corn mill debate by the medical officer of health reflected the ambiguity of colonial urban policy in Accra in the early twentieth century. In the case of Mr. Kwantreng, the medical officer of health (MOH) and other European members of the Town Council cited a number of issues related to public health and sanitation—the mill was located in a residential compound, and the compound itself was "full of shacks and old lorry parts and other filth and was therefore injurious to health."[29] In their protests, African councillors did not debate the sanitation question. Mark Addy suggested, for example, that the shacks might be removed to conform with sanitary regulations. T. Jones-Nelson and Solomon Odamtten likewise suggested that the owner of the corn mill could relocate it to another site if given sufficient time (i.e., six months). In supporting various means to redress the situation, African councillors tacitly embraced Town Council President E. Norton Jones's call to "rely on the advice of the Medical Officer of Health in matters of public health."[30]

African representatives, however, did complain about what they saw as a lack of recognition of the social and cultural practices of urban residents. Councillors described the complex history of ownership and use rights associated with this particular corn mill and, in the process, spoke to a broader culture of space among Ga residents. While African land tenure has often been described as

Figure 3.2. Women on the beach sort fish for smoking. People and Cities, March–April 1968. Source: Photographic Archive, Information Services Office, Ministry of Information, Accra R/R/8158/12.

"communal"—in which chiefs hold land in trust for communities and individuals petition for the right to use land—the practices of ownership and spatial order here might more appropriately be defined as social. Mr. Kwantreng, it turns out, did not own the corn mill, but he did own the compound where the corn mill was located. Rather, Councillor Odamtten noted that the mill had been owned by Mrs. J. S. Bruce Vanderpuye, who willed it to a Mr. Teymani. Teymani himself had apparently consulted the MOH before he installed the mill inside Mr. Kwantreng's compound. At the time of the complaint the mill was being used by Mr. A. W. Simons, who was a pensioner. In fining Mr. Kwantreng and ordering that the corn mill be taken down, European town councillors and the regulations

Figure 3.3. Widely varied commercial enterprises existing side by side in Accra. Various Places in Accra, 1975. Photograph by Ben Kwakye. Source: Photographic Archive, Information Services Office, Ministry of Information, Accra PS/1834/2.

they enforced flattened African sociospatial relationships in ways that ignored the complex social and economic dynamics of the city. In labeling corn mills a "nuisance," the MOH also seemed to condemn the foodways of Accra residents. As J. Kitson Mills noted, "Corn-mills generally catered for the staple food of the people of Accra (Kenkey) and much inconvenience would be caused if the corn-mills were removed."[31] These mills provided maize for household food production, but they also served as important revenue sources for community members. Women produced and sold kenkey in markets, providing critical supplementary income for families.[32] Pensioners like Mr. Simons, who had access to corn mills, relied on that income to supplement insufficient pensions and provide for a wide range of dependents.[33]

Figure 3.4. Cooked food seller. Market Scenes, 1984. Photograph by Felix Antonio. Source: Photographic Archive, Information Services Office, Ministry of Information, Accra PS/3004/6.

Figure 3.5. Cooking area inside a compound. Street Scenes, 1955. Source: Photographic Archive, Information Services Office, Ministry of Information, Accra R/2200/3.

The debate over corn mills, then, reflected a complex urban politics in Accra, which was rooted in an increasingly powerful form of definitional violence that simultaneously sought to capture and codify diverse economic practices as an "industry" and reform or restrict its function as a "nuisance." In many ways, the debates of the 1940s had their roots in Accra's early town planning practices that linked urban sanitation, spatial order, and social control. By the mid-1930s, the Town Council had passed a number of new rules and procedures that regulated a wide range of African socioeconomic practices, from curing fish, selling palm wine, and slaughtering livestock to building practices and tenancy agreements. Many of these regulations were aimed at removing commercial activities from residential zones. The Town Council built new slaughterhouses and markets in order to concentrate and more effectively control activities that were seen to be directly connected to concerns about public health. However, as the debate about the corn mill demonstrates, some of these practices were built into the patterns and practices of daily life, not easily separated out from the social concerns of the household.

When the ATC considered the draft bill that would regulate the sale of palm wine in October of 1930, councillors raised a number of questions that highlighted some of the contradictions and varied perspectives in operation through urban governance. European councilmembers were primarily concerned about the redundancy of the bill—was palm wine not covered by the existing Wine and Beer License? Was a license even necessary for establishments selling palm wine? Councillors were perplexed as to how and whether to regulate the sale of palm wine, for example, which was clearly alcoholic and thus potentially subject to liquor ordinances but was also sold in the streets and open markets rather than established shops. In 1930 councillors agreed that palm wine should remain under the regulatory authority of the chiefs, but their debates highlighted that the boundaries of legitimate oversight and authority over African practices were clearly shifting. African councillors looked beyond the technical parameters of the bill. Councillor Kojo Thompson questioned the state's motives. If, as the government argued, palm wine production was destroying trees, wouldn't it be better to educate the people on better strategies for tapping palm wine rather than introducing regulations that would create further hardship for local peoples? Regulation would not only be a hardship for palm wine sellers but would also inhibit the work of breadmakers who used palm wine.[34]

Other practices were more directly connected to space. Council officials and technocrats regularly debated the siting and organization of various kinds of spaces that were critical to local economies of food production, from processing meat and curing fish to selling cooked foods and agricultural products, which they attempted to control with varying degrees of success.[35] Cattle kraals and markets, in particular, generated considerable debate. As we saw in relation to the corn mill, some of that debate was about the health consequences of mixed-use development. Bread baking, fish curing, animal meat processing, and other types of activities that provided food for the city's population also produced pollutants that British officials worried would negatively impact the health of the already congested districts of Jamestown and Ussher Town. The ATC made plans to relocate these activities on the edge of the city, reshaping the social and economic landscape of food production in significant ways. However, individuals working in cattle kraals and abattoirs also provided an essential service in the city and thus presented an opportunity to generate revenue for the colonial state. British members of the ATC repeatedly attempted to raise fees in the cattle kraals. For British officials, investments to improve the infrastructure of the cattle kraals justified increased cost; however, African councillors pointed repeatedly to the welfare of the people. If, as health officials had insisted, the cattle kraals and abattoirs had to be relocated outside of the city in order to ensure the health of the people, Dr. Nanka-Bruce argued that "it was expected that the expenses incurred in that direction should be borne by the Council and not made a means of revenue."[36] These increased costs also rankled in light of new competition from European firms. In order to cut costs the Gold Coast Hospital at Korle Bu had begun to purchase its meat from the Accra Ice Company, an expatriate firm, rather than purchasing it from local butchers, creating hardships for a local economy that had grown in size over the first decades of the twentieth century in order to service the expanding colonial economy.[37] While the fee increases were taken off the table, this kind of commodification of space was part of a broader expansion of expatriate enterprise in the capital.

While the ATC sought to regulate markets in similar ways, traders proved much more vocal and organized in response to proposed changes. In some cases, traders sent petitions and engaged in direct protest. Sixty Ga women sent a petition to the secretary for native affairs in 1909, objecting to the relocation of fish smoking and curing to a small village called Tsokor, located outside of the city. Women marched in protest on Christiansborg Castle in 1923 to protest their removal from the old Salaga Market (built in the early 1880s) to the newly constructed Selwyn Market (named after the controversial sanitary officer).[38] However, traders also often outright refused to use newly constructed sites as a more passive form of protest against the ATC's attempts to control the markets. These actions often frustrated ATC officials and highlighted many of the rifts on the Council between European/official and African/unofficial members.

Councillors frequently debated the best strategies for encouraging local traders to occupy newly constructed markets. As early as 1931, traders in Selwyn Market petitioned the Town Council to reduce market fees. African councillors

Figure 3.6. Area view of the Old Kaneshie Market. Area View of the old and new Kaneshie Markets, 1975. Photograph by Ben Kwakye. Source: Photographic Archive, Information Services Office, Ministry of Information, Accra PS 1693/2.

like the Hon. Dr. Nanka-Bruce made arguments in economic rather than social or cultural terms. The general depression, he argued, had lowered rents around the city, and he felt that the city's markets should respond accordingly to attract traders who could afford to rent the stalls.[39] These debates, however, did not raise questions about the desirability of these new infrastructural forms: Did African traders even *want* these markets? African councillors, it seems, had bought into the logics of colonial spatial planning even if urban residents had not, reinforcing the suspicion that the Accra "crowd" had raised in their protests about the Municipal Corporations Ordinance.

In 1932 Councillor Kitson Mills noted that the market at Korle Gonno, which was set aside during the general planning of the neighborhood, had been sitting unused since its construction in 1929. As a new market, traders who relocated their business to Korle Gonno took a financial risk, which was amplified by the fees that the ATC charged for all sellers. The ATC president, who was also the district commissioner of Accra, reached out to the Jamestown Manche and other chiefs to get their feedback.[40] The Manche's response did not seem to elicit any particular urgency, so the council decided to drop the matter, but Kitson Mills persisted.[41] As he argued, "The market had been built, and it would go to ruins—to the loss of the Council—if it remained unoccupied."[42] Drawing on the kinds of arguments that British councillors had made about the financial implications of cattle kraals and abattoirs, Kitson Mills renewed his argument on financial grounds the following year: "The market had been built at some expense by the Council for the use of the people in Korle Gono, and it would go to ruins if unoccupied. He had asked before that the people should be induced by the Council to make use of the market by demanding no market fees for the present until at a stage when they had got used to the amenities of a proper market. He thought it was the duty of the Council to educate the people in such matters and he asked that the matter should be reconsidered."[43] In a motion placed before the council, Kitson Mills argued that allowing the market to be used for free would induce women sellers to use the market until they had become used to the new site. Kitson Mills pointed to the maternity hospital as an example of a public service that had originally provided services for free before successfully introducing fees that led to a noted increase in revenue. Councillor Akiwumi pointed to similar changes in bus fares between Labadi and the post office in successfully promoting ridership. Reducing costs would "confirm new habits."[44] "Official" members, including appointed African "official" Councillor de Graft Johnson, were resistant to the idea of suspending fees for fear of raising protest in other city markets and "creating an undesirable precedent."[45] In order to operate the market, the ATC had to hire a market clerk and scavengers, which would be sunk costs for the council if the site was not generating revenue. And yet, this abandoned market provided an opportunity to show residents of the city that the ATC was working "in the interests of the people." As he argued, "Many people still thought that Town Councils merely existed for the purpose of collecting taxes and yet they began 40 years ago. Here was an opportunity for the Council to disprove such an allegation."[46] These kinds of challenges brought opportunities to be creative. De Graft Johnson suggested temporarily handing over the market to the Jamestown Manche to manage for six months as an experiment before the ATC again considered whether they should reinstitute fees. Individuals who already possessed hawkers' licenses would be allowed to use the market for free. Still others supported the suspension of fees as a form of education and encouragement to adopt this new spatial and economic infrastructure.[47] Being outside of the business district, the ATC would not lose much. Otherwise, the medical officer of health postulated, people would prefer to use the London Market instead. Ultimately, everyone decided: they had nothing to lose.

Even as they constructed new markets in areas outside of the commercial core, the ATC and their allies increasingly acted to reshape what commerce looked like in the old town center. In the 1930s the ATC also began to dismantle some of the traders' stalls in order to make space for new "shops" that were leased by the Council to expatriate firms. Eighty applications were submitted for the five shops built in Selwyn Market in the early 1930s.[48] While some of these firms, like the United Africa Company and Messrs. Shaul & Coy, were owned by Europeans, others like Messrs. S.A. Turqui Bros and Messrs. Zahn & Kassab were part of a growing population of Syrian traders who were operating in the country. As ATC members debated the leasing of five shops in the Selwyn Market in 1931, African councillors like Kojo Thompson objected to consideration of tenders from Syrian traders "on the grounds that such aliens do not materially help the country." For European members, these questions were baffling. In the minutes of these meetings, British officials questioned Thompson: "Why not? They pay taxes and assist trade." The president of the ATC observed that "the matter was a question of funds and that the tenders would be considered on their merits." However, Thompson insisted that his objection be recorded.[49] While the language of "aliens" might suggest xenophobia, Thompson's concerns should be read in light of broader changes in state support for the market and the spaces available to Ga residents of Accra. Expatriate British firms were one thing, but, in supporting new populations as competition in Accra's busy markets, Thompson worried that Ga people were being pushed out altogether. There were few African tenants in the shops—a striking contrast to several decades before when Ga merchants dominated the city's commercial landscape.[50] These changes raised important new questions about how "market" was defined, who operates in market spaces, and how that is distinguished from "shops."

From a purely economic perspective, these new stores were hugely successful. The ATC obtained a revenue of at least £144/year for each shop—paid in advance—and shop owners were responsible for the interior fittings and maintenance of the buildings. The profits generated from the shops inspired the council to build more in 1932. For "official" members, the destruction of "petty trader's" market stalls to make way for more "established" business was a wise investment.[51] As economic difficulties in the 1930s presented challenges for shop owners, some, like Messrs. Shaul & Co., appealed for a rent reduction. As Councillors Johnston and Kitson Mills noted, "Times are hard, and profits are small." The low level of trade and the high cost of spirits licenses made it difficult for many businesses to remain open.[52] While Shaul & Co. ultimately terminated their lease and gave up occupation of the shop, others moved in behind them, and the government built additional shops in London Market.[53]

Figure 3.7. Market stalls surrounded by shops and stores. Views of Accra, 1955. Source: Photographic Archive, Information Services Office, Ministry of Information, Accra G/856/5.

The earthquake that devastated large parts of Accra in 1939 seemed to exacerbate contention over these issues. At a December meeting, the council passed a motion "that the authority of the Council be given to the Medical Officer of Health to remove certain corrugated iron temporary shacks used as corn-mills, palm wine shops and business purposes as per list submitted by him."[54] The MOH again objected to the sanitary conditions of the shacks. "Speaking from a sanitary standpoint," he argued, "the existence of the unauthorized corrugated iron shacks should now be discouraged because they were unsuitable for the purposes for which they had been erected. Besides, they harboured rats and flies and were in most cases very dirty. Dirt carried disease which at times may become epidemic."[55] From the perspective of the British members of the Town Council, the temporary structures were an understandable development after the earthquake but also set a dangerous precedent with the potential to undermine the Council's efforts and authority. J. Kitson Mills and Solomon Odamtten objected to the action and intent behind the motion and foresaw a different sort of precedent embedded in the Council's proposed direct action against African communities. As Kitson Mills noted, "If the Council took advantage of the earthquake and ordered the removal of the shacks it seemed to him other buildings would soon be attacked."⁵⁶ This move represented a lack of consideration for the suffering of Accra residents in the aftermath of the earthquake and the broader financial depression that had crippled the colony for at least a decade. But it also highlighted once again the lack of consideration for African socioeconomic practices. The very activities and spaces that British councillors considered a public health threat to the city's residents were central to the lives of those residents. Far from a "nuisance," the activities that took place in these corrugated iron structures were central to the livelihoods and daily lives of many urban residents. Owners of corn mills were essential to producing kenkey, and palm wine sellers "earned an honest livelihood" out of those "shacks." Destroying them would entail significant hardship in a way that would cut to the heart of the socioeconomic life of Accra's population. "The sympathy of the Council," Odamtten argued, "should go in favour of the people of the Municipality."⁵⁷

At the heart of this contestation was a critical double standard. Councillor Odamtten pointed this out directly in relation to the corn mill debates. "Those who lived near the Union Trading Company's Workshop, like Dr. J.H. Murrell," he argued, "had not urged the removal of the Union Trading Company's machinery as a nuisance. Likewise it was unfortunate to molest those who have erected corn-mills to cater for the needs of the people." Odamtten's words echoed complaints that would be reiterated in the debates about Mr. Kwantreng's corn mill a month later—African corn mills were a nuisance, but the nearby Accra Ice Company, which was extremely noisy, was apparently free to operate under European ownership. African-directed occupation and adaptation of public space was subject to public health scrutiny in part because it seemed to defy (or at least operate outside of) colonial visions of authority and order. Like African lorry drivers who were labeled "pirates" because they traveled on public roads and operated passenger services to supplement the municipal bus system, corn mills and distilleries were a "nuisance" not because their activity was objectionable in itself but because they represented the persistence of Africans operating outside of the imagined order. When African councillors complained about the conditions surrounding markets in order to improve the conditions of food sellers or explain the unpopularity of spaces reserved by the Town Council for market activity, questions of sanitation seemed remarkably less urgent. "If the women sellers would protect their foodstuffs as required by the bye-laws, there would be nothing to complain of," the Council concluded.⁵⁸

These attacks on the livelihood of workers raised questions about the priorities of the Town Council at the same moment when its power was being consolidated and extended in new ways. In demolishing essential means of livelihood for urban residents, the Town Council drew attention to broader concerns about African wages and the limitations placed on African earning potential and advancements through racialized policies of imperial governance. Such issues had come to a head in 1936 when the town clerk—one of the highest-ranking and best-paid positions available to Africans in the city—was convicted of embezzling Council funds and removed from office. The Council president, within the purview of his authority, appointed a new town clerk—a European, Mr. Duncan MacDougall, who had previously been employed by the Basel Mission Society. The outrage that followed highlighted frustration over opportunity, representation, and authority in the growing city, split (at least in this case) clearly along racial lines.[59]

EXPATRIATE ENTERPRISE, ORDERED MODERNITY, AND THE POLITICS OF URBAN DEVELOPMENT

These contestations over spatial order and urban reform were shaped by competing notions of what was "legitimate." Over the course of four decades, Council members used their authority to enshrine their particular visions for the city in law—"illegitimate" became "illegal" and "illicit."[60] Reinforced through regulations and systems of licensing and permitting, Council legislation, priorities, and preferences had real consequences for African residents. Demolished buildings, property seizure, fines, and jail time deeply affected individuals and families—a consequence reflected in the regular petitions from residents appealing for consideration in response to infractions. Much to the frustration of councillors, however, legal codes were not wholly effective means of enacting social change. Town Council regulations marked the boundaries of acceptable behavior in emerging colonial urban society, but the exercise of regulatory power was unable to effectively change existing behaviors and practices—at least not with the immediacy that councillors desired. Councillors expressed persistent frustration, confusion, and sometimes indignation over African behaviors that failed to conform to the new spatial order. Councillors complained that market women who protested fees or refused to operate in new public markets, for example, simply did not understand the purpose of new municipal structures. African councillors, in particular, advocated for greater public education around issues of sanitation, public health, and public safety, arguing that if sanitation officers or building inspectors would put more effort into explaining the rationale behind new regulations, urban residents might more readily comply.[61]

The more immediately consequential Town Council interventions were connected to the provision of public services and the control over new public space. Particularly in markets and lorry parks, councillors leveraged access to resources in order to change behavior and enforce regulations. By 1936, the Town Council had opened five markets around the city and employed eight market clerks who maintained order in the market, managed space, and collected fees.⁶² In setting aside public land for markets and building sheds for sellers, the Town Council expanded its control over the provision of public services and more clearly defined the boundaries of "appropriate" public action. Creating specially designated spaces for commercial activity, in other words, allowed officials to justify more rigorous policing of activities that occurred outside the boundaries of those commercial zones. Hawkers, petty traders, and food sellers were required to pay licenses and fees to operate in the city, and their activities were generally confined to public markets. Lorry drivers were subject to similar regulations, including licenses and fees to use public lorry parks located primarily near major public markets. When lorry drivers began parking along roadsides and picking up passengers, the Town Council called on the city police force to crack down on offenders. By 1936, the totality of licenses and taxes constituted nearly one-third of the Town Council's total revenue. Expenditure on lorry parks, by contrast, accounted for only three one thousandth of the Council's budget.

This form of regulatory oversight was an extension of the broader commodification of land in Accra over the course of the early twentieth century. The Town Councils Ordinance of 1894, which established the ATC, empowered councillors to collect rates on properties in the municipality in order to generate revenue to fund city services, maintenance, and infrastructural development.⁶³ The accurate collection of rates required annual assessments of the city's built structures, including homes and businesses. This assessment provided the basis for Town Council revenue, but it also created functional maps of city resources, which councillors used to inform policies and development plans, including, of course, the policies that encouraged the construction of more "high-quality" buildings that would simultaneously contribute to the "ordered modernity" of the town and draw increased rates on property. The assessment and rate system also redefined the relationship between space, the built environment, and value through the framework of money and the possibilities for wealth generation. The expansion of town boundaries to incorporate new areas like Labadi was directly tied to the presence of a good number of "rateable properties," which marked these districts as part of the "modern" city.

For colonial officials, the commodification of space created new opportunities to generate revenue from public space. The Town Council rented out kiosks at bus stations to companies like The Anglo-African Aerated Waters, Ltd., to sell iced mineral waters, snacks, and cigarettes.⁶⁴ They signed exclusive leases for advertising space on buses and bus shelters with private companies like West African Publicity Limited.⁶⁵ And throughout the 1930s, the Town Council built new shops within markets, which they leased to a number of expatriate (largely European and Syrian) companies on a yearly basis.⁶⁶ The construction of these new shops perhaps best exemplified the motivations behind the Town Council's plans for Accra's development. Even as the Council claimed that they were unable to lower market fees due to the depression, they built new stores in the Selwyn Market to lease out "on very favourable terms." As demand increased in 1932, the Council demolished petty traders' stalls in order to construct additional shops that would generate revenue and provide space for expatriate enterprise at the center of the city's busiest commercial districts.[67] Roads, too, were commercialized and commodified spaces, which the Council rigorously policed.[68]

This process of commoditization and regulation created clear categories of economic activity, which privileged expatriate enterprise and marked a significant shift from earlier models of integrated African-European commerce. Up through the end of the nineteenth century, commercial operations in Accra required the cooperation of African merchants and traders who obtained goods from European firms on credit. As the profit margins diminished around the 1890s, European firms asserted direct control over coastal trade.[69] Town Council development priorities echoed this shift away from cooperation and integration toward a system of spatial and regulatory governance that privileged expatriate enterprise in the name of creating "ordered modernity" and funding the city's further development. This seemingly limited scope of effective action had enormous consequences in defining new expectations of legitimacy and legality in the colonial city—a form of definitional violence in which African practices were increasingly judged as being outside of "legitimate frameworks."[70] In doing so, they consolidated a particular form of colonial capitalism, situated at the intersection of expatriate enterprise and ordered modernity, and enshrined in law and backed by the regulatory, policing, and enforcement power of the state. In licensing and regulating daily life through the strategic control and investment in public space, the Town Council effectively marginalized Africans as "other" or aberrant within colonial society and created systems that structurally disenfranchised Africans within the political and economic frameworks of urban colonial governance.

URBAN CONSTITUENCIES AND THE DIFFUSION OF COLONIAL AUTHORITY

The expanding regulatory authority of the Town Council generated spirited opposition from those who found themselves operating outside of colonial spatial visions. Many of those protests were directed through African councillors, who had been elected by ratepayers to represent the interests of residents in the city's various districts. The regulation of corn mills and distilleries also generated a debate that seemed to fall along easily assumed racial lines as African councillors urged European officers to exercise restraint in dealing with African residents like Mr. Kwantreng and Mr. Simons and to extend consideration to the people of Accra more broadly. These racialized political divides were inscribed in the very language of the Council itself, which labeled European appointed representatives as "Official Members" and elected African representatives as "Unofficial Members."[71] While these labels reflected the individual's role in relation to the official structures of colonial governance, it also mapped closely onto increasingly segregated spatial politics.

African councillors often spoke out against Town Council policies, bringing forward complaints from ratepaying constituents and voting as a united opposition bloc against new forms of regulation and enforcement, which, they argued, were short-sighted, culturally insensitive, or unduly harsh. In doing so, outspoken councillors like J. Kitson Mills and Kojo Thompson highlighted the persistent gap between the city councillors imagined and the city people actually used—a gap that echoed the seemingly contradictory responsibilities of the Town Council as an institution of both social engineering and representative governance.

However, these same councillors just as frequently used their connections with and understandings of African socioeconomic conditions to suggest alterations to Council policy in ways that reinforced and expanded the influence of colonial spatial and infrastructural authority. By the 1930s, large-scale active resistance seemed to have died down, but African residents regularly used public space to register their discontent with Council policies. The willful destruction of property was often explained by African and European councillors alike as a misunderstanding. When young men destroyed trees and shrubs that had been newly planted by the Department of Agriculture using Council funds, the president of the Town Council appealed to African councillors and chiefs to help intervene and stop the practice.[72] However, when the young men of Labadi destroyed oil lamps in frustration over the Council's failure to provide the town with electric lighting in 1936, councillors had to grapple with a much more direct critique of their policies and the difficult balance between infrastructural promise and limited resources in the growing town.[73] Particularly as new communities were incorporated into the municipal boundaries, demands for infrastructure increased rapidly. Incorporation meant that the Town Council collected rates in communities like Labadi. In exchange, urban residents expected voting rights and infrastructural development that reflected community priorities.[74]

The broader debates around infrastructure, regulation, and spatial planning suggest that the actions of Accra residents defied easy categorization. In their petitions and representations to the Town Council, Accra residents made claims to infrastructure and space based on their position as ratepayers. African councillors and Accra residents alike strategically mobilized colonial discourse about public safety and public health in their claims for basic infrastructure. Infrastructural services like electric lighting and public latrines were the "built forms around which publics thicken."[75] In the colonial context, that form of public investment posed both an opportunity and a threat within the frameworks of an institution like Accra. Residents who demanded access to the infrastructure of "ordered modernity" represented, in the minds of British and African officials alike, the success of colonial social engineering. However, these infrastructural demands also placed new pressure on organizations like the Town Council to shape more responsive urban development plans. Infrastructures might be, as Anand argues, "the material articulations of imagination, ideology, and social life,"[76] but they are also embedded within highly contested structures of power and authority. Latrines were an excellent example. Not only did the demand for sanitation infrastructure place financial and political pressures on the Town Council, but the spatial and social politics related to the siting of latrines—where they were located, how they were maintained—presented new kinds of challenges. British officials welcomed African embrace of sewage and sanitation systems in Accra; Town councillors appealed to the Governor's Office for additional funding to erect public latrines and sewers in the city throughout the 1930s. But as material infrastructure expanded, these objects, services, and spaces generated new forms of public critique, which directly or indirectly challenged the vision and authority of the Council.

These tensions were most obvious in debates over the organization and regulation of space for African economic activities. As a trading town, markets and streets played a particularly important role in local economies, facilitating mobility and exchange among the city's diverse residents. They were, in other words, simultaneously economic and social spaces. In the eyes of British and African councillors alike, setting aside distinct public spaces for markets and establishing formal public transport like the municipal bus system was an extension of the infrastructural work of ordered modernity that latrines and electric lights represented. However, town councillors noted that many of the newly constructed markets, for example, sat unused months after they opened.

DISTURBANCES IN THE GOLD COAST (WATSON COMMISSION)

Despite the broader infrastructural and economic investments of the interwar years under Guggisberg's Ten Year Plan, residents of Accra saw their economic opportunities further eroded, thanks in part of a focus on rural development and investment in new global trade networks. The war provided additional challenges. Imports tightened as Britain itself faced rationing and redirected investments toward the war effort. Lord Swinton traveled to West Africa in the early years of the Second World War to make a case for controlling the import-export trade as part of the war effort.⁷⁷ Even those merchants, traders, and farmers who did make money during the period had very few outlets for investment or consumption. Short-term sacrifice in the context of war was understandable, but when demobilized soldiers returned to the Gold Coast, many expected the colonial government to make good on long-promised investment and opportunity. When that investment was hampered by the challenges of Britain's own recovery efforts, people across the Gold Coast grew increasingly frustrated.

By the late 1940s, economic discontent spilled over into boycotts, protests, and violence. On February 28, a group of ex-servicemen who had fought in the Gold Coast Regiment marched to Christiansborg Castle with a petition demanding jobs and compensation that had been promised at the beginning of the war. Gold Coast police, led by Police Superintendent Imray, stopped the soldiers at the crossroads near Christiansborg, claiming that they did not have a permit for their march. When the protesters refused to turn around, Imray opened fire. Three men—Sergeant Adjetey, Corporal Attipoe, and Private Odartey-Lamptey—were killed. Dozens of others were wounded. Outraged and frustrated, the people of Accra and other Gold Coast towns took to the streets and attacked European and Asian businesses. Nationalist political parties sought to seize the opportunity, writing to the secretary of state for the colonies that "unless Colonial Government is changed and a new Government of the people and their Chiefs installed at the centre immediately, the conduct of masses now completely out of control with strikes threatened in Police quarters, and rank and file Police indifferent to orders of Officers, will continue and result in worse violent and irresponsible acts by uncontrolled people."⁷⁸ The United Gold Coast Convention (UGCC) offered to take charge of government in the name of the people and called for immediate political reform and self-government.

The governor declared a state of emergency on March 1, and the government passed a new Riot Act. However, the protests persisted for several more days. Believing that the UGCC's "Big Six" had orchestrated the protests, the governor had the political leaders arrested. However, in the inquiry that followed the protest—the Watson Commission—extensive testimony from the community made clear that the frustration and motivations captured a much more popular and widespread sentiment than the UGCC's elite "Big Six" could possibly mobilize. Concerned about the long-term consequences of the riots, the governor appointed a committee on April 7, 1948, under the Commissions of Enquiry Ordinance "to enquire into and report on the recent disturbances in the Gold Coast and their underlying causes; and to make recommendations on any matter arising from their enquiry."⁷⁹

The extraordinary testimony collected in the files of the Watson Commission includes perspectives from politicians and chiefs, goldsmiths and traders,

Africans and Europeans. While there was significant disagreement about the level of coordination and the political motivations behind the protests, it was clear that the events of February 28 grew out of deep economic discontent, rooted in both broader patterns of colonial exploitation and more specific forms of spatial and economic inequality ingrained in and reinforced by systems and structures of urban governance in Accra. The committee, comprising Andrew Dalgleish (a well-known trade unionist in England), Mr. Keith Anders Hope Murray (head of Lincoln College, Oxford), and Andrew Aiken Watson (lawyer and king's counsel), embraced the wide scope of their inquiry and investigated "every aspect of life in the Colony which we may deem relevant for our purpose," from the activities of the UGCC and the details of the ex-servicemen's protest to the research on swollen shoot disease.[80]

While issues like swollen shoot disease—a virus that devastated cocoa crops throughout the colony—resonated in the cocoa growing regions of the interior, in Accra residents were more squarely focused on commercial activities. This discontent did not begin in 1948. As we have seen, Accra residents and communities elsewhere in the colony increasingly vocalized their discontent over economic regulations, taxation, and municipal governance throughout the 1920s, 1930s, and 1940s. Government, however, seemed reluctant to respond in ways that addressed residents' concerns and advanced more equitable, inclusive, and representatives forms of development. When railway workers went on strike in 1946 and government refused to act, members of the Legislative Council including Dr. J. B. Danquah and ATC Councillors Akilagpa Sawyerr and Nanka-Bruce, intervened to bring an end to the strike. However, Danquah argued that this incident highlighted the importance of fundamental economic reorganization to address mass dissatisfaction. And it led to a mass meeting that would culminate in the form of a new political party—the United Gold Coast Convention (UGCC)—which would revive "the spirit of our ancestors, the founders of the Fanti Confederation and of the Gold Coast Aborigines Rights Protection Society and . . . place the country's affairs on a sound basis."[81] Colonial officials were convinced that the UGCC's "Big Six" were members of a "Communist organization overseas" (or had allowed themselves to be co-opted by an organization overseas) in order to "establish a Communist Government in the Gold Coast as a unit in a Union of African Socialist Republics."[82] The increasing unrest after the war and the concentration of action in 1948, they argued, must have been the result of political coordination.

Despite protests from Danquah and other UGCC leaders, the commission's report insisted that the UGCC and Nkrumah were dedicated to the advancement of communism. These accusations, and the general obsession that the British government had with Nkrumah's past party affiliation, highlighted the fragility of colonial governance. In Accra in particular, the thin veneer of authority and control, backed by regulatory and legal structures, cracked under the weight of popular protest. The commission was ultimately unable to make a determination about whether the UGCC had coordinated the series of disturbances that rocked the capital in 1948, but, in targeting colonial policies related to land, trade, and labor, Accra citizens challenged the very foundations of colonial authority and control.

The railway strikes and the ex-servicemen's protests were both informed by a broader discontent around employment practices after the war. Government created elaborate plans for the demobilization of ex-servicemen at the end of the war, giving special consideration to ex-service army drivers with civilian driver's licenses in applying to purchase new lorries and providing training in industrial occupations. Demobilization and resettlement schemes created paths to employment in public works, railways, education, posts and telegraphs, medicine, mixed farming, agriculture, trade, and clerkships.[83] For the government, ex-servicemen who criticized these programs were lazy and entitled, unwilling to provide any capital to support their training or pursue entrepreneurial or private sector opportunities. For ex-servicemen and their allies, these measures were too slow in coming, especially considering the extraordinary service and personal sacrifice of soldiers in the war.[84] In their petition, submitted by BEA Tamakloe and five others, ex-servicemen also noted that these measures sidestepped grassroots organizations like the Gold Coast Ex-Servicemen's Union in favor of government-sponsored organizations like the Gold Coast Legion. After having been asked to recruit soldiers to fight in the war, the union felt that they were discarded when the fighting ended. The petition argued that these new government agencies and the European officers they employed were "not a true representative of the ex-Servicemen of this country" because they "know nothing of the conditions of life of the ex-Servicemen,"[85] which were notably harder due to the increased cost of living. By pushing ahead with policies and processes without proper consultation or involvement of existing African-initiated organizations, groups like the Legion undermined the very processes and spirit they sought to engender. But, importantly, the Gold Coast Ex-Servicemen's Union noted the difference in African and European benefits at the end of the war and called for greater Africanization of the West African Frontier Force, including greater numbers of African officers.[86] Despite the popular unrest that followed the shooting, government insisted that the Ex-Servicemen's Union was not officially recognized because they had not submitted a constitution.[87] In a move that seemed to echo protest over the authority of the Town Council and the chiefs, the Legion, it seemed, would continue to dominate the demobilization and resettlement process.

Ex-servicemen were not alone, however, in their concerns about labor conditions and employment opportunities. Like the railway workers who had gone on strike in 1946, workers across the colony protested low wages and abusive work conditions. During the war, Gold Coast residents had willingly sacrificed in order to support the larger war effort, but now that the war was over, these sacrifices seemed more like exploitation and oppression as African merchants and traders "still suffer unnecessarily and Government has been (quite) recently looking on with complacent reserve."[88] As Gbese Mantse Nii Ayitey Adjin III noted, "Syrian and Indian Firms employ one clerk to perform three clerks and three labourers' work, with meagre salary, now call it rather wages."[89] Accra residents paid high tax rates from their meager wages, which the ATC used to employ government officials at higher rates and invest in projects with few clear benefits to African residents.[90] G. N. Alema argued that "our Government's schemes for developments in the interest of the people have always been on paper except when it comes to a matter of employing men from the United Kingdom for posts in the Civil Service and building bungalows for these employees.... Actually the proposal to Africanize the service is all an eye wash, a sham and a mockery. The people of this country are convinced that our Government have no real goodwill towards them. There is more attention paid to the needs of Europeans than to those of the Africans."[91] While the urgency and frustration were now more intense, L. Val Vannis argued that concern over unemployment and work conditions had been building since at least 1938, drawing connections between the conditions that led to the cocoa hold-ups and the protests of 1948.[92] For many, limited economic growth and limited opportunities were made all the more frustrating by expanding opportunities for Europeans in the Gold Coast. As Eugene Ugboma wrote in the *African Morning Post*, "It seems that the Government is rather only interested to find jobs for Europeans, as their increasing number in the Service is quite noticeable. What with the creation of so many unnecessary posts. As for the fat salaries of the Europeans coupled with their numerous allowances and comforts, as compared to the meagre salaries of the Africans and their hardships, I presume that you have already had sufficient information. I need not also mention the opposite of Africanization of service, which is going on."[93] The promise of self-government through town councils and taxation seemed to benefit only Europeans, while Africans continued to struggle to secure opportunities and realize their visions for the future.

Employment issues were also directly connected to frustrations about the structure of retail trade. In particular, memoranda submitted to the Watson Commission frequently cited the Association of West African Merchants (AWAM) as the primary source of tension. Formed in 1916, AWAM was a trade association of European firms operating in the Gold Coast. Including the three largest trading firms on the coast—the United African Company (UAC), United Trading Company (UTC), and G. B. Ollivant—AWAM members signed merchandise agreements that limited competition and set minimum prices and commissions. The association effectively formed a monopoly, buying up smaller competitors and fixing minimum prices.[94] As Joseph Meyers noted: "The suppression of trade and debarment of Africans from ordering their requirements from overseas and exporting their produce for sale in the markets of the world by themselves as before and the withholding of the amount of difference between the locally paid price and the price paid overseas by Government is an oppression to and not good for us, and we don't agree."[95] African traders and merchants complained that "trading without competition is cheating."[96] Merchandise agreements made it impossible to compete in the sale of imported European goods, and limited access to the dollars generated through the export of raw materials prevented African traders from competing through the importation of American goods. For local merchants who felt pushed out of the import/export business, this monopoly symbolized a broader pattern of unequal and preferential treatment, through which the colonial government propped up European firms while limiting opportunities for Africans.[97] In opening up a new branch in Ashanti in 1947, AWAM leaders bragged publicly about their "excellent relations with Government," allowing them to "enjoy the fullest confidence of Government and maximum cooperation."[98] The government granted subsidies and special access for European merchants, echoing earlier complaints in the ATC about access to markets and taxation on hawkers and other African entrepreneurs. The editors of the *Ashanti Pioneer* argued that the AWAM "killed trade": "Importing firms that would have been competitive incentives have all been gulped down, and those who are too heavy for the whales belly have had to face a persistent barrage of unfair attacks and painful trade contraptions of all sorts."[99] Even if the AWAM was a private enterprise, the government appeared to be "under the influence of AWAM spell."[100]

The Gold Coast public actively protested AWAM and called for the government to restore free trade. In 1947 accusations of corruption in the Gold Coast Supplies and Customs Departments prompted the governor to convene the Martindale Commission. Through its investigation, the commissioners found that government officials had granted special favors to some firms, giving them preferential access to import licenses and foreign exchange. While the public criticisms had been levied primarily at AWAM and the principle of "past performance" through which the government gave foreign firms privileged access to quota import licenses, the Martindale Commission Report blamed Lebanese and Syrian firms like A.G. Leventis as the source of corruption—part of a broader pattern in which the government scapegoated non-European traders for the inflation and black-market practices that agitated African merchants and traders.[101] The individuals, offices, and firms accused of corruption immediately protested that the commission's proceedings had been "improper; and that this report contained . . . 'misstatements . . . so fundamental as to strike at the roots of . . . the reliability of the report.'"[102] The governor quickly convened the Sachs Commission that effectively reversed the conclusions of the Martindale report. As one writer expressed in the *Spectator Daily*: "The results of the Martindale Commission which gracefully skirted around past performance because the AWAM themselves took no notice of it, should have educated the government on the futility of the regulations. The Martindale Report, as a matter of fact, should be thrown to a dark neglected corner and forgotten entirely. It has done no good to the so-called elite that lead our society and, emphatically, has not made a good advertisement of the local government itself."[103] While the "past performance" policy was discontinued as a result of the Martindale Commission, little else seemed to change, and, in maintaining the status quo, these investigations seemed to highlight the weakness and futility of government processes in addressing the exploitation of expatriate firms. AWAM remained a barrier—"one more river to cross" in order to address long-standing issues of inflation and price fixing.[104] As a writer in the *Daily Echo* argued, the labor unrest "is only one of the symptoms of the serious inflation which no amount of halfhearted official measures by way of unenforceable price fixtures in the Gazette can combat."[105]

Frustrated by these trade conditions, Nii Kwabena Bonne III, Osu Alata Manche, and Oyokohene of Techiman, began collecting information and organizing.[106] While others had called for boycotts and other forms of public action throughout 1947, they lacked the public profile, power, and connections to mobilize such a wide range of constituents.[107] Bonne, however, was both a respected chief in Accra and a merchant with thirty-six years' experience on the coast as businessman with a successful enterprise in England, engaging in international commerce across Europe, Asia, and the Far East. Upon closer investigation, he was shocked by trading conditions in the Gold Coast and the prevalence of the black market, which had particularly devastating consequences for poorer citizens who "could not clothe themselves and the majority of them were almost in rags."[108] Bonne, like many others, concluded that the high cost of imported goods most commonly consumed by Africans was unnecessarily inflated and became an undue hardship on the people, being deliberately raised to an "unbearable high level" to generate more profits for European and Asian traders.[109] As Madam Eugenia Kai Sasraku, Madam Dora Afuah Quarshie, and other women retailers at Makola Market explained, government permitted the AWAM to make as much as 75 percent profit on all commodities, and petty traders, who were not allowed to buy directly from suppliers, were expected to resell goods purchased at company stores at the same price they had purchased them for, realizing no profit.[110] At the same time, the government doubled the rents on market stalls. Bonne approached the Ga Native Authority with his information and plans. Having received their support, he launched the boycott as an anti-inflation campaign in Accra in October 1947.

Much like earlier labor movements and protests, the government and merchant firms did not initially take the campaign seriously. The power of the firms was immense. Bonne and others accused them of questionable or corrupt trade practices in order to control the market—"'passbook' customers, clandestine sales behind the counter, cash sales by chits of essential goods which the firms ingeniously made to be in short supply, conditional sale of stagnant lines and other tricks and trade to suit the whims and caprices of the firms."[111] Echoing earlier critics, he also argued that they had a "gentlemen's agreement" with the government to engage in these practices in order to generate more profit. But when the campaign extended beyond the "9 days wonder," it became clear that Bonne had "forged a 'bridgehead'" among Ga people. Bonne testified that he received threats and that the firms attempted to "hush him up" and "hoodwink" his efforts.[112] Buoyed by popular support that now extended to the boycott of imported textiles, Bonne approached the Joint Provincial Council at Dodowa on December 20, 1947, for permission to extend his campaign and boycott to other areas of the colony. The colony-wide boycott began on January 26, 1948, and quickly expanded to Kumasi with the support of the Ashanti Confederacy Council.[113]

Trade came to a near standstill. In Bonne's words, "the spirit of unity which pervaded the whole campaign in the colony and Ashanti were simply national, and the public demonstrations conducted nonviolently to the end were testimony of our being inherently law abiding people."[114] A.G. Leventis & Co approached Bonne on February 3, 1948, with a list of reductions in the prices of goods sold by their firm.[115] Other firms, however, went on the attack. The UAC instituted criminal proceedings against Asere Manche Nii Teiko Ansah—an action that was widely viewed as retribution for the boycott. These attacks further inflamed the public. After the Asere Manche's case was adjourned on February 17, the crowd began to protest and, when it was clear that the police were on strike and not prepared to respond, some individuals began to riot.[116] Increasingly concerned about the unrest, representatives of the Chamber of Commerce, the Boycott Committee, the Joint Provincial Council, and the government met with the colonial secretary in Accra to hammer out an agreement for reducing the price of textiles and implementing effective price controls for general goods. A mass meeting was called in Bukom Square on February 26, 1948, in which Bonne announced that the consumer had won and that the boycott would end on February 28, 1948. The government gave chiefs and native authorities great power to address black marketing and profiteering, and prices were reduced by 50 percent.[117]

February 28, then, was a confluence of several major events that exemplified the economic discontent of the people and their protest against the unevenly distributed power and protection of government. By now "increasingly suspicious of any measure or proposition coming from the authorities,"[118] women "went out from store to store on the lookout for the reduced prices."

> They declared that the prices were the same and started to shout *"Wohee,"* meaning "we are not buying." each textile store of the firms, Syrians and Indians were thronged, with hundreds of women mingled with a few men inspecting prices. At the UAC central stores the crowds duced, gambolled, and hooted at every European merchant that came out of the yard, and roundly denounced UAC and AWAM, UI and John Holt for fixing their prices and so the crowds were thick at these stores, SCOA had fewer people, another big crowd was seen at AC Leventis. All along the women cried down the inflation and demanded a continuation of the boycott.[119]

At G. B. Ollivant, the surging crowd shouted *"Agbene wo hie etserewo"* ("Now we are awake") and told journalists on site to "let them know about it."[120] At Selwyn Market, two shoppers—a woman and a young man—who purchased cloth and essential commodities were attacked by the mob. Stores began to close.[121]

The riots lasted for several days. By the time the crowds had calmed down and the looting had ceased, dozens of people had died, and the violence had spread to cities throughout the colony. Government officials and other foreign observers struggled to understand the actions of the mob. They were at once seemingly wild and uncontrolled while also coordinated. While government officials and some chiefs and members of the public insisted the series of events were too coincidental and must have been part of a larger political plot, orchestrated by the UGCC, the commission was unable to come to any conclusions. Bonne and the representatives of the Ex-Servicemen's Union both distanced themselves from the riots and condemned the violence.[122] Danquah and other political leaders insisted that they had not coordinated the events, even though they had been involved in some way in organizing the Ex-Servicemen's protest and had used the opportunity to advance a call for self-government.[123] As Danquah himself acknowledged and chiefs and other members of the public confirmed, there was too little agreement between the various constituencies involved for true coordination to be possible.[124] It is much more likely that the confluence of events marked a release of long-held frustration on the part of Accra residents and others throughout the colony, particularly after so many years of sacrifice during the war.

Far from an uncontrolled mob, individuals submitting memoranda and testimony to the commission and writing into the newspapers demonstrated a nuanced understanding of the issues at stake in the Gold Coast. In the long sessions—often 8 a.m. to 6 p.m.—in which the commissioners heard testimony from any individual or organization "wishing to give evidence concerning the causes of the recent disturbances in the Gold Coast" and in the follow-up meetings they conducted on special subjects, the commissioners noted "the high minded purpose and obvious care with which the views of youth organizations, students and last but not least the Ex-Servicemen were presented."[125] In passing out alcohol to prisoners, storming the gates of Ussher Fort Prison, calling for the release of jailed ex-servicemen, looting stores, and shouting down government officials, protesters highlighted deep connections between the carceral state, colonial capitalism, urban spatiality, and increasing levels of poverty in the city as the foundations of exploitative and oppressive structures. The larger events regularly invoked in relation to the riots were amplified further by smaller indignities—discriminatory statements by the chief veterinary officer, the construction of a European-only school, the unfounded dismissal of African employees—which further exacerbated frustrations and highlighted the systemic and structural nature of the concerns.[126] As Enoch mourned in the *West African Monitor*, "in a few years this God given land of ours will slip away altogether into European hands."[127]

While the governor coordinated a response to the protests, the ATC remained notably silent. Their only contribution to the Commission of Enquiry was in response to formal information requests, which included questions about housing, slum clearance, building permits, shortages of building materials, the organization and operation of markets, market revenues, and trade licensure.[128] In a confidential meeting held on March 16, 1948, the president of the ATC argued that the Council had nothing to add to the government's statements. Other European official members condemned the disturbances and supported the government's action, while calling on elected members to make the same kinds of statements. African Councillors Akwei, Quist, Jones-Nelson, Ollennu, Adumua, and Peregrino Brimah all walked a fine line, expressing their support for self-government and for their allies in the UGCC, while also condemning the violence. The Council ultimately unanimously passed a resolution stating that:

> We, the undersigned elected and nominated members of the ATC, do hereby register our total disapproval of the violence, communal thefts and lawlessness which pervaded this town during the last two days of February. We wholly support those measures which the government was immediately bound to adopt to bring successfully the disturbances in Accra to an end. We respectfully offer our sincere sympathies to His Excellency the Governor in the exceptionally heavy and onerous responsibilities which have beset him since his recent arrival in the colony. We further extend our sympathies to those commercial firms and merchants within the municipality who have suffered loss and damage as a result of the disturbances. To those who have suffered bereavement as a result of these disorders we offer our most sincere condolences. We declare our most profound belief in the policy of the Gold

Coast government which seeks the self government of this country in due course through proper constitutional channels. Finally, we pledge ourselves willing to undertake any duties which the government may call upon us to fulfill in the interest of the law, order and good government of this town.[129]

In doing so, town councillors reinforced long-standing public skepticism about the degree to which their elected officials—members of the city's elite class—actually understood the realities of their lives or supported their concerns. What did self-government really look like? Whose interests did it protect?

Throughout the inquiry, members of the Watson Commission expressed considerable sympathy with the public's plight. Watson himself protested that the testimony summaries circulated to the Legislative Council had been edited in a way that misrepresented the facts, and he regularly spoke with the public about their intention to listen carefully and their great appreciation for the general cooperation and thoughtfulness of the Gold Coast people in this sensitive investigation. The *Report of the Commission of Enquiry into Disturbances in the Gold Coast* captured a number of the political, economic, and social issues conveyed through the 187 memoranda and hours of oral testimony from 81 witnesses given to the Watson Commission, from the disturbances themselves and the nature of government response to issues of immigration, trade, inflation, swollen shoot policies, economic development, education, housing, and, finally, political, legal, and constitutional reform. As the commission noted, "The spread of liberal ideas, increasing literacy and a closer contact with political developments in other parts of the world" required a new approach to self-government and an increase in the pace of Africanization.[130] The state's resistance to reform led the public to develop a deep general suspicion about government policies and intentions, and government seemed to reinforce those ideas through clumsy messaging. It was time for change.

The government in London read the report as radical. In a published response, government representatives argued that "it is an axiom of British colonial policy that progress, whether, political, social or economic, and whether in local affairs or at the centre of government, can be soundly achieved only on two conditions: first that it rests on the foundations of tradition and social usage which already exist, and second that changes and developments carry with them the substantial acceptance of the people."[131] While the commission emphasized the urgent need for change, government advocated for a more measured approach with change introduced gradually in stages and rooted in the power of the chiefs. The commission's understanding of the Gold Coast government's "tardiness in meeting popular demand for progress," they argued, was a reflection of the political activists they interviewed rather than a general condition in the colony. The policies of the administration were appropriate.

Undoubtedly, those who participated the most in the activities of 1948 were politicized in new ways. The government's response, however, underestimated how widespread that politicization had become. What was once—and still imagined to be—an elite movement (i.e., the "Big Six") was now increasingly "popular," encompassing individuals from a wide range of socioeconomic backgrounds and with highly varying levels of political power and authority. The union of market women, merchants, ex-servicemen, chiefs, and educated elites in the economic discontent represented the emergence of a new national consciousness that was firmly rooted in a desire for economic opportunity.

CONCLUSION

In connecting the political, legal, and regulatory power of the state with the economic exploitation and oppression faced by its citizens, Accra residents and other protesters in 1948 drew on a long history of contestation over economic opportunity and authority in the colonial capital. This politics of exclusion and marginalization—enshrined in law and backed by the financial and policing power of the state—lay at the foundation of an unfolding process of informalization, which was central—not merely incidental—to the structures and practices of colonial government. But, as Accra residents' petition protests make clear, this process was not the product of a lack of engagement with the infrastructures, technologies, and economies of modern city life or the regulatory politics of the municipal and colonial state. Rather, in applying the regulatory power of the state to delegitimize African spatial and economic practices, Town Council members—British and African alike—sought to protect the interests of expatriate enterprise and realize imperial visions of ordered modernity. By tracing the ways in which the Town Council sought to use laws and regulations to redefine corn mills and distilleries as illegal and illegitimate, we see the process of informalization unfold. Informality, in other words, is not a naturalized economic phenomenon but rather a by-product of ongoing spatial, regulatory, cultural, and economic politics, which have their roots in the colonial period.

As the history of urban development in Accra suggests, informalization was less about incorporating Africans into global capitalism than it was about supporting expatriate visions of economic, social, and spatial order. While some urban residents managed to find opportunities within the new order, many others found themselves increasingly marginalized in social, economic, and political terms within the new regulatory regime—a structurally precarious position, inscribed into the frameworks of global capitalism, the economics of governance, and the politics of space in cities like Accra. Their experiences simultaneously reflected the specificity of Accra and its integration into a global economic order through the networks of imperial power and the structures of colonial governance. Ultimately, they also fueled new and increasingly popular forms of protest that would, in a moment of extraordinary public agitation, spill over into riots and radical politics; these protests would create a new sense of urgency about the political and economic future of Accra and the Gold Coast more broadly.

It is critical that we have a realistic idea of the power and effectiveness of colonial Accra's political institutions. The emerging political and economic structures of the colonial capital were shaped and contested by British colonial officials, town councillors, and a diverse array of urban residents in ways that highlighted the weakness of the colonial state, the economic power of urban residents, and the persistence of Indigenous economic and spatial cultures. Ongoing contestation over the parameters of regulation, however, does not negate the violence of categorization inherent in this process. On the contrary, these debates around the development of a new spatial order, the redefinition of economic opportunity, the commodification of space, and the mobilization of racialized class politics over the first several decades of the twentieth century evidence the emergence of a political system that marginalized African practices and created economies of extraversion through the politics of space.[132] These debates—and this period—represent the consolidation of the regulatory power of the Town Council and the broader social, economic, and legal structures that would shape the experiences of Accra residents long after the end of colonial rule.

In the context of contemporary debates about urban development, these historical perspectives are critical to the development of new and more just policies and regulatory frameworks. As Mayne argues for the term "slum," the reproduction of these terms in academic discourse risks reproducing or reinforcing the social disadvantages and structural inequalities that they describe.[133] While Mayne sees potential in "informal economy" as an alternative analytic through which to understand the lived experiences of the urban poor, "informal economy," like "slum," has a history. It was *produced* as a category of social, economic, and legal marginalization, generated through the unfolding processes of colonization and the expansion of global capitalism. Tracing the histories of these practices is essential to understanding their contemporary instantiations in an academic sense or to imagining alternative political and economic futures that do not merely incorporate these practices into profoundly unjust structures but rather use them as inspiration for a completely new framework.

The production of the "informal economy" is foundational to informalization in both a social and spatial sense. In discussing the process of informalization, scholars of the contemporary city seek to understand the ways that urban citizens adapt to changing economic systems in order to "access opportunities and, at the same time, maintain social coherence."[134] This structuralist approach highlights the processes of social, economic, and cultural construction that generate the "reserve army of urban unemployed and underemployed" and shape their economic activities.[135] Keith Hart and the many scholars that followed him employed "informal economy" as an analytic that helpfully captured the labor and practices that operated outside or on the margins of the wage economy and, thus, "escape enumeration by surveys."[136] Much of the work on informal economic activities in Africa and elsewhere expands on this notion, tracing the origins of economic activities like market trading and exploring their significance as a means of both survival and accumulation in the context of persistent economic uncertainty.[137] However, as these debates in colonial Accra show, this process took root many decades before.

FOUR

OF PIRATE DRIVERS AND HONKING HORNS

ON MAY 31, 1940, THE president of the Accra Town Council (ATC) wrote to the colonial secretary, complaining that "pirate passenger lorries" were plying the roads between the Gold Coast's capital, Accra, and the eastern suburb of Labadi:

> I have the honour to inform you that for some time there has been considerable competition by 'pirate' lorries from Labadi with the Council's buses, and efforts made to put an end to this competition have been only partially effective in view of the fact that certain roads not covered by the Municipal Bus Service routes, which were approved by the Governor-in-Council on the 11th August, 1927 are used by the "pirate" lorries as a means of avoiding the restrictions imposed by the order in Council. In consequence of this, in a number of cases it has not been possible for the Police to institute prosecutions. Since the routes mentioned in paragraph 1 were approved, new roads have been opened and it is now possible for a lorry to convey passengers from the centre of Accra to practically the other side of Christiansborg without traveling over route 1 of the Schedule of roads appropriated to the bus service.[1]

A heavily traveled route, the road between Labadi and Accra was used to lorry traffic. Labadi functioned as an eastern gateway to the capital—the first stop for lorries bringing produce and people from the productive eastern interior. Labadi was also seen as a headquarters for drivers. In the early twentieth century, hundreds of Labadians had taken up driving work, and the suburb emerged as a primary (perhaps preeminent) center for training drivers in the colony. Thus, it was not the presence of lorries on the road itself that troubled colonial officials. The drivers that caught the attention of colonial officials were troublesome because they blurred the distinctions of colonial urban space and order—goods versus passengers, public versus private, commercial versus residential—and threatened the colonial state's power to command the road, control revenue, and effectively regulate the mobility practices of urban residents. They were mobile urban "pirates" who skirted the established order and subverted the authority embodied in state-run urban bus services. In picking up passengers along the roadside, these drivers brought the problems and challenges of motor transportation to the heart of colonial power.

The president of the ATC's complaint was only the latest in a long-running debate about "illegal competition" in the municipality's transportation system, dating back to 1932. Even more broadly, however, this concern about "pirate passenger lorries" and "illegal competition" was part of a much larger technopolitical contestation over African mobility and spatial practices in the colonial capital—an unfolding but highly contested process of informalization in which the colonial state sought to use regulation to exert authority over the spatial and social landscape of the city in new ways. By invoking the language of piracy, colonial officials highlighted the deep unease with which they operated in the city and the tenuousness of their authority. The dominance of African owner-operators in the motor transport industry of the Gold Coast enabled drivers and passengers to assert control over how and where they moved, empowering them to act as autonomous entrepreneurs that provided real and valuable alternatives to state-run services. However, in defining their movement within the city, these drivers and passengers also found themselves in direct conflict with representatives of the British colonial state, whose attempts to normalize and rationalize the city had created an alternative framework of laws and practices. Based on British practices and values, this urban plan failed to account for African understandings of the city.[2] As a result, motor transportation was situated at the center of larger technopolitical debates about urban life, mobility, and spatial practice in the colonial capital.

This chapter explores two high-profile examples of conflict—horn honking and "pirate passenger lorries"—as a way to understand the issues at stake for colonial officials, elite Ga Town Council representatives, and the African drivers and passengers who dominated the commercial motor transport sector. These colorful examples were certainly not the only nodes of contestation. As I have detailed elsewhere, drivers regularly protested licensing restrictions and fares, and city residents complained about the conditions of roads and access to affordable transportation services.[3] However, these issues of horn honking and pirate passenger lorry service stand out from the more general policy discussions of the archival record, giving us a glimpse into the practices of African mobility and colonial anxiety over the limits of British authority often obscured through more mundane policy documents.[4] The often-emotional reactions and frustrations of

British colonial representatives highlight both the symbolic and practical importance of technology and mobility practice in the city. British officials and ATC representatives clearly understood mobility as an extension of the state's efforts to develop the spatial and technological infrastructure and culture of Accra. But Accra residents also had their own unique visions of urban life—what Garth Myers calls "the local frame of awareness."[5] Rather than merely resisting an imposed colonial order, African urban residents actively shaped that very order by asserting the validity of long-standing and widely embraced spatial and mobility practices.

This chapter looks beyond what Mavhunga describes as the "banal mobility" of objects to a broader understanding of mobility that sometimes shaped but was not defined by technological objects.[6] Infrastructural technology like roads and motor vehicles both produces and are produced by the "untheorized practices of everyday life,"[7] through which urban residents negotiate the use and meaning attached to space. Through mobility politics, Accra residents asserted their own visions for their city and negotiated colonial politics within and outside of the formal elite structures of elected town councils, legislative assembles, or chieftaincy politics. To capture these overlapping processes of technopolitical rhetoric, technological planning, and technology-in-use,[8] I place archival sources in conversation with oral histories from drivers and passengers who began their careers in the late-colonial period and whose lives and work shaped the culture of urban mobility in question in the debate over pirate passenger lorries.[9] Many of these drivers came from La, where they identified as the sons, grandsons, nephews, and cousins of drivers. Their history of driving, in other words, was a profoundly personal history, and their narratives highlight the importance of motor transport technology to the occupational and social lives of both themselves and their passengers. Drivers who narrated their own life histories as drivers provide an important counterpoint to the archival record of regulation and infrastructural development that dominated the concerns of British colonial officials. By framing their technological practice through the movement of their passengers, these drivers also push us to think about space—not just the objects that operate within space—as both political and technological.

While we do not have many records of the voices and stories of individual drivers and passengers, their actions speak loudly through the complaints and frustrations of colonial officials and town ouncil members. Through motor transportation, a range of African residents in Accra spoke to and interacted directly with British colonial officials; in debating how the road should be used and how space should be defined, these two means of "enframing the city" came into conflict and conversation.[10] In doing so, urban residents shaped the emergence of a distinctly *Accra* culture, embracing the possibilities of cosmopolitan technologies while remaining firmly rooted in local practices and values.

MOBILITY, REGULATION, AND MOTOR TRANSPORTATION IN EARLY TWENTIETH-CENTURY GOLD COAST

As a preeminently European introduction, colonial officials in the early twentieth century felt relatively comfortable with their control over motor transport practice in Accra. Longer histories of urban residence and Indigenous politics placed Africans in a position of power in Accra, often undermining European attempts to redesign the city as the new colonial capital at the end of the nineteenth century.[11] However, motor transportation was new and unfamiliar to both the Indigenous Ga population of the city as well as to the migrant labor populations who were increasingly attracted to the colonial capital. Government officials believed that this newness would allow them to shape African appropriation of the technology from the very beginning—a confidence rooted in colonial control of railways, which dominated colonial communications and transportation infrastructure beginning in the mid-nineteenth century.[12] Building on practices throughout Britain's African colonies, representatives of the colonial state sought to encourage the development of the railway, both as a means of resource extraction and revenue generation as well as a tool for controlling African mobility.[13] At the same time they discouraged the development of motor transportation, resisting calls to build roads in the colony and creating road breaks and neglecting maintenance on existing roads to discourage their use throughout the 1910s and early 1920s.[14]

However, colonial officials grossly underestimated African interest and enthusiasm for motor vehicles, as well as the influence of spatial patterns and mobility practices that had predated the advent of motor transport. Europeans were ambivalent about the usefulness of motor vehicles in both metropole and colony after their introduction at the turn of the twentieth century. As Jo Guldi demonstrates, this ambivalence was rooted in eighteenth-century British infrastructural politics; however, European ambivalence to motor transportation was echoed in other parts of the continent as well.[15] The focus on railways over roads contrasted with American reactions to the new technology; in the United States, roads had been readily embraced as an expression of not only technological modernity but also American identity, particularly after the introduction of the Ford Model T, which had democratized access to motor transport technologies in America by the 1930s.[16] However, as late as the 1940s, automobile cultures and regulations were still relatively inchoate in much of the world. European colonial officials who sought to reorganize urban space according to the new technologies were doing so through a process of experimentation and debate at home as well as in their colonies. And yet, the possibilities provided by motor transport technologies—and particularly the promise of autonomy and mobility that accompanied the new technology—took on a different form of urgency in colonies where governmental authority and legitimacy were far less secure and autonomy and mobility represented threats to tenuous order rather than the promise of a new future. Instead, in colonies in India and Africa the British sought to construct narratives of modernity rooted in the railway, even as railway policies differed significantly across the British Empire in terms of cost, scale, accessibility, passenger versus freight, and so on.[17]

In the Gold Coast, however, diverse groups of Africans appropriated the technology of motor transport in rapidly increasing numbers and used motor vehicles to reshape the control of mobility and space in the colony. As I've argued elsewhere, motor transportation provided an important alternative to the railway, which allowed African entrepreneurs to assert and maintain control over the flow of goods from rural production zones to coastal ports, increasing their profits and resisting British attempts to control trade in the colony. A few elites in coastal society used their wealth to purchase private vehicles. However, many other Africans embraced motor transportation as a new form of commercial investment—providing goods and passenger transport between and within rural and urban areas. Vehicles numbered only 16 in 1908. By 1932, there were 4,141 commercial motor vehicles and 1,618 private cars and taxis registered in the Gold Coast. By the end of the 1930s, there were over 5,501 commercial vehicles and 2,076 private cars and taxis.[18] The number of drivers in the colony also grew and, in fact, even outpaced the number of registered vehicles. By 1945 a single vehicle could have well over twenty-five different licensed drivers associated with it, as well as potentially a much larger number of mates (or apprentices) who helped the driver maintain the vehicle and its cargo (goods and/or passengers).[19]

This rapid pace of growth occurred in spite of mediocre road conditions.[20] When the first car was imported at the turn of the twentieth century, it was barely usable on Accra's uneven road surfaces. A few decades later, things had scarcely changed. As one observer wrote in the *Gold Coast Independent*:

> Accra in 1918! What a spectacle its streets present! So far as the business quarter of the city is concerned, not town planned streets remember, but roads carried along the foundations of age worn Bush tracks impressed by the feet of men when houses were few and other shelter, none; And the journeyman's main aim was to cut across anywhere and anyhow to gain the brief shade of a friendly tree somewhere in the vicinity of this course. With the knowledge that the High Street and other roads in Accra grew in the manner indicated, their abrupt corners and bends, as it were in deference to every point of the compass, should not cause greater surprise than the fact that little improvement—certainly no appreciable improvement, has been affected in the march of years[21]

Figure 4.1. The driver, Murphy, waits patiently for his turn while his mate cleans the bonnet. A Day in the Life of a Tro-Tro Driver. Photograph by Ben Kwakye. Source: Photographic Archive, Information Services Office, Ministry of Information, Accra PS/1877/6.

And yet, as this same commentator noted, the diversity of vehicles on the road was immense—"a clash of medievalism and of the 20th century!"—as buses and trucks with large six-cylinder engines and motorcycles by Harley Davidson and Triumph operated alongside sheep and goats. It was a veritable "war zone" in which all—people and animals alike—are "turned loose by someone who is responsible for their welfare" with few safeguards for protection.[22] Regulation, the writer argued, was necessary to bring some order to the roads and minimize the related risks: "Why are these obsolete methods in Accra not done away with? Why has the municipal or other authority responsible not brought us up to date? Why is the traffic not regulated. Why are the sheep and goats allowed to remain? Is it because the risk is negligible as compared with the illustration of danger resulting from lack of foresight or judgment at the seat of war?"[23] "The bad management of traffic in our streets" led to accidents like the one that killed Reverend John Edmund Boggis when his motorcycle collided with a car driven by

Mr. Soper, acting agent of Messrs. Cadbury Bros.[24] However, "A Citizen" argued in the pages of the *Gold Coast Independent* that the advent of motor cars also led rulers to be more disconnected from the people—a different kind of danger. If previous governors had walked or ridden horses or carts through the streets of the capital and had to directly encounter their citizens, the speed of motorized transport made that much more difficult and increasingly insulated colonial leadership from public opinion.[25]

This early twentieth-century account depicts a highly dynamic form of street life in the city, which incorporated Africans as both drivers and passengers. In other parts of the continent, the high cost of motor vehicles and the low wages and limited economic opportunities available to Africans restricted African access to motor transport technologies; at the same time, colonial policies—or, in the case of settler colonies, the policies of white minority rule—were attempting to control African mobility.[26] In the Gold Coast, European companies and the colonial state imported the earliest motor vehicles in the first decades of the twentieth century.[27] However, access to the new technology was not restricted to the colonial elite. In the interior of the Gold Coast, wealthy Akan cocoa farmers in the early twentieth century, who benefited directly from the colonial economy of extraction, often invested the profits of their farms in lorries, marking the beginning of what Polly Hill calls the "lorry age" (post-1918).[28] Initially, cocoa farmers purchased motor vehicles to transport cocoa to train stations and buying agents. Echoing an earlier use of head carriers to transport produce, however, farmers were soon bypassing colonial railways altogether, using motor vehicles and roads to take their produce directly to coastal ports where they could maximize profit.[29] Motor transportation provided a new way to connect urban and rural areas within the colonial economy, facilitating the emergence of new trading practices and opening up new possibilities for rural farmers and villagers, even as the new technology built on much older networks.

While peripheral roads often connected farms and small villages to regional markets throughout the colony, the larger paths of automobility led to Accra, as the political capital, major market, and international port. People from all over the colony traveled through the city as they made their way to the central lorry park with goods and passengers from rural production zones or regional markets. Unsurprisingly, then, these commercial drivers reflected the broader diversity within the colony. By the 1930s and 1940s, drivers had been registered in all regions of the Gold Coast; however, registered drivers were particularly concentrated in the southern half of the colony where agricultural production and the cocoa industry motivated the construction of roads, financed the purchased of imported lorries, and provided steady work for drivers.[30]

In Accra Indigenous Ga people dominated the motor transport industry. The suburbs of La and Teshie were considered headquarters for drivers, where generations of families entered the industry through apprenticeship and professional training and regulated the professional standards of the industry through trade unions that governed driver behavior and negotiated working conditions with the government. Drivers came from all over the colony to be trained in La, which was considered the home of the colony's first and most respected drivers.[31] As they came to Accra from other regions, these young men were absorbed into the Ga community and the professional community of drivers in Accra through apprenticeship networks. For drivers—many of whom had left their hometowns and defied their parents to pursue driving work—it was this occupational identity as drivers that mattered most as they made decisions about their economic, social, and political lives.[32] Technological expertise, professional skill, and occupational experience served as a shared language among the ethnically diverse and mobile population of drivers in Accra and throughout the Gold Coast.

Some expatriate firms operated motor transport services in the early twentieth century. In 1906 Messrs. Scheck and Barker began operating three-ton Daimler motor lorries on the Dodowah Road.[33] Messrs. Miller's Motor Transport Department began running a regular service between Accra and Christiansborg in 1918, leaving from both their commercial headquarters and the post office and operating until 8 p.m.[34] By the early 1920s Elders Road Transport Company had begun using lorries to transport cocoa from the railway station to the coast, eliminating the need for cart operators. Still others, like the Basel Mission Trading Company ran their own transport departments and operated throughout the colony, moving goods between rural production zones and urban markets. However, the vast majority of the colony's transport industry lay in the hands of African entrepreneurs who either drove their own vehicle or, if they had been particularly successful as drivers or businessmen, owned a small fleet that they let out to young drivers, often still in training. The tremendous growth of the industry, in other words, was a reflection of African entrepreneurialism rather than expatriate or government investment.

Colonial ambivalence to motor transportation in the early part of the twentieth century necessitated retroactive attempts at regulation during the 1930s. Having failed to stem the rising tide of commercial motor transportation, colonial officials in the 1930s sought to regulate and rationalize a motor transport industry that had emerged outside of the restrictions of colonial policy. Africans shaped motor transport practice to suit their own social and economic interests, drawing on older systems of Indigenous transportation such as head carriers to organize the industry and create standards for training and expertise that reflected understandings of how to be a (good) driver.[35] British colonial officials, by contrast, were influenced by European expectations and practices of motor transportation, as well as by broader concerns about control and authority over the emerging industry.[36] New efforts to regulate driving culminated in the 1934 Motor Traffic Ordinance, which dictated not only road conditions and standards for vehicle maintenance and operation but also attempted to define who could and could not be a driver.[37] Literacy requirements, physical examinations, and certificates of competency challenged African understandings of the skills required to be an effective driver, resulting in protests from newly emerging motor transport unions throughout the colony.[38]

BUILDING MOBILITY INFRASTRUCTURE

These regulatory efforts followed a broader pattern of governance in Accra. Ato Quayson argues that early resettlement efforts were "reactive" in response to crisis (e.g., disease, earthquakes, rapid urbanization).[39] As we've seen, by the 1930s and 1940s, however, Town Council members and colonial technocrats had begun to articulate a more rigorously organized and coherent government policy in Accra and other Gold Coast towns, rooted in concerns about sanitation and public health and evidenced in wide-ranging regulations on trade and housing. The plan for the town, which was supported by the ATC and the British colonial government in the early twentieth century, reflected the shifting priorities of the colonial state in providing social welfare. Rather than one central policy statement, the plan for Accra was a set of interrelated policy efforts that reflected what historian Fred Cooper calls "development colonialism."[40] Building on the reformist work of Governor Gordon Guggisberg in the 1910s and 1920s, the British administration increasingly invested in infrastructural, economic, and social development projects. In the city itself, building projects and road construction sought to reshape patterns of urban residence and sociability by changing the built environment. The city's expanding boundaries and investments in infrastructural development raised new questions about urban mobility, particularly for members of the ATC, which held primary responsibility for urban development and infrastructure.[41]

Road construction was of central importance for both mobility and public health infrastructure. Wider, well-planned, well-built roads enforced proper distances between houses and reduced the incidence of mosquitoes. But roads also facilitated the movement of people and goods into and out of the city. The multilayered function of roads complicated questions about the responsibility for building and maintaining them. When Councillor de Graft Johnson highlighted the poor condition of main roads in Accra in 1930 and questioned whether the money being spent to build the Labadi-Teshie Road might be better used to build roads in the town, the acting senior public health engineer noted that government was responsible for the construction of roads and drains.[42] However, in the context of the "prevailing financial stringency" of the Great Depression, Public Works Department funds for road construction and maintenance were dwindling.[43] Funding shortages meant that offices were forced to balance basic infrastructural provision with pressing public health concerns, and maintenance costs only increased as the road network grew. By the mid-1930s, the combination of incomplete and poorly maintained roads in the city had created a crisis.

Incomplete roads were a particular subject of discussion and complaint, echoing broader patterns of incompleteness and obsolescence that hampered colonial development efforts and undermined British arguments about public welfare. The ATC and the Public Works Department were unable to keep up with the rapid pace of urbanization in the city by the 1920s and 1930s, and road infrastructure was often not completed due to a lack of funds. In 1932 Councillor Kojo Thompson complained that a large gap remained at the end of Boundary Road. Councillor Dr. Reindorf had himself paid to have the road built, at a cost of £150 and several lawsuits from residents who accused him of trespassing. Having now taken on the road as their responsibility, Thompson argued, it was only fair that the government should complete the work since they had not paid for the original construction.[44] When the Council debated the condition of Boundary Road again in 1933, Akilagpa Sawyerr described the state of the road as "disgraceful" and urged the members of the Council to protest. The municipal engineer said that he had made three requests for funds to complete the three hundred yards of road and had been turned down repeatedly. The president once again wrote to the government. African councillors were diligent in their complaints about road maintenance, particularly in African middle-class neighborhoods like Adabraka.[45] These kinds of complaints rarely manifested in changes, however. By 1934 the ATC convened a small committee to assess the state of city streets and get the attention of the government. The committee, led by the medical officer of health, listed more than twenty-three streets in Accra, Adabraka, and Korle Gono.[46]

Funding debates within the ATC took place within the context of a reorganization of funding responsibilities within the colonial government. While the ATC sent requests for road construction, the governor consistently decreased the Council's "grant-in-aid" and increased its annual contribution to the maintenance of town roads. Instead, government increasingly directed their funds to the construction of new neighborhoods outside the congested quarter, echoing broader patterns in colonial housing policy. When the ATC president asked the director of public works about infrastructure plans for the town, it was clear that the construction of a new layout in Christiansborg and a new road to the cemetery—spaces that were central to colonial plans for the reordering of urban life—were more important than more established neighborhoods.⁴⁷

MOVING THROUGH MODERN SPACES

Elected members' concerns about road construction highlighted many of the concerns of their constituents who demanded equitable access to infrastructure. However, ATC transport policy, often shaped by the interests of official members, was primarily focused on *how* people moved—the technology of mobility practice. While the city's urban elite embraced the ostentatious display of horse-drawn carriages and, later, private motor vehicles as a way to show off their wealth and status throughout much of the nineteenth and early twentieth centuries, most residents of Accra had been walking from their homes to the markets and workplaces of the relatively compact old town core (Jamestown, Usshertown, and Osu). Market traders, who carried large quantities of goods from their homes to market stalls, often operated in nearby markets rather than the larger markets established in the center of town (e.g., Salaga Market, Makola Market).⁴⁸ Wage laborers walked along roadsides or cut through fields and neighborhoods using well-trodden paths. The conditions of the dirt roads led residents of Station Road to petition the governor, demanding that the roads be watered down multiple times a day to avoid "the dust arising from the powdered condition of the roads, which by all means when swallowed into the air passages is dangerous to health and may likely spread consumption."⁴⁹ By the 1920s and 1930s, even those office workers who possessed bicycles to aid in their travel to and from work complained that the long distances and rough conditions meant that they arrived to work late, hot, and dirty—a condition that often resulted in sanction by employers. In response to public discontent and in order to supplement Town Council revenues, the ATC created a municipal bus service in 1927.⁵⁰ Based out of a lorry park near the central post office, this bus service ran along all of the major thoroughfares in the city, connecting residents of central Accra to its newly developing suburbs (especially Adabraka and Ridge) as well as some of the broader Ga littoral to the east (e.g., La, Teshie).⁵¹

The municipal bus system quickly became a symbol of colonial visions for the city in the interwar period. The British-style buses, bus shelters, lay-bys, and lorry parks evoked an urban modernity considered suitable and respectable for the capital of Britain's "model colony." The system of bus stops facilitated the emergence of a new spatial awareness in the capital, now increasingly determined by bus shelters and routes, and encouraged debates about visibility and safety, which culminated in the acquisition and expansion of street lighting.⁵² This new spatial awareness also necessitated the construction of lorry parks throughout the city, decentralizing both commercial and passenger transport and placing greater emphasis on local markets and urban commuters.[53] Bus passengers from all walks of life queued at bus stops and purchased tickets from ticket collectors and bus conductors at established prices. In a culture where barter still dominated most economic transactions, the municipal bus system marked a new form of sociability, both in terms of the economic exchanges it encouraged but also in the social interaction that the buses facilitated. Seen as a suitably "modern" transport system, the bus service even occasionally attracted European residents and tourists who negotiated the expanding city alongside African residents of varied classes, genders, and ethnic groups.

For town councillors, these new spaces and forms of sociality created new demands and opportunities for revenue. Much like public markets, the bus stations themselves were commodified spaces. In 1931 the ATC leased the entire bus station across from the General Post Office to Anglo-African Aerated Waters, Ltd., converting their old refreshment kiosk into an open-air refreshment garden that would provide significant additional revenue (£120 per year) for the Council.[54] In the same year the Council granted permission for the German Drug Company to erect more than one hundred "illuminated advertisement columns." As the company described it, the signs, which were supposed to be made of cast iron and glass, stood "8 feet high and 18 inches square with the words 'BUS STOP' embossed on each of the four side of the roof. One side of the panels would be reserved to the Council for the Bus Time Table whilst the other three would be used for advertisement purposes." The German Drug Company would pay for the installation, upkeep, and electricity, keeping the signs lit until 10 p.m. every night, but they also reserved the right to sublet the three advertisement panels. After seven years they would transfer ownership to the Council, who would rent them for £1 per column per year.[55] In 1934, the president of the Council attached advertisement boards to buses to increase revenue. The contract arranged with Messrs. Shaul and Coy for £50 per year was perhaps smaller than the Council had hoped, and the president noted that commercial firms had been slow to take advantage of the opportunity.[56] However, the Council managed to secure a new client the following year: West Africa Publicity Limited.[57] Importantly, the leasing out of bus signs for advertising also represented a new phase of commercializing public space—a public instantiation of the overlapping interests of government and commercial firms, selling a private company sole rights to advertising on public property. Similar sorts of advertising boards were placed at bus stops and stations and leased out accordingly. Advertising on buses themselves, however, took the quest for profit on the road as public buses were transformed into mobile billboards that brought advertising and commercial interests to all parts of the city. By utilizing their authority over public lands, infrastructure, and services, the Council granted European firms access to land and created important footholds for expatriate enterprise in the middle of important African commercial and residential districts, expanding and protecting the interests of European capital. Collaboration with corporate interests—an early form of public-private partnership—allowed the Council to secure more funding for public works in the midst of ever-tightening budgets. However, in securing additional advertising opportunities for companies, the Council advanced a particular kind of capitalism.

The new system also demanded new infrastructures to support the safety and comfort of residents. African councillors like Akiwumi argued for public seats to be installed at bus stations at intervals along the Accra-Christiansborg Road because, as he observed, "It was a long distance from Accra to Christiansborg, and it would be a relief for people travelling on foot on that road to rest on the seats."[58] Roads and bus systems, in other words, were not just about passengers. Official members of the ATC were less sympathetic about the needs of the pedestrian public; the expenditure could not be justified without a revenue. When Councillor Akiwumi appealed that the "matter was an urgent one as far as the users of the road were concerned," the president dismissed the urgency and argued that the question should wait—a refrain that reoccurred repeatedly throughout the 1930s.[59]

Other infrastructure demands were less easy to dismiss, however. The provision of street lights in neighborhoods like Sabon Zongo and Abossey Okai, for example, were about more than mere convenience. As Akiwumi noted, police reports in local papers had highlighted issues of crime in these neighborhoods because "Sabon Zongo and Abossey Okai had afforded hiding places for thieves and all sorts of rogues; and because of the absence of lights in those localities, the police had been experiencing great difficult in tracing them."[60] The installation of lights would facilitate the work of the police and guarantee the security of private property—two key pillars of "liberal imperialism" in Accra.[61] But, as Councillor Kitson Mills noted, the residents of these neighborhoods were also ratepayers who deserved to be protected, particularly since residents were investing in the growth of their neighborhoods and the construction of "many good and substantial buildings." It was "only fair" that they received investment.[62]

For residents, however, the modern appeal of a bus system and its attendant infrastructure competed with the realities of cost and convenience. As early as the 1930s, African councillors called for reductions in fares by roughly a third on underperforming lines in order to attract more patronage.[63] Rate reductions began in 1932 on the underperforming route between Labadi and the post office as part of a one-month pilot program. The Council engaged in a publicity campaign to spread knowledge about the change in bus fares. Manchemei beat the gong

gong, Council staff put up notices, and local newspapers ran stories announcing the news.[64] These pilot programs exceeded expectations. After a fare reduction proposed by Kojo Thompson to encourage ridership on new bus routes along Boundary Road in 1935, the municipal engineer noted that fare reduction actually led to a 25 percent increase in revenue—30 percent of which was profit. The Council approved a plan to extend the reductions to additional lines as deemed appropriate and feasible by the Engineering and Accounting Departments, and the municipal engineer congratulated Councillor Thompson on his excellent proposal.[65]

These fare reduction experiments were part of a broader project to encourage African residents to regularly patronize the bus system. Councillors also proposed adjusted and extended routes that reflected the needs and daily patterns of residents. Given the extraordinary foot traffic on Boundary Road—eighty-four-hundred passengers over four days in 1935—councillors agreed to an experimental bus service, which was later extended in 1936 as part of a new regular bus route between the post office and the booming suburb of Adabraka.[66] But fare reductions seemed to be the only intervention that significantly improved ridership. As councillors noted in 1931, "The falling off in the bus takings was due to people not having enough money to use on them." Councillors Booth, Quartey-Papafio, and Thompson "were certainly sure that more people could not travel on the buses now as they could not afford the high rates."[67] In taking up their proposals, the Council dramatically increased the profits generated through the bus service, from £2,553 in 1931[68] to £4,160 in 1936—pure profit that constituted 10 percent to 25 percent of the Council's total revenue.[69]

Conversations about bus fares and the profitability of the bus service differed significantly from other financial debates within the Town Council. Town councillors, technocrats, and residents alike often cast ongoing controversies over ratepaying for property or basic utilities like water as a question of civic responsibility. The difficult financial realities of the Council and the constant need for revenue were recast as an investment in the welfare and growth of the city. Every ratepaying resident contributed to the future that the Town Council sought to build—a future defined by modern self-government. In conversations about bus fares and the revenue of the bus service, however, councillors were often much more explicit about the profit motive behind this public good. Profits from the bus service far outpaced those collected at markets and lorry parks, providing a critical source of revenue for a Town Council that had been overwhelmed by the financial responsibilities of town planning and maintenance since the governor's office transferred responsibility for town roads and decreased Council subsidies in the late nineteenth century. At a minimum, the Council needed to recoup its costs in the municipal bus service. Ideally, however, the bus system would generate profits that could supplement the Council's meager budget, funding road construction and maintenance among other infrastructural costs.[70]

Questions about fares and ridership were only one part of that calculation. Expanding new routes, purchasing new buses, and providing benches for waiting passengers were all part of the cost of operating and maintaining an effective public service.[71] While infrastructural costs often dominated Council discussions, African councillors also highlighted the investments of labor that kept infrastructure like the bus service in operation. As the global depression dragged on, Councillor Kitson Mills called for an end to the levy on bus employee wages and improvement in the employment conditions of employees in a 1935 meeting, stating that "the bus service contributed a great deal towards the revenue of the Council, and therefore the people engaged in the bus service should be well paid. They received fair wages before but they were reduced during the depression days and levies laid in some cases. They were quite willing, so far, to help in the economic situation which faced the Country. When prosperous time came it was considered that they should receive back what they had contributed, but that had not been the case."[72] Kitson Mills and the employees he represented embraced the rhetoric of public service, responsibility, and shared sacrifice that had been so central to government rhetoric in the midst of global and financial crisis. African councillors argued that higher pay would "encourage them to give good service" and annual leave would enable these essential workers to "recoup their health."[73] Official members, however, seemed unmoved by these arguments. Councillor Roberts dismissed the need for leave by pointing to the workers' status as day laborers who, he argued, "were not entitled to annual leave.... They could not be placed on the same basis as clerical staff."[74] If the Council were to increase wages and introduce an annual leave for bus service employees, "it would create awkwardness to both Government and mercantile firms when artisans and labourers would demand vacation leave with full pay."[75] Councillor Sutherland pointed to his own firm—the United Africa Company, Ltd.—who paid lower wages than the Council without complaint. After all, Roberts noted, "The bus service was, at present, being run on a very narrow margin. During prosperous years the Council subscribed heavy sums to the depreciation fund, but that had not been the case during the past three years—in fact, no moneys had been paid in as the vehicles were old."[76] Roberts argued that increasing wages would make it difficult to generate a profit on the bus service, which was "being run on a very narrow margin."[77] Old buses could not be replaced, and private companies provided competition for municipal services. While councillors were willing to invest projects that advanced their visions, they were often reluctant to spend smaller sums to address issues of public concern. Councillors readily manipulated fares to convince people to use poorly sited markets or expensive bus services but would refuse to raise wages, provide appropriate seating and street lighting, or extend electricity to communities. In a pattern that echoed through other parts of the socioeconomic sphere, employees and passengers were stuck between the demands of social hierarchy, private sector interest, and public sector profitability.

These concerns about the cost of the bus system were further complicated by what town councillors and other government officials often referred to as "competition."[78] Municipal buses were certainly not the only motor vehicles present in the city. Alongside numerous private vehicles owned by the town's wealthier inhabitants, taxis and mammy lorries (or mammy wagons) were seen plying city streets. Drivers of both taxis and mammy lorries reflected broader patterns and practices of motor transportation in the colony. Outside of the municipal bus system, African owner-operators dominated commercial motor transportation in Accra and operated largely outside of any system of comprehensive regulation (beyond basic requirements of licensing, speed, and vehicle condition established through the 1934 Motor Traffic Ordinance and its subsequent amendments). Any car could operate as a taxi, providing it was registered with the government, its driver possessed a taxi license, and the driver displayed a lighted taxi sign on the top of the vehicle. The limited physical markers for taxis enabled drivers to easily move into and out of the taxi industry; however, this subtlety also caused significant confusion when a passenger sought to hail a cab, unable to distinguish a taxi from a private car.[79] More commonly, it seems, passengers of means called for taxis when they needed to carry large, heavy or unwieldy goods, rather than attempting to utilize the municipal bus service.[80]

As a center for trade and a major coastal port, Accra also served as a transportation hub for mammy lorries from all over the colony. With their imported metal engine and chassis and locally constructed and painted wooden body, mammy lorries ferried goods (and some passengers) from rural production areas to urban markets. Mammy lorries were frequently used by market women ("mammies") who traveled with drivers into the interior to trade dried and salted fish for other foodstuffs like tomatoes and yams, which could then be sold in Accra. However, farmers also employed mammy lorries themselves, as farmers of cocoa and other products transported their produce directly to Accra's port for sale and export. While lorries shared the road, they were expected to travel directly to the city's central lorry park to load and unload goods and passengers.

Thus, Accra's streets were busy and diverse, catering to a wide range of motor transport users through a system of overlapping networks. Drivers and passengers alike moved freely between these networks, in response to shifting socioeconomic circumstances. In setting up the municipal bus system, Town Council members assumed that passengers would prefer the slick cosmopolitanism and technological sophistication of new, imported buses and that drivers would value the economic stability of waged employment in the "formal" sector. In practice, however, for many passengers like Felicia, a trader from Keta who traveled to Accra for work, deciding whether to ride in a municipal bus or a lorry was a question of convenience and accessibility:

> Everybody at all can take any of the car that he wants. If you want to take the bus and you get to the bus stop and it's full up and it can't stop, if you want you wait for another one to come. But if you don't want to wait you just go and look for a lorry and go wherever you are going. Everybody joined the buses. And if you go to the market and you buy food and you have a load that is not too much, then you feel you can join a bus and put it on your thighs. Or if it's too much you can go and join a lorry.[81]

Drivers, likewise, often used salaried positions (or what they referred to as "company work") driving for the municipal bus service, government agencies, or private companies to save money to purchase their own wooden-sided mammy lorries—a testament to the value attached to economic independence of entrepreneurial driving. Drivers and passengers alike identified mammy lorry drivers as the real professionals—"real drivers," as men in La referred to them—due to their knowledge of the vehicle and their skill in negotiating the dangers of the road. However, a catastrophic accident, family misfortune, or financial emergency could easily bankrupt drivers who often operated based on small profit margins. As a result, throughout their careers, drivers might have to shift back and forth several times between taxis, company cars, municipal buses, and mammy lorries in response to available work and capital investment.

Throughout the 1930s and 1940s, members of the ATC and even the colonial governor expressed concern about possible competition with the municipal bus service. The bus service provided a sizable proportion of the ATC's revenues, and the Council sought to protect their interests in the bus service by restricting alternative forms of public transportation and claiming urban public transportation as a site of colonial control and authority; this would limit African drivers' participation in the urban transport sector.[82] These colonial justifications for the protection of the municipal bus system reflected the dual concerns of colonial governance—capitalism and civilization.[83] The municipal bus system was inextricably bound up in this project, moving residents in the capital of Britain's "model colony." In laying out bus routes; establishing bus shelters, lay-bys, and lorry parks; and importing British-style buses, the ATC attempted to regulate and shape the mobility patterns and practices of urban residents while also soliciting new forms of revenue from Accra residents to fund their visions for the city's future.

THE PRACTICES OF MOBILITY: HORNS, BRAKES, AND RESIDENTIAL SPACE

Even as they negotiated bureaucratic solutions and maximized profits, town councillors felt their control over the practice of mobility slip further in the growing city. In response to demand from the rapidly growing and increasingly suburbanized populations of Accra, new primary and secondary roads were cut through emerging residential areas, incorporating urban residents into a mobile network. While such roads were intended to provide more direct and efficient routes to the city center for city residents, drivers of mammy lorries, who sought to avoid traffic congestion on older roads that directly connected the city to rural areas, quickly appropriated these new urban roads. For municipal bus and taxi drivers, residential roads were central to an emerging practice of urban mobility, marked by slower speeds, frequent stops, and shorter distances. Buses and taxis were integral parts of the new spatial imagining of the city, facilitating the mobility of urban residents from their homes to the city's various commercial, entertainment, industrial, and governmental districts for work and pleasure, and urban residents walked from their homes to sensibly placed bus stops. They were, in short, uniquely urban forms of mobility and sociability.

The drivers and passengers of mammy lorries, by contrast, had a markedly different relationship to the city. Unlike municipal buses and taxis defined by their role in urban mobility, mammy lorries connected village and city, carrying goods and passengers from rural production zones to urban centers of trade and consumption and back again. This sort of periurban mobility was central to the lives of both rural and urban residents and facilitated economic, social, and cultural connections between areas that were considered politically and administratively distinct within the British system of indirect rule.[84] Food, family members, imported goods, and ideas were all transported by mammy lorries, bridging the socioeconomic and sociocultural distance created by the "bifurcated state"[85] of indirect rule and bringing rural and urban areas into regular conversation.

Ultimately, however, neither the drivers nor passengers of mammy lorries associated mobility with residency. For many of the traders who patronized mammy lorries and markets and the drivers who carried them to and from the city, Accra was a space moved through or visited, not lived in. Even for those who did live in the city, the constant movement of trade meant that many saw the city as a sort of node within a periurban sphere of circulation and exchange, connecting rural and urban areas through social, economic, and cultural ties. These alternative spatial understandings and mobility practices, in turn, shaped very different understandings of the relationship between motor transportation and city space. Colonial police and members of the ATC regularly complained about lorry drivers who parked along roadsides and impeded the flow of traffic or drove too quickly through streets and around corners in urban areas where pedestrians frequently walked in, along, or across the road.[86] In 1935 the commissioner of police announced the introduction of new parking regulations in Accra "owing to the increasing number of motor accidents in the busy thoroughfares of the town."[87] While the new regulations caused some councillors to worry about the impact on the loading and offloading of goods in front of business premises, such infractions proved easy enough to police as the Town Council and the Legislative Council imposed reduced speed limits for Accra and urban areas, and the colonial police force introduced a Motor Traffic Unit, tasked with enforcing local traffic laws and regulations. Rather, the most vexing problems for colonial officials—both police and legislators—was not the danger and inconveniences of urban motor transportation itself but the politics of respectability, order, and control that were threatened as mammy lorries transgressed the boundaries between rural and urban, commercial and residential.

Emerging structures of mobility and new spatial understandings came into direct conflict at urban crossroads and intersections. The construction of new roads that accompanied the development and expansion of residential areas provided alternative pathways for the drivers of mammy lorries traveling to the capital. In an effort to bypass the traffic and rough conditions on major roads, drivers explored new residential streets as shortcuts. Accustomed to limited foot and vehicle traffic outside of the city and attempting to increase the time and fuel efficiency of their driving, lorry drivers employed common strategies to ensure safe passage along these new routes. Rather than stopping at intersections, drivers merely slowed down and honked as they approached, warning other vehicles of their passing. Widely accepted and often recommended on rural roads and in smaller towns, such honking quickly proved to be both a nuisance and a danger in the more urbanized capital.[88] By 1936, the inspector general of police noted, "It is beyond dispute that many local drivers make excessive and unnecessary use of the horns on their vehicles, and that this is markedly so in the case of a few lorry drivers who regularly use the Dodowah Road in the early hours of the morning."[89] These observations were punctuated by noise complaints from a number of European civil servants living in bungalows within earshot of the road.[90]

In response to complaints, the director of public works was ordered to widen major streets, such as the Dodowah Road; the conservator of forests was asked to evaluate the whether foliage obstructed visibility at intersections and to plant hedges and trees to dampen the effect of traffic noise on nearby residents; and the inspector general of police placed traffic constables at major intersections to direct traffic.[91] When none of these tactics reduced traffic noise, colonial officials were confounded. For the inspector general of police, these failures raised

Figure 4.2. Accra Views, 1958. Photograph by Paul Anane. Source: Photographic Archive, Information Services Office, Ministry of Information, Accra R/6208/2.

questions about race and the capability of African traffic constables.[92] For others, the persistence of horn honking in the city defied all understanding. The commissioner of the Western Province complained in a letter to the colonial secretary in 1936: "I should like to point out, however, that it is not always a fact that drivers of motor vehicles sound their horns owing to lack of visibility. For instance, there is a stretch of road behind the Residency over which it is possible to see a long distance ahead and in the early morning lorry drivers appear to sound their horns out of the sheer joy of living apparently, the noise at times being terrific."[93] It was not necessarily the horn honking itself that confused colonial officials. Government officials had also been puzzling over the issue of horn honking in Britain—a reflection of the relative newness of motor transport practice and the necessary negotiations and regulations that would define expectations of drivers, passengers, pedestrians, and the state.[94] Rather, it was the inability of the colonial state to regulate and reform the practices of African lorry drivers that frustrated colonial officials. The failure to regulate drivers and curb the practice of horn honking highlighted fundamentally different cultures of urban space and mobility, as well as the tenuousness of colonial authority. In this particular case, African lorry drivers used horn honking not only to communicate warnings to pedestrians and other motorists but as the basis for a broader system of communication between drivers.[95] While honking in this particular context was undoubtedly a safety strategy, drivers used their horns as part of a fairly wide-ranging system of communication: to warn about police officers ahead, greet fellow drivers, or express appreciation for a vehicle's appearance or the drivers' skill and reputation. Drivers were closely identified with the vehicular inscriptions and decorations on their vehicles, and drivers honked to greet each other when they saw someone they knew on the road. Some drivers looking to pick up passengers along the roadside might honk to alert pedestrians. And in rural areas or small towns where there were few vehicles and roads were often used for walking as much as for motor transportation, drivers would also honk to encourage pedestrians to clear a path in the road. As I've documented elsewhere, failure to do so sometimes resulted in catastrophic accidents and death.[96] In some cases (and in the absence of indicators or efficient mirrors), honking alerted other vehicles that a driver was about to pass. Drivers also used horn honking as a form of protection, alerting each other to the presence of police, or scaring off wildlife while repairing a vehicle in rural areas. Some of these systems of horn honking were transformed over time into unique cultural practices.[97] However, horn honking also pierced the social boundaries between the road and residential space. In the process, it placed European expectations about urban residential space and African cultures of the road into unanticipated conversation and conflict, requiring a revision of urban plans and assumptions about the organization and function of urban space.

CONTROLLING SPACE: PIRACY, MOBILITY, AND AUTHORITY

Archival documents suggest that government officials spent most of their time puzzling over how to regulate lorries; however, photographs and the memories of Accra residents indicate that the municipal bus service was used on a regular basis by people from a diverse range of socioeconomic backgrounds. There was always anxiety among ATC members, the governor, and other colonial officials about the revenues generated by the bus service, and passengers seemed to move freely between municipal buses and lorries—motivated more by convenience and utility than class, prestige, or other sorts of socioeconomic markers. Drivers, likewise, often moved between municipal buses and lorries depending on what employment was available. However, the bus service regularly turned a profit throughout the 1930s and 1940s. Such profit was guaranteed by a monopoly system established under the Omnibus Authority Act in 1927, which limited the participation of independent vehicle owners in the urban public transport industry by refusing to grant commercial licenses to vehicle owners who sought to establish independent bus services in the capital.[98] Such protectionist policies preserved the "handsome revenue" of the ATC in the short term; however, even as late as 1943–44, colonial officials recognized that the state was unable to introduce a "complete and comprehensive general transport system."[99] The expansion and reorganization of the city's residential areas led to greater demands for alternative and expanded forms of public transportation by the town's African residents. Meanwhile, colonial officials were complaining about the difficulties involved in organizing and regulating such a system given African practices that blurred the boundaries between goods and passenger transport and the difficulty of enforcing new regulations due to staff and funding shortages. The frustrations of colonial officials over regulations indicated more fundamental tensions in the ATC's vision for and understanding of the urbanity and mobility practices of Accra's population.

In the realm of public transportation, as elsewhere in colonial economy, society, culture, and politics, colonial officials often failed to take into account African practices when crafting policies that restricted and regulated African lives.[100] For many of Accra's residents, the municipal bus service did not adequately reflect how they experienced and negotiated urban space. In other words, as colonial officials obsessed over *how* they moved, Accra residents made technological choices based on *why* they were moving. Wage laborers and office workers might have found the bus services' routes convenient, connecting the city's residential neighborhoods with centers of business and administration and facilitating transportation to and from work. Still others might have traveled at night or on weekends to partake in the enticements of urban popular culture in dance clubs, cinemas, and football pitches.[101] However, for many Accra residents, mobility was intimately connected to their activities in the city's numerous markets. Traders traveled daily between their homes and markets throughout the city with their sales goods in tow.[102] The wealthiest traders hired taxis to transport their goods directly from their homes to the market stalls. Others who lacked the means to regularly hire a taxi attempted to carry their goods on the municipal bus, either holding their goods on their lap throughout the ride or cramming bundles in the small boot at the rear of the bus. When the storage available on the bus proved insufficient, some traders carried their goods to market, with the help of assistants, children, and other family members and dependents. Women who purchased foodstuffs and other goods in the central market likewise faced

Figure 4.3. Women climb through the open sides of a tro-tro in Accra. Feature Stories on Transportation in Ghana, 1966. Photograph by George Alhassan. Source: Photographic Archive, Information Services Office, Ministry of Information, Accra R/R/7179/10.

difficulties in securing adequate public transportation.[103] Thus, the municipal bus service proved insufficient or unusable for a large number of the city's most mobile residents.

The blurring of boundaries between goods and passenger transport reflected a more fundamental understanding of urban space and mobility among Accra residents. In contrast to the system of indirect rule, which assumed strict divisions between rural and urban authority, the residents of Accra understood their town as an extension of the countryside, bound together by close ties forged through trade, transportation, and sociability. The highly educated African men who comprised the ATC were wealthy ratepayers with very different opportunities and priorities in relation to the city and colonial government. These *manbii* were financially invested in the welfare of Town Council investments—their taxes (or rates) went to pay for these services. But they were also invested in a particular sort of symbolic spatial culture in the city—Westernized, living much like European residents in similar parts of the city, early to move into the newly developing suburbs. Drivers, by contrast, were largely drawn from the non-ratepaying class of people, from the bush or *kose*—the regions that lay outside of the core of Ga urbanity (Kinka, Nleshi, and Osu). They were often "school leavers" (individuals who had dropped out of school, often for financial reasons) who were connected to city life through the networks of farming, fishing, and trade, which had facilitated movement in the region for generations. They did not own property, but lorry drivers, at least, did often own their vehicles, and they dedicated themselves to securing the highest profits possible with their investments. Their priorities were influenced by their own profit motives, as well as those of their passengers—often market women who were traveling between Accra and the rural hinterland and within Accra itself.

By the late 1920s and early 1930s, market women and other urban residents began pursuing alternative forms of urban transportation. Mammy lorries, which entered the city carrying goods from the farms of the interior, made initial stops and unloaded goods at the outskirts of the city, moving between markets and wholesale yards to distribute produce for farmers and traders. La, also known by colonial officials as "Labadi," was one of the most important gateways into the city from the cocoa-producing eastern interior. As one of the first major urban markets as well as a center for motor transportation, La was a node connecting rural and urban transport networks. Drivers stopped at La as one of the first in a series of stops as they made their way along the main coastal road to the central market and lorry station in downtown Accra.[104]

Both market women and drivers who had long-established relationships in long distance trade and transportation, seized on the possibilities of the mammy lorries in forging new motor transport practices in the city that better suited local patterns and practices of mobility and urban residence. For drivers who offloaded goods at a peripheral market like La, driving through town with a partially empty truck highlighted lost potential profit. As their lorries emptied, some enterprising drivers sought to replace their loads by offering their services to urban traders who were attempting to transport their trade goods to the central market. For market women, the opportunity to arrange cheaper transportation that was closer and more convenient proved appealing. By the 1930s, colonial officials reported that one could see traders standing with their goods at the roadside waiting to hail a passing lorry.

ATC members and other colonial officials viewed this practice as an extension of a perceived laziness on the part of lower-class African urban residents. In the context of a colonial urban plan, such practices made little sense. Bus stops had been placed within easy walking distance and buses ran at regular intervals; there seemed to be no need to wait on the roadside for a ride on a mammy lorry when bus shelters and modern buses were available. Furthermore, mammy lorries charged more for their services (as much as three pence within Accra city limits) than the municipal buses, whose fares were just over one pence. However, colonial logic failed to take into account the cost and trouble of headloading goods from homes to bus stops and again from lorry parks to market stalls. For many traders, the ease of use more than compensated for the elevated cost, providing traders with a more affordable alternative to the taxi and a quicker alternative to the municipal bus, for which passengers often waited in long lines during peak traffic times at the beginning and end of the workday. Lorries, which were built to transport goods, also provided necessary storage space that was absent for municipal buses focused on passenger transport. Thus, in appropriating mammy lorries into the urban transport industry, traders highlighted the conflation of categories of goods and passenger transport in the mobility practices of Accra residents.

As early as 1932, such practices began to raise concerns among members of the ATC, who feared that mammy lorries would cut into ATC revenues provided by the municipal bus services.[105] Echoing colonial fears about the role of independent motor transportation as competition with colonial railways in rural areas several decades earlier, the ATC immediately sought to limit the operations of "innumerable lorries ... plying for hire for the carrying of passengers within the Municipal Boundaries."[106] By 1940, much of this illegal competition seemed to be located on the road between La and Accra—a route dominated by well-organized and highly skilled Ga drivers.[107] That the center of this practice seemed to be La only strengthened colonial desires to restrict it. La's role as a market and transportation center was paralleled by its reputation as a site of unrest for colonial administrations as far back as the 1920s when La residents allegedly attempted to bomb the colonial governor.[108] ATC members lobbied the governor to introduce new transport regulations that not only restricted passenger transport to the municipal bus services but also criminalized practices like stopping to load and unload along roadsides. Passenger transport along the routes of the municipal bus service was restricted to that service alone, while mammy lorries and other commercial vehicles were expected to proceed directly to the central lorry park in downtown Accra without stopping.

As the president of the ATC's letter attests, drivers quickly found alternative routes that bypassed colonial attempts to protect the municipal bus service through road scheduling. Passenger transport operations other than the municipal bus service were banned on major transport arteries that ran through the city. ATC members assumed that police enforcement on scheduled roads would eliminate the practice. While scheduling and enforcement did succeed in limiting the operation of alternative passenger transport services along municipal bus routes, it did not eliminate the practice entirely. Instead, lorry drivers merely moved onto Accra's expanding residential road infrastructure, crafting alternative pathways through the city that ran through the heart of the emerging residential districts. There, concerns about honking horns and pirate lorries overlapped in the complicated web of frustrated urban governance.

The language of piracy suggests the degree to which these passenger lorries threatened the authority of the colonial state and the foundations of the colonial order. Regulatory measures like road scheduling failed to halt the actions of mammy lorry drivers and passengers. For colonial officials and Accra residents alike, these failures highlighted the tenuousness of colonial control over urban mobility and space. British colonial officials freely admitted the limitations of their direct authority in rural areas, where they negotiated with chiefs who served as the indirect enforcers of colonial power. But in the city, colonial officials sought more direct control over African residents, seeking to influence the institutions and practices of politics, economics, society, and culture in pursuit of their "civilizing" mission. Particularly at the center of colonial power—the capital—the actions of drivers and passengers who used mammy lorries as passenger vehicles provided a direct challenge to colonial authority and asserted African ownership over Accra as a social and economic space. Africans not only worked around colonial restrictions in ways that were meaningful and useful to them, creating spaces for themselves to succeed and live that often defied expectations of colonial authorities, but their persistence also fundamentally reshaped colonial policy and the expectations of colonial authority.

CONCLUSION

The drivers and motor vehicle passengers in Accra provided important challenges to colonial authority at precisely the moment that the British colonial state sought to extend its influence over African lives and African spaces. After decades of conflict over urban residential redevelopment, state officials at the end of the 1930s finally began to reshape the city to reflect modernizing visions of sanitation, efficiency, and order. But new residential patterns raised new questions about the way that Africans lived in and moved through urban space. The tenacity of African drivers and passengers who sought alternative forms of urban mobility in order to better fit their needs and values, and the inability of the colonial state to suppress these alternatives, highlight the degree to which, even in the colonial capital at the height of investment in "development colonialism," colonial hegemony remained elusive. Even as Africans embraced the technologies and spatial practices of modernization—the physical and social symbols of "civilization"—they did so through local frames of awareness and practice.[109]

While market women and drivers did sometimes go on strike or protest as a form of political expression during this period, horn honking or the operation of pirate passenger lorries were not expressly political acts. However, in unapologetically embracing technology to pursue their own interests, lorry drivers and their passengers did shape a different kind of technology story. In a colonial context, European officials often ignored, underestimated, denigrated, or denied African capacity to operate effectively and on their own terms in "modern" society. British officials in the Gold Coast and European colonial agents around the continent saw their role as that of "civilizers"—bringing light to a dark continent. In cities like Accra, spatial networks and technological systems embodied the promise of a colonial modernity just as much as churches and storefronts. British officials and the Ga elites who served as their representatives on the ATC assumed that technology operated effectively only within a predetermined Western set of values and practices.[110] Drivers and passengers who embraced the utility of lorries in urban settings, however, challenged these assumptions and shaped a new vision for urban mobility.

Telling stories of what Clapperton Mavhunga calls "everyday innovation" in Africa is critical in order to understand African experiences outside of these colonial frameworks.[111] As the debates over horn honking and pirate passenger lorries highlight, these quotidian practices often had political consequences, even if African agents did not frame them as political acts. As such, they reshaped the life of the city far beyond the mundane realities of daily life—going back and forth to the market, traveling to work, transporting goods, picking up passengers, making money. In using vehicles and roads in ways that Europeans could never have envisioned, drivers and passengers in Accra highlighted the limitations of British control and asserted a uniquely African practice of motor transportation and mobility. In the process, they reshaped the urban plan. In other words, Accra was an African city not only because of its precolonial roots but also the persistence of Africans in shaping the plan for the city long after it became the colonial capital because, as Myers argues, "The decisions of ordinary, low-income citizens are the creative heart of African urban form."[112] In some cases, those decisions were part of an intentionally political engagement that spawned factions and debates around town. In others, as we see here, the actions of urban residents, united in their pursuit of mobility and prosperity, were less controversial for urban residents than they were for British representatives, who often failed to consider the interests and aspirations of the city's lower-class population.

In Accra, "pirate passenger lorries" and honking horns were the early foundations of an emerging *African* urban mobility, simultaneously rooted in the past, the constantly evolving present, and competing visions of the future. By the time British colonial rule was effectively consolidated in the 1920s and 1930s, Accra was both a colonial port city and a Ga town. As Parker argues and as the struggles over pirate passenger lorries suggest, these were not distinct forms of urbanism. Nor was the African influence on urban life suppressed by the technological wonder of the "colonial sublime."[113] Rather, debates over the infrastructure and use of motor transport and urban planning technologies and the persistence of pirate passenger lorries highlight the existence of a distinctive *Accra* culture, which, by the 1930s and 1940s became a touchstone for the entire colony.

FIVE

BUILDING HOMES IN THE "NEW ACCRA"

AT 7:23 P.M. ON JUNE 22, 1939, an earthquake struck Accra. As Assistant Colonial Secretary Harold Cooper recounted in the *Times*:

> There was no warning of its approach and it started, not with the subdued rumble which increased in volume as the uneasy minute past, but with the sudden deafening clamor which pursued a monotonous and nerve wracking course until it ceased as abruptly as it had begun. The noise may most appropriately be compared (and this is an analogy which sprang instantly to the mind of almost every European in Accra) to that of a giant underground train plunging madly through a vast hollow station built only a few feet below the earth surface; And the monstrous clatter of the wheels of this imaginary vehicle was punctuated from time to time by solitary staccato explosions as if the rails upon which it traveled were splitting under the strain. The moment that all obscuring reverberation of the tremor had subsided it was succeeded by a shrill and eerie wail, now for the first time audible, from the African Township; But this in its turn sank quickly into a muffled chorus of dismay. Almost at the very start of the tremor the electricity supply failed in the ensuing darkness added to the general horror. Immediately after the shot could ceased police whistles began to blow in almost every part of the town and cars could be seen racing down from the residential area towards the crowded Jamestown and Asere quarters, which were expected to present a scene of appalling confusion. It is not unusual for natural upheavals of this magnitude to be followed, and aggravated, by rioting on the part of a frenzied, grief-stricken populace. In Accra, however, there was no such distressing aftermath, and the first government officials to reach the African Township found the streets choked with excited but orderly throngs, whose only desire seemed to be to unite in a mutual effort to alleviate the suffering which had so bafflingly descended upon them.[1]

Twenty-two people died, more than one hundred were injured, and thousands more lost their homes. Government buildings were damaged, and road and water infrastructure required urgent repair. However, the biggest concern was with housing. In the aftermath of the earthquake, Governor Arnold Hodson quickly mobilized official engineers and volunteers to conduct a house-to-house inspection. More than 1,500 houses needed to be demolished and 600 more were uninhabitable. There were 15,500 people who needed rehousing. The governor immediately sent pleas for relief funds, both to the Colonial Office and to the British public, aided by notable political and commercial imperial leaders.[2] People in the town also responded quickly. Volunteers showed up to inspect houses, provide food, and distribute milk; African railway employees transformed carriages into temporary accommodations; African soldiers in the Gold Coast regiment quickly built "roundhouses" made from palm leaves in open spaces around the town.

Governor Hodson noted these extraordinary contributions in his dispatches to Malcolm MacDonald, the secretary of state for the colonies. Despite the significant losses, Hodson was optimistic about the future and felt that he "had the earthquake problem well in hand." Much like the fires of 1894, the devastation of the earthquake also presented an opportunity. As Hodson noted, "In one way, in spite of all the suffering and loss, it is a good thing as we shall now have the opportunity of turning Accra into a town which everyone will be proud of."[3] Central to Hodson's proposals for disaster recovery and relief was a massive new rehousing scheme that would mitigate some of the future risk of earthquake damage but also provide long-term interventions to change the shape of the town. Because the scale of the devastation left many Accra residents homeless and necessitated extensive demolitions, Hodson argued: "It is, of course, inconceivable the work of reelection and repair should be allowed to result in the resurrection of a town the disposition and conditions of which would be similar to those which obtained prior to the recent catastrophe. My policy is, therefore, directed towards securing at the same time not only the reparation of the earthquake damage and the rehousing involved their end but also the clearance and replanting of those congested areas which would have had to be dealt with by 'slum clearance' schemes in the near future."[4] Temporary measures in the immediate aftermath of the earthquake were just that—temporary. However, they would lay the groundwork for a more wholescale remaking of the city through rebuilding its residents' housing.

This situation was simultaneously entirely novel and wholly predictable. The scale of the earthquake's devastation was relatively exceptional—though not quite as severe as the damage from a quake in 1862 that destroyed much of the town. Hodson's visions were also probably much grander and more fully realized than any previous attempts. But, in trying to leverage crisis or disaster to implement reforms in the built landscape of the city, Hodson also drew on a number of precedents that were connected to ongoing narratives about sanitation, public health, and urban governance. As Quayson argues, Hodson followed a long line of governors and other colonial leaders who sought to leverage disaster management protocols in order to effect major interventions in the built environment of the city.[5] These moments of disaster at least temporarily transformed the spatial politics of the town and created opportunities to reshape the city by exploiting the vulnerability of Accra residents to control the process of rebuilding. However, these moments of emergency intervention and the expansion of spatial power were less typical and rarely as successful as colonial officials hoped. Rather, the day-to-day realities with which Accra residents grappled to secure and maintain housing and assert their rights to land in the city were more immediately and intimately connected to the regulations and rates that had, by the late nineteenth and early twentieth centuries, become a central part of urban governance. The Town Council structure was deeply connected to the assessment and regulation of residential properties, both for the collection of revenue and the identification of eligible voters and office holders. The assessment of properties and the expansion of regulation and oversight in and around the home sought to reframe what it meant to live in the city.

This chapter explores the ways in which a wide range of government officials—from African representatives and colonial government leaders to nationalist politicians—sought to construct a "modern" city through the regulation of housing and its relationship to their vision of town planning. These spatial and social politics certainly reflected different—and changing—conceptions of land, and those politics in many ways intensified and transformed at independence. But regulation and planning also often produced the very problems that they purported to solve. The "slums" that Hodson was so invested in clearing by 1939, I argue, were often the product of both disinvestment and misguided interventions. If African town councillors pushed back on the enactment of these policies in the 1920s and 1930s, by the end of World War II, "town planning" policies had become deeply ingrained in the practice of colonial urban governance and visions for a postcolonial future, influenced by shifts in emerging transnational professional practice and discourses of development. However, the persistence of "slums" were not evidence of the perceived "disarray" of African residential patterns that colonial officials and technocratic experts assumed. Rather, in asserting their own visions for city life through the form and organization of housing, African residents advanced a different understanding of spatial politics that was often deeply rooted in Ga conceptions of land and community. As members of the Ga Shifimo Kpee nationalist party suggested in their shouts of "Ga land for Ga people!," the "new Accra" envisioned in the plan for the town often ignored the values and visions of the people who represented its core. Instead, by the 1940s and 1950s, African and British leaders alike embraced the promise of modernist planning and architecture as the path toward a modern, prosperous future, which required all members of the community to embrace the notion of "self-help." This democratic narrative of community participation echoed the embrace of "vernacular architecture" and construction methods by early town planning advisers like Maxwell Fry and Jane Drew. But for local residents, this rhetoric often rang hollow in light of persistent disinvestment and accelerating urbanization, which placed new pressures on the built environment and sociocultural landscape of the town and made it increasingly difficult to build homes in the town in both the physical and social sense.

LAND

The fees gathered through trade and transport constituted a large portion of the Town Council's revenue by the 1930s, but this new form of urban governance was built on a new system of rates, or property taxes. The 1894 Town Councils Ordinance laid out a comprehensive plan for assessing the value of property in the town. As soon as the ordinance was extended to the town, the governor would appoint an assessor who would "ascertain and assess the annual value of the houses in such town, and take the names of the owners and occupiers of such houses."[6] The appraiser had the right, in the discharge of his duties, to enter any house between 6 a.m. and 6 p.m. "on any lawful day" and require the owner or occupier to provide full name and address. The assessor would then deliver an alphabetical list of ratepayers to the district commissioner.

This assessment of the town's houses connected new definitions of urban citizenship and new understandings of property ownership. The list of ratepayers was both a financial and a political instrument. The list was used by Town Council officials to track the payment of rates. But ratepayers were also eligible voters under the ordinance, and only those who were up-to-date on their rates were eligible to run for one of the elected positions on the Council. After an initial period of public viewing, individuals who wished to contest the list had to pay a shilling to inspect it, file a formal written notice with the district commissioner, and attend a public meeting to plead their case. Or if they still did not feel that their case had been heard fairly, these people had to appeal to a divisional court judge as a final authority. This bureaucratic approach to governance leveraged the growing power of the state—notably the courts—to reinforce compliance with the new system. Those who did not cooperate with (or who actively obstructed) the assessor's work could be fined twenty shillings. Those who refused to pay could have their house seized and sold.[7]

While colonial officials frequently pointed to the democratic nature of the Town Council as an example of progressive leadership in the Gold Coast, African residents of Accra immediately resisted the rates. Far from being a democratic process, the rates were instituted "for the purpose of raising the means of carrying out the provisions of this ordinance"—an ordinance that, in various forms, diverse Accra residents had contested fiercely for decades. The 1894 Bill was, Sarah Balakrishnan argues, interpreted in light of the Public Lands Bill, which a wide range of townspeople had protested as an attempt to seize land for the colonial state.[8] A group of local leaders wrote directly to Queen Victoria protesting the new Town Councils Ordinance, arguing that the tax (2.5 percent of rentable value) would place an unfair burden on a population that was already struggling from political and economic changes that undercut the wealth of African leaders, and elected members of the Town Council would be in the minority. As elite members of the community complained, people were being taxed without proper representation. But even more urgently for the vast majority of Accra residents, new taxes endangered various forms of social, cultural, and economic value invested in property. Due to the unpopularity of the new ordinance, the governor struggled to find individuals who were willing to stand for election out of the town's 225 ratepayers. Taki Tawia rallied the town to resist, but when the colonial state deployed Hausa soldiers to disperse meetings and put down rebellions—and other members of the Muslim community joined in support—Accra's elite residents worried about the threat of mob violence and attempted to diffuse the conflict. As the town scrambled to respond to the new rates, and the state refused to back down, these same elite residents stepped in at the last minute to pay the rates of Ga Mantse Taki Tawia, Osu Mantse Noi Ababio, and other Ga leaders so their houses would not be seized. Worried about arrest, other residents soon followed.[9]

The system of rates—and the debates about housing regulation, development, and planning—that emerged in the aftermath of the Town Councils Ordinance was part of a broader attempt by the British colonial state to grapple with the persistent problem of land in the Gold Coast. Unlike other colonies where the British seized, conquered, or purchased land on which capitals were built, Ga residents and their chiefs continued to control the vast majority of the land in the Gold Coast. Policies like the Public Lands Ordinance and the Town Councils Ordinance effectively commodified land, attaching value and creating new processes for asserting and contesting the ownership of land. But British land administration models were ill-equipped to deal with the highly complex politics of land ownership in Accra. As the British established their new position in Accra in the 1870s and 1880s, they encountered large numbers of private landowners—a marked difference from other territories.[10] Ownership of land as a sign of wealth, rather than status through "ownership in people," became increasingly important as the practice of slavery declined at the end of the nineteenth century—a period that coincided with the selection of Accra as the colonial capital.[11] Former slave trading elites sought to capitalize on the new "legitimate trade," purchasing or otherwise securing land for commercial agriculture.[12] Families also made new kinds of investments in private or family houses, increasingly grand and built of stone. This commodification of land in Accra complicated long-standing Ga understandings of land tenure, in which land was held by a "chief" (or elected family head) on behalf of the lineage/family (*we*). All family members had the ability to make claims on family or stool land for use, and the chief (in consultation with the elders) would often reallocate land upon the death of a family member.[13] By the late nineteenth century, however, individuals increasingly asserted more permanent control over their land in the town, building more permanent homes and burying family members within the walls of the family compound: this rendered the site both economically, socially, and spiritually sacred.[14]

The growing presence of the colonial state in Accra certainly influenced changing notions of land tenure in the late nineteenth and early twentieth centuries. The Public Lands Ordinance allowed the state to claim land (and compensate owners) for public use—a right that was increasingly exercised as British officials sought to expand infrastructure, construct new neighborhoods like Victoriaborg, and implement new town plans.[15] However, as Sarah Balakrishnan argues, Ga leaders and city residents also embraced new understandings of land tenure in order to secure opportunity for themselves.[16] Chiefs like Taki Tawia began to cede large tracts of land to the colonial state, commercial firms, or other influential allies, often in exchange for payment, in order to consolidate his own authority and power in the city.[17] Increasing urbanization also placed new pressures on land in the town. Having no connection to family lineages and thus no inherent right to family or stool lands, early settlers like the Tabon negotiated with Ga leaders to secure usufruct rights for their communities and were thus integrated into existing Ga systems.[18] But new migrants in the nineteenth and early twentieth centuries often arrived as individuals seeking economic opportunity on the coast and had less favorably positioned to negotiate with the powerful stools or lineage heads. Instead, they sought to buy or rent land. Ga townspeople in the late nineteenth century began to use the colonial court system to assert ownership of land, which they could then sell.[19] Ga entrepreneurs could also mortgage property to secure advances from trading companies and mercantile firms—money which, Sackeyfio-Lenoch argues, they later reinvested in more urban real estate.[20] The rapid pace of "land alienation" in Accra significantly reshaped the urban landscape in the late nineteenth and early twentieth centuries.[21] The commodification of land certainly enabled the colonial state to purchase land to expand the boundaries of the city and develop new public works facilities and infrastructure; however, this was far from straightforward. Ga residents and other urban migrants also asserted their rights to the town in ways that heavily constricted British officials' ability to control city space. In building outside of the city, British officials tacitly acknowledged that they were unable to control the city center because, as numerous observers marveled, the entire town was owned by Africans.[22]

REGULATION

Possessing little direct control over the city and its residents, British officials and town councillors often focused on the creation of rules and categories that could provide the foundation for (at least the illusion of) "bureaucratic efficacy and order." The Town Council's Ordinance provided some foundational structures and responsibilities for both the governing class and the governed; however, as Bissell notes, "Developing an integrated and comprehensive legal framework was well beyond the means of local officials" and colonial regulations were often extended in a "patchwork fashion" in response to specific emergencies rather than part of any forward-thinking plan.[23] African residents in colonial towns often saw regulations as money grabs that extracted additional wealth from Africans through taxes, fees, and fines, rather than a means for protecting the welfare of the general public or advancing collective interests. But that did not mean that regulation was inconsequential. Much like the mosquito inspections that brought Accra residents face-to-face (often, quite literally) with British colonial power and created unprecedented new forms of oversight and regulation over the intimate spaces and daily lives of individuals and families, regulations regarding the assessment, construction, and maintenance of buildings and their immediate surroundings represented a direct assault on the autonomy of the city and its residents.

Given the long history of British fears of poor health and sanitation and their association with the congestion of the old town core, it is unsurprising that most of these regulations focused on African housing. Houses were assessed based on size and the perceived value of the property, rather than the income of the resident. Many "family houses" had been inherited from wealthier family members or, particularly in light of the changing economic fortunes of many merchants and political leaders in nineteenth- and twentieth-century Accra, had been built when the owner himself had been much wealthier. Chiefs and lineage heads were obligated to keep large houses for political reasons, but dwindling income had made maintenance difficult.[24] Homeowners who did not or could not pay their taxes had their houses seized.[25] In 1930 alone, more than three decades after the imposition of rates, Joseph William Blankson, town clerk for Accra, appeared before the court. He reported that, having followed the process laid out in the Town Councils Ordinance for the assessing and levying of rates, he had "here on the 24 sheets of paper which I produced, all initialed by me, the names of ratepayers who have not paid their rates duly assessed upon them together with particulars of their house numbers and the amounts." Noting that a notice had been placed on the houses for twenty-one days, he was in the court to "apply for an order for the sale of the houses and lands," which the court duly granted "to defray the rates set out on the lists."[26]

Rates were undoubtedly important to the Town Council; they constituted at least a quarter of the Council's total revenue by the late 1920s and 1930s,[27] and nearly 90 percent of those rates were assessed on nongovernment property.[28] Fines and the seizure of property provided an important "stick" with which the Council could reinforce the collection of this critical revenue and maintain their other expenditures. Ambiguously defined "nuisance" found in compounds could also lead to steep fines. If homeowners were unable to pay the fines, Town Council officials seized their homes for sale or demolition. The Council's sanitary and public health responsibilities gave city officials broad authority over the prosecution of "insanitary" spaces, and officials often took advantage of the vague definitions of these categories to declare properties "insanitary." Properties labeled as "wastelands" or "ruins" were often seized, demolished, and the property resold.[29] In other cases, inspectors seized and destroyed the contents of houses. Residents were rarely fully compensated for their dispossession, and numerous residents were left homeless.[30] African residents identified these practices as extensions of the broader land grab the British had been engaged in throughout the Gold Coast since at least the 1870s, and colonial officials readily admitted that the laws governing sanitation and public health were more expedient in clearing land than the Public Lands Ordinance.[31]

In 1933 the Accra Ratepayers Association appealed to members of the Town Council to address the rapid increase in demolition notices. As elected African town councillors attested, the global depression had wreaked havoc on the financial security of Accra residents. Demolitions were inconsiderate in light of ongoing hardship; building conditions reflected the impoverished state of many residents who simply did not have the resources to maintain their buildings. In other cases, they argued, demolition seemed like an overzealous execution of regulation by Council officials. Mr. Addy, for example, appealed to Councillor Dr. Reindorf when he was facing a demolition notice. He complained that he had been asked to demolish a portion of his building because he had not obtained a building permit before beginning construction. While technically the property was in contravention of the law, Dr. Reindorf went and inspected the veranda in question himself and found it to be sound. He and Addy asked whether the homeowner should have to demolish a perfectly sound structure merely because he had been late in obtaining a permit? Particularly in light of the depression, such financial waste seemed both cruel and unwise.[32] Councillor Kitson Mills also appealed for mercy on behalf of those whose corrugated iron buildings were set for demolition. While Kitson Mills acknowledged that the health officers were well intentioned and technically accurate in executing their duties to protect the health of the town, the "ruthless demolition of these shanties were causing more harm than good. It would be far better for one to live in a shanty than to remain unprotected at the mercy of sun, wind, and rain." When their structures were demolished, dispossessed persons, who were in these iron shacks because did not have enough resources to build a proper house in the first place, would be forced to find housing in the already congested areas of the towns, where there were simply not enough resources or rooms.[33]

For many Accra residents, regulations that addressed housing felt like a particular threat. For the British, rules that governed construction methods and building safety were critical to ensuring the broader safety of the public. The municipal engineer, president of the Accra Town Council (ATC), medical officer, and other European officers often defended the actions of the Council and its representatives in demolishing houses that contravened regulations. In the ongoing debate about the fairness of demolition orders, the acting municipal officer for health pointed to a building that had recently been divided into multiple rooms that were smaller (by 4.5 inches) than the allowed size in the building regulations. "The owner of the property was warned when he commenced the alterations, but he disregarded the warning," the municipal engineer complained when he was questioned about the citation.[34] For these "official" European officers, the cause of the hardship was often the actions of African residents themselves who failed to follow the rules. These regulations were a manifestation of the underlying British vision of colonial rule as a form of trusteeship—a vision that remained dominant through the first several decades of the twentieth century.[35] African councillors regularly appealed to the Council to not "adhere too strictly to the regulations, but to exercise reasonable discretion in the matter" given that money was scarce. As Kojo Thompson noted, "Masons generally make mistakes in laying the foundations of buildings, and it would be a hardship to ask the man to pull down the wall which must have been expensive to erect. In view of the hardness of the times and taking into consideration that the dimensions of the rooms were only 4.5 inches short of the requirements of the regulations, he asked that the owner of the building should not be penalized."[36] Mr. Addy's case was held for further investigation as Dr. Reindorf conferred with other officials to determine the safety of the structure. Others questioned the appropriateness of the process and urged the Town Council to consider individual cases more carefully rather than deferring to the municipal engineer or the medical officer.[37] However, in response to these kinds of appeals, the president of the ATC and other European officers more often pointed to the letter of the law and the processes laid out in the ordinance. People hid, the president argued, to avoid being served demolition notices, and they often ignored warnings when constructing sheds, rooms, verandas, and other ancillary structures that contravened the regulations.[38] "They had received verbal warnings from the Building Inspector which is more than need had been done for them, and shows that these cases are dealt with sympathetically," he stated.[39] There was no need to change existing practices.

Particularly in light of the depression, "temporary structures" like corrugated iron shacks were often marked as "dangerous buildings" and slated for demolition, which compounded the hardship for the city's most vulnerable residents. In the eyes of the medical officer of health, these structures were an immediate threat to public health and welfare, which necessitated more urgent action. When Kojo Thompson argued that "every consideration should be given to the people in these hard times, and not to follow the letter of the law in every instance," the president of the ATC remarked that "the Building Regulations were made to be enforced. People could not be allowed to build before putting in Building Permits. The Regulations had to be enforced, and the Council had not the power to waive them."[40] More detailed investigations and consideration "caused useless and valueless discussion and unnecessary work to the staff of the Council."[41] At the core of these debates, however, were fundamental misunderstandings about the significance of houses for Ga people. For many Accra residents building and housing regulations not only provided new kinds of intrusions into the built spaces of their households and family life, but these regulations also often had a profound impact on the spiritual and ritual world the family was a part of. As Balakrishnan notes, "The house was a space of safety for the ancestors, a site of guardianship and protection," in contrast to the "public sphere" or the areas outside of the boundary of the town, which carried significant risk and were widely considered a "zone of danger."[42] Family members were buried in the house, chiefs held court in their houses, and many rituals were connected to the house.[43] In seizing property and seeking to reorder the social life of the household through its built space, then, colonial officials violated sacred boundaries and often polluted important ritual sites.

Colonial officers, town councillors, and other elites who envisioned a new "modern" future for Accra, then, faced a considerable challenge. Even with the support of the African members of the Town Council, colonial officers were still heavily reliant on the goodwill of Ga chiefs and other city residents in securing access to land by the 1930s and 1940s, and practices of "intramural burial" made residents reluctant to relocate or cede ground. The 1888 Cemetery Bill sought to shift burial practices to new public cemeteries and make land more "fungible"; however, these rules were incredibly difficult to enforce and required constant policing well into the 1940s.[44] Housing regulations, then, were a tool, backed by the authority of the Town Council and the power of the courts, which colonial officers used to justify increasing interventions in housing practice. In 1936 alone, demolition notices were signed for 389 properties in Accra for a variety of reasons, a dramatic escalation from the previous year. Whereas the Town Council had previously authorized demolition for a wide range of reasons, including "danger," contravention of the regulations, and unauthorized structures, by 1936 demolitions were almost exclusively targeted at unauthorized structures. For town planners, building inspectors, municipal engineers, and public works officers, demolitions created an opportunity to address the organization of the compact old town core, which they often described as congested and unhealthy.[45] If individuals would not willingly relocate or sell their property, the Town Council found other means to create and control space through demolition, permitting, and the regulation and policing of private space.

SLUMS

In diagnosing persistent housing and building challenges in Accra, colonial technocrats and political figures—like those in many other African colonies—tended to blame what they considered to be inherent African sociocultural forces. As Bissell describes for Zanzibar, sanitary reformers and colonial planners worked from a set of assumptions that "naturalize[d] social conditions, treating particular historical configurations as if they were the result of essential or inherent forces."[46] To some degree, this narrative of chaos, dysfunction, disorder, and danger was an urban manifestation of European observers and colonial officials' widespread stereotypes and assumptions about Africans, which crystallized (and were increasingly racialized) in the late nineteenth and early twentieth centuries. As we saw in debates over health and sanitation, which formed the foundation of new ideologies of colonial urban governance, British officials often used scientific advancements as cover for explicitly racist practices, pathologizing African bodies and sociocultural practices in order to reinforce notions of European cultural superiority and justify increasing levels of intervention in the daily lives of urban residents. British observers frequently noted the mud and thatch construction of "swish" houses, the mixed-use organization of the city, and the narrow footpaths between houses, all of which were seen as symbols of the fundamental differences at hand in these colonial encounters. However, colonial officials often interpreted these conditions through what Mayne describes as "the stereotypes of slumland difference and repulsion that were familiar to them in their homeland."[47] In nineteenth century Britain, "slum" discourse highlighted the fundamental "inequalities and environmental degradations underpinning modern capitalist cities"; however, rather than addressing the root causes of inequality, politicians, philanthropists, and social activists often shifted blame instead to the urban poor who, they argued, could and should be reformed. Spatial reform would reinforce broader perceived needs for moral reform. By the late nineteenth century, so-called slum reformers had become increasingly confident in their ability to design a modern spatial order.[48] In colonial cities, these same policies—developed by newly professionalized technocratic fields like public health, social work, architecture, urban planning, engineering, and education—informed new approaches to urban governance that placed authority in technical experts to find solutions to perceived public "problems."[49]

Technocratic officials and other observers increasingly described Jamestown and Ussher Town as "unfit for human habitation" and requiring new forms of regulation to bring conditions in those communities up to "modern" standards.[50] Throughout the documents preserved in the colonial archive, officials utilized passive language to describe housing conditions in "slums." Frustrated by their lack of direct control over land and their inability to fundamentally remake the city, British officials complained about the "congested areas" of town in justifying residential segregation on public health grounds in the late nineteenth and early twentieth centuries. However, by the 1940s, technocratic advisers, town councillors, and British officers alike referred regularly to "slums." Architect Maxwell Fry's captured much of this attitude in writing to the resident minister for West Africa about his 1945 report on the proposed town planning scheme for the city:

> Slums at their worst exist at Ussher Town, Jamestown and areas generally inhabited by the Hausa or Mohamedan communities, and bad housing with filthy lanes exist at Labadi. Conditions such as these may be accounted for by poverty and ignorance. Labor immigration has been greatly increased since the war mainly on account of military developments. This necessitated existing buildings in the neighborhood of such being overcrowded and spacing compounds being led to accommodate shacks of all kinds. This is specially noticeable in Riponsville (Korle Woo), Sabon Zongo where, according to the medical officer of health report for 1942, some 100 people were sleeping in the open and on verandahs.[51]

Maxwell's report echoed the passive language found throughout the colonial archives—these conditions "existed" without a clear (or admitted) cause. Clearly the only solution, officials argued, was "slum clearance."

In reality, the situation was much more complicated. Overcrowding was a symptom of rapid urbanization, benign neglect, and intentional disinvestment. Having been both unable and unwilling to invest in public infrastructure and services in preexisting Ga neighborhoods in the early years of colonial rule, British colonial and Accra municipal leaders directed the limited resources dedicated to urban development into the construction of European and elite African neighborhoods; however, these neighborhoods were inaccessible to the new migrants beginning to flood the city in the 1920s and 1930s. In search of cheap housing, migrants settled in Jamestown, Ussher Town, and to some degree, Osu, straining the capacity and infrastructure of the old neighborhoods and exacerbating sanitation and public health challenges. By the 1940s the population in neighborhoods like Sabon Zongo, Adabraka, Agbogbloshie, and Christiansborg had dramatically increased.[52]

Even in the face of these persistent housing challenges, British officials were often uncompromising in their adherence to building regulations and planning logics. A number of economic disturbances—from the string of cocoa holdups between 1916 and 1937–38[53] to the global depression—further weakened an economy already struggling to adjust to changes wrought by the end of the slave trade and transformations in the operation of mercantile firms on the coast[54] in ways that dramatically impacted many Accra residents' economic prosperity. At the same time, Accra continued to attract migrant laborers, both from the centuries-old community of circulating laborers who moved between trading ports and coastal cities, and among young men and women in rural areas looking to break from tradition and access wealth through opportunities and promises of city life.[55] Facing housing shortages and high prices, many residents erected corrugated iron structures as a form of temporary housing. These structures were frequent targets of building inspectors who sent warnings and approved notices for demolition because, within public health guidelines, these structures were a danger to the health of the community. "Swish" structures were also frequently targeted for citations, fines, and demolition. The housing shortages and congestion were exacerbated by ongoing property seizures and demolitions in which owners were rendered homeless when they were unable to pay taxes or violated building codes.

As African town councillors repeatedly pointed out, the need for these structures highlighted a fundamental contradiction between the ideal form enforced through regulation and the reality of resources on the ground. Many individuals were unable to afford to build the cement block houses called for in town building regulations—wages were too low, trade was too weak, and the cost of imported materials was too high. When Councillor Kitson Mills asked for the Town Council to suspend demolition of corrugated iron buildings "until the change for the better in present affairs and people could afford to put up substantial buildings," he recognized the health concerns raised by inspectors but argued that "the ruthless demolition of these shanties was causing more harm than good." He also asserted, "It would be far better for one to live in a shanty than to remain unprotected at the mercy of sun, wind and rain. There was another aspect to the situation the sanitary officers had lost sight of—congestion. All along, the authorities had been trying to avoid congestion, and it was an uncontested fact that when these shanties were demolished, the inmates were bound to seek shelter in the already congested areas."[56] Kitson Mills made similar arguments about "swish" buildings, calling for an amendment to the building regulations to allow for the construction of these buildings in Sabon Zongo because "the people are not in a position to put up cement block buildings owing to the prevailing depression."[57] Unlike the iron structures, there was considerable evidence to suggest that these mud and thatch structures could be healthy and climatically appropriate structures. As Kojo Thompson noted, experts at Achimota Training College had successfully completed an experiment with swish buildings.[58] The Basel Mission Church in Osu used swish buildings to house European staff with no ill health effects, and Ga people had lived to an old age in swish houses for centuries with no problems. Other African councillors echoed Kitson Mills's appeals throughout the 1930s to no avail. The medical officer and other European councillors argued that migrants would not invest in properly built homes due to their temporary status. Furthermore, following Simpson's recommendations from 1908, the medical officer argued that swish buildings "harboured rats, termites, and other pests, and that after these houses had been built, dangerous borrow pits were left."[59] The state would continue to demolish temporary structures that contravened the building codes: making an exception at this point would be "a retrograde step in the development of the town."[60] But importantly, while they were having ongoing discussions about a proposal for a "housing scheme," the government had consistently been unable and unwilling to allocate funds to construct new houses or provide funds and support for dispossessed peoples. Faced with competing priorities, European town councillors, who were in the majority, and other British officials directed the limited available funds to developing European residential areas in the interests of health and safety; meanwhile, African neighborhoods continued to decay as a result of underinvestment and overuse. In strictly adhering to the building regulations, these officials effectively produced the very "slum" conditions they decried.

DISASTER MANAGEMENT AND SLUM CLEARANCE

In light of these persistent housing issues, disasters presented both challenges and opportunities for urban governance. Simpson's public health guide provided a framework for disease-related interventions that served as a planning handbook for early colonial officers. Early colonial policies and investments focused on the development of segregated neighborhoods like Victoriaborg and Ridge, which grew quickly in the first few decades of the twentieth century with the construction of both government buildings and European bungalows. Older neighborhoods like Jamestown and Ussher Town remained relatively unchanged in terms of major infrastructure works or construction projects, even as the populations of those neighborhoods grew and spilled over into new developments like Sabon Zongo. The 1894 fire was an opportunity in the minds of colonial administrators who quickly drew up proposals to replan the cleared area with a widened street and a new layout of houses and other buildings. Disease epidemics in 1908, 1911, and 1918 also provided cover for more aggressive interventions, including the demolition of houses and the resettlement of certain populations.[61] New neighborhoods emerged in the context of crisis—Korle Gono, most notably, in response to the plague.[62] While the colonial government seemed to eagerly embrace Simpson's advice and began a campaign of reconstruction around the harbor at Jamestown, the energy quickly waned as finances were redirected to more urgent projects, often dedicated to the improvement of European neighborhoods, government buildings, or trade infrastructure.

The earthquake that devastated Accra marked both a continuation and a radical departure from these earlier disasters. This was not, of course, the first time that an earthquake had devastated the city. The region had a history of well-documented earthquakes, including two particularly severe events in 1862 and 1906. The July 10, 1862 quake almost completely destroyed the city, as well as the areas around Weija due to unstable geological formations of sand and clay that were common in these areas. British officers writing from Accra in the aftermath of the earthquake noted that "there is not a whole stone house left, and our fine old castle is a wreck." While swish houses largely survived, "every stone house there (of which there is a considerable number and some very fine ones) is without exception irretrievably injured and damaged. The walls of all of them are split and cracked from the foundation to the roof; the verandahs are separated from the main walls; the partitions . . . were thrown down, and in many the roofs have fallen completely in."[63] One officer who had been stationed at the British garrison noted that the "whole of Accra"—including soldiers and officers—were "in tents or wood huts." He went on to say, "You won't find me living in a stone house on coast again for some time."[64] The damage to such sturdy and "fine" stone structures shocked Europeans on the coast, including the destruction of Christiansborg Castle, which then lay abandoned for several decades. In the midst of all of the rubble, a mud hut with a thatched roof seemed preferable to a tent, shack, or shed made out of the ruins of stone buildings.

More than seventy years later, informed in part by Simpson's vision of disease control and public health through planning as well as increasingly racialized notions of architecture and spatial development, colonial officials seemed to have forgotten the lessons of the last disaster. Building regulations that mandated the use of cement block in construction left little room for alternative materials or designs. When the earthquake struck Accra on the evening of June 22, 1939, an enormous section of the town was destroyed. Twenty-two people died, and another hundred or more sustained serious injuries. Government buildings and the city's waterworks were damaged, but the most urgent issue was housing. Thousands of homes were destroyed and tens of thousands of residents were left homeless, sheltering first in temporary accommodations under tables, market sheds, and shacks constructed out of rubble. Soldiers built temporary grass huts and railway workers opened up goods carriages to house displaced residents. Tremors continued for several weeks, inhibiting repair work,[65] but the governor, Sir Arnold Hodson, quickly mobilized labor and addressed the more urgent challenges. Electricity and water were restored, and repairs on government buildings proceeded quickly, as did temporary housing for the dispossessed. As Assistant Colonial Secretary Harold Cooper wrote in the *Times*, "The immediate problem may now be regarded as solved. Temporary shelter has been found for all refugees. But there remains the vastly more difficult problem of the rebuilding of Accra. [Governor Hodson] was to provide new homes for these people, the majority of whom are too poor to build again on their own account?"[66]

In writing to the Colonial Office in London, Hodson immediately and eagerly seized on the possibilities that the earthquake presented. Widespread destruction meant that the city's residents *needed* government assistance. The scale of the damage meant that large sections of the city could be cleared and rebuilt along new lines. Geologists and seismologists suggested that the government might consider moving the capital some distance outside of Accra in order to minimize the chances of future damage from inevitable earthquakes.[67] But for Hodson, this catastrophe meant that the "slum clearance schemes" that had "long been on the mind of government" might actually be achievable. Plans that had been drawn up in preparation for this "slum clearance" in Accra years before were now abandoned—layouts for communities on the outskirts of town—West of Accra, adjoining Korle Bu and Korle Gono, at Kaneshie to the northwest, at Adabraka to the north, and to the north and east of Christiansborg. Hodson's strategy sought to use earthquake relief as a sort of urban development Trojan horse. In reality, this project to transform Accra into a model city was actually made up of two plans: the first, for rehousing residents who were dispossessed by the earthquake, and the second, for other residents who lived in congested areas.[68] Hodson called for the construction of an initial set of temporary structures for immediate relief, which would later be demolished to make way for more permanent structures.

Hodson's dreams of a new city were tempered by technocratic officers who urged the government to invest in practical construction in order to avoid waste and future loss. As Gold Coast seismologist N. R. Junner argued, "From a study of the damage done to buildings and other structures in and near Accra it is clear that the damage and concomitant loss of life and injury to persons would have been much less if the design and construction of buildings—small and large alike—had been simpler and better." Ornamentation and decoration (ornamental facades, columns, parapets, balustrades, copings, towers, gables, etc.), often utilized in construction by owners to convey status, became dangerous in the earthquake, leading to injury and deaths among the population and damage to buildings. While these architectural features had figured prominently in European observations about the fine stone houses in the city, according to Junner, "Stricter control and supervision of the design and construction of all buildings other than single-storey, inferior-type buildings is advocated, and the following facts, based largely on the experience gained in regions subject to severe earthquakes, should be taken into account when permanent re-building of Accra is being considered":

a) A building should be of simple design and ornamentation with all the parts well tied together, and should be so rigidly constructed that it will move as a whole in an earthquake.
b) Buildings should be as nearly square and as low as is conveniently possible. Square buildings are more suitable than long buildings because the direction of the earthquake waves cannot be predicted and because they afford the best opportunity for symmetrical bracing.
c) The foundations of substantial buildings resting on clay, silt, sand and soft earth should be particularly strong and rigid, as the amplitude of seismic vibrations in this type of ground may be large. Deep foundations are also preferable for large buildings as the movements caused by the earthquake are usually much greater at the surface than they are at a depth of 10–20 feet. Where the underlying material is sand, silt or mud the foundations of large buildings should be in the form of a strong concrete raft. Suyehiro has shown that in earthquakes in Tokyo the movement of a rigid building on a massive foundation block may be much smaller than the movements of the underlying sand, silt or mud.
d) All unnecessary ornamental work and additions to buildings should be avoided.
e) Walls should be light and strong. Arches, windows, and doors are sources of weakness in walls. The use of arches is not to be recommended and windows should be as small and as few as conveniently possible.
f) Roofs should be light and rigid and should not be steeply inclined.
g) The piers of buildings and bridges may be a great source of weakness unless they are soundly constructed. In seismic areas arched piers should not be used and all piers of important structures should be constructed to withstand an acceleration of at least three feet per second from any direction;

in other words the width at the base of the pier should be at least one-tenth of the height of the pier. Tapered piers are advisable in seismic areas and stronger cement may be used near the base of a pier.

h) Well constructed wooden buildings will oscillate greatly but will withstand anything but a very severe earthquake unless they are built on unconsolidated materials.
i) Good-quality building materials and workmanship are essential.
j) Inferior-quality buildings should not be of more than one storey.[69]

Outside of the governor's office, British officials expressed cynicism and skepticism about Hodson's dreams of a "permanent scheme" for the "new Accra." As one officer noted, "On the information given us it might be anything from the 'really first class town' of Sir Arnold Hodson's dream to an eruption of bungalows not unlike the environs of the Slough Housing Estate." Having seen these dreams wither before, more seasoned officers were hesitant to dive into a plan that would ultimately falter before the "permanent" vision was realized, leaving the town with a series of unsightly and poorly constructed "temporary" accommodations that would never be improved.[70] Others, like GLM Ransom, feared that "the earthquake has made it almost impossible for us to put the check on this wild governor than would otherwise have been desirable." Even so, he noted, "We should do our best."[71]

Coming late to the project, technical officers worked quickly to clarify the financial costs of the project and brought in Major Orde Browne, an ethnographer and linguist with expertise on labor conditions in East Africa, to consult on the project.[72] The notion of temporary structures were immediately abandoned as a waste of money. Instead, engineers insisted, small houses could be built at equal cost and later expanded in response to owner demand. People displaced by the earthquake would be placed into these houses and allowed to live there for free for a defined period of time, after which they would be allowed to purchase their houses through a hire-purchase arrangement, paying back the government for the cost of construction plus interest. Other details, however, they believed, would be the source of conflict. In making plans, local officers turned not to community members or even Town Council representatives to assess needs and preferences. Instead, they pointed to other examples—from Port of Spain in Trinidad to Belize to Japan to the Slough Housing Estate in the UK—and called on government to bring in additional specialized technical advisers with experience in town planning but little to no direct experience in Accra. In considering the design and materials used for the houses, for example, Orde Browne noted:

> Details of the houses are not available, but it is to be hoped that these will not be prejudice by too great attention to economy; For instance, a lining to the iron roofs, and some sort of composition, will make a great difference to the comfort

of the occupants; instances have occurred in East Africa where laborers have refused to occupy houses with unlined iron roofs. Alternatively, there are various composition sheets which replace corrugated iron; they are rather more expensive, but last far better, particularly in a tropical sea climate, and they require no painting. The improvement in the temperature of the building which attends their use is, of course, immense.[73]

Similar sorts of observations were made about communal kitchens, which had been unpopular in Gambia. In order to avoid "family quarrels" and support "the resultant contentment of the housewife," government officials agreed to construct separate iron structures behind each building to serve as a kitchen. Communal bathrooms seemed to elicit no such concern, but officials did emphasize the importance of gardens and recreational areas, as well as markets and other public amenities. Planning the town was just as important as constructing the houses in order to advance new visions of ordered urban living and prevent the reemergence of "slums."

If, in July 1939, Governor Hodson did not "envisage any difficulty in turning Accra into a really first class town," the realities of what that plan would and could look like changed dramatically with the beginning of the Second World War. Hodson had promised that interest payments would be to the government's advantage as part of the scheme; however, the conflict placed a strain on both financial and material resources available for development projects. Government was responsible for the provision of roads, electricity, and water infrastructure, but those developments were delayed because materials and equipment could not be delivered. Once Italy entered the war, the Gold Coast could no longer work with Italian contractors to complete the project, and the limited remaining building materials and manpower was needed to build facilities for the military. As Hodson noted, "At the present time the demands of the Services must have priority over civil requirements.... Financially too, the present moment is inopportune for embarking upon further expenditure on buildings which are, strictly speaking, not essential for the welfare of the public."[74] Instead, Hodson proposed to use the remaining funds to complete essential infrastructure projects and convert a small number of "temporary" structures into upgraded, permanent buildings in order to guarantee some income; he also needed to demonstrate that the government continued to embrace the possibilities and seriousness of the longer-term vision.[75] Secretary of State Malcolm Maxwell, however, construed the pause as another opportunity:

> I know that before the war it was your desire to turn the disaster of the earthquake to good advantage by the rebuilding of the town in a manner worthy of the capital of one of the larger British colonies. The war may make any large scale building program impracticable for the present. At the same

time, the very fact that rapid development is impracticable may make the present moment a particularly propitious one for working out an up-to-date town planning scheme, and for taking any legislative or administrative action that may be necessary for its eventual carrying out. I shall be happy to be of any assistance I can to you in this matter which, as I am sure you will agree, is one of considerable importance.[76]

Waiting, in other words, allowed government to design a truly comprehensive plan that was backed by state power.

HOUSING DEVELOPMENT

Hodson admitted that, in the aftermath of the earthquake, plans were prepared quickly and were not always as meticulous as they could have been, resulting in endless revisions and modifications. Yet Hodson remained noticeably disappointed in admitting that the plan needed to be drawn back considerably. African communities were also disappointed in the end result. As Hodson himself noted, further surveys of damage in the town showed that more higher-end housing was necessary than officials originally anticipated. Africans who had invested in the building standards prescribed in British regulations found themselves relegated to substandard housing stock, left to fend for themselves in restoring their former houses.[77] And yet, even if this vision of a new town was, once again, unrealized, 1939 marked a major turning point in the colonial state's approach to urban development; it was part of a broader shift in British imperial policy from "trusteeship" to "development."[78] In the Gold Coast this work was prefigured by the interventions of Governor Gordon Guggisberg, who invested heavily in infrastructure and social services throughout the colony. However, many of Guggisberg's investments were targeted at rural development—strategic investments in education and infrastructure that he believed would encourage widespread development, decelerate urbanization, and improve self-sufficiency in the colony. As sites of danger and bad influence, cities—and the accelerating rate of urbanization—were considered more of a challenge than an opportunity before the war. The earthquake, however, shaped a new kind of language around urban development. Colonial officers acknowledged the challenge ahead. In discussions about the earthquake rehousing, Eastwood noted that:

> I do not want to cavil at a scheme which, as far as a layman can judge, looks broadly alright, but I must confess that I'm a bit appalled by our helplessness in dealing with schemes of this kind. Here are proposals for the expenditure of large sums of money which will permanently affect the amenities and conditions of life in one of our major colonies and we have no expert knowledge on which to draw for advice whether the proposals are soundly conceived. If it

were a question of engineering we should go to the ground agents; if it were one of health or labor we have advisors on those subjects. But the present question covers a wider field than any of those subjects, though they all of them enter into it, and we have no one who is a real expert on it to whom we can turn for advice. This question of housing in the layout of towns is one which is going to be of increasing importance.[79]

Eastwood's concerns, however, were soon addressed. While the war scuttled Hodson's grand plans and hampered direct investment in the early 1940s, by the end of the war the Colonial Office was funneling unprecedented amounts of money and staff into new town planning initiatives in Accra and throughout the British Empire. The war further exacerbated urbanization, placing extraordinary strain on cities like Accra and creating a new urgency around urban housing development in the colonies.

Governor Alan Burns wrote to the Colonial Office in 1944 requesting £800,000, spread over four years, for a new rehousing and slum clearance scheme in various Gold Coast towns. The war, once again, prevented progress on the project; however, Burns wrote in January 1944, "I propose to push on with the work as soon as circumstances permit." The plan involved the design, building, management, and administration of government housing estates—the latter, the governor noted, to ensure that standards for government housing were maintained and rents were collected in a timely fashion. In order to realize these plans, however, changes would have to be made, Burns argued. Local government was not currently equipped to plan and manage housing estates. The governor created a new housing department with its own director and called for the establishment of new local housing authorities, which would work with the community and the local government to advise management. This new centralized approach—a clear department from previous practices that involved a wide range of offices including the Labor Department, Public Works, Lands and Medical Departments, the Town and Country Planning Board, local political administration and the Town Council—would allow for better control of the process and encourage research and experiments in construction. As Burns noted: "I feel that on general social grounds, apart from particular causes such as the spread of tuberculosis, the provision of improved housing for the people, by methods that will both ensure and demonstrate the permanent value of the work, as if such importance that it cannot be left to the present uncoordinated machinery and that it requires a special department to deal with it."[80] Burns's plans coincided with the appointment of Maxwell Fry, a well-regarded British modernist architect, as town planning adviser for British West Africa in 1944 who, with his wife Jane Drew, quickly began to assess the form and function of the towns of the colony, including Accra.

This was not the first time that housing development and town planning had been considered in Accra. In addition to the large-scale rehousing and urban reform proposals that emerged in the wake of disease and natural disaster (the earthquake, for example), the government had invested in housing developments in European residential areas like Victoriaborg, Christiansborg, Ridge, Cantonments, and Ringway Estates in the 1910s and 1920s as well as newer African neighborhoods like Adabraka. The Public Works Department had established plans and construction practices for various classes of bungalow, as well as barracks and other communal housing for lower-level state employees. However, the government lacked significant experience or adequate standards for constructing African housing.[81] As Fry noted in his survey of existing housing: "Government housing in West Africa for Africans, with the notable exception as parts of the Accra rehousing schemes for which the emergency they were intended to meet is a justification, is of low standard but relatively high cost, being built in permanent materials. The problem of raising the standard of accommodation while keeping within an economic rent is one that must be approached from various angles and will be solved by the efforts of many people working over a series of years."[82] New standards for African housing, he argued, were needed, including adequate living and sleeping space, kitchens in or near the house, private latrines and washing facilities, verandas, security, lockable storage of various types, and space for a garden and an area for children to play. Even as Fry advocated for higher standards, he acknowledged that single-room dwellings with shared kitchens and latrines would still be necessary for lower-waged workers. The gap between the cost of housing development and the reality of low African wages meant that government could not provide the high-quality housing that Fry recommended without a significant subsidy—one that they were not prepared to provide.

Fry was fairly ruthless in his assessment of existing colonial housing stock. In African communities, housing development had largely been "reactive" in its response to disaster and disease and stood in sharp contrast to the more intentionally planned and provisioned European neighborhoods.[83] In the Gold Coast he felt that money had been wasted on unnecessarily long access roads, an excessive focus on larger houses, and a disregard for the terrain. Echoing criticisms by African town councillors a decade before, he also argued that the high building standards set for the center of town made it impossible for African property owners to maintain their buildings and that standards should be relaxed in order to maintain the town's appearance.[84] Instead of trying to force everyone to meet the same high standards set out in regulation, available housing should reflect the range of income levels of the individuals living in the town, and the integration of these different housing types would avoid the development of "low-class"

Figure 5.1. Older housing stock in planned neighborhoods in Accra. Street Scenes, 1955. Source: Photographic Archive, Information Services Office, Ministry of Information, Accra R/2200/2.

neighborhoods or slums in segregated areas of the town. Community buildings and other essential social infrastructure like schools and churches would allow the city's diverse population to interact, facilitating social cohesion.[85] In looking around, however, Fry was also uninspired by African building methods. He claimed that there was not "any architecture worthy of the name, nor any background of architecture."[86] Traditional African architecture resembled "that of architecture in the dark ages in Europe"[87] and was "unsuitable for the development of a modern civilization."[88] In response, Fry proposed a series of standard designs—a "typical labourers compound," single-room houses, two- and three-room self-contained and terrace style houses, and mixed development housing estates—for Accra and other cities in Ghana.[89]

Fry's approach echoed new policy orientations in the Colonial Office. Building additional housing would help alleviate the pressures of rapid urbanization during the war, but construction could also serve as a form of economic development, introducing new kinds of industries and crafts into colonies: from the production of cement blocks to the provision of water and electricity. Despite Fry's assessment that African construction materials were unsophisticated and unsuitable for modern living, the war made it difficult to transfer Colonial Development and Welfare Act funds from Britain and disrupted trade, necessitating the incorporation of local construction methods and expertise; factors like these forced architects to rethink some of Fry's assumptions about design and construction.[90] These realities were further complicated by the low wages of many Africans. While Accra did have a larger number of wealthy and middle-class African residents (as compared with colonial cities of settler colonies in East and Southern Africa, for example) who were able to construct and maintain impressively elaborate houses, income inequalities were significant. Many workers in the city found themselves unable to afford even a single room, and the most vulnerable migrant workers often lived "in the streets," sleeping in doorways, verandas, and market stalls at night.[91] The value (and cost) of housing in segregated residential areas reflected these unequal opportunities. The description of housing that Acquah provided in Accra in the 1950s likely also applied to the range of housing options available in the 1940s:

> At one extreme there is an imposing home of an African professional man, built on the pattern of an English country mansion having spacious and well-kept gardens and all the modern comforts and conveniences available. At the other extreme are metal sheeting or swish huts devoid of floor covering, many of which are in an advanced state of dilapidation. These lack amenities of light, water and sanitation. Between these two extremes is a variety of swish, wooden, concrete and brick buildings of varying size and quality. Rooms differ considerably in the space they provide and the circulation of air they allow. In Adabraka and other suburbs, windows are usually large and ceilings relatively high. In Ussher Town and in the other old parts of the municipality, windows are usually small and ceilings low. Consequently, households who occupy only one room in Adabraka or the other suburbs have a healthier environment than those occupying one room in Ussher Town irrespective of the floor space. Buildings in the old parts are packed close together. Except for the main highways, streets or lanes are narrow. There are no gardens. On housing estates and in the new suburban areas, houses stand in plots of land which allow for gardens, but the space is usually left as dry earth or concreted. It does, however, provide a place for children to play, whereas in the older parts they are usually obliged to play on the streets and near the gutters.[92]

While government investment had been higher in many of these European areas, cost was often lower for European residents whose rents were heavily subsidized by the government. The value of land in planned neighborhoods was also significantly higher than in the old town quarters, further exacerbating income inequalities.[93]

In order to implement Fry's plans, the government passed a new Town and Country Planning Ordinance in 1945, which sought to clarify responsibility and authority for town planning. Based on examples from Trinidad, the new ordinance called for a Town and Country Planning Board, which was composed of "a president appointed by the governor, the heads of the medical, public works and lands departments or their representatives and not less than too nor more than four other members appointed by the Governor."[94] The board was required to meet with the relevant town council and native authority before presenting any proposed schemes to the governor and Legislative Council. The board could also appoint a planning committee to prepare planning schemes and were empowered to survey land and execute schemes approved by the governor. Importantly, this new ordinance allowed the board to seize lands when the owners refused to purchase them and expanded rights to "betterment" from and compensation for the owners of properties whose property values were impacted as a result of planning and housing development.[95]

MODERNISM AND TOWN PLANNING

In 1946, Fry described the state of Accra in the journal *African Affairs*:

> There is a large old-established reservation and open space on one side of the town; on the other, the rapidly expanding residential area. As things are going at the moment, houses with jut along the entrance roads from Accra and elsewhere, in ribbon development, and the town will become most unbalanced with a large spread in one direction and a big gap in the other, so that public service of every kind have to be cut and run at a loss. ... Accra is a town like Freetown. During the war, its water and electric services have had to do double work, and it has surprised me that they have managed to go on working at all. Town is developing rapidly and the need for housing is felt every where. Any knowledge of rents is never very accurate, and it is difficult to obtain information because the records are few, but we know that Africans are paying very large sums for terrible accommodation in Accra, for they cannot go too far outside to find new houses. So here the problem is very largely a housing—and we found certain things already prepared for us. The terrain is a series of undulating hills, valleys and marches and watercourses, and these have been used to introduce a water system.[96]

Figure 5.2. Modern terraced houses in Accra. Aerial Views of Accra, 1994. Photograph by Iddi Braimah. Source: Photographic Archive, Information Services Office, Ministry of Information, Accra PD/802/10.

These challenges prompted a new plan for the town, both in terms of its organization—a new ring road and new housing developments laid out around the European sections of town, widened roads, new parkways—and the construction of houses for its residents. Fry applauded the work of Mr. Alcock, the chief engineer in Kumasi, who had been carrying out a number of experiments on housing developments.[97]

These new plans were part of the expanding influence of modernism on architecture and town planning in British colonies. Fry and Drew established themselves early as leaders in this emerging field through their work as Accra town planning advisers and architects in the Gold Coast. Committed to modernist principles that privileged "the integration of formal and functional requirements with environment so as to develop specific expression of purpose and structure mediated by an abstract aesthetic capable of multiple rather than singular ... responses,"[98] they fully embraced the power of modernism to shape the future.[99] As a "major instrument of government," town planning could help ensure a more equitable form of urban development and lay the foundation for future development toward independence.[100] Fry and Drew's ideas—like those of other architects of the period—were both inherently imperial and wholly independent.[101] Members of the Architectural Association (AA), located in central London, were at the forefront of the new "international" movement embodied in the Congress Internationale d'Architecture Moderne (CIAM). But they also had close working relationships with the School of Hygiene and Tropical Medicine, as well as their own experiences working in the colonies. Fry himself had spent part of his national service in the Gold Coast before being hired as a town planning adviser.[102]

Fry and Drew are often remembered today for their embrace of vernacular architectural styles and their insistence on adapting modernist principles to the conditions of the "tropics." For the most part, this strategy reflected a keen interest in the relationship between climate, environment, and architecture. Their approach—later termed "tropical architecture"—sought to use design to address the comfort levels of those living in warm, humid climates. Passive cooling, ventilation, and air flow were all critical concerns for those working in "tropical architecture." However, they were often equally noted for their consideration of sociocultural conditions—in both urban and rural areas—in shaping housing designs and town plans. Drew, in particular, was highly respected for her perceived rapport with local peoples. While they initially followed other colonial technocrats and municipal leaders in rejecting the compound house (or *agbonaa*) as an "unfathomable" way to organize living arrangements, Fry began to question that decision as early as 1947.[103] By the early 1950s, they had embraced an approach to design and planning that emphasized "first, people and their needs; second, climate and its attendant ills; and third, materials in the means of building."[104] The compound, they argued, provided a local model of the modernist idea of the "free plan," which was both socially and culturally relevant and, when constructed well, appropriate for the climate. Local workmen, they acknowledged, were exceptionally adaptable and skilled.[105]

In villages they were even more straightforward in their embrace of local building practices. Echoing the ideas of a Mr. Frank Samuel, Fry criticized the high cost of building in cities and argued that "in the village, where there was space, [Africans] were allowed to pursue their own ideas; building almost entirely from the local materials available the villager was able to build himself a reasonably spacious house—it certainly required replacing fairly frequently, but he could do it by his own labor, helped by his family, at virtually no cost at all."[106] In cities, Fry and Drew called for more affordable building materials and the relaxation of regulatory standards in order to improve affordability and increase class diversity in neighborhoods. And in their educational and commercial commissions, they sought to account for local conditions in ways that both ordered social and spatial relationships and allowed for flexibility and growth, testing some of the assumptions of modernism.[107]

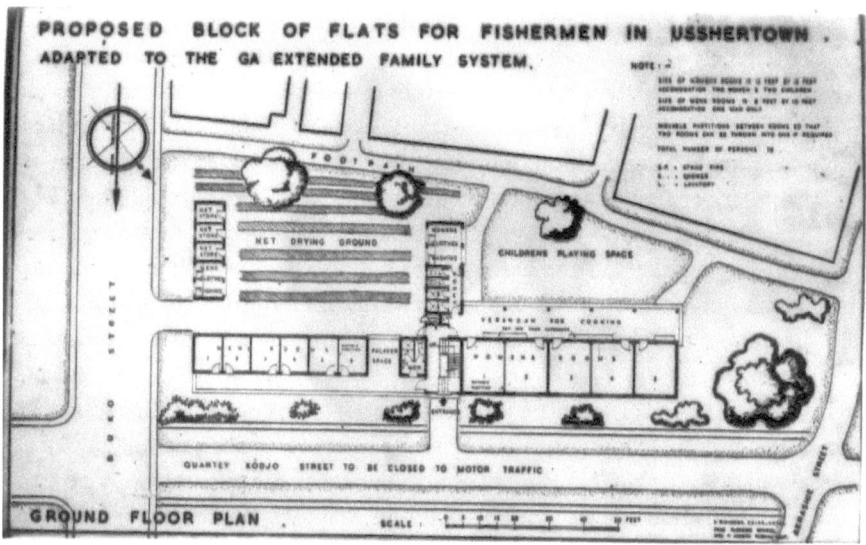

Figure 5.3. Model of Proposed Block of Flats for Fishermen, Usshertown, Accra, 1953. Source: Photographic Archive, Information Services Office, Ministry of Information, Accra G/307/1.

And yet, as Ola Uduku argues, Fry and Drew's approach was shaped through an understanding of architecture through a "them" (those being built for) and "us" (those who were designing the buildings) frame.[108] Their work "presupposed a European-Western supremacy over local knowledge and local architectural tradition"[109] and called for the import of expertise, ideas, and forms to enhance local living.[110] In *Tropical Architecture* they praised the role of architecture in bringing about "new community life based less on family and communal sanctions, since the new division of labor must be accepted as a necessary element of westernized production, by introducing new skills and crafts by means of which self-respect and personal dignity may be restored."[111] "Once more mankind is on the move towards new objectives, and people who for centuries have lived under the shadow of one or another form of surveillance now undertake the management of their own destinies and shoulder the compelling responsibilities of government."[112] Modernism provided a tool with which African communities could transition to political and cultural independence—neither "African" nor "colonial" but "modern."[113] Housing was central to this project. As Fry argued, "The needs of the family are expressed first in the dwelling itself and then as an extension from the dwelling in terms of paths and roads, markets, shops, recreation, etc."[114] "Ideal Home" exhibits communicated similar ideas in the domestic sphere. Modern technologies, modern methods, modern clothing, modern living was the future.¹¹⁵ Like other architects working during the period, Fry and Drew believed in the power of modernist architecture and planning to "rationalize the use of space and regulate social life," and they eagerly put those principles to work in advancing late colonial development priorities to improve living standards, public welfare, and environmental protection.¹¹⁶ They were part of a transnational network of architects, planners, and technocrats, both through the CIAM and through the networks of empire. Information, data, people, and ideas flowed not only between Europe and the colonies but also between different colonies, through conferences and professional networks, Colonial Office postings, laws and directives, and the circulation of research through scholarly and colonial publications.¹¹⁷

In attempting to consider the local context, Drew argued that they sought "to design in a way which, without in any sense copying African detail, gives a response which is African."¹¹⁸ This presumed neutrality or aculturality is a defining feature of plans themselves. As Bissell argues, "In their final incarnation, plans and maps take on a form of appearance that nowhere reflects their processes that brought them into being or their eventual impact on the city. In retrospect, they may seem nothing less than coherent and compelling—every bit the rationalizing and modernizing instruments of urban reform they claim to be."¹¹⁹ Planning was ultimately driven by the tangible, physical, and material. Proper policies and procedures would provide the illusion of order and control; even as plans repeatedly failed, officials sought new and better regulations, organized in a "town plan" that would both ward against the "sickness that overtakes those who live in unbalanced urban conditions"¹²⁰ and provide an overarching view of and guidebook for the future. Like the colonial officials described by Bissell, Fry and Drew were unable to fully see the problems with the system in which they operated.¹²¹ Despite their efforts to create new institutions to train local architects in the Gold Coast/Ghana and elsewhere, "African architecture" included very few African voices or perspectives, and non-African "modernist" paradigms continued to be predominant in architectural and planning education in the Gold Coast and beyond.¹²² However, hesitation about the new plan was widespread. While Fry argued that "the exhibition of the Accra plan showed that there is plenty of goodwill among all classes of people," it was clear that ongoing engagement was necessary and that property owners would need to be persuaded to follow the plan by rebuilding or setting back their property lines with little or no compensation beyond the benefits and long-term security that would accrue from being part of a "good plan."¹²³ Africans quickly reframed many of the aesthetic features of the tropical architecture style. "Social life," Margaret Peil noted several decades later, "is not centered on a set of rooms but on the space outside them."¹²⁴ Balconies, hallways, and other "public" areas were frequently repurposed for other uses.¹²⁵ Residents in Sabon Zongo adapted the grid plan to better reflect the spatial and social requirements of their spiritual practice.[126] Families in Tema Manhean refused to relocate to new housing estates. Implementing the plan was clearly going to be a very different—and more contentious—process than the work of imagining it.

Fry and Drew's plan for ordered growth in Accra, released in a 1945 report, centered on the construction of a ring of settlements radiating out from the city center, connected by a new ring road, as well as a new government center, which would be both a site of new monuments and a center of circulation for the increasingly traffic-congested city. This infrastructure planning would lay the groundwork for slum clearance and large-scale redevelopment to take place in Jamestown and Ussher Town. Open areas were to be preserved, and new neighborhoods were to be developed with their own local centers in mind, complete with community buildings, markets, clinics, recreation areas, and schools. The area covered would house a population of 250,000 with an average density of thirty-five persons per acre. Keeping the plan compact would make service provision more financially feasible for the Town Council.[127]

These were, in many ways, issues that government could control. By contrast, Fry argued, "Control over the appearance of the center of the town is [a] problem not easy of solution."[128] Convincing business owners of "the benefits of good architecture" was critical to enforcing some standards on the main streets of the town, but planning the entire town was impossible. Regulation and standardization, he argued, were the solution.[129] By investing in new town centers that could provide a model, the planners hoped to positively influence others to come in line. Within residential neighborhoods, Fry and Drew focused on community planning. The complicated web of activities in the town was directly related to the needs of the family, they argued. Slums and poverty were the result of the government's failure to satisfy these needs or other forms of strain on the capacity of the family. Self-sufficiency required self-contained communities that could provide for families' needs. If government wanted individuals and families to embrace new modern lifestyles and standards, they had to make those standards and resources attainable. Government had to simultaneously step back and take charge.[130] In order to make the most rapid impact on the lives of residents, Fry proposed a prioritized list:

1. Erection of new government and municipal offices
2. Improvement of existing and construction of proposed main thoroughfares
3. Slum clearance and rehousing at Jamestown and Ussher Town
4. Extension of markets
5. Construction of marine drive and improvement of the foreshore
6. Construction of the sports stadium[131]

Implementing these proposals would require courage, but, as he argued, it also "depends in the last resort on the people's will." In light of limited resources, however, "haphazard development" was a luxury that the government simply could not afford.[132]

NATIONALISM AND HOUSING

Government quickly went to work operationalizing the recommendations of his report. Fry requested that an ad hoc town planning committee be formed in 1944, which included members of the ATC (F.C. Lander, Richard Akwei, V.B. Annan, and K. Adumua-Bossman), the town engineer (A.T. Flutter), and the medical officer of health.[133] In 1945, the Legislative Council passed the new Town and Country Planning Ordinance, which was to take a "broader view of planning ... orderly and progressive development of land, town and other areas, whether urban or rural to preserve and improve the amenities thereof and other matters connected therewith."[134] Upon the passage of the ordinance, the governor ordered that planning areas be declared in Cape Coast and Accra.[135] In 1945 the Colonial Office approved a massive rehousing program for the Gold Coast, at the cost of £800,000, to create new government housing estates and establish a new housing department.[136] By 1946, the acting colonial secretary noted that the Accra Planning Committee was using Fry's report to inform an intensive planning process.[137]

After the war, however, residents grew increasingly frustrated by the obvious gaps between planning visions and realistic implementation. Residents who were paying rent on the "temporary buildings" that had been erected in new government housing estates after the 1939 earthquake began agitating for the realization of the "permanent" housing scheme they had been promised after the earthquake. In January 1948, in response to the government's failure to act, residents began refusing to pay rent. Chiefs appealed to colonial officials to allow residents to purchase their properties, even in this "temporary" state, so that they could complete the improvements themselves. Government officials refused, however, arguing that the temporary structures needed better roofs that and private sale would almost certainly guarantee a return to "slum conditions," even as they continued to refuse to invest in the permanent housing scheme.[138] Chiefs like Nii Ayikai II, the Akumajay Mantse, also called out government for not realizing promises made upon executing deeds for land. Ayikai sued the government to regain control of land that had been deeded for public use, arguing that government had failed to erect buildings on the property and thus violated the terms of the lease.[139] Ayikai's case generated enormous attention in Accra and seemed to mobilize anticolonial resentment across social and economic categories. These kinds of complaints highlighted the persistence of land challenges and the inability or unwillingness of the state to make good on its promises of investment and "development." As Enoch noted in the *West African Monitor* in the same year, "British government, therefore, have now voted large sums of money for colonial development. It is not a development in the interest of the natives. No. It is a vote for making the colonies congenial by whatever scientific means possible to afford a permanent home for the surplus British population now that India, Burma, and Ceylon have closed their gates."[140] The unevenness of implementation and investment inspired significant and understandable cynicism among a wide swath of Accra's population who grew increasingly frustrated by the lack of opportunity.

These frustrations were amplified in the context of rapid urbanization after the war. The housing estates built in the aftermath of the earthquake, and mobilized further through the war, resulted in a considerably expanded municipality. New housing estates at Korle Gonno, Christiansborg, South Labadi, Kaneshie, Sabon Zongo, and Abossey Okai were made available to African residents through hire-purchase or rentals. Labadi was incorporated into the municipality in 1943. The Airport Residential and Cantonments neighborhoods expanded considerably during and after the war, largely through the construction of government, quasigovernment, and commercial bungalows and flats. However, Ioné Acquah's *Accra Survey* noted in the 1950s that "in spite of the houses built by Government, firms and private persons within the urban areas and beyond it, there is still an acute housing shortage with its attendant problems of high rentals and overcrowding."[141] Housing in the city was wide ranging in 1954—from imposing buildings in the style of an English country mansion to huts made out of metal sheeting or swish. Spatial arrangements, likewise, were widely diverse—from closely packed buildings in the old town quarters to the large plots of land on housing estates.[142] In 1952, Acquah notes, the town planning department classified almost all of the houses in Ussher Town as "poor."[143] This widespread spatial inequality—not to mention the economic concerns noted by the Coussey Commission—informed the discontent that spilled over into riots in 1948, and that discontent continued to simmer as new African leaders were elected in 1951. Like the technocrats before him, Kwame Nkrumah embraced some version of modernism as a tool for future development. Seeking to redress perceived gaps in colonial urban development and transform Accra into a modern capital city worthy of the "Black Star of Africa" that could be showcased on Independence Day, March 6, 1957, Prime Minister Kwame Nkrumah commissioned a new plan for the town and assembled a team led by B. A. W. Trevallion and Alan G. Hood.

Accra: A Plan for the Town, published in 1958, articulated a nationalist vision for the city, both in the built environment and through the forms of urban culture and urban experience that this built environment would make possible, echoing the discourses of "tropical architecture" and colonial development that circulated in the late 1930s and 1940s. Nate Plageman argues that in the years that immediately preceded independence major newspapers like the *Daily Graphic* served as important sites where the new nation and its future were imagine and where newspaper staff shaped discourses about the political, social, cultural, and economic possibilities of the nation-to-be.[144] In the pages of the *Graphic*, newspaper staff detailed Accra's "ever-changing face" through descriptions of infrastructural development, urban planning, and architectural design—descriptions that linked "Accra's physical environment to the colony's growing prospects of national independence."[145] In the process, he argued, newspaper staff projected an image of an independent, urban modernism that ignored the realities of many Gold Coast residents—including many of those living in Accra. But for these writers, new buildings and infrastructural development were "markers of progress" and signs that Accra had "come of age" as a city in and of the world.[146]

For some, built space and a well-planned town created modern citizens—an embrace of some of the core tenets of modernism. *Graphic* writers saw sanitation infrastructure as a means of creating a new citizenry that could bridge the dramatic inequalities characteristic of urban life through greater cleanliness.[147] Kwame Nkrumah, likewise, embraced this modernist rhetoric and encouraged the development of new structures and institutions that would convey a new vision of Ghana's capital and its citizens. New department stores like Kingsway would create "modern consumers," as Bianca Murillo argues, by placing the new Kingsway store in the middle of a major new thoroughfare (now known as Independence Avenue), Nkrumah sought to put "consumerism on display" in order to help "legitimize Ghana as a new nation and establish Accra as a desirable destination."[148] A new airline, steamship, and other forms of transport infrastructure, as well as hydroelectric dams and industrial manufacturing plants, sought to project a vision of the nation both at home and abroad. But for others, modernism was an experience. Highlife music and dance, cinema and film, fashion, and other expressions of urban life created a vision of cosmopolitan nationalism, which drew on global trends to articulate the aspirations, ideals, and values of local audiences: it was a form of modernism simultaneously elitist and populist, institutional and experiential, creating and created.

The Trevallion-Hood plan, then, seemed to embody both colonial-era reform and postcolonial aspiration for the growing city. Minister of Housing Inkumsah encouraged Accra residents to remember "the moral as well as the physical importance of clean, well-designed and efficiently maintained towns, and to ask all our citizens to remember that our daily environment means a very great deal to us." "In this age of material well-being, motor-cars and advertisements we are inclined to overlook spiritual and aesthetic factors and I ask every citizen of Ghana to consider the need for beauty in his town or village and to be insistent that everything in that town from the largest building to the smallest road sign or advertisement is designed in good taste in order that the result will be towns and villages worthy of our State and one of which posterity can be proud."[149] In doing so, he articulated a vision of urban planning as both infra/structure and experience. In revising the 1944, the authors, likewise, sought to integrate "local knowledge acquired in the recording of day-to-day development over the last twelve years, the rise in the standard of living, the greater importance of the motor vehicle and up-to-date techniques of planning"—producing a plan that was, at least tacitly, both local and global.[150] And, as Town Planning Adviser W. H. Barrett noted in the preface, the plan represented an extension of existing town planning—"a modest design to improve present conditions and to give scope for future development to be carried out in a manner fitting to the dignity of a capital city which is also practical and economically feasible."[151] This plan was not, in other words, a completely new vision for the city but rather a continuation and improvement upon the old, simultaneously capitalizing on the "present political buoyancy and enthusiasm of the public" for urban development and modernization while tempering expectations of a brand new capital city that would saddle the country with unrealistic financial burdens.[152]

The plan identified thirteen different categories of development (Communications, Open Space, Industry, Population and Housing, Commerce, Markets, Educational Facilities, Health Services, Cultural Requirements, Land Tenure and Compensation, Government Development, Services, Central Area Development), which would distinguish Accra as a "capital city" rather than an "industrial city"—a designation that the plan's authors say would be better applied to neighboring Tema with its deepwater port.[153] Accra, in other words, should not be the site of large-scale economic activity but, rather, a genteel city that projected state power and cultural sophistication. Attention and development efforts centered on the Central Business District—the quarter of a square mile enclosed by High Street, Kwame Nkrumah Avenue, Rowe Road, and Boundary Road—where some 75 percent of road users traveled to Tudu Lorry Park, the General Post Office, Kwame Nkrumah Avenue (South), High Street, Selwyn Market, Pagan Road, and the Supreme Court.

The plan made predictable recommendations about transportation infrastructure, sanitation, and other public projects, while projecting a pattern of urban growth over the next several decades. But the real vision for the city was shaped by the proposed "open space system" and the redevelopment of government sites in the center of town. The long coastal strip, which extended the length of the city, as well as "green wedges" that separated residential areas and provided urban residents with spaces for recreation and relaxation, were the most important elements to be retained from the original 1944 planning strategy. Trevallion and Hood argued that these green spaces must be cultivated and maintained in order to preserve the aesthetic value of the city's design, making Accra a more desirable place by creating "microclimates" of lower temperature within the city, providing recreation areas to serve the growing interest in sports among urban residents, ensuring the development of distinctive cultures within neighborhoods, and preventing the overdevelopment of residential areas (as exemplified by older neighborhoods like Jamestown and Ussher Town).[154] Particularly in the center of the city, open land was often sited on government property (ministerial properties, the Supreme Court). In some cases, this land was identified as shale, which was dangerous as a foundation for further building due to the risk of earthquakes. Protecting that property, however, also required careful cultivation and maintenance. Young men would not play football in a garden and traders would not hawk their wares on public lands if they were well-tended and if there were alternative accommodations provided, the authors argued.

If the "open space system" was a continuation and extension of colonial-era urban design and town planning, the redevelopment of the city center represented a more clearly delineated nationalist vision. In particular, the redevelopment of the central area would highlight the power and position of the newly independent government and mark Accra as an administrative, legislative, commercial, educational, and cultural center as well as a center of "communications" (both transport and information). The area would not change substantially—the city center already ordered activities into different zones or sectors. Rather, redevelopment would address what the plan's authors identified as "major failings of the central area at present": "the lack of imposing features in the form of civic squares and other open spaces in the commercial area, the low standard of design of the buildings, the presence of certain inappropriate uses of land and the inadequacy of the present road system and of facilities for car and lorry parking."[155] The most imposing and impressive sites like the Supreme Court and its surrounding gardens would be preserved and extended so as to "dominate the area." The new Aglionby Library, designed intentionally so as to not compete with the grandeur of the Supreme Court structure, would be joined by other major new sites of construction, including the Ghana Commercial Bank, the Law School and Law Library, a new Magistrates' Court, and a proposed Ministry of Information site (which was not, ultimately, built here). The area would also serve as the site for a new parliament complex, an International Conference Center, and other ministerial buildings (also ultimately sited much farther to the north).

Figure 5.4. High Street Scenes. Views in Pictures, 1975. Photograph by V.S. Katapu. Source: Photographic Archive, Information Services Office, Ministry of Information, Accra PS/1913/17.

While impressive as a symbol of the newly independent government's power, these plans for the modernization of Accra seemed to do little to address the real housing needs of its residents. In 1953 55 percent of households paid rent, and percentages were much higher in neighborhoods that were dominated by migrants. With the exception of Sabon Zongo, rent prices per room rose significantly as one moved from the old town center into new residential developments. In migrant neighborhoods like Sabon Zongo where many residents lived on meager wages, individuals rented dwellings that were "unauthorized structures of swish, metal sheeting and wood."[156] While these individuals struggled in the face of high rents, army officers, European commercial employees, wealthy Syrian and Lebanese traders, and government workers often paid subsidized fees for rent and utilities.[157] These contradictions rankled in light of government rhetoric about "self-help." While focused primarily on rural housing development, films like *Mr. Mensah Builds a House* (1955) produced by the Gold Coast Film Unit sought to instill a new ethic around housing construction in the country. Created on behalf of the Ministry of Housing, the Information Services Department used cinema vans to screen the film in communities around the country, complemented by practical demonstrations by government departments, as well as photographs, pictures, and booklets.[158] Educational films like *Mr. Mensah* and *The Boy Kumasenu*[159] warned of the dangers of the city, the risks of irresponsible use of money, and the dangers of trusting disreputable people. When Mr. Mensah's irresponsible nephew wastes all of his money and materials by drinking, buying his girlfriend expensive gifts, and gambling at the track, Mensah faces a crisis. Having retired from his job as a shopkeeper, Mensah and his wife pack up their belongings and travel to their new rural home—only to find that the building is incomplete. However, an African government worker who happens to be on site provides Mensah with an opportunity—a new Department of Rural Housing will help him complete his house as long as he can secure the assistance of the community. Reluctant at first, having been burned numerous times by government promises, the elders of the community ultimately agree and Mensah's house is complete. Community members also begin construction on other houses in the community. As the song that weaves throughout the film warns, "Build your house and build it quick and see you build it well. Own your home and love your wife, you get some happiness in your life."[160]

Meanwhile government workers prioritized the construction of new monuments and roads—prestige projects to be "tackled now" in preparation for the independence festivities, while others were reshelved as part of "a long term policy for development."[161] The £1 million budget for the reconstruction of Accra was cut to £600,000 in order to ensure that funds could be distributed to support development projects in other parts of the country.[162] The government's grandiose redevelopment plans were scaled back. These had included a new sewerage system, slum clearance, housing and infrastructural development, road construction, market construction, and the organization of planning in Nima and Lagos Town, which, officials recognized, would only product a "cleaner, tidier town, eventually provided with an impressive waterfront and up-to-date sanitation" but not a "first class modern city with wide streets, attractive squares and well laid out gardens and open spaces."[163] In order to meet deadlines, officials chose to focus on the infrastructure for key sites like the new Accra Hotel, the development of marine drive, the construction of a new entertainment hall and the Accra Sports

Figure 5.5. Accra Changing Skyline, 1973. Photograph by George A. Alhassan. Source: Photographic Archive, Information Services Office, Ministry of Information, Accra PS/1458/21.

Stadium, renovation of Accra Airport terminal buildings, and a new Independence Memorial Hall built near the community center.[164]

While many eagerly embraced Nkrumah's new vision for the future, Ga residents in Accra viewed the plan with more skepticism, rooted in a decades-long engagement with urban and spatial politics. Accra had changed considerably over the last seventy years. High rates of urbanization brought diverse new populations into the city. The population of the city roughly doubled between 1921 (38,049) and 1931 (61,558) and doubled again by 1948 (135,926).[165] Unlike older migrant communities in Accra, these new migrants were not incorporated into Ga social, cultural, and political structures. Rather, they found space for themselves within the emerging colonial economy. Acquah noted that Indigenous occupations like agriculture and fishing were not as important anymore, the obligations of kinship were weakened, and new social, political, cultural, and economic institutions had emerged that catered to this increasingly diverse population. Forty-eight percent of the population in 1948 were non-Gas, a cosmopolitan city with residents from across the colony and around the world.[166] This population growth, Acquah argued, was characterized by high rates of inequality in income and housing, homelessness, poverty, destitution, rent exploitation, and crime.[167] The pressure on land and housing was particularly acute for Ga peoples who often housed large extended families.[168]

In the 1951 elections for the first national African-dominated parliament, Ga inhabitants of Accra voted for Kwame Nkrumah as their minister of parliament in the hope that Nkrumah's subsequent appointment as prime minister and the triumph of his Convention People's Party (CPP) would result in an improvement in conditions for Ga citizens in Accra. However, by 1957, when the former colony of the Gold Coast officially gained its independence from Great Britain, six years of Nkrumah-led CPP governance made it clear to Ga people that their interests were not being represented in government. A mere five months after independence (and only a few months before the release of this new plan for Accra), Ga people gathered in Bukom Square in Central Accra (Nkrumah's own constituency) to elect leaders for a new political party—the Ga-Adangbe Shifimo Kpee—which sought to restore resources, respect, and opportunity to Ga people and to challenge the Akan ethnic dominance in national political and economic life. The slogans of this new political party—*Ga shikpon gamei anoni* (Ga land for the Gas) and *Gboi mli gbweo* (The strangers are crushing us)—highlight the centrality of land and spatial politics to broader political concerns among Accra residents. While the Shifimo Kpee described itself as a nonpolitical association, founding members like Attoh Quarshie argued that Nkrumah's desire to establish Ghana as a unified, democratic nation-state actually served to marginalize Ga peoples and institute a system of corruption and nepotism.[169] Organizing themselves as an ethnic nationalist party, the Ga Shifimo Kpee sought to unite all Ga-Adangbe peoples and to guarantee the protection of their birthright (both in terms of land and access to resources and jobs). The fight over land and the right to the city continued well after the British left, articulated through the politics of regulation and the promises of modernist futures.

CONCLUSION

Trevallion and Hood noted that the structure of the town at the time of writing in the 1950s provided a good foundation or plan for continued growth. As a plan rooted in colonial models of spatial control, "Accra: A Plan for the Town" provided both a resource and a challenge for the leaders of the newly independent country. It was, on the one hand, a reflection of the persistent legacy of colonial spatial politics, which chafed against Nkrumah's critiques of neocolonialism and calls for Africanization and development through "African personality" and "African socialism." It also raised new kinds of concerns among Accra residents who struggled to assert their own visions for the city in the midst of nationalist reimaginings. While Nkrumah's own town planning policy seemed to embrace many of the broader points of the plan—the importance of imposing civic structures and open squares, the development of distinct neighborhoods, the siting of industrial development in Tema rather than Accra—his government was unable to significantly redevelop what is often referred to as "Accra Central," the old Ga quarters of town and the center of Ga political, social, economic, and cultural power. In 1960, government officials estimated that in Accra alone approximately three thousand unauthorized buildings were erected each year, as the expansion of the city outstripped the government's ability to implement plans and provide proper drainage, roads, and other infrastructure/services.[170] The building regulations, the engineer-in-chief noted, "were made at a time when little, if any, modern construction other than simplest concrete block houses, warehouses, etc, were being built outside municipalities"; however, by 1960 that had clearly changed as he argued that "there is a vast amount of building taking place throughout the country in all districts and a great use is being made of concrete."[171] While the engineer-in-chief was arguing to extend building regulations to the entire country, he acknowledged that "whilst many building permits are issued and applied for, it is not correct to assume these regulations are being properly administered."[172]

To some degree, those failures were rooted in the same kind of government inefficiency and ineptitude that William Bissell describes as "chaos" in colonial Zanzibar.[173] As Quayson notes, the large financial cost of such redevelopment and the financial challenges faced by the newly independent government certainly inhibited their ability to fundamentally redevelop the city's downtown core, echoing the financial struggles of the British government in the 1930s and 1940s. At the same time, however, the "modernist aesthetic vision" of the plan—its embrace of modernization in the form of infrastructural design, architectural style, and urban planning—reflected a broader attitude toward technology among postcolonial leaders, development experts, and urban planners. The plan's authors argued that this plan was an important revision of previous plans because it took into account local experiences and practices, which had been collected and recorded in the decade since the original plan was drafted. In theory, this would mark a radical departure from colonial planning efforts. In reality, however, the recording of local experience seemed to mean collecting user data, which was used to justify the proposed plan. The authors failed to interrogate any of the fundamental assumptions, concepts, values, or categories that influenced their plan.

As Quayson points out, this singular vision ignored the "multi-synchronicity" of urban development in Accra, which was shaped by the diverse town-planning policies of the early colonial period, as well as the "culturally saturated character" of the coastal area, which was imbued with "cultural signification" and ritualistic purpose.[174]

Quayson argues that, through this oversight, Trevallion and Hood "sought to project the process of urban formation as the *posterior effect* of central planning, rather than the dialectical product of the messy mixings of planned and unplanned processes."[175] However, the inconsistent implementation of the plan also reflected the ambiguities and contradictions of Nkrumahist development plans and the realities of postcolonial political visions. In viewing urban development as a dialectic between planned and unplanned, we continue to privilege the importance of Western discourses of "planning" while ignoring the importance and viability of systems and structures that developed out of the values and practices of African communities. As Parker and Sackeyfio-Lenoch note, these structures were essential in the formation of early colonial authority in Accra. But, in many cases, they also provided viable alternative models, which continue to chafe against persistent attempts to westernize urban spatial politics and practice in Accra—the trotro system and market trading being the most prominent. By embracing the logics of Western urban planning and "modernization" as universalizing technologies with inherent value and meaning, we cast these local examples of innovation and entrepreneurial creativity as part of the "informal economy" and obscure their value as examples of "anibue" or "eye-opening": aspirational visions for the future, rooted in African logics.

CONCLUSION

ON JULY 1, 2021, BULLDOZERS and demolition crews rolled into Agbogbloshie, a community located on the east side of the Odaw River, near the Korle Lagoon, adjacent to the old city center. Appearing on colonial-era maps as an open wetland, Agbogbloshie became a site of unregulated settlement and economic activity as the city expanded rapidly in the 1960s. Inhabited largely by migrants from rural areas in northern Ghana, the residential section of the community is known as Old Fadama; however, the community is more popularly known as "Sodom and Gomorrah," a reference to the perceived debauchery and decay associated with the neighborhood. The site has long been associated with a prominent market for onions and yams, transported from northern Ghana through community networks in rural homelands. However, in the last several decades, Agbogbloshie has become infamously synonymous with e-waste. International organizations regularly site Agbogbloshie as the world's largest e-waste site and a symbol of poverty and desperation within the global economy: "Welcome to Hell" and "Inside the Hellscape Where Our Computers Go to Die" are just some of the article headlines about Agbogbloshie.[1] However, as numerous researchers have made clear, the difficult living conditions in Agbogbloshie obscure a robust and dynamic socioeconomic organization through which residents work as individuals and communities to creatively remake both the materials and infrastructures of social and economic life in a city with high rates of unemployment and low housing stock. While many of us might take our cellphones and TVs—or our functioning bureaucracy and piped water—for granted as forms of connection in the world, residents and workers in Agbogbloshie have to reimagine their relationship to these technologies and infrastructures. Young men and boys scramble among the e-waste and other industrial waste, searching for

Figure concl 1.1. E-Waste and Recycling at Agbogbloshie, 2018. Photograph by the author.

salvageable materials that are stripped and repurposed in a highly organized scrapyard. Members of the Greater Accra Scrap Dealers Association transform waste into recycled materials and manufacture local consumer goods like stoves. And grassroots civil society organizations mobilize communities to organize housing and social services and advocate for investment and support in local government.[2] And yet, in the international media and among local politicians and elites, Agbogbloshie and Old Fadama are obvious targets of blame—the cause of flooding and pollution—and a site of opportunity for reform through demolition and redevelopment.

The demolition exercise on July 1, 2021, was initially targeted primarily at the onion market. The Greater Accra Regional Minister, Henry Quartey, had instructed traders at the onion market to relocate to Adjen Kotoku—a market that had been built more than a decade before in an effort to decongest the city's old neighborhoods and commercial districts but that had remained unoccupied.[3] The move was part of Quartey's Let's Make Accra Work project, which aimed to clean up the city and relocate traders off city streets and into state-sanctioned markets.[4] Market women begged for more time, but Quartey pushed forward. When bulldozers arrived on the July 1 deadline, however, community members were shocked as they moved beyond the onion market to demolish the nearby scrapyard. Scrap dealers argued that they had never been part of the relocation plan and had received no notification from the task force in charge of the project.[5] They also argued that they had not received the same resources allocated to the onion sellers in order to aid in the move. Instead, their shops were destroyed, and they were left without businesses. Quartey denied the accusations, pointing to public statements and arguing that the entire demolition exercise would have been "an exercise in futility if we leave all these structures and leave scrap dealers to be here. Then what is the point?"[6]

On the one hand, Quartey's campaign to clean up Accra reflected a real and urgent need to address ongoing flooding, which has repeatedly resulted in damaged property and death during the annual rainy season. Waste that blocks gutters prevents the proper flow of storm water, and unsanctioned settlements in floodplains further exacerbate drainage issues while putting local residents at risk. The government had undertaken demolitions in Agbogbloshie before with limited success,[7] but this time, Quartey insisted, things were different. "Read my lips—no one is coming back; it is done and no one is coming back,"[8] he asserted. And yet, as the scrap dealers' appeals suggest, the government provided few real alternatives for individuals who had not been able to secure economic opportunities and affordable housing in the sanctioned city sphere. Quartey himself acknowledges that people would return if the clearance was not rigorously enforced. By April 2022, contractors began erecting a fence to "secure the land" to "prevent encroachment,"[9] and Quartey put a plan before the government at Jubilee House to redevelop the land in a way that would be "fitted into the development plans of Accra."[10] While the overall plan was "to bring immense life to the area" and build "a new Agbogbloshie that we all will be proud of," the specific details still needed to be worked out with the various agencies.[11] A new Agenda 111 Hospital was designated for a portion of the land, but while Quartey argued that this project "was the best thing that could happen to a society" in "not just reclaiming the land but ... [using it] to benefit society more than it used to be," critics pointed out that regardless of the development plans, the well-documented soil contamination in Agbogbloshie—with lead concentrations one hundred times higher than normal levels[12]—was unsuitable for any redevelopment without significant remediation efforts.[13] The site design images of a futuristic campus released in government statements raised additional questions about who exactly this redevelopment would benefit.[14]

FROM COLONIAL EXPERIMENTS TO INTERNATIONAL MODELS

In many ways, Quartey's campaign was nothing new. Numerous government agencies had sought to clear Agbogbloshie and Old Fadama in order to make way for new development: this was part of a neoliberal approach to urban governance that privileges foreign investment. However, in attempting to assert control over land and redirect its use, Let's Make Accra Clean also strongly echoed the rhetoric of technocrats and British government officials in the debates of the Accra Town Council (ATC) nearly a century earlier. Quartey, of course, is not a colonizer, and his language is not "colonial" in a conventional sense. Rather, in reviving the language of colonial urban development, Quartey and his colleagues highlight the degree to which the policies and regulations implemented under British rule in Accra were part of a much broader growth of technocracy, which emerged in and through the colonial project. These "imperial durabilities" are, Ann Laura Stoler argues, sometimes clearly evident—the persistence of administrative units, engineering projects, and legal frameworks that "mark the social geography" of postcolonial life. However, she argues that "colonial entailments may lose their visible and identifiable presence in the vocabulary, conceptual grammar, and idioms of current concerns."[15] Currently, many of the most pressing issues "are features of our current global landscape whose etiologies are steeped in the colonial histories of which they have been, and in some cases continue to be, a part."[16]

The new approach to urban development, emerging in the late nineteenth and early twentieth centuries, coincided with both the formation and professionalization of new technocratic fields like urban planning, architecture, engineering, public health, and social work and with the expansion and consolidation of colonialism in Africa and elsewhere. These new fields were deeply connected to the cultures in which they were formed; they were "cultural practices" just as much as they were technological or scientific ones.[17] As Porter argues for planning, seeing these fields as cultural practices recognizes that they are "specific to particular peoples, life views, times and spaces," even as their theories and models "mythologize its universal features and norms."[18] Technocratic professions and the technologies, infrastructures, models, and policies they promoted were inherently connected to and produced through and with colonialism. They were certainly "tools of empire,"[19] as historians of technology have argued, but practitioners in these fields also carried with them the philosophies and ideologies of empire, translating those abstract ideas into spatial forms. These "conceived spaces," as Lefebvre described them, translated colonial intention into a plan of action, reorganizing space and social life in ways that advanced British goals to expand "expatriate enterprise" and "ordered modernity."[20] As a "technology of rule," twentieth-century infrastructure represented a particular form of urban governmentality through sanitation and public health, influencing "the conditions of possibility of urban life."[21] In urban infrastructure, material and social engineering were united in particularly powerful ways. In cities like Accra, the built form of the city and the technologies through which it operated were part of a new form of urban governance in which "notions of the contaminated city" were used to introduce and enforce "different cultural understandings of public and private, sacred and profane, appropriate and inappropriate behaviors."[22] Planners, architects, engineers, and others saw colonies as "laboratories of modernity" and often used the freedom that colonies offered to experiment with new ideas that, in turn, influenced practices in Europe.[23] In the process, British officials, technocrats, and their elite allies crafted a vision of the city that was defined by what Matthew Gandy calls "incomplete modernity"—a sense of unfulfilled potential that required reform and regulation, highlighted and "repeatedly justified through the use of cultural distinctions between modernity and tradition"—that sat at the core of the urban "civilizing mission."[24]

In Accra, as in other colonial cities, city builders used evidence of what they viewed as "nuisance" in order to justify reform and regulation that would reinforce the "rational and efficient use of space."[25] The ordinances that created and empowered institutions like the ATC were inspired by "an authoritative promise of the better city yet to come," giving these new institutions of urban governance the power to seize land and institute policies in the name of sanitation and public health.[26] Urban scholars have often emphasized the power and importance of cartography as a "science of domination" that "established boundaries and secured norms, treating questionable social conventions as unquestionable social facts."[27] These archival remnants—along with buildings, roads, and plans—certainly exemplify or embody colonial ideologies,[28] but a focus on buildings, plans, and maps alone ignores the complex urban politics that form city space and urban life.[29] Effective urban governance required much more than a map or a plan. As the preceding chapters make clear, officials often failed to realize the "perception" or "conceived space" laid out on paper; infrastructure symbolized "an imminent modernity, even as that modernity was endlessly deferred."[30] Rather, I argue, it was the power of regulation and the reframing of urban governance as a technical act that had a more powerful lasting influence on city life.[31] Through imported technocratic discourses of urban planning and regulation, British officials and town councillors reframed Indigenous notions of spatial organization and governance in Accra as problems, which, they argued, posed threats to public health and welfare and inhibited growth.[32] This new reframing privileged expatriate capitalism and carved out space for city elites, reorganizing the infrastructure, residential patterns, social dynamics, and economic processes around the demands of the "colonial-capitalist city."[33]

If early colonial policies were more "trial by fire," by the late 1920s and 1930s, technocratic fields had cohered around a core set of policies, principles, and procedures that were increasingly integrated into the institutions of empire. When Lord Passfield sent his circular to colonial officers recommending town planning as "an orderly and scientific method of controlling work already in progress or inevitable in future, in a manner which secures the best and most far reaching economic results from current expenditure as it takes place," he secured the importance of planning and allied fields in the logics and practices of colonial governance.[34] But as the history of urban development in Accra makes clear, these processes were far from straightforward. Colonial officials often projected their anxieties about the unruliness of city space generally on cities like Accra, reacting to rather than reflecting on the complex dynamics of the town and its residents' needs. As Robert Home notes, "The physical form of African towns was shaped by laws and regulations imported or transplanted from elsewhere, but developing in a local context."[35] Local residents could not be "cajoled" into new urban forms of living. In Accra, long histories of urban settlement and urban governance shaped a form of city life that was deeply rooted in the political, social, cultural, and economic practices of Ga people, even as it readily incorporated outsiders and embraced transnationalism. Colonial officials and technocratic experts often expressed frustration over their inability to fundamentally remake the town. They regularly blamed their failures on "tradition"—forms of social, economic, and cultural practice that contrasted sharply with the "modernity" of colonial visions.[36] And yet, in their demands for sanitation, economic opportunity, housing, and transport infrastructure, Accra residents argued that it was not the technology and infrastructure of modernity itself they rejected but rather the perception through which it was conceived.[37] Colonial officials encountered, not a blank slate, but a form of Indigenous urbanism with its own cultures of placemaking, logics of infrastructure, expectations of technology, patterns of organization, and values of order that represented a form of "lived space"—an alternative understanding of what the city was and who it would be for.[38]

Robert Home points to the importance of these histories: "The initial processes which create towns live on and their subsequent story, inscribed as a sort of DNA of an urban form, entwining history with the social production of space."[39] Certainly, as he argues, "the legacy of colonialism is still etched on the landscape and practices" of cities like Accra.[40] But in Accra, precolonial urban morphologies shaped a generic conception of a "colonial town form" into something that was uniquely Accra. This was more than mere resistance—the push and pull of urban residents. It is a set of fundamental values, patterns of movement, interaction, and spatiality that insistently shapes the urban form. The words from William Kentridge's 2018 installation at the Zeitz MOCAA Museum in South Africa— "A nicely built city never resists destruction"—seems to capture this complex dynamic. On its surface, it points to the importance of progress. Like colonial technocrats and postcolonial government officials, Kentridge suggests that destruction is a necessary component to development. And yet, in the context of the installation in which shadowed figures trudge through sparse landscapes carrying their belongings, pushing carts, and holding signs, Kentridge also suggests a more skeptical interpretation from the perspective of local residents who— like residents of early twentieth century (and now early twenty-first century) Accra—are questioning whether the city is, in fact, "nicely built" and whether the destruction was worth it.

Colonial officials had limited success in physically reshaping the old Ga town. And while their efforts at reform and planning were often plagued by incompetence, this book argues that new technocratic approaches did have significant lasting impacts on the form and function of city life. Surviving buildings and roads might be the most obvious reminders of colonial presence in Accra, but the lasting impact of colonial power was—and continues to be felt—in the ordinances and regulations that shaped even the most mundane details of both public and private life in the city. A history of regulation and governance in Accra is, effectively, a documentation of the unfolding of a historical process of informalization, through which members of the colonial-capitalist class enshrined their own privileges and visions of city life. And in passing regulations and reshaping the legal landscape of urban governance, I argue that colonial officials, technocrats, and their elite allies effectively marginalized and criminalized Indigenous African practices, marking them as "nuisance" and subjecting them to new forms of oversight, policing, and reform.

In many ways, the histories laid out in this book were unique to Accra. Ga residents held unusual amounts of political, economic, social, and cultural power in the city for much of its history, and their ability to persist and preserve long-standing practices (seen here in trade, transportation, and housing) even as they embraced new technologies, infrastructures, and influences is a testament to the proudly urban identity of the city's residents, which is both profoundly cosmopolitan and distinctively Ga. As a result, the ways in which imported ordinances, technologies, and infrastructures were debated, adapted, or discarded reflected both the strong sense of identity and organization in Ga communities as well as the specific historical conditions of Accra (and the Gold Coast, more broadly) in any given moment. Accra's unique urban politics was also shaped by the power of early nationalist organizations and other political leaders, as well as the relative economic autonomy of Indigenous entrepreneurs in the Gold Coast—the foundations of early anticolonial organizing that helped mobilize local populations and articulate powerful alternative visions.

And yet, the ordinances and regulations, technologies and infrastructures at the center of these debates were also part of new and powerful global processes. As Keller Easterling argues about infrastructure more broadly, "Beyond the activity of the humans within it, the arrangement itself rendered something significant and others insignificant. The organization was actively *doing something* when it directed urban routines. It made some things possible and some things impossible."[41] As a result, infrastructure serves as an important link between different regimes. Far from being "hidden" or "unremarked," infrastructures often help us trace the persistent politics of space and the assumptions that technocratic officials carry with them about the city.[42] These new technocratic infra/structures created a framework of ideas that as historians of development have shown, became "deeply embedded in international policies and institutions in the decades following the end of colonial rule."[43] If this new class of expert began using conferences and consultancies to share information and ideas in the context of colonial rule, the books and articles they wrote and the policies and practices they initiated became key reference works for policymakers and practitioners in the late colonial and early postcolonial period, transforming their "philosophical assumptions and apocalyptic narratives" into "conventional wisdom in the lexicon of contemporary development."[44] That language of development and technocratic social engineering was embedded in national and global political institutions, as "experts" defined what James Scott calls "high modernism" as the primary form of "seeing like a state."[45] At independence, colonial bureaucrats and technocratic experts found employment in newly established international institutions, taking their experience and assumptions with them to create the foundations of new professional fields and forms of international governance.[46] These ideas and practices were reinforced through new international technical and governmental standards, which became the dominant marker not only of progress but of quality—the "basic template for city building," which enabled planners and other officials to "understand, examine, and modify the city, or a part of it."[47] Increasingly, too, they have been embedded in a broad-based bourgeois class consciousness, shaping "political will, economic priorities, socio-spatial differentiation, and materialities" of middle-class residents in ways that echo the conflicts between educated elites and "the crowd" in colonial Accra.[48] It is part and parcel of a theory of modernization and development that claims its own universality and demands universal application, even as it remains grounded in the specific historical experiences of Western industrial capitalism.[49]

WHAT'S NEW ABOUT THE "NEW ACCRA"?

Today's urban politics echo these historical trends rooted in colonial spatial logics and the complicated legacy of decolonization, even as they reflect the new realities of global political economy. As Sharan argues, "Reflection on the contemporary city requires that we recover the ways in which we ordered our cities in the past, not with a view of a return but to excavate their traces in our everyday habits and ways of inhabiting the city."[50] What, then, does that mean in contemporary Accra? How can we use these historical lessons to think about the plans of the present and the possibilities of the future? If the UN Sustainable Development Goals have reenergized conversations about urban futures and opened up new possibilities for thinking about equitable and inclusive urban development, what does that mean for how technocrats, scholars, residents, and government officials think, talk, write, plan, and act in cities like Accra?

As you drive down Accra's High Street from the old commercial district and the historically Ga districts of Jamestown and Ussher Town toward the modern center of cosmopolitanism on Oxford Street, you travel around a roundabout. Independence Arch rises from the middle of the roundabout, a symbol of the promise of an independent Ghana, atop which stood Kwame Nkrumah on March 6, 1957, declaring that "Ghana, your beloved country is free forever!" Travel just a little further, and you reach a branch in the road that leads to Christiansborg Castle, the seat of both colonial and postcolonial government. Between Independence Arch and the Castle, the Accra Metropolitan Assembly (AMA) has erected a new sign with a new sort of promise, proclaiming, A NEW ACCRA FOR A BETTER GHANA.

The "new Accra" signals a renewed political commitment to urban planning and development in the city, embodied in the 2013 National Urban Policy. And things certainly do seem to be changing. Particularly in the city's most elite districts, old buildings are being torn down and long-vacant properties are being cleared to make way for new high-rises of glass and concrete. Within the existing city, new districts like Airport City have grown rapidly, distinguished by award-winning architecture, international hotel chains, and upscale restaurants and shops. In 2017, the city began work on plans for a massive urban extension into the Ningo-Prampram District to the east of Accra. The construction boom coincides with what some have labeled a "cultural renaissance"—art galleries, street art festivals, fashion boutiques, cafés, bistros, cocktail bars, and music venues cater to a tight-knit community of artists, architects, intellectuals, and designers.[51]

Spurred by the promises of growth in a neoliberal Ghana, the "new Accra" is all about construction, from high-rise office buildings and skyscrapers to planned

Figure concl 1.2. A New Accra for a Better Ghana, 2016. Photograph by the author.

"communities" and new shopping malls. Some—Kente Tower, Gold Coast City, Adinkra Heights, Switchback Park, Appolonia, Cantonments City, Jamestown Boxing School—evoke the rich cultural and economic history of the city and its diverse population. And a select few—"Point of No Return" in Tema and a new Ghanaian National Museum on Slavery and Freedom—engage that history directly by creating sights for historical reflection and, undoubtedly, tourist dollars. Others highlight the global aspirations that informed their planning, with names like Riviera Residence, Infinity Tower, Accra Twin Towers, and Hope City. Still others evoke the corporations that the new construction will house—Unibank, Ecobank, MTN, etc.[52] These new projects are flashy and forward-looking, designed by innovative, award-winning young architects from within and outside of the continent. These structures are going up alongside a slightly older set of buildings, like the World Trade Center Accra or Accra Mall, the worn appearance of which belies their central role in what feels like a real-life Monopoly game (an Accra version of which is currently for sale at Accra Mall and other high-end retail shops around the city).[53]

On the surface, these new construction projects seem to be the realization of the promise of "A New Accra for a Better Ghana." The "new Accra" embraces the tenets of "new urbanism" among the city's developer class and policy elites. Glittery new buildings, sleek architectural designs, upscale shops, and sustainable landscaping anchor new developments that promise "walkable blocks and streets, housing and shopping in close proximity, and accessible public spaces."[54] While new urbanism casts itself as a rejection of modernism, these movements share a belief in the importance of the built form and its ability to reshape behavior; this is done by creating new parameters of urban life, articulated through models and principles, and enacted through urban plans.[55] It is, in other words, the newest iteration of urban politics.

Developers are proposing not mere buildings but communities. Devtraco Plus, Ltd., which has been developing the East Cantonments Village property on 8.9 acres in the middle of one of the city's wealthiest and most desirable districts, aims to create a livable, walkable, sustainable development with a strong identity. The development at East Cantonments was intended to be an example of a well-planned, mixed-use development that could appeal to international buyers, inspired by the Buckhead Atlanta project in Atlanta, Georgia. The project included plans for apartments, townhomes, a sports facility, a hotel, retail, and boutique offices that will provide residents with a place for greenspace, stay/residential, live/play, and commuting. This kind of property is not geared toward low-income residents or, in fact, even Ghanaians. Townhouses call for rooftop infinity pools, residences are insulated from the noise of the street, and jogging paths cut through the development. But this is more than a refiguring of space and spatial practice. This vision for a sustainable community of tasteful, powerful global citizens represents a sort of spatial occupation by the capitalist class. "New Accra" is, apparently, an empty playground for cosmopolitan urban imaginaries, unmoored from the realities of the vast majority of city residents even as it claims to cultivate community.

While, in theory, new urbanism's focus on creating walkable, sustainable developments is modeled on the inclusiveness of the village, in practice, this approach has created a sort of omnibus of planning models. Some of those models have become hegemonic in themselves. The focus on bus rapid transit in urban plans to the exclusion of both local mobility systems/solutions and other possible technological alternatives, for example, has been a waste of resources in many cities like Accra. These cities can ill afford the loss, and these kinds of transportation issues divert attention from the central issues facing mobile urban residents. Driven by the interests of private corporations and Western urban planners, these models take on imperialistic overtones.[56] In a sort of parallel to critiques of gentrification, the preference for more expensive Western models marginalizes the majority of urban residents who are unable to afford access to new housing developments, transit systems, and other amenities.

The slick design of these new developments, the affluence of their residents, and the cosmopolitan appeal of the cupcake stores, boutiques, art galleries, and coffee shops surrounding them have attracted the attention of government officials and international journalists alike. Not unlike the attention given to Accra as the capital of Britain's "model colony" or the new capital of the "black star of Africa," Accra has now been branded Africa's "capital of cool"—part of a new cultural and economic resurgence on the continent, with its own global investors, stylists, and tastemakers.[57] However, this language of cosmopolitan "cool-ness" and the rapid economic growth of a new oil economy obscures a much more complicated urban politics. These changes are unevenly distributed and embraced in the city, and official and journalistic commentary rarely reflects on who is left out in the "new Accra." These unresolved questions of inclusion and marginalization are connected to these much longer histories of precolonial urbanism, colonial planning, and postcolonial modernization in the city. The rapid pace of construction and the remarkable consistency of developer plans and architectural styles are driven by global tastes and investor preferences. The city has no current and coherent master urban plan.

In carving out their own visions for the city, these developers participate in elite variations of managing. While scholarship on African urbanism tends to focus on the actions of lower-class residents who are often excluded or marginalized in government plans, the city's affluent neighborhoods—Ridge, Cantonments, Spintex, Airport Residential, Dzorwulu, East Legon, and the like—themselves also highlight the varying ways in which urban residents have shaped city life. Some of these neighborhoods have their roots in colonial plans and draw their prestige from their historical connection to European residence in colonial segregation planning: the quintessentially British colonial urban form of the cantonment, for example, or the larger projects and grander structures of the Ridge. Dzorwulu and Airport Residential, for example, are planned neighborhoods that emerged after independence, growing up around prestige sites like Kotoka International Airport or the University of Ghana. Others, like Spintex, are recent additions, more directly connected to the recent spate of urban redevelopment.

Spintex today looks much like the rest of these neighborhoods, with relatively well maintained roads, expensive houses, and heavy concentrations of upscale retail and services. However, the neighborhood emerged in the early 2000s (noticeably around the same time that the Accra Mall was under construction) when wealthy Accra residents began building large homes on vacant land alongside the Accra-Tema Motorway—an area that was zoned for industrial rather than residential use and that had not been approved by government. Widespread condemnation did not stop construction. While more informal settlements (often labeled as "slums") might have been cleared by bulldozers when residents failed to heed government warnings about building in flood plains or otherwise unzoned parts of the city, the Accra government was unable to demolish the large concrete homes of some of Accra's wealthiest and most powerful residents.[58] Instead, residents carved out their own road and later pressured the government to pave it.

New developments, sprinkled throughout the city center and its sprawling suburbs and hinterlands, engage in a similar form of elite managing, negotiating competing claims to land, inadequate infrastructure provisions, and municipal bureaucracy using a wide range of strategies. Many local property owners, particularly in popular elite neighborhoods like Osu and Cantonments, seem eager to cash in on the new property boom. In Osu popular spots like Bywell Bar have been torn down to make way for new developments. Other property owners have chosen to refurbish colonial-era buildings as hotels and Airbnb rentals, drawing on some form of colonial nostalgia to market their properties. Other expats or returnees have set up roadside cocktail bars, live music venues, and private clubs, which draw on the ubiquitous material culture of the city's lower classes but are inaccessible to those urban residents. The members-only club Front/Back, for example, asks members to enter through a shipping container identical (on the outside) to those that the city regularly targets for removal around markets. The club is decorated with roadside mirrors, local toys, and recycled materials that are so central to the life of the street, and yet the exorbitant membership fees exclude all but the most elite in Accra who use the space to network and play. A recording of Ngugi reading *Things Fall Apart* plays on repeat in the bathroom. Chimamanda Adichie novels sit on the shelves alongside books about Ghanaian art and critiques of development culture.

On the surface, these new developments seem to further exacerbate the social and economic inequalities that have long defined city life in Accra. Today an estimated 43 percent of Accra metropolitan residents live in "slums,"[59] and an estimated 80 percent of the country's workforce finds employment in sectors like market trading and transport.[60] Accra's urban poor operate side businesses out of their homes, purchase food in open-air markets, cook over coal fires, use underfunded public transportation, live without water or electricity, and send their children to apprenticeships with family members or keep them at home because they cannot afford school fees. Elite residents, by contrast, have access to a much wider range of resources and infrastructures at the local, national, and global level. Their children attend elite, private schools in Ghana and abroad. They access the internet on smart phones, own their own cars, purchase imported food from grocery stores, work in air-conditioned offices, buy water to fill giant tanks, and run generators. As elite residents travel between work, home, shopping malls, bistro, cafés, and clubs in air-conditioned comfort, largely insulated from the lived realities of the street outside, they reproduce a sociospatial inequality rooted in colonial residential and social segregation policies.

These inequalities are indeed real, and the income gap in cities like Accra seems to have grown at an accelerated pace in the last ten years, reinforced and reproduced through infrastructure and urban spatial forms. Inequity has also been exacerbated by neoliberal economic policies, weak commodity markets, and currency redenomination. In response to this politics of extraversion, "southern urbanism" or urban theory from the Global South has set its sights on the practices of the local, which are cast as forms of resilience and resistance in the face of global hegemonies that marginalize local residents and local knowledge. In particular, academics, policymakers, journalists, and planners often categorize the adaptations of poor urban residents in this context as manifestations of "informality" and target urban planning analysis and intervention on lower-class neighborhoods, markets, transport systems, and other infrastructure. This association of informality with poverty, I argue, is an oversimplified characterization of Keith Hart's original formulation, which obscures a much more complex urban politics in the city and rooted in a much longer history of urban residence in Accra. By exploring this history of urban politics, we can better understand how many Accra residents claim a "right to the city," often bridging the gaps and blurring the boundaries between the sociospatial inequalities inscribed in urban planning policy and practice. Accra residents describe these daily acts as "managing."[61] In contrast to phrases like "making do" or "getting by," which are often associated with informal practices and imply survivalism, managing "highlights the ways in which participants engage in meaningful acts, strategically harnessing the resources at hand not only to accomplish objectives but also to construct satisfying lives."[62] Acts of managing transcend the distinctions of socioeconomic class in the city, uniting Accra's population in a process of grassroots placemaking, simultaneously reifying and resisting the city's economic inequalities.

WHAT IS THE CITY?

If the model city—the foundation of urban theory—is grounded in the expectations and assumptions of Western urbanism, what, then, does "the city" mean in a place like Accra? In focusing on the local and tracing the politics of "development" and the unfolding process of informalization in Accra, this book seeks to also shed light on the global. Of course, Accra, like other African cities, was and remains part of global flows of goods, people, and ideas in ways that are still underrecognized and underappreciated by many politicians, practitioners, and theoreticians; to some degree, this book seeks to open some space for thinking about those global connections, even if I do not explicitly trace them here. However, I would argue, the history of Accra also helps us think about the ways in which concepts are formed, flourish, and fail on a global scale. As Robinson and Srivastava have both pointed out, cities in poorer countries are often cast as "other" because city life seems to differ so significantly from Western urban experience—a space in need of "development" in contrast to the "modernity" of Western cities and an exception or aberration within narratives that claim "universality."[63]

Indeed, there is often "a disconnect between the stories and promises associated with the technology and what the urban space is actually doing," and "modern" technologies and infrastructures often do function differently in African cities.[64] But, in treating examples like Accra (or, for that matter, nearly any African city) as an extraordinary exception, we miss opportunities to enrich our understanding of city life and challenge some deep assumptions and ongoing structural violence, rooted in the history of colonialism and empire. Rather than examples of "failed urbanism," cities like Accra (or Bombay, Calcutta, Columbo, or Lagos) may actually be more honest representations of the rule, which our urban theory should be revised to accommodate.[65] We should, as Murray argues, be open to considering that there might be more than one form of urbanization and more than one type of city in the context of "global urbanism."[66] But we should also consider that maybe the seemingly rapid transformations in twenty-first-century urban development—"where metropolitan landscapes are increasingly fragmented into distinct zones characterized by concentrated wealth, global connectivity, excess, and fantasy, on the one side, and neglect, impoverishment, and deprivation on the other"—might be less of an "emergent post-urban moment" and more like a supreme realization on long-standing urban processes that had, before the twenty-first century, been experienced unequally around the world.[67]

The history of urbanism in Accra suggests that these processes are both new and old—a blatantly unequal form of urbanism that might be seeing a new moment of widespread embrace, but the roots of these global processes of urban fragmentation lay in the colonies where the inequalities and abuses of capitalism and their connection to governance were laid most bare and were at their most extreme. Jacobs argues that "it was in outpost cities that the spatial order of imperial imaginings was rapidly and deftly realized."[68] If, for a long time, the economic power of the West meant that US and European cities could protect themselves by profiting from the exploitation of colonies, the deterritorialization of capitalism and shifts in the global distribution of power in the twenty-first century means that the old "wealthy metropolitan centers of global finance" are no longer safe.[69] These twenty-first-century cities are—as "colonial" cities always were—both implicated in these broader processes of exploitation and exclusion while also being profoundly variable and local.[70] In their "fragmentation" they are exemplifying a global process of informalization that is much older than we realize.

AFRICAN PASTS AND URBAN FUTURES

In his introduction to *Under Siege*, Okwui Enwezor argues that African cities "are collision points between tradition and modernity, between African development and external pressures; the new site for the reformulation of old and new influences, and the opportunity for the symbolic production of post-colonial identities." Enwezor acknowledges that "as a consequence of their colonial legacy, many African cities still remain administrative systems, although disconnected from the city dynamics." However, he argues, "the syntax of these cities today is not defined by the 'modern' grammar inherited from colonialism, nor by the assumption of an organic connection between individual and collective memory, of testimonies and beliefs. In these cities, where everything is interpreted and outlined by the apparent chaos of the everyday, where forms of self-organizing procedures, parallel and informal economies, and the resilience and inventiveness of urban dwellers have relentlessly kept many cities still functional."[71]

Enwezor's assertion of the disconnection of administration from the realities of everyday life is an attempt to grapple with the failures of urban governance and the ubiquity of alternative systems of social, political, and economic order, often glossed as the "informal sector." In focusing on the syntax of African cities, Enwezor seeks to understand what these cities actually *are*—not as failures or aberrations or sites of incompleteness, but on their own terms. In doing so, he is part of a much larger scholarly conversation about the parameters of "southern urbanism" that seeks to place the "informal city" at the center of policy debates and scholarly analysis. In interrogating the "informal city," theorists like Simone, Pieterse, and Enwezor rightly emphasize the experiences of the "urban majority," who are largely left out of (or explicitly criminalized by) planning and policy processes. However, in embracing the framework of the "informal economy," these scholars reify the artificial categories that have come to shape development practice but that often obscure the much more complex sociospatial histories of African cities.

These scholarly engagements with the "informal economy" seem to ignore the wider range of activities that the term originally sought to capture and explain. Keith Hart's original formulation of the "informal economy" in Ghana was defined primarily by self-employment. In response to a lagging wage labor sector, Hart argued, many Ghanaians pursued more precarious economic opportunities that were not easily accounted for in economic surveys. While some of this work was, indeed, low-wage, Hart acknowledged that "informal activities encompass a wide-ranging scale, from marginal operations to large-scale enterprises."[72] The broader economic conditions that shaped the labor market and economic opportunities of 1970s Accra have not improved significantly in the last forty years. And yet, today the term "informal economy" and the broader category of "informality" are exclusively associated with the urban poor. Market traders, *trotro* drivers, cooked-food sellers, and beer brewers are all "underemployed" members of an "informal economy"—in Ga, *kobolo*, a good-for-nothing street lounger who embodies the precarity of "urban crisis."[73] Independent social media managers, café owners, fashion designers, and Uber drivers are more often "entrepreneurs," even if their work carries the same risk.

In Accra, as elsewhere, this politics of categorization has meaningful consequences for urban residents. As Hart notes, "Most enterprises run with some measure of bureaucracy are amenable to enumeration by surveys, and—as such—constitute the 'modern sector' of the urban economy. The remainder—that is, those who escape enumeration—are variously classified as 'the *low productivity* urban sector,' 'the reserve army of *underemployed and unemployed*,' 'the urban *traditional* sector,' and so on. These terms beggar analysis by assuming what has to be demonstrated."[74] Today, "informal economy" and "informality" seem to have fallen into the same trap. In defaulting to these terms as a way explain contemporary African cities, we reify and reproduce categories that have been deployed in oversimplified and highly politicized ways by government institutions and development organizations. While scholars often use these terms to identify and demarcate groups that are underrepresented in development policy and yet are vital to the economic and social life of African cities, those same forms of demarcation have also been used by politicians and others to criminalize the activities of the urban poor, transforming them into targets of government sanction, demolition, and, at times, violent attack.

As the history of Accra's urban politics demonstrates, this exclusive focus on the urban poor and the persistent use of "informality" as a frame of analysis obscures more fundamental questions about the systemic and structural violence of the built form and the power of spatial politics. In Accra, this politics cut across class, as rich and poor residents alike sought to make space and opportunity for themselves in a city that was increasingly not planned with their interests in mind. In tracing the unfolding of informalization as a historical process rooted in colonial-era urban governance, we are able to better understand the systemic or structural conditions that shape urban inequality and underdevelopment in cities like Accra and focus attention on possible alternative models and visions for the city, rooted in local understandings of space, infrastructure, technology, and community. But they also highlight complicated contemporary politics, in which "Westernization" often stands in for "formal," privileging citizens of means, criminalizing the urban poor, and perpetuating imperialistic systems of urban underdevelopment.

NOTES

INTRODUCTION

1. The National Archives (UK): Public Records Office (hereafter cited as TNA: PRO) CO 99/8 1893–1894 Gold Coast Gazette.
2. TNA: PRO CO 99/8 1893–1894 Gold Coast Gazette.
3. TNA: PRO CO 99/8 1893–1894 Gold Coast Gazette.
4. Parker, *Making the Town*.
5. As such, colonial regulatory regimes and practices in Accra were part of a broader imperial project in which, as T. J. Tallie argues for the "global nineteenth century Anglophone settler project" (2) and its particular incarnation in colonial Natal, colonial governments around the world sought to "cordon off indigenous land reserves and enshrine African custom in a static and separate legal code" (1). Tallie illustrates the important ways in which white settler presence and power shaped the particular execution of these aspirations in colonies like Natal, but in attempting to realize a new form of order and control land, they also evidence an important connection with other "commercial" colonies as part of a larger imperial project. See Tallie, *Queering Colonial Natal*.
6. Parker, *Making the Town*, xvii.
7. Dakubu, *Korle Meets the Sea*, 100–101.
8. Odotei, "External Influences on Ga Society and Culture," 61; Dakubu, *Korle Meets the Sea*, 101; Parker, *Making the Town*, 8.
9. Dakubu, *Korle Meets the Sea*, 101; Parker, *Making the Town*, 8.
10. Sackeyfio-Lenoch, *Politics of Chieftaincy*, 23.
11. Parker, *Making the Town*, 6; Sackeyfio-Lenoch, *Politics of Chieftaincy*, 23.
12. Parker, *Making the Town*, 9–10.
13. Odotei, "External Influences on Ga Society and Culture," 61; Parker, *Making the Town*, 9–10.
14. Parker, *Making the Town*, 9–10; Robertson, *Sharing the Same Bowl*, 28–30.
15. Parker, *Making the Town*, 9–10.
16. Quayson, *Oxford Street, Accra:* 41–42; Parker *Making the Town*, 2, 4.
17. Parker, *Making the Town*, xviii.
18. Parker, *Making the Town*, 2.

19. Robertson, *Sharing the Same Bowl*, 28–30.
20. Barbot, *A Description of the Coasts of North and South Guinea*.
21. Parker, *Making the Town*, 10.
22. Parker, *Making the Town*, 6; Kilson, *Kpele Lala: Ga Religious Songs and Symbols*, 238.
23. Parker, *Making the Town*, 6; Kilson, *Kpele Lala*, 10.
24. Barbot, *A Description of the Coasts of North and South Guinea*, 70–72. Barbot noted that "could the Akim and Akwamu blacks agree, as they are continually at variance, about the annual tribute the former demand of the latter, by virtue of their feudal right over them, the trade would yet be greater at Accra than it is: but the Akwamus will by no means submit to it, lest a concession of this nature might, in time, cost them the loss of their whole country; and their king is such a politician, as to sow discord between the governors of Akim, by means of fair words and large gifts, whereby he preserves his country in peace, and in a condition to enjoy a beneficial trade" (70–72).
25. Barbot, *A Description of the Coasts of North and South Guinea*, 70–72.
26. Hawthorn, *Journal of an African Cruiser* in Wolfson, *Pageant of Ghana*, 123–124.
27. Huntley, *Seven Years' Service of the Slave Coast of Western Africa*, in Wolfson, *Pageant of Ghana*.
28. Kilson, *Kpele Lala*, 7.
29. Robertson, *Sharing the Same Bowl*, 28–30.
30. Robertson, *Sharing the Same Bowl*, 28–30; Quayson, *Oxford Street, Accra*, 47.
31. Robertson, *Sharing the Same Bowl*, 28–30.
32. Parker, *Making the Town*, xvii.
33. Quayson, *Oxford Street, Accra*, 41–42; Parker, *Making the Town*.
34. Quayson, *Oxford Street, Accra*, 38.
35. Quayson, *Oxford Street, Accra*, 54, 57; Parker, *Making the Town*, 14; Brooks, *EurAfricans in Western Africa*; Dumett, "African Merchants of the Gold Coast," 1860–1905; Ray, *Crossing the Color Line*; Ipsen, *Koko's Daughters*.
36. Quayson, *Oxford Street, Accra*, 121.
37. Parker, *Making the Town*, 14, 16.
38. Osei-Tutu, *Asafoi (Socio-Military Groups) in the Histoyr and Politics of Accra (Ghana) from the 17th to the 20th Century*.
39. Parker, *Making the Town*, 22.
40. Parker, *Making the Town*, 17.
41. Parker, *Making the Town*, 22–23.
42. Parker, *Making the Town*, 19.
43. Robertson, *Sharing the Same Bowl*, 28–30.
44. Parker, *Making the Town*, 7.
45. Kilson, *African Urban Kinsmen*, 3.
46. Parker, *Making the Town*, 7.
47. Parker, *Making the Town*, 7.
48. Parker, *Making the Town*, 6.
49. Kilson, *African Urban Kinsmen*, 3.
50. Parker, *Making the Town*, 6; Kilson, *Kpele Lala*, 238.
51. Parker, *Making the Town*, 16.
52. Kilson, *Kpele Lala*, 7.
53. Parker, *Making the Town*, 16.
54. Kilson, *Kpele Lala*, 7; Parker, *Making the Town*.
55. Quayson, *Oxford Street, Accra*, 41–42.

56. Dumett, "African Merchants of the Gold Coast"; Murillo, *Market Encounters*.
57. Robertson, *Sharing the Same Bowl*, 32.
58. Parker, *Making the Town*, xviii.
59. Parker, *Making the Town*, xviii.
60. Parker, *Making the Town*; Ferguson, *Expectations of Modernity*; Field, *Search for Security*.
61. See for example: White, *Comforts of Home*; Cooper, *Struggle for the City*; Cooper, *On the African Waterfront*.
62. White, *Comforts of Home*; Lyons, *The Colonial Disease*; Cooper, *On the African Waterfront*; Mamdani, *Citizen and Subject*; Demissie, *Colonial Architecture and Urbanism in Africa*, 2. The garden city movement was arguably the most ordered and well-documented example of technocratic urban form, which Bigon and Katz argue highlights "the relationship between colonialism and modern planning." See Bigon and Katz, *Garden Cities and Colonial Planning*, 3.
63. Lugard, *The Dual Mandate in British Tropical Africa*; Crowder, "Indirect Rule – French and British Style," 197–205.
64. Mamdani, *Citizen and Subject*, 37–61.
65. Balakrishnan, *Anticolonial Public*.
66. TNA: PRO CO 96/740/1 1937 Municipal Affairs: A Petition by the Ratepayers of Accra regarding the Appointment of Mr. D. McDougall as Town Clerk.
67. Bissell, *Urban Design, Chaos, and Colonial Power in Zanzibar*.
68. Fair, *Reel Pleasures*, 9; Lefebvre, *Le Droit à la ville*.
69. Bissell, *Urban Design, Chaos, and Colonial Power in Zanzibar*, 1.
70. As Dalston notes in her commanding history of rules in the Western world, "We are, all of us, everywhere, always, enmeshed in a web of rules that supports and constrains" (1). However, she notes that "the universality of rules does not imply their uniformity, either across cultures or within historical traditions" (2). Rules, then, predated the expansion of British government in Accra, even if they looked quite different from British understandings. And the choice of which rules to create and how they should be implemented and enforced represented distinct and intentional choices on the part of government leaders, as "rules can either be thick or thin in their formulation, flexible or rigid in their application, and general or specific in their domain" (3). As "rules with their sleeves ruled up, the ones that get things done on the ground," regulations generate particular attention both from the governing and the governed since "we bark our shins against regulations almost every day" (152). Daston, *Rules: A Short History of What We Live By*.
71. Mitchell, *Colonizing Egypt*, ix.
72. Stanley, *Coomassie and Magdala* quoted in Quayson, *Oxford Street, Accra*, 40; Sackeyfio, *The Politics of Chieftaincy*, 1.
73. Horton, *West African Countries and Peoples, British and Native*, 137.
74. Bissell, *Urban Design, Chaos, and Colonial Power in Zanzibar*, chap. 1.
75. Adas, *Machines as the Measure of Men*, 263.
76. Adas, *Machines as the Measure of Men*, 261–262.
77. Adas, *Machines as the Meassure of Men*, 263–264.
78. Adas, *Machines as the Measure of Men*; Headrick, *The Tools of Empire*; Headrick, *Power over Peoples*; Mitchell, *Rule of Experts*. As Daston argues, the vision of modernity as articulated through and embodied in the science and technology of the nineteenth century was predated by an earlier definition of modernity that was fixated on orderliness, predictability, and rules; colonial officials and other Western observers just as often fell back on this older definition in talking about modernity (or the lack thereof) in African cities like Accra (Daston, *Rules*, 181).

79. Myers and Muhair, "Afterlife of the Lanchester Plan," 113; Mitchell, *Rule of Experts*.

80. Rankin, *After the Map*. Daston argues that the rise of regulation in Western cities was driven by three factors: "First, quickening trade swelled purses and kindled new desires. . . . Second, burgeoning urban populations strained old infrastructures of streets and sanitation. . . . Third, the political consolidation of nation-states from the seventeenth century to the present day enforced uniformity on what were previously disparate territories, not only legally but culturally" (Daston, *Rules*, 153).

81. Home, "Colonial Urban Planning in Anglophone Africa"; Mitchell, *Rule of Experts*; Adas, *Machines as the Measure of Men*; see also Scott, *Seeing Like a State*, 55.

82. Walkowitz, *City of Dreadful Delight*; Fyfe, *By Accident or Design*; Bigon and Katz, *Garden Cities and Colonial Planning*, 54–55.

83. Porter, *Unlearning the Colonial Cultures of Planning*, 52.

84. Wright, "Tradition in the Service of Modernity," 322–45; Stoler, "Tense and Tender Ties," 848; Bigon and Katz, *Garden Cities and Colonial Planning*, 20; Silva, "Urban Planning in Sub-Saharan Africa," 9–10. See also Tilley, *Africa as a Living Laboratory*.

85. In the realm of architecture, Kuukuwa Manful argues that "colonial architectural domination was realized in a number of ways, four of which I discuss in detail. . . . These are (1) the diminishing, erasure and demolition of existing African architectures; (2) the erection of imposing and intimidating European architectures; (3) the juridical and bureaucratic control of the built environment through planning, permits and licenses and; (4) the influence and imposition of European hegemonies of aesthetic taste" (233). While the scope of this book extends well beyond architecture, Manful's schematic provides a helpful framework here to think about the strategies of spatial governance. Manful, "Afterword: Theorizing the Politics of Unformal(ized) Architectures."

86. Quoted in Home and King, "Urbanism and Master Planning," 82.

87. Bigon and Katz, *Garden Cities and Colonial Planning*, 15–16, 83.

88. Silva, "Urban Planning in Sub-Saharan Africa," 9–10.

89. Home, "Colonial Urban Planning in Anglophone Africa," 62; Demissie, *Colonial Architecture and Urbanism in Africa*, 3–4; Manful, "Afterword," 233.

90. de Boeck, "Infrastructure: Commentary from Filip de Boeck"; Harvey and Knox, *Roads: An Anthropology of Infrastructure and Expertise*, 5.

91. Easterling, *Extrastatecraft: The Power of Infrastructure Space*, 11.

92. Easterling, *Extrastatecraft*, 73.

93. Myers, *Verandahs of Power*, 88; Silva, "Urban Planning in Sub-Saharan Africa: An Overview," 11–18; Home, "Colonial Urban Planning in Anglophone Africa," 22.

94. Bissell, *Between Fixity and Fantasy*, 225–226. In a Western, noncolonial context, Daston also argues that this is, in many ways, inherent in the nature of rules and regulations because they are always seeking to "bridge the chasm between the universal idea of good order and the most minute particulars in real life" (*Rules*, 154).

95. This reflected a broader strategy among colonial powers across the continent. As Silva writes, "Even when the planning law was not openly segregationist, plans tended to gradually introduce a functional and a social zoning, and what can be termed a defacto racial segregation. Besides the application of basic principles related to public hygiene, urban planning was expected to promote the separation of lifestyles. Racial segregation was also present in the annual budgetary decisions related to the location of the new infrastructures, and in the level of infrastructures and social equipments, frequently different in the European and in the African quarters: water inside home versus public fountains; WC versus public latrines; water collection systems versus open air disposal of dirty waters." Silva, "Urban Planning in Sub-Saharan Africa: An Overview," 18.

96. Mitchell, *Rule of Experts*, 4–5.
97. Scott, *Seeing Like a State*, 6. See also Myers, who argues that elite actors in British colonial states in East Africa developed city plans by "ignoring the everyday spatial life-world of the majority of the residents" (*Verandahs of Power*, 160), which resulted in the constant reframing of the city—a process that highlighted the failures of "orders without framework" and guaranteed a "persistence of disorder."
98. Hodge, *Triumph of the Expert*, 15–17.
99. Njoh, *Planning Power*, 10–11.
100. Mavhunga, *What Do Science, Technology, and Innovation Mean from Africa?*, 4–5.
101. Scott, *Seeing Like a State*, 6.
102. Cooper, *Struggle for the City*.
103. Mavhunga, *Transient Workspaces*, 4; Mavhunga, *What Do Science, Technology, and Innovation Mean from Africa?*; Oliver, "Vernacular Know-How," 113–126.
104. For an example of a similar process in a more rural area of Ghana, see Konadu, *Our Own Way in This Part of the World*. Daston argues that this sort of failure represents the failed transitions of rules into *norms* that are internalized as implicit conventions that have become second nature (*Rules*, 154–155).
105. Murunga, "Review of *Verandas of Power*," 210.
106. Mavhunga, *What Do Science, Technology, and Innovation Mean from Africa*, 9.
107. Mitchell, *Colonizing Egypt*, 165.
108. See also Janet Roitman, who argues that "economic knowledge about and of the economy is always organized against other, contending orderings"; See Roitman, *Fiscal Disobedience*, 8–9.
109. Bigon, "From Metropolitan to Colonial Planning," 84.
110. Roitman, *Fiscal Disobedience*, 3.
111. Roitman, *Fiscal Disobedience*, 3. Daston likewise describes regulations as "rules in action" (*Rules*, 154).
112. Roitman, *Fiscal Disobedience*, 3.
113. Home, "Colonial Urban Planning in Anglophone Africa," 53–54; Home, *Of Planting and Planning*, 3.
114. As Dirks argued, "Colonial knowledge both enabled colonial conquest and was produced by it." See Dirks, *Colonialism and Culture*, 3.
115. Home, "Colonial Urban Planning in Anglophone Africa," 54.
116. Njoh, *Planning Power*, 59–60; Home, "Colonial Urban Planning in Anglophone Africa," 54.
117. Mitchell, *Colonizing Egypt*, 13.
118. Burton, "Unfinished Business of Colonial Modernities,"3.
119. Mitchell, *Colonizing Egypt*, 33; Myers, *Verandahs of Power*, 3.
120. Sharan, "In the City, Out of Place," 4906.
121. Parker, *Making the Town*.
122. McFarlane, "Governing the Contaminated City," 415–435.
123. Simone, "Straddling the Divides," 102–117; Meagher, "Introduction: Special Issue on 'Informal Institutions and Development in Africa," 405–418.
124. Hart, "Informal Income Opportunities and Urban Employment in Ghana," 61.
125. Hart, "Informal Income Opportunities and Urban Employment in Ghana," 68.
126. Examples of such studies in Ghana include, for example: Clark, *Onions Are My Husband*; Robertson, *Sharing the Same Bowl*; Pellow and Chazan, *Ghana: Coping with Uncertainty*.
127. Mayne, *Slums*, 8.
128. Mayne, *Slums*, 16.

129. Mayne, *Slums*, 9–11.
130. Perera, "Planners' City," 57–73; Marris, "Meaning of Slums and Patterns of Change," 419–441; Manful, "Afterword," 232.
131. Mavhunga argues that "the dilemma of knowledge production in Africa centers on how its structures, practices, and concepts came to be informalized while inbound European ones were rendered formal." Mavhunga, *What Do Science, Technology, and Innovation Mean from Africa?*, 10.
132. Mitchell, *Rule of Experts*, 7.
133. Tilley, *Africa as a Living Laboratory*.
134. See, for example: Gandy, "Planning, Anti-planning and the Infrastructure Crisis Facing Metropolitan Lagos," 371–396. There is a persistent reliance on these binaries even when the analysis disproves them.
135. As Roitman argues in *Fiscal Disobedience*, "By looking at the institutionalization of certain concepts and practices—for instance, the institutionalization of 'tax' and 'price' in Cameroon—we can glimpse the various ways in which specific economic concepts and metaphors have been assumed and performed by local actors. And by studying the institutionalization of these concepts or historical institutions, we see how their practices involve various modalities, or how they are both assumed and yet disputed as forms of knowledge, which carry political and socioeconomic consequences for those involved. Instead of presenting representations and metaphors of the economy as an underlying generative system that induces behavior and leads to certain forms of organization, I show how, despite their efficacy, they tend to instability due to their fundamental ambivalence as institutions or political techniques" (7).
136. Marr, "Worlding and Wilding," 3–21.
137. Comaroff and Comaroff, *Theory from the South*, 7; Marr, "Worlding and Wilding," 6.
138. Stoler, *Along the Archival Grain*, 2; Plageman, "Colonial Ambition, Common Sense Thinking, and the Making of Takoradi Harbor, Gold Coast," 321; Stoler, "Colonial Archives and the Arts of Governance," 87–109.
139. Stoler, "Colonial Archives and the Arts of Governance," 87–109.
140. Writing about economic regulation in the midst of significant instability in Chad, Roitman similarly argues that multiple histories of the economy "are most evident to us in times of conflict, when the terms of logical practice are interrogated and the intelligibility of the exercise of power is not necessarily taken for granted" (*Fiscal Disobedience*, 3).
141. Plageman, "Colonial Ambition, Common Sense Thinking, and the Making of Takoradi Harbor, Gold Coast"; Daston, *Rules*, 176.
142. Clifford, *Our Days on the Gold Coast in Ashanti*; Coe, *Dilemmas of Culture in African Schools*.
143. Newell, *Literary Culture in Colonial Ghana: "How to Play the Game of Life."* Paul Schauert uses the Ghanaian concept of "managing" to describe the way that individuals utilized the state for the purpose of self-fashioning. See Schauert, *Staging Ghana*.
144. For additional analysis of colonial petitions as historical sources elsewhere in other British colonies in Africa, see Korieh, "May It Please Your Honor," 83–106.
145. Korieh, "May It Please Your Honor," 97.
146. Korieh, "May It Please Your Honor," 97; Lawrance, Osborn, and Roberts, *Intermediaries, Interpreters, and Clerks*.
147. Korieh, "May It Please Your Honor," 88.
148. Plageman, "Accra Is Changing Isn't It?"; Newell, "Newspapers, New Spaces, New Writers: The First World War and Print Culture in Colonial Ghana," 2.
149. Newell, "Newspapers, New Spaces, New Writers," 2; Lorang, *Writing Ghana, Imagining Africa: Nation and African Modernity*.

150. Barber, *Africa's Hidden Histories*.

151. Tania Murray Li describes at least some of these groups as "parties beyond 'the state' that attempt to govern," particularly in the context of high modernism. ("Beyond 'The State' and Failed Schemes," 383–394).

152. Satia, *Time's Monsters*; Tilley, *Africa as a Living Laboratory*; Mitchell, *Rule of Experts*; Scott, *Seeing Like a State*; Pels, "Anthropology of Colonialism: Culture, History, and the Emergence of Western Governmentality," 163–183.

153. Cooper, *Colonialism in Question*, 8–9; Roitman, *Fiscal Disobedience*, 7.

154. Appadurai, *Social Life of Things*.

155. Roitman, *Fiscal Disobedience*, 10.

1. "FRUITY" SMELLS, CITY STREETS, AND THE POLITICS OF SANITATION

1. *Gold Coast Leader*, July 12, 1902, 2.
2. *Gold Coast Leader*, July 12, 1902, 2.
3. Parker, *Making the Town*, 99–100.
4. Grace, "Poop."
5. Parker, *Making the Town*, 99–100.
6. Parker, *Making the Town*, 99–100.
7. Bissell, "Between Fixity and Fantasy," 220.
8. Bissell, "Between Fixity and Fantasy," 216.
9. Bissell, "Between Fixity and Fantasy," 225–226; Bissell, *Urban Design, Chaos, and Colonial Power in Zanzibar*.
10. Berry, "Hegemony on a Shoestring," 327–355.
11. Casely-Hayford, *Gold Coast Native Institutions*.
12. Griffith, "1892 Towns and Public Health Ordinance," in *Ordinances of the Gold Coast Colony*, 738.
13. Griffith, "1892 Towns and Public Health Ordinance," in *Ordinances of the Gold Coast Colony*, 739.
14. Casely-Hayford, *Gold Coast Native Institutions*, 382–388.
15. Casely-Hayford, *Gold Coast Native Institutions*, 382.
16. Griffith, "1892 Towns and Public Health Ordinance," in *Ordinances of the Gold Coast Colony*, 746–747.
17. Griffith, "1892 Towns and Public Health Ordinance," in *Ordinances of the Gold Coast Colony*, 748.
18. While they may exist somewhere in the archive in Accra, there are currently no archival records available that comprehensively track the outcome of inspections, fines, or other forms of regulatory enforcement. Our sense of their power can only be gleaned from rare moments of debate or discussion within the Town Council minutes.
19. TNA: PRO CO 99/8 1893–1894 Gold Coast Gazette.
20. TNA: PRO CO 99/8 1893–1894 Gold Coast Gazette.
21. "Municipality for Accra," *Gold Coast Chronicle*, September 19, 1896, 2.
22. "(Official) Municipality Ordinance," *Gold Coast Chronicle*, October 16, 1896.
23. In some cases, the editorial boards of newspapers that had been publishing articles in favor of the "Municipality Ordinance" changed their tune in response to public outcry. As the editors of the *Gold Coast Chronicle* noted: "On the press, it came to our knowledge that the Kings, chiefs and the townsmen of Accra and Christiansborg have expressed their

unwillingness to accept the 'Town Council Ordinance' in any shape or form, as it will prove a great hardship to the majority, if not to all of them. We have thought it prudent therefore to discontinue the insertion in our columns, of the remaining and unpublished portion of the letter of our correspondent that has appeared in our columns under the above heading [The (Official) Municipality Ordinance]." November 28, 1896.

24. *Gold Coast Chronicle*, November 25, 1899, 3.

25. Fortescue, "Accra Crowd, the Asafo, and the Opposition to the Municipal Corporations Ordinance, 1924–25," 351; Parker, *Making the Town*.

26. Dumett, "African Merchants of the Gold Coast"; Fortescue, "Accra Crowd, the Asafo, and the Opposition to the Municipal Corporations Ordinance, 1924–25."

27. Fortescue, "Accra Crowd, the Asafo, and the Opposition to the Municipal Corporations Ordinance, 1924–25."

28. Hart, *Ghana on the Go*, 58–59.

29. Hart, *Ghana on the Go*, 59; PRAAD: NAG (Accra) CSO 14/2/126 1932–1933 Boundary Road, Accra.

30. Casely-Hayford, *Gold Coast Native Institutions*, 382–388.

31. Bissell, *Urban Design, Chaos, and Colonial Power in Zanzibar*.

32. Bissell, *Urban Design, Chaos, and Colonial Power in Zanzibar*, 2.

33. The *nom de plume* Vortigern likely referenced Arthurian stories in which a series of kings called Vortigern make consistently foolish decisions with disastrous consequences for themselves and their kingdoms. Lupack, "Vortigern." https://d.lib.rochester.edu/camelot/theme/Vortigern.

34. *Gold Coast Chronicle*, July 28, 1894.

35. *Gold Coast Chronicle*, November 15, 1898, 2.

36. "We ask the Colonial Office authorities in England to follow us further on to the time in 1887 when Colonel B.P. White, the mention of whose name is associated with some pleasurable feelings, was administering the Government. We remember that he employed a large number of women to carry water from Beulah in the dry season, but the times are changing and who can predict what the prospect of the dry season will be in 1894." *Gold Coast Chronicle*, July 28, 1894.

37. *Gold Coast Chronicle*, July 28, 1894; *Gold Coast Chronicle*, November 15, 1898, 2.

38. *Gold Coast Leader*, March 20, 1909, 3.

39. "The (Official) Municipality Ordinance," *Gold Coast Chronicle*, October 16, 1896, 3.

40. *Gold Coast Chronicle*, March 29, 1901, 2.

41. *Gold Coast Chronicle*, March 29, 1901, 2.

42. *Gold Coast Chronicle*, September 10, 1896.

43. "Governor's Address on the Annual Estimates," *Gold Coast Leader*, December 25, 1909, 2–3.

44. "Governor's Address on the Annual Estimates," *Gold Coast Leader*, December 25, 1909, 2–3.

45. "Extract of the Minutes of the Legislative Council Held at Accra, 28th October 1910," *Gold Coast Leader*, January 21, 1911, 3.

46. *Gold Coast Leader*, November 22, 1913, 4. This critique was part of a broader condemnation of the Public Works Department in the colony: "It seems to us that there is a great deal of energy, mental and physical, misdirected and wasted in the public works due partly to want of interest by the officers of the Public Works Department in their business and mainly to the absence of co-ordinated and well arranged plans or schemes of work."

47. *Gold Coast Leader*, November 22, 1913, 4.

48. *Gold Coast Leader*, January 4, 1913.

49. *Gold Coast Leader,* January 4, 1913.
50. TNA: PRO CO 96/730/1 1936 Water Supply—Extension of Accra Water Works.
51. *Report on Accra Drainage Scheme* (Government Press), 1917; TNA: PRO CO 96/387/1 1929 Sewerage Scheme for Accra, Gold Coast Sessional Paper III 1916–1917.
52. TNA: PRO CO 96/775/11 1942–1943 Accra Sewerage Scheme.
53. TNA: PRO CO 96/730/1 1936 Water Supply—Extension of Accra Water Works.
54. TNA: PRO CO 96/730/1 1936 Water Supply—Extension of Accra Water Works.
55. TNA: PRO CO 96/730/1 1936 Water Supply – Extension of Accra Water Works.
56. TNA: PRO CO 96/730/1 1936 Water Supply – Extension of Accra Water Works.
57. TNA: PRO CO 96/730/1 1936 Water Supply – Extension of Accra Water Works.
58. TNA: PRO CO 96/730/1 1936 Water Supply – Extension of Accra Water Works.
59. *Report on Accra Drainage Scheme* (Government Press), 1917 TNA: PRO CO 96/387/1 1929 Sewerage Scheme for Accra, Gold Coast Sessional Paper III 1916–1917.
60. *Report on Accra Drainage Scheme* (Government Press), 1917 TNA: PRO CO 96/387/1 1929 Sewerage Scheme for Accra, Gold Coast Sessional Paper III 1916–1917.
61. *Report on Accra Drainage Scheme* (Government Press), 1917 TNA: PRO CO 96/387/1 1929 Sewerage Scheme for Accra, Gold Coast Sessional Paper III 1916–1917.
62. TNA: PRO CO 96/389/2 Gold Coast Colony Korle Lagoon Reclamation Scheme Report and Estimate, Percy Hall, Director of Public Works 3-1-29.
63. Public Records and Archives Administration Department: National Archives of Ghana (ACCRA) (hereafter cited as PRAAD: NAG (Accra)) CSO 20/1/3 1932–36 Minutes of Meetings, Accra Town Council.
64. PRAAD: NAG (ACCRA) CSO 20/1/3 1932–36 Minutes of Meetings, Accra Town Council.
65. PRAAD: NAG (ACCRA) CSO 20/1/3 1932–36 Minutes of Meetings, Accra Town Council.
66. PRAAD: NAG (ACCRA) CSO 20/1/3 1932–36 Minutes of Meetings, Accra Town Council.
67. PRAAD: NAG (ACCRA) CSO 20/1/3 1932–36 Minutes of Meetings, Accra Town Council.
68. PRAAD: NAG (ACCRA) CSO 20/1/3 1932–36 Minutes of Meetings, Accra Town Council.
69. PRAAD: NAG (ACCRA) CSO 20/1/3 1932–36 Minutes of Meetings, Accra Town Council.
70. Pexbroke Playfair, "The Public Health and Sanitation," *The Gold Coast Independent,* August 26, 1922, 12.
71. "Our Town Councils," *Gold Coast Leader,* June 21, 1913, 4.
72. "In the year 1911 the receipts of the Accra Town Council amounted to £7,780.4.11. £1,000 of this amount was grant-in-aid from the Government and the balance is derived from revenue got from licences on spirit, wine, and beer, etc., taxes on houses and wheels, fees derived from slaughter houses, market dues, penalties on prosecutions, sale of water, etc. The expenditure for the year 1911 totalled £7,558.18.9. In the items under Receipts in 1911 we note that the penalties on prosecutions yielded the sum of £348.18.0 or about 22% of the total receipts of the Town Council. We consider the policy as very unsound which makes collection of penalties a principal source of revenue of the Town Council. The native Sanitary Inspectors employed by the Council in 1911 received all put together £433 in salaries and this is about £84 less than the total sum collected from sanitary prosecutions, or in other words the revenue derived from sanitary prosecutions yield about 80% of the salaries paid to all the native Sanitary Inspectors combined. Or if we take as a basis of comparison the salaries paid to the Municipal and Assistant Municipal Inspectors who received £425 as wages in 1911, we find that the revenue derived by Town Council from sanitary prosecutions yielded a little over 82% of the cost of the employment of these two European officers. There are complaints all over the Colony of unnecessary sanitary prosecutions and excessive fines for sanitary offences. Natives are being ground down, persecuted, and oppressed in the name of Sanitation. 'They

do not keep their places clean,' 'they allow water receptacles to breed mosquitoes, and so on and so forth,' say the Sanitary Inspectors. Little or nothing is done to teach the people what is required of them, and it does appear that the object of the Sanitary authorities in subjecting the people to merciless prosecution for sanitary offences is not to correct insanitary habits, but by an irregular method to make people pay additional taxes for the upkeep of the Town Council, or contribute in non-Town Council towns towards the salaries of Sanitary officers." *Gold Coast Leader*, May 25, 1912, 5.

73. Pexbroke Playfair, "The Public Health and Sanitation," *Gold Coast Independent*, August 26, 1922, 12.

74. "Another Latrine Incident," *Gold Coast Chronicle*, September 19, 1896, 3.

75. "Notes and Comments," *Gold Coast Nation*, December 9, 1915, 4; see also *Gold Coast Leader*, June 22, 1912, 2.

76. "Notes and Comments," *Gold Coast Nation*, December 9, 1915, 4.

77. *Gold Coast Leader*, May 25, 1912, 5.

78. PRAAD: NAG (ACCRA) CSO 20/1/3 1932–36 Minutes of Meetings, Accra Town Council.

79. PRAAD: NAG (ACCRA) CSO 20/1/3 1932–36 Minutes of Meetings, Accra Town Council.

80. Gold Coast Sessional Paper III, 1916–1917, Report on Accra Drainage Scheme (Government Press), 1917 TNA: PRO CO 96/387/1 1929 Sewerage Scheme for Accra.

81. TNA: PRO CO 96/775/11/1942–1943 Accra Sewerage Scheme.

82. PRAAD: NAG (ACCRA) CSO 20/1/3 1932–36 Minutes of Meetings, Accra Town Council.

83. PRAAD: NAG (ACCRA) CSO 20/1/3 1932–36 Minutes of Meetings, Accra Town Council.

84. PRAAD: NAG (ACCRA) CSO 20/1/3 1932–36 Minutes of Meetings, Accra Town Council.

85. PRAAD: NAG (ACCRA) CSO 20/1/3 1932–36 Minutes of Meetings, Accra Town Council.

86. PRAAD: NAG (ACCRA) CSO 20/1/3 1932–36 Minutes of Meetings, Accra Town Council.

87. PRAAD: NAG (ACCRA) CSO 20/1/3 1932–36 Minutes of Meetings, Accra Town Council.

88. *Gold Coast Chronicle*, September 8, 1894, 4.

89. *Gold Coast Chronicle*, September 8, 1894, 4.

90. PRAAD: NAG (ACCRA) CSO 20/1/3 1932–36 Minutes of Meetings, Accra Town Council.

91. PRAAD: NAG (ACCRA) CSO 20/1/3 1932–36 Minutes of Meetings, Accra Town Council.

92. PRAAD: NAG (ACCRA) CSO 20/1/3 1932–36 Minutes of Meetings, Accra Town Council.

93. PRAAD: NAG (ACCRA) CSO 20/1/1 1930–31 Minutes of Meetings, Accra Town Council.

94. The most extreme and contentious example of this division was seen in debates over the malfeasance (embezzlement of council funds) by the appointed town clerk, who had long been an African employee. African councillors joined together as a bloc to protest the president's appointment of a European as a replacement clerk because the action seemed to unjustly ascribe criminality to the entire African population based on the actions of one person and because the appointment of a European represented a loss of one of the only pensionable positions for Africans within the ATC. The president of the ATC and other official members consistently pointed to the regulations to justify his upholding of the rights and responsibilities of his office and denied the accusations of discrimination levied by African councillors, but the conflict tainted the work of the council for a number of years and spilled over into other debates throughout 1935–1936. PRAAD: NAG (ACCRA) CSO 20-1-1 1930–31 Minutes of Meetings, Accra Town Council, PRAAD: NAG (ACCRA) CSO 20/1/3 1932–36 Minutes of Meetings, Accra Town Council.

95. PRAAD: NAG (ACCRA) CSO 20/1/3 1932–36 Minutes of Meetings, Accra Town Council.

96. Parker, *Making the Town*, 222.

97. Parker, *Making the Town*, 222; Fortescue, Accra Crowd, the Asafo, and the Opposition to the Municipal Corporations Ordinance, 1924–25.

98. TNA: PRO CO 96/381/1 1929 Report on Accra Drainage Scheme (Government Press), 1917, Sewerage Scheme for Accra, Gold Coast Sessional Paper III 1916–1917.

99. TNA: PRO CO 96/381/1 1929 Report on Accra Drainage Scheme (Government Press), 1917, Sewerage Scheme for Accra, Gold Coast Sessional Paper III 1916–1917.

100. TNA: PRO CO 96/381/1 1929 Report on Accra Drainage Scheme (Government Press), 1917, Sewerage Scheme for Accra, Gold Coast Sessional Paper III 1916–1917.

101. PRAAD: NAG (ACCRA) CSO 20/1/3 1932–36 Minutes of Meetings, Accra Town Council.

102. PRAAD: NAG (ACCRA) CSO 20/1/3 1932–36 Minutes of Meetings, Accra Town Council.

103. TNA: PRO CO 96/775/11 1942–1943 Accra Sewerage Scheme.

104. TNA: PRO CO 99/8 1894 Gold Coast Gazette; CO 1018/15 1943 The Accra Town Council Ordinance; TNA: PRO CO 96/772/20 *Municipal Affairs: Accra Town Council Legislation*.

105. Grace, "Poop."

106. TNA: PRO CO 96/687/1 1929 Sewerage Scheme for Accra; Joshua Grace, "Poop," *Somatosphere* http://somatosphere.net/2017/poop.html/.

107. Gold Coast Sessional Paper III, 1916–1817, Report on Accra Drainage Scheme, Gold Coast (Government Press, 1917), TNA: PRO CO 96/387/1 1929 Sewerage Scheme for Accra.

108. Grace, "Poop."

109. Bissell, "Between Fixity and Fantasy," 2–3.

110. Bissell, "Between Fixity and Fantasy," 4.

111. Grace, "Poop."

112. PRAAD: NAG (ACCRA) CSO 20/1/2 1931–32 Minutes of Meetings, Accra Town Council.

113. All road construction and maintenance was placed under the control of the Director of Public works in 1895. See Jennifer Hart, *Ghana on the Go*, 44.

114. Jennifer Hart, *Ghana on the Go*, 48.

115. PRAAD: NAG (ACCRA) CSO 14/1/76 1933 Public Works Extraordinary Estimates, 1933–34.

116. PRAAD: NAG (ACCRA) CSO 14/1/75 1931 Public Works Extraordinary Estimates, 1932–33.

117. PRAAD: NAG (ACCRA) CSO 14/1/76 1933 Public Works Extraordinary Estimates, 1933–34.

118. PRAAD: NAG (ACCRA) CSO 14/1/75 1931 Public Works Extraordinary Estimates, 1932–33.

119. PRAAD: NAG (ACCRA) CSO 14/1/75 1931 Public Works Extraordinary Estimates, 1932–33.

120. PRAAD: NAG (ACCRA) CSO 20/1/1 1930–31 Minutes of Meetings, Accra Town Council.

121. PRAAD: NAG (ACCRA) CSO 20/1/1 1930–31 Minutes of Meetings, Accra Town Council.

122. PRAAD: NAG (ACCRA) CSO 20/1/2 1931–32 Minutes of Meetings, Accra Town Council; PRAAD: NAG (ACCRA) CSO 20/1/3 1932–36 Minutes of Meetings, Accra Town Council.

123. PRAAD: NAG (ACCRA) CSO 20/1/3 1932–36 Minutes of Meetings, Accra Town Council.

124. PRAAD: NAG (ACCRA) CSO 20/1/2 1931–32 Minutes of Meetings, Accra Town Council.

125. PRAAD: NAG (ACCRA) CSO 20/1/3 1932–36 Minutes of Meetings, Accra Town Council.
126. PRAAD: NAG (ACCRA) CSO 20/1/3 1932–36 Minutes of Meetings, Accra Town Council.
127. PRAAD: NAG (ACCRA) CSO 20/1/3 1932–36 Minutes of Meetings, Accra Town Council.
128. PRAAD: NAG (ACCRA) CSO 20/1/3 1932–36 Minutes of Meetings, Accra Town Council.
129. PRAAD: NAG (ACCRA) CSO 14/2/115 1932–35 Roads in Accra—Drainage and Maintenance of.
130. PRAAD: NAG (ACCRA) CSO 14/2/115 1932–35 Roads in Accra—Drainage and Maintenance of.
131. PRAAD: NAG (ACCRA) CSO 14/2/115 1932–35 Roads in Accra—Drainage and Maintenance of.
132. PRAAD: NAG (ACCRA) CSO 14/2/115 1932–35 Roads in Accra—Drainage and Maintenance of.
133. PRAAD: NAG (ACCRA) CSO 14/2/115 1932–35 Roads in Accra—Drainage and Maintenance of.
134. PRAAD: NAG (ACCRA) CSO 14/2/115 1932–35 Roads in Accra—Drainage and Maintenance of.
135. PRAAD: NAG (ACCRA) CSO 14/2/115 1932–35 Roads in Accra—Drainage and Maintenance of.
136. PRAAD: NAG (ACCRA) CSO 14/2/115 1932–35 Roads in Accra—Drainage and Maintenance of.
137. PRAAD: NAG (ACCRA) CSO 14/2/115 1932–35 Roads in Accra—Drainage and Maintenance of.
138. PRAAD: NAG (ACCRA) CSO 14/1/75 1931 Public Works Extraordinary Estimates, 1932–33.
139. PRAAD: NAG (ACCRA) CSO 14/2/115 1932–35 Roads in Accra—Drainage and Maintenance of.
140. PRAAD: NAG (ACCRA) CSO 20/1/3 1932–36 Minutes of Meetings, Accra Town Council.
141. PRAAD: NAG (ACCRA) CSO 20/1/3 1932–36 Minutes of Meetings, Accra Town Council.
142. PRAAD: NAG (ACCRA) CSO 20/1/3 1932–36 Minutes of Meetings, Accra Town Council.
143. PRAAD: NAG (ACCRA) CSO 20/1/3 1932–36 Minutes of Meetings, Accra Town Council.
144. PRAAD: NAG (ACCRA) CSO 20/1/3 1932–36 Minutes of Meetings, Accra Town Council.
145. PRAAD: NAG (ACCRA) CSO 20/1/3 1932–36 Minutes of Meetings, Accra Town Council.
146. PRAAD: NAG (ACCRA) CSO 20/1/3 1932–36 Minutes of Meetings, Accra Town Council.
147. PRAAD: NAG (ACCRA) CSO 20/1/3 1932–36 Minutes of Meetings, Accra Town Council. It took several more years for construction to actually begin after the DPW and Government approved the proposal. Warrants were executed for the extension in 1940. PRAAD: NAG (ACCRA) CSO 14/1/78 1934 Public Works Extraordinary Estimates 1935–36;

PRAAD: NAG (ACCRA) CSO 14/1/79 1936 Public Works Extraordinary Estimates 1936–37;
PRAAD: NAG (ACCRA) CSO 14/1/80 1937 Public Works Extraordinary Estimates 1937–38;
PRAAD: NAG (ACCRA) CSO 14/1/361 1940 Special Warrants Under Head—Public Works Extraordinary: Special Warrant Under Head—Public Works Extraordinary, Sub-Head – Extension of Hansen Road to Hero Cemetery, Accra.

148. PRAAD: NAG (ACCRA) CSO 20/1/3 1932–36 Minutes of Meetings, Accra Town Council.
149. de Boeck, "Infrastructure"; Harvey and Knox, *Roads*, 5.
150. *Gold Coast Nation*, April 10, 1913, 270.
151. *Gold Coast Leader*, April 22, 1922, 9.
152. *Gold Coast Nation*, September 2, 1915, 7.
153. *Gold Coast Leader*, June 21, 1913, 4.
154. *Gold Coast Aborigines*, January 31, 1900, 2.

2. "HEALTH IS THE FIRST WEALTH"

1. "Sanitary Instructions for the Tropics," *Gold Coast Leader*, February 17, 1912, 2.
2. Newell, *Histories of Dirt*.
3. Fielding-Ould, "Observations at Freetown, Accra, and Lagos." Quoted in Patterson, "Health in Urban Ghana," 251–268.
4. Fielding-Ould, "Observations at Freetown, Accra, and Lagos," Quoted in Patterson, "Health in Urban Ghana."
5. Vaughan, *Curing Their Ills*:2.
6. Collingwood, *Imperial Bodies*, 1–2.
7. Collingwood, *Imperial Bodies*, 6.
8. Newell, *Histories of Dirt*, 7–9; Amoako-Gyampah, "Household Sanitary Inspection," 278–301.
9. Roberts, *Sharing the Burden of Sickness*, 19–21, 236–237; Tilley, *Africa as a Living Laboratory*.
10. Roberts, *Sharing the Burden of Sickness*, 143–151; Newell, *Histories of Dirt*, 7–9.
11. Newell, *Histories of Dirt*, 17–18.
12. Festus Cole, "Sanitation, Disease, and Public Health in Sierra Leone, West Africa, 1895–1922," 240.
13. "Gold Coast Colony," *Gold Coast Aborigines*, March 5, 1898, 4 (Paper on the Gold Coast Colony read by Mr. T. H. Hatton Richards, late assistant colonial secretary of the colony, at the Royal Colonial Institute, November 23, 1897).
14. Newell, *Histories of Dirt*, 35; Echenberg, *Plague Ports*, 11–12.
15. Francis Hart, *Gold Coast: Its Wealth and Health*, 239.
16. Amoako-Gympah, "Inherently Diseased and Insanitary?," 1–25.
17. Dumett, "Campaign against Malaria and the Expansion of Scientific Medical and Sanitary Services in British West Africa, 1898–1910," 167.
18. Roberts, *Sharing the Burden of Sickness*, 107–110.
19. Roberts, "Korle and the Mosquito," 344–346.
20. Roberts, "Korle and the Mosquito," 344–346; Roberts, *Sharing the Burden of Sickness*; Newell, *Histories of Dirt*, 19.
21. Roberts, "Medical Exchange on the Gold Coast during the Seventeenth and Eighteenth Centuries," 484.

22. Roberts, "Medical Exchange on the Gold Coast during the Seventeenth and Eighteenth Centuries," 484.
23. Curtin, "Medical Knowledge and Urban Planning in Tropical Africa," 596–597.
24. Roberts, *Sharing the Burden of Sickness*, 21.
25. Curtin, "Medical Knowledge and Urban Planning in Tropical Africa," 596–597.
26. Roberts, *Sharing the Burden of Sickness*, 8–11.
27. Roberts, "Medical Exchange on the Gold Coast," 490; Hart, *Gold Coast: Its Wealth and Health*, 239.
28. Dumett, "Campaign against Malaria," 155–156.
29. Roberts, "Medical Exchange on the Gold Coast," 490.
30. Dumett, "Campaign against Malaria," 156–157; Hart, *Gold Coast: Its Wealth and Health*, 239.
31. Sir Patrick Manson, "The Royal Colonial Institute," *The Gold Coast Commerce*, November 24, 1900.
32. Dumett, "Campaign against Malaria," 158–159.
33. "Notes on Current Events," *Gold Coast Chronicle*, May 11, 1895, 2. A similar sentiment was echoed in the August 7, 1895 issue of the *Gold Coast Chronicle* in an article titled "A Mystery" (see p. 2).
34. Dumett, "Campaign against Malaria," 155–156.
35. Rankin, *Healing the African Body*, 49.
36. Dumett, "Campaign against Malaria," 155–156.
37. Vaughan, *Curing Their Ills*, 29–30.
38. Festus Cole, "Sanitation, Disease and Public Health in Sierra Leone," 253; Dumett, "Campaign against Malaria," 167.
39. Newell, *Histories of Dirt*, 7–9.
40. Dumett, "Campaign against Malaria," 158–159; Hart argued, for example, that colonial officials should remove "native huts" when they are a menace to European residents, following the advice of leading public health, medical, and scientific officials (see *Gold Coast: Its Wealth and Health*, 238).
41. Newell, *Histories of Dirt*, 7–9.
42. Patterson, *Health in Colonial Ghana*, 38–40.
43. Bashford, *Imperial Hygiene*, 6; Hart, *Gold Coast: Its Wealth and Health*, 239.
44. Rankin, *Healing the African Body*, 6–7.
45. Manson, "The Royal Colonial Institute."
46. Manson, "The Royal Colonial Institute."
47. These movements were part of nineteenth- and early twentieth-century definitions of national identity through a politics of difference at home and throughout the empire. Bashford argues that "the pursuit of 'health' has been central to modern identity formation. It has become a way of imagining and embodying integrity and, problematically, homogeneity or purity of the self, the community, and especially in the early to mid 20th century, the nation" (Bashford, *Imperial Hygiene*, 4). "Public health," she argues, "is historically contemporaneous with, and part of, modern rationalities of government: political economy, liberal rule, nationalism, new politics of citizenship" (7).
48. Chamberlain claimed that he wanted "to show the colonies that the days of apathy and indifference" were over. See Festus Cole, "Sanitation, Disease and Public Health in Sierra Leone," 239–240.
49. Hart, Gold Coast: Its Wealth and Health, 236–237.
50. Manson, "The Royal Colonial Institute."

51. Manson, "The Royal Colonial Institute."
52. Bashford, *Imperial Hygiene*, 4–5; Collingwood, *Imperial Bodies*, 3–4.
53. Bashford, *Imperial Hygiene*, 4–5, 9.
54. Hart, *Gold Coast: Its Wealth and Health*, 238–239.
55. Dumett, "Campaign against Malaria," 161. Manson made a similar argument in his call for the development of the London School of Tropical Medicine in 1900: "This school strikes, and strikes effectively, at the root of the principal difficulty of most of these tropical colonies – disease. It will cheapen government and make it more effective. It will encourage and cheapen commercial enterprise. It will conciliate and foster the native." Hart, *Gold Coast: Its Wealth and Health*, 236–237.
56. "The Liverpool School of Tropical Medicine. Second Annual Report—1900," *Gold Coast Chronicle*, 3.
57. Dumett, "Campaign against Malaria," 161.
58. Francis Hart, *Gold Coast: Its Wealth and Health*, 236–237.
59. "Recognition by the Government," *Gold Coast Chronicle*, 3.
60. Bashford, *Imperial Hygiene*, 9.
61. Bashford, *Imperial Hygiene*, 1.
62. Echenberg, *Plague Ports*, 11–12.
63. Bin-Kasim, *Sanitary Segregation*.
64. Bashford, *Imperial Hygiene*, 7.
65. Patterson, *Health in Colonial Ghana*, 11.
66. Patterson, *Health in Colonial Ghana*, 12–13.
67. Quoted in Patterson, *Health in Colonial Ghana*, 11.
68. Patterson, *Health in Colonial Ghana*, 11–12.
68. Patterson, *Health in Colonial Ghana*, 11.
70. Hart, *Gold Coast: Its Wealth and Health*, 239–240.
71. Tilley, *Ordering Africa*, 3–4.
72. Tilley, *Ordering Africa*, 6–7.
73. Bashford, *Imperial Hygiene*, 4–5.
74. "Health is the First Wealth," *Gold Coast Aborigines*, January 31, 1900, 2.
75. Roberts, *Sharing the Burden of Healing*, 82–83; Swanson, "Sanitation Syndrome."
76. "Health Is the First Wealth," *Gold Coast Aborigines*, January 31, 1900, 2.
77. "Health Is the First Wealth," *Gold Coast Aborigines*, January 31, 1900, 2.
78. John Parker, *In the Time of Dying*.
79. Balakrishnan, "Building the Ancestral Public," 1–25; Parker, *In the Time of Dying*.
80. "Health Is the First Wealth," *Gold Coast Aborigines*, January 31, 1900, 2.
81. *Gold Coast Chronicle*, July 6, 1897, 4.
82. Tilley, *Africa as a Living Laboratory*.
83. Tilley, *Africa as a Living Laboratory*, 3; Bashford, *Imperial Hygiene*, 9.
84. Tilley, *Africa as a Living Laboratory*, 3; Hart, *Gold Coast: Its Health and Its Wealth*.
85. Bin-Kasim, *Sanitary Segregation*, 19; Curtin, "Medical Knowledge and Urban Planning in Tropical Africa."
86. "The Gold Coast Colony," *The Gold Coast Aborigines*, March 5, 1898, 4. This is a paper on the Gold Coast Colony read by Mr. T. H. Hatton Richards, late assistant colonial secretary of the colony, at the Royal Colonial Institute, November 23, 1897.
87. "The Gold Coast Colony," 4.
88. Patterson, *Health in Colonial Ghana*.
89. Dumett, "Campaign against Malaria," 166–167.
90. Dumett, "Campaign against Malaria," 166–167.

91. Tilley, *Africa as a Living Laboratory*, 11–12.
92. Rankin, *Healing the African Body*, 5.
93. Headrick, *Tools of Empire*.
94. Echenberg, *Plague Ports*, 2–4.
95. Tilley, *Africa as a Living Laboratory*, 11–12; Roberts, *Sharing the Burden of Sickness*; Konadu, *Our Own Way in this Part of the World*.
96. Roberts, *Sharing the Burden of Sickness*, 8–11.
97. Roberts, *Sharing the Burden of Sickness*, 15–18.
98. Patterson, *Health in Colonial Ghana*, 21.
99. Patterson, *Health in Colonial Ghana*, 20.
100. Roberts, *Sharing the Burden of Sickness*, 19–21.
101. Echenberg, *Plague Ports*, 278.
102. Echenberg, *Plague Ports*, 11–12; Myers and Ali Muhair, "Afterlife of the Lancaster Plan," 106.
103. Newell, Histories of Dirt, 27–28. For further discussions about the politics of soap in the empire, see Timothy Burke, *Lifebuoy Men, Lux Women: Commodification, Consumption, and Cleanliness in Modern Zimbabwe* (Durham, NC: Duke University Press, 1996); Anne McClintock, *Imperial Leather: Race, Gender, and Sexuality in the Colonial Contest* (New York: Routledge, 1995).
104. Newell, *Histories of Dirt*, 19, 35.
105. While there is some elision in colonial discourse, I seek to distinguish sanitation from medicine in this chapter and the one preceding. While both might fall under the umbrella of "public health," and may sometimes reinforce one another, they generally represented different spheres of expertise and authority.
106. Patterson, *Health in Colonial Ghana*, 20.
107. Newell, *Histories of Dirt*, 20–21.
108. Fielding-Ould, "Observations at Freetown, Accra, and Lagos," quoted in Patterson, "Health in Urban Ghana: The Case of Accra 1900–1940."
109. Francis Hart, *Gold Coast: Its Wealth and Health*, 236.
110. Francis Hart, *Gold Coast: Its Wealth and Health*, 236.
111. Roberts, *Sharing the Burden of Sickness*, 107.
112. Roberts, *Sharing the Burden of Sickness*, 109–110.
113. Roberts, *Sharing the Burden of Sickness*, 110–111; White, *Speaking with Vampires*.
114. Francis Hart, *Gold Coast: Its Wealth and Health*, 242.
115. Patterson, "Health in Urban Ghana," 257.
116. PRAAD: NAG (Accra) CSO 20/1/2 1931–32 Minutes of Meetings, Accra Town Council; PRAAD: NAG (Accra) CSO 20/1/3 1932–36 Minutes of Meetings, Accra Town Council.
117. "Public Hygiene in Its Relation to the Medical Profession," *Gold Coast Independent*, August 3, 1918, 3–4.
118. That is, "whether he likes it or not."
119. "Public Hygiene in Its Relation to the Medical Profession," *Gold Coast Independent*, August 3, 1918, 3–4.
120. "Public Hygiene in Its Relation to the Medical Profession," *Gold Coast Independent*, August 3, 1918, 3–4.
121. Roberts, "Medical Exchange on the Gold Coast," 507–509.
122. Roberts, "Medical Exchange on the Gold Coast," 507–509.
123. Patterson, *Health in Colonial Ghana*, 27.
124. Roberts, "Medical Exchange on the Gold Coast," 507–509; Patterson, *Health in Colonial Ghana*, 27.

125. Roberts, *Sharing the Burden of Sickness*.
126. Konadu, *Our Own Way in This Part of the World*, 3–12; Patterson, *Health in Colonial Ghana*, 27.
127. Kilson, *African Urban Kinsmen*, 89.
128. Kilson, *African Urban Kinsmen*, 94.
129. Roberts, *Sharing the Burden of Sickness*, 158.
130. For other scholarship on African science and medicine, see Osseo-Asare, *Bitter Roots*; Osseo-Asare, *Atomic Junction*; Mika, *Africanizing Oncology*; Livingston, *Improvising Medicine*.
131. Similar conditions were noted across British West Africa. See, for example, Cole, "Sanitation, Disease and Public Health in Sierra Leone," 238–266.
132. Cole, "Sanitation, Disease and Public Health in Sierra Leone," 238.
133. PRAAD: NAG (Accra) CSO 20/1/3 1932–36 Minutes of Meetings, Accra Town Council. A year earlier, Kitson-Mills drew parallels between the acculturation of Africans into hospital care and what he argued was a necessary education process to encourage the use of new market spaces and trading practice (PRAAD: NAG (Accra) CSO 20/1/3 1932–36 Minutes of Meetings, Accra Town Council). For more information on leprosy in the Gold Coast, see Gundona, *Coping with This Scourge*.
134. Dumett, "Campaign against Malaria," 173.
135. War and depression created new kinds of constraints for funding and often led to reductions, as well as more autocratic forms of policy and practice in order to combat disease. See Cole, "Sanitation, Disease and Public Health in Sierra Leone," 245.
136. Roberts, *Sharing the Burden of Sickness*, 192, 197.
137. Patterson, "Health in Urban Ghana," 252–253.
138. *Gold Coast Leader*, January 25, 1908, 2.
139. Echenberg, *Plague Ports*, 281–282; Patterson, *Health in Colonial Ghana*, 47–49.
140. Echenberg, *Plague Ports*, 13.
141. Roberts, "Black Death in the Gold Coast," 12.
142. Echenberg, *Plague Ports*, 13; Roberts, "Black Death in the Gold Coast," 12.
143. Simpson, *A Treatise on Plague*; Roberts, "Black Death in the Gold Coast," 12.
144. *Gold Coast Leader*, January 25, 1908, 2.
145. "Bubonic Plague," *Gold Coast Leader*, January 25, 1908, 3.
146. "Professor Simpson on the Plague," *Gold Coast Leader*, March 7, 1908, 3.
147. Patterson, *Health in Colonial Ghana*, 47–49.
148. As other articles in the same issue of the *Leader* noted, it is more difficult to exterminate insects like fleas than to get rid of rodents. "Rats and Disease," *Gold Coast Leader*, March 7, 1908, 4.
149. "Professor Simpson on the Plague," *Gold Coast Leader*, March 7, 1908, 3.
150. *Gold Coast Leader*, March 28, 1908, 3.
151. *Gold Coast Leader*, November 29, 1913, 5.
152. Roberts, *Sharing the Burden of Sickness*, 119.
153. Roberts, *Sharing the Burden of Sickness*, 119.
154. Roberts, *Sharing the Burden of Sickness*, 121.
155. Roberts, *Sharing the Burden of Sickness*, 121; Roberts, "Black Death in the Gold Coast," 17–18.
156. "Concerning Accra and Plague," *Gold Coast Leader*, June 20, 1908, 3.
157. Roberts, *Sharing the Burden of Sickness*, 122.
158. Roberts, *Sharing the Burden of Sickness*, 122.

159. "Concerning Accra and Plague," *Gold Coast Leader*, June 20, 1908, 3.
160. "Concerning Accra and Plague," *Gold Coast Leader*, June 20, 1908, 3.
161. "Concerning Accra and Plague," *Gold Coast Leader*, June 20, 1908, 3.
162. Roberts, *Sharing the Burden of Sickness*, 123.
163. Home, "Colonial Urban Planning in Anglophone Africa," 49.
164. Curtin, "Medical Knowledge and Urban Planning in Tropical Africa," 608.
165. Roberts, "Black Death in the Gold Coast," 4–5.
166. Roberts, "Black Death in the Gold Coast," 4–5; Bin-Kasim, *Sanitary Segregation*, 35, 27–28.
167. Curtin, "Medical Knowledge and Urban Planning in Tropical Africa," 596.
168. Curtin, "Medical Knowledge and Urban Planning in Tropical Africa," 595–596.
169. Bashford, *Imperial Hygiene*, 1–2. As Curtin notes, segregation was "only one thread among many" in Western town planning and segregation was motivated by both sanitary, social, economic, and racial concerns. While sanitary segregation was a common justification in West African cities, it was not the only concern: race and class were also important. ("Medical Knowledge and Urban Planning in Tropical Africa," 613).
170. Bin-Kasim, *Sanitary Segregation*, 49.
171. Curtin, "Medical Knowledge and Urban Planning in Tropical Africa," 605.
172. Bin-Kasim, *Sanitary Segregation*, 50–52.
173. Patterson, *Health in Colonial Ghana*, 47–49; Roberts, *Sharing the Burden of Sickness*, 118–125.
174. Patterson, "Health in Urban Ghana," 252–253; Bin-Kasim, *Sanitary Segregation*.
175. Roberts, *Sharing the Burden of Sickness*, 118–125.
176. Roberts, "Black Death in the Gold Coast," 28–30.
177. "Some Extracts from the Minutes of a Meeting of the Legislative Council Held on the 26th March Last," *Gold Coast Leader*, July 19, 1913, 4.
178. Patterson, *Health in Colonial Ghana*, 20.
179. Roberts, "Black Death in the Gold Coast," 30–31.
180. "Government Gazette of January 6, 1912," *Gold Coast Independent*, July 27, 1918, 3–4; "Legislative Council Debates," *Gold Coast Independent*, August 3, 1918, 4.
181. Bin-Kasim, *Sanitary Segregation*, 162; "The Accra Town Council and the Towns Ordinance 1894," *Gold Coast Independent*, July 27, 1918, 3.
182. Newell, *Histories of Dirt*, 22–23.
183. "Sanitary Progress," *Gold Coast Nation*, April 10, 1913.
184. Patterson, "Health in Urban Ghana," 255–256.
185. Patterson, "Health in Urban Ghana," 255–256.
186. Roberts, *Sharing the Burden of Sickness*, 115–118. The half-mile separation was "calculated to be more than a mosquito flight away from the Korle Lagoon," a standard that was later questioned by medical researchers (Roberts, "Korle and the Mosquito," 348–350).
187. Quoted in Dumett, "Campaign against Malaria," 170–171.
188. Dumett, "Campaign against Malaria," 170.
189. Dumett, "Campaign against Malaria," 170–171.
190. *Gold Coast Leader*, January 13, 1906, 5; *Gold Coast Leader*, December 25, 1909, 3.
191. Roberts, "Korle and the Mosquito," 348–350.
192. Quoted in Newell, *Histories of Dirt*, 40–41; Bin-Kasim argues for a more nuanced interpretation of Clifford's position: he was not inherently opposed to residential segregation but *was* skeptical about the medical arguments for segregation and concerned about the effects on African neighborhoods and opposition from Ga landowners (*Sanitary Segregation*, 61–65).

193. "Who Are Responsible?," *Gold Coast Nation*, June 26, 1913, 335.
194. "Destruction of Mosquitoes Bill," *Gold Coast Leader*, April 15, 1911, 3.
195. Patterson, "Health in Urban Ghana," 256; "Destruction of Mosquitoes Bill," *Gold Coast Leader*, April 15, 1911, 3.
196. "Destruction of Mosquitoes Bill," *Gold Coast Leader*, April 15, 1911, 3.
197. "Destruction of Mosquitoes Bill," *Gold Coast Leader*, April 15, 1911, 3.
198. Patterson, "Health in Urban Ghana," 256.
199. Patterson, "Health in Urban Ghana," 256.
200. Newell, *Histories of Dirt*, 29.
201. Patterson, "Health in Urban Ghana," 256.
202. *Gold Coast Leader*, May 25, 1912, 5.
203. "Editorial Notes," Gold Coast Leader, May 10, 1913, 4.
204. "Some Extracts from the Minutes of a Meeting of the Legislative Council held on the 26th of March Last," *The Gold Coast Leader*, July 19, 1913, 4.
205. Roberts, *Sharing the Burden of Sickness*, 151–153.
206. Roberts, *Sharing the Burden of Sickness*, 151–153.
207. PRAAD: NAG (Accra) CSO 20/1/3 1932–36 Minutes of Meetings, Accra Town Council.
208. PRAAD: NAG (Accra) CSO 20/1/3 1932–36 Minutes of Meetings, Accra Town Council.
209. PRAAD: NAG (Accra) CSO 20/1/3 1932–36 Minutes of Meetings, Accra Town Council.
210. PRAAD: NAG (Accra) CSO 20/1/3 1932–36 Minutes of Meetings, Accra Town Council.
211. Patterson, *Health in Colonial Ghana*, 21.
212. Newell, *Histories of Dirt*, 20–21. Wolé means "enter" in Yoruba; wolé wolé evokes the sanitary officers' practice of entering houses and compounds for inspections.
213. For more detailed accounting of the rates of sanitary inspection and the relative effectiveness of larval control, see: Akwasi Kwarteng Amoako-Gyampah, "Household Sanitary Inspection, Mosquito Control and Domestic Hygiene in the Gold Coast [Ghana] from the Late-Nineteenth to the Mid-Twentieth Century," *Social History of Medicine* 35, no. 1 (2021): 278–301.
214. PRAAD: NAG (Accra) CSO 20/1/3 1932–36 Minutes of Meetings, Accra Town Council; *Gold Coast Leader*, May 25, 1912, 5.
215. *Gold Coast Leader*, May 25, 1912, 5.
216. PRAAD: NAG (Accra) CSO 20/1/3 1932–36 Minutes of Meetings, Accra Town Council.
217. Quoted in Patterson, *Health in Colonial Ghana*, 38–40.
218. "Letters to the Editor," *Gold Coast Leader*, July 27, 1943, 7.
219. "Health Week Propaganda," *Gold Coast Independent*, October 14, 1922, 12.
220. Patterson, *Health in Colonial Ghana*, 38–40.
221. Patterson, *Health in Colonial Ghana*, 38–40.
222. "The Unofficial Members on the Governor's Address on the Estimates," *Gold Coast Leader*, February 24, 1912.
223. "Yellow Fever," *Gold Coast Leader*, January 9, 1915, 2.
224. "Yellow Fever," *Gold Coast Leader*, January 9, 1915, 2.
225. F. V. Nanka-Bruce and C. E. Reindorf, "Yellow Fever at Accra," *The Gold Coast Leader*, July 15, 1911, 5.
226. F. V. Nanka-Bruce and C. E. Reindorf, "Yellow Fever at Accra," *Gold Coast Leader*, July 15, 1911, 4.
227. F. V. Nanka-Bruce and C. E. Reindorf, "Yellow Fever at Accra," *Gold Coast Leader*, July 15, 1911, 4.
228. "Yellow Fever Panic in the Making," *Gold Coast Nation*, July 3, 1913, 341–342.

229. "The Estimates of Revenue and Expenditure for 1919—The Governor's Message. Address to the Legislative Council," *Gold Coast Leader*, March 9–April 5, 1919, 4. Governor Hugh Clifford had assessed the situation quite differently. Upon taking office in 1912, Clifford argued that the senior sanitary officer was an obstruction to governance and had acquired too much power, emboldening him to act outside of or in defiance of the governor's orders (Bin-Kasim, *Sanitary Segregation*, 61–65).

230. "The 'Mosquito Propaganda' and Segregation," *Gold Coast Leader*, August 12, 1911, 3, 26; Patterson, *Health in Colonial Ghana*, 38–40; Bin-Kasim, *Sanitary Segregation*, 41–42; Roberts, *Sharing the Burden of Sickness*, 151–153.

231. "Some Extracts from the Minutes of the Legislative Council Held on the 26th of March Last," *Gold Coast Leader*, July 19, 1913, 4.

232. Patterson, *Health in Colonial Ghana*, 38–42.

233. Bin-Kasim, *Sanitary Segregation*, 41–42.

234. Roberts, *Sharing the Burden of Sickness*, 143–151.

235. Patterson, *Health in Colonial Ghana*, 38–40.

236. *Gold Coast Chronicle*, January 22, 1897, 3.

237. *Gold Coast Chronicle*, January 22, 1897, 3. For a similar position, see Governor F. M. Hodgson, "The Gold Coast—Its Present Conditions and Prospects," *Gold Coast Aborigines*, May 13, 1899, 3. Also an address to the Africa Trade Section of the Liverpool Chamber of Commerce.

238. Patterson, *Health in Colonial Ghana*, 33–34; Hart, *Gold Coast: Its Wealth and Health*, 243.

239. Dumett, "Campaign against Malaria," 157–158.

240. Dumett, "Campaign against Malaria," 164.

241. Patterson, *Health in Colonial Ghana*, 35–36.

242. Dumett, "Campaign against Malaria," 165.

243. Newell, *Histories of Dirt*, 40–41.

244. Echenberg, *Plague Ports*, 11–12.

245. "Tropical Malaria and the Mosquito Theory," *Gold Coast Aborigines*, November 11, 1899, 3.

246. Newell, *Histories of Dirt*, 33–34.

247. Newell, *Histories of Dirt*, 40–41.

248. Newell, *Histories of Dirt*, 33.

249. Dumett, "Campaign against Malaria," 167–169.

250. "Sir William MacGregor at the Glasgow University," *Gold Coast Leader*, January 10, 1903, 3.

251. Patterson, *Health in Colonial Ghana*, 36–37.

252. "Prevention of Malaria," *Gold Coast Nation*, April 10, 1913, 272; "Homeopathic Treatment for the Malarial Fevers of West Africa. Dr. Hayward's Address to the African Trade Section of the Incorporated Chamber of Commerce of Liverpool," *Gold Coast Chronicle*, February 5, 1897.

253. Hart, *Gold Coast: Its Wealth and Health*, 243; Roberts, *Sharing the Burden of Sickness*, 115–118; 143–151.

254. *Gold Coast Leader*, September 6, 1913, 6.

255. "The Accra Town Council," *Gold Coast Chronicle*, March 29, 1901.

256. "Report on Accra Drainage Scheme (Government Press), 1917, Gold Coast Session Paper III 1916–1917," PRAAD: NAG (Accra) CSO 96/387/1 1929 Sewerage Scheme for Accra.

257. TNA: PRO CO 96/689/2 Gold Coast Colony, Korle Lagoon Reclamation Scheme.

258. Roberts, "Korle and the Mosquito," 348–350; Patterson, "Health in Urban Ghana," 256.
259. Roberts, "Korle and the Mosquito," 346–347.
260. Roberts, *Sharing the Burden of Sickness*, 226–228; Roberts, "Korle and the Mosquito," 348–350.
261. Patterson, "Health in Urban Ghana," 256.
262. Roberts, *Sharing the Burden of Sickness*, 226–228; "Letter from the Governor to LS Amery (Colonial Office) 7th May 1929," "Minutes 7/5/29," TNA: PRO CO 96/689/2 1929 Accra (Korle) Lagoon Reclamation Scheme.
263. "Letter from the Governor to LS Amery (Colonial Office) 7th May 1929," "Minutes 7/5/29," TNA: PRO CO 96/689/2 1929 Accra (Korle) Lagoon Reclamation Scheme.
264. "Extract from Report by the Acting Director of Public Works to the Acting Colonial Secretary 25/9/28" TNA: PRO CO 96/687/1 1929 Sewerage Scheme for Accra.
265. "Minutes 7/5/29," PH Morris, 4/6/29 TNA: PRO CO 96/689/12 1929 Accra (Korle) Lagoon Reclamation and Deepening Scheme.
266. "Minutes 7/5/29," Draft Letter from Sidney Webb to Governor of the Gold Coast, 17/6/29, TNA: PRO CO 96/689/2 1929 Accra (Korle) Lagoon Reclamation Scheme.
267. Roberts, *Sharing the Burden of Sickness*, 226–228.
268. Patterson, "Health in Urban Ghana," 256.
269. Roberts, "Korle and the Mosquito," 346–347.
270. For a more detailed accounting of this incident, see Roberts, "Korle and the Mosquito."
271. Quoted in Patterson, "Health in Urban Ghana," 256–257.
272. Quoted in Roberts, "Korle and the Mosquito," 359.
273. Roberts, "Korle and the Mosquito," 359.
274. Roberts, "Korle and the Mosquito," 344–346.
275. Roberts, "Black Death in the Gold Coast," 30–31.
276. Newell, *Histories of Dirt*, 24–26.
277. Dumett, "Campaign against Malaria," 172–173; Newell, *Histories of Dirt*, 24–26; Patterson, "Health in Urban Ghana," 252.
278. *Gold Coast Nation*, December 9, 1915, 1172.
279. "Current Events," *Gold Coast Independent*, August 19, 1922, 9.
280. Roberts, *Sharing the Burden of Sickness*, 143–151; Patterson, *Health in Colonial Ghana*, 11–12.
281. Roberts, *Sharing the Burden of Sickness*, 143–151.
282. "Current Events," *Gold Coast Independent*, August 12, 1922, 9.
283. Bashford, *Imperial Hygiene*, 7.
284. Roberts, *Sharing the Burden of Sickness*, 171–175.
285. Vaughan, *Curing Their Ills*, 11, 25.
286. Tilley, *Africa as a Living Laboratory*, 4–5.
287. Tilley, *Africa as a Living Laboratory*, 7–8; Vaughan, *Curing Their Ills*, 6.
288. Tilley, *Africa as a Living Laboratory*, 13.
289. Tilley, *Africa as a Living Laboratory*, 14. See also Vaughan, *Curing Their Ills*; Luise White, *Speaking with Vampires: Rumor and History in Colonial Africa* (Los Angeles: University of California Press, 2000); Nancy Rose Hunt, *Colonial Lexicon: Of Birth Ritual, Medicalization, and Mobility in the Congo* (Durham, NC: Duke University Press, 1999); Livingston, *Improvising Medicine*; Roberts, *Sharing the Burden of Sickness*; Konadu, *Our Own Way In This Part of the World*; Osseo-Asare, *Bitter Roots*; Osseo-Asare, *Atomic Junction*; Mika, *Africanizing Oncology*.
290. Quoted in Patterson, *Health in Colonial Ghana*, 15.

291. Newell, *Histories of Dirt*, 13, 19.

292. Newell argues that this sort of quiet resistance was common throughout towns in British West Africa (*Histories of Dirt*, 22–26).

3. AFRICAN TRADE AND EXPATRIATE ENTERPRISE IN THE COLONIAL CITY

1. Minutes of the General Monthly Meeting, January 8, 1940. PRAAD: NAG (Accra) CSO 20/1/8 1941 Minutes of Meetings, Accra Town Council.

2. Minutes of the General Monthly Meeting, January 8, 1940. PRAAD: NAG (Accra) CSO 20/1/8 1941 Minutes of Meetings, Accra Town Council.

3. H.S. Newlands, Report on the Objections Lodged with the Colonial Secretary against the Application of the Municipal Corporations Ordinance, 1924, to the Town of Accra with Minutes of Evidence (Gold Coast: Government Printing Office, Accra, 1925).

4. Sharan, "In the City, Out of Place," 4906.

5. Parker, "Making the Town."

6. McFarlane, "Governing the Contaminated City."

7. Fortescue, "Accra Crowd," 349.

8. Murillo, *Market Encounters*.

9. Fortescue, "Accra Crowd," 351.

10. Fortescue, "Accra Crowd," 351.

11. Fortescue, "Accra Crowd," 352.

12. Parker, *Making the Town*, 222.

13. GH PRAAD ADM 11/1/889 Municipal Corporations Ordinance—Protests against Application of to Accra, 1924.

14. GH PRAAD ADM 11/1/889 Municipal Corporations Ordinance—Protests against Application of to Accra, 1924.

15. CO 966/56 Municipal Corporations Ordinance Protests H.S. Newlands, *Report on the Objections Lodged with the Colonial Secretary Against the Application of the Municipal Corporations Ordinance, 1924, to the Town of Accra with Minutes of Evidence* (Gold Coast: Government Printing Office, Accra, 1925).

16. CO 966/56 Municipal Corporations Ordinance Protests "Minutes of Evidence," Adjabeng Lodge, Accra, November 20, 1924. H. S. Newlands, *Report on the Objections Lodged with the Colonial Secretary against the Application of the Municipal Corporations Ordinance, 1924, to the Town of Accra with Minutes of Evidence* (Gold Coast: Government Printing Office, Accra, 1925).

17. CO 966/56 Municipal Corporations Ordinance Protests "Minutes of Evidence," Adjabeng Lodge, Accra, 20 November 1924. H. S. Newlands, *Report on the Objections Lodged with the Colonial Secretary against the Application of the Municipal Corporations Ordinance, 1924, to the Town of Accra with Minutes of Evidence* (Gold Coast: Government Printing Office, Accra, 1925).

18. CO 966/56 Municipal Corporations Ordinance Protests "Minutes of Evidence," Adjabeng Lodge, Accra, 20 November 1924. H. S. Newlands, *Report on the Objections Lodged with the Colonial Secretary against the Application of the Municipal Corporations Ordinance, 1924, to the Town of Accra with Minutes of Evidence* (Gold Coast: Government Printing Office, Accra, 1925).

19. GH PRAAD ADM 11/1/889 Municipal Corporations Ordinance—Protests against Application of to Accra, 1924.

20. GH PRAAD ADM 11/1/889 Municipal Corporations Ordinance—Protests against Application of to Accra, 1924; Balakrishnan, *Anticolonial Public*, 197; Parker, *Making the Town*, 222.

21. Quoted in Fortescue, "Accra Crowd," 354–355.
22. Fortescue, "Accra Crowd," 353.
23. Quoted in Fortescue, "Accra Crowd," 355.
24. Fortescue, "Accra Crowd," 356.
25. Emmanuel Akyeampong, "Bukom and the Social History of Boxing in Accra: Warfare and Citizenship in Precolonial Ga Society," *International Journal of African Historical Studies* 35, no. 1 (2002): 44.
26. Fortescue, "Accra Crowd"; Robertson, *Sharing the Same Bowl*, 12–17; Pellow, *Women in Accra*, 38–63.
27. Fortescue, "Accra Crowd," 359–360.
28. Guggisberg, *Keystone*.
29. Minutes of the General Monthly Meeting, January 8, 1940. PRAAD: NAG (Accra) CSO 20/1/8 1941 Minutes of Meetings, Accra Town Council.
30. Minutes of the General Monthly Meeting, January 8, 1940. PRAAD: NAG (Accra) CSO 20/1/8 1941 Minutes of Meetings, Accra Town Council.
31. Minutes of the General Monthly Meeting, January 8, 1940. PRAAD: NAG (Accra) CSO 20/1/8 1941 Minutes of Meetings, Accra Town Council.
32. Robertson, *Sharing the Same Bowl*.
33. Minutes of the General Monthly Meeting, January 8, 1940. PRAAD: NAG (Accra) CSO 20/1/8 1941 Minutes of Meetings, Accra Town Council.
34. PRAAD: NAG (Accra) CSO 20/1/1 1930–31 Minutes of Meetings, Accra Town Council
35. Robertson, *Sharing the Same Bowl*, 82.
36. PRAAD: NAG (ACCRA) CSO 20/1/2 1931–32 Minutes of Meetings, Accra Town Council.
37. PRAAD: NAG (ACCRA) CSO 20/1/2 1931–32 Minutes of Meetings, Accra Town Council.
38. Parker, *Making the Town*, 120–222.
39. Minutes of the General Monthly Meeting, November 9, 1931. PRAAD: NAG (Accra) CSO 20/1/2 1931–32 Minutes of Meetings, Accra Town Council.
40. PRAAD: NAG (ACCRA) CSO 20/1/3 1932–36 Minutes of Meetings, Accra Town Council.
41. PRAAD: NAG (ACCRA) CSO 20/1/3 1932–36 Minutes of Meetings, Accra Town Council.
42. PRAAD: NAG (ACCRA) CSO 20/1/3 1932–36 Minutes of Meetings, Accra Town Council.
43. PRAAD: NAG (ACCRA) CSO 20/1/3 1932–36 Minutes of Meetings, Accra Town Council.
44. PRAAD: NAG (ACCRA) CSO 20/1/3 1932–36 Minutes of Meetings, Accra Town Council.
45. PRAAD: NAG (ACCRA) CSO 20/1/3 1932–36 Minutes of Meetings, Accra Town Council.
46. PRAAD: NAG (ACCRA) CSO 20/1/3 1932–36 Minutes of Meetings, Accra Town Council.
47. PRAAD: NAG (ACCRA) CSO 20/1/3 1932–36 Minutes of Meetings, Accra Town Council.
48. PRAAD: NAG (ACCRA) CSO 20/1/2 1931–32 Minutes of Meetings, Accra Town Council.
49. PRAAD: NAG (ACCRA) CSO 20/1/2 1931–32 Minutes of Meetings, Accra Town Council.

50. PRAAD: NAG (ACCRA) CSO 20/1/2 1931–32 Minutes of Meetings, Accra Town Council; PRAAD: NAG (ACCRA) CSO 20/1/3 1932–36 Minutes of Meetings, Accra Town Council.

51. PRAAD: NAG (ACCRA) CSO 20/1/3 1932–36 Minutes of Meetings, Accra Town Council.

52. PRAAD: NAG (ACCRA) CSO 20/1/3 1932–36 Minutes of Meetings, Accra Town Council.

53. PRAAD: NAG (ACCRA) CSO 20/1/3 1932–36 Minutes of Meetings, Accra Town Council.

54. "Motion by the Medical Officer of Health," Minutes of the General Monthly Meeting, December 11, 1939. PRAAD: NAG (Accra) CSO 20/1/7 1938–1940 Minutes of Meetings, Accra Town Council.

55. "Motion by the Medical Officer of Health," Minutes of the General Monthly Meeting, December 11, 1939. PRAAD: NAG (Accra) CSO 20/1/7 1938–1940 Minutes of Meetings, Accra Town Council.

56. "Motion by the Medical Officer of Health," Minutes of the General Monthly Meeting, December 11, 1939. PRAAD: NAG (Accra) CSO 20/1/7 1938–1940 Minutes of Meetings, Accra Town Council.

57. "Motion by the Medical Officer of Health," Minutes of the General Monthly Meeting, December 11, 1939. PRAAD: NAG (Accra) CSO 20/1/7 1938–1940 Minutes of Meetings, Accra Town Council.

58. Minutes of the General Monthly Meeting, May 12, 1930. PRAAD: NAG (Accra) CSO 20/1/1 1930–31 Minutes of Meetings, Accra Town Council.

59. Minutes of the General Monthly Meeting, August 10, 1936. PRAAD: NAG (Accra) CSO 20/1/3 1932–36 Minutes of Meetings, Accra Town Council; Minutes of the General Monthly Meeting, September 14, 1936. PRAAD: NAG (Accra) CSO 20/1/3 1932–36 Minutes of Meetings, Accra Town Council.

60. As Keith Hart's foundational 1973 article notes, these categories often overlap in the "informal economy," broadly construed. See also Jennifer Hart 2014.

61. Minutes of the General Monthly Meeting, May 14, 1934. PRAAD: NAG (Accra) CSO 20/1/5 1933–35 Minutes of Meetings, Accra Town Council.

62. Minutes of the General Monthly Meeting, May 11, 1936. PRAAD: NAG (Accra) CSO 20/1/3 1932–36 Minutes of Meetings, Accra Town Council; Minutes of the General Monthly Meeting, June 13, 1932. PRAAD: NAG (Accra) CSO 20/1/3 1932–36 Minutes of the Meetings, Accra Town Council; Minutes of the General Monthly Meeting, July 7, 1930. PRAAD: NAG (Accra) CSO 20/1/1 1930–31 Minutes of Meetings, Accra Town Council.

63. Parker, *Making the Town*, 141–142.

64. Minutes of the General Monthly Meeting, December 8, 1930. PRAAD: NAG (Accra) CSO 20/1/1 1930–31 Minutes of Meetings, Accra Town Council.

65. Minutes of the General Monthly Meeting, May 12, 1930. PRAAD: NAG (Accra) CSO 20/1/1 1930–31 Minutes of Meetings, Accra Town Council.

66. Minutes of the General Monthly Meeting, November 9, 1931. PRAAD: NAG (Accra) CSO 20/1/1 1930–31 Minutes of Meetings, Accra Town Council; Minutes of the General Monthly Meeting, October 12, 1931. PRAAD: NAG (Accra) CSO 20/1/1 1930–31 Minutes of Meetings, Accra Town Council; Minutes of the General Monthly Meeting, April 13, 1931. PRAAD: NAG (Accra) CSO 20/1/1 1930–31 Minutes of Meetings, Accra Town Council; Minutes of the General Monthly Meeting, March 9, 1931. PRAAD: NAG (Accra) CSO 20/1/1 1930–31 Minutes of Meetings, Accra Town Council; Minutes of the General Monthly Meeting, June 11, 1935. PRAAD: NAG (Accra) CSO 20/1/3 1932–36 Minutes of Meetings,

Accra Town Council; Minutes of Meetings, Accra Town Council, March 11, 1935. PRAAD: NAG (Accra) CSO 20/1/3 1932–36 Minutes of Meetings, Accra Town Council; Minutes of the General Monthly Meeting, September 12, 1932. PRAAD: NAG (Accra) CSO 20/1/3 1932–36 Minutes of Meetings, Accra Town Council; Minutes of the General Monthly Meeting, August 10, 1932. PRAAD: NAG (Accra) CSO 20/1/3 1932–36 Minutes of Meetings, Accra Town Council; Minutes of the General Monthly Meeting, July 11, 1932. PRAAD: NAG (Accra) CSO 20/1/3 1932–36 Minutes of Meetings, Accra Town Council; Minutes of the General Monthly Meeting, April 11, 1932. PRAAD: NAG (Accra) CSO 20/1/3 1932–36 Minutes of Meetings, Accra Town Council; Minutes of the General Monthly Meeting, March 14, 1932. PRAAD: NAG (Accra) CSO 20/1/3 1932–36 Minutes of Meetings, Accra Town Council; Minutes of the General Monthly Meeting, February 8, 1932. PRAAD: NAG (Accra) CSO 20/1/3 1932–36 Minutes of Meetings, Accra Town Council; Minutes of the General Monthly Meeting, August 13, 1934. PRAAD: NAG (Accra) CSO 20/1/5 Minutes of Meetings, Accra Town Council; Minutes of the General Monthly Meeting, January 8, 1934. PRAAD: NAG (Accra) CSO 20/1/5 Minutes of Meetings, Accra Town Council; Minutes of the General Monthly Meeting, December 11, 1933. PRAAD: NAG (Accra) CSO 20/1/5 Minutes of Meetings, Accra Town Council.

67. Minutes of the General Monthly Meeting, March 14, 1932. PRAAD: NAG (Accra) CSO 20/1/3 1932–36 Minutes of Meetings, Accra Town Council.

68. Minutes of the General Monthly Meeting, March 14, 1932. PRAAD: NAG (Accra) CSO 20/1/3 1932–36 Minutes of Meetings, Accra Town Council; Minutes of the General Monthly Meeting, June 11, 1934. PRAAD: NAG (Accra) CSO 20/1/5 1933–35 Minutes of Meetings, Accra Town Council.

69. Asante, "Nested Patriotism," 347–364; Murillo, *Market Encounters*.

70. PRAAD: NAG (Accra) CSO 20/1/1 1930–31, Minutes of Meetings, Accra Town Council.

71. As Parker (2000) notes, early incarnations of the Town Council did include an occasional African "Official Member," appointed by the colonial governor. By the 1920s, however, this practice had ceased altogether.

72. Minutes of the General Monthly Meeting, August 12, 1935. PRAAD: NAG (Accra) CSO 20/1/3 1932–36 Minutes of Meetings, Accra Town Council; Minutes of the General Monthly Meeting, November 14, 1932. PRAAD: NAG (Accra) CSO 20/1/3 1932–36 Minutes of Meetings, Accra Town Council.

73. Minutes of the General Monthly Meeting, January 13, 1936. PRAAD: NAG (Accra) CSO 20/1/3 1932–36 Minutes of Meetings, Accra Town Council; Minutes of the General Monthly Meeting, July 13, 1936. PRAAD: NAG (Accra) CSO 20/1/3 1932–36 Minutes of Meetings, Accra Town Council; Minutes of the General Monthly Meeting, September 13, 1936. PRAAD: NAG (Accra) CSO 20/1/3/ 1932–36 Minutes of Meetings, Accra Town Council.

74. Minutes of the General Monthly Meeting, September 21, 1931. PRAAD: NAG (Accra) CSO 20/1/2 Minutes of Meetings, Accra Town Council.

75. de Boeck, "Infrastructure: Commentary from Filip de Boeck."

76. Anand, "Pressure: The Politechnics of Water Supply in Mumbai," 542–564.

77. L. Val Vannis on behalf of the Freedom Defence Society, April 30, 1948 CO 964/15 1948 Memoranda received from members of the public—Accra and district.

78. "The Riots of 28th February 1948," *Today in History*, https://praad.gov.gh/index.php/the-riots-of-28th-february-1948/.

79. BNA: PRO CO 964/1 1948 Commission of Enquiry—Composition of the Committee and Administrative Arrangements.

80. BNA: PRO CO 964/1 1948 Commission of Enquiry—Composition of the Committee and Administrative Arrangements.

81. Memorandum by Dr. JB Danquah on his Apprehension, Removal, and Detention, and Reply to the Reasons so Far Assigned by Government for Such Action, BNA: PRO CO 964/2 1948 Gold Coast Commission of Enquiry—Causes of the Disturbance.

82. Memorandum by Dr. JB Danquah on his Apprehension, Removal, and Detention, and Reply to the Reasons so Far Assigned by Government for Such Action, BNA: PRO CO 964/2 1948 Gold Coast Commission of Enquiry—Causes of the Disturbance.

83. BNA: PRO CO 964/9 1948 Gold Coast Commission of Enquiry—Labour and Resettlement.

84. "Ex-Servicemen Rally Hist Arms Collection" BNA: PRO 964/5 1948 Gold Coast Commission of Enquiry—Press and Public Relations.

85. BNA: PRO 964/2 1948 Gold Coast Commission of Enquiry—Causes of the Disturbance.

86. BNA: PRO 964/2 1948 Gold Coast Commission of Enquiry—Causes of the Disturbance.

87. BNA: PRO 964/2 1948 Gold Coast Commission of Enquiry—Causes of the Disturbance.

88. V.B. Annan, Proprietor and Managing Director V.B. Annan & Co Ltd., Accra BNA: PRO 964/15 1948 Memoranda received from members of the public—Accra and district; L. Val Vannis on behalf of the Freedom Defence Society, 30 April 1948 BNA: PRO 964/15 1948 Memoranda received from members of the public—Accra and district; Joseph Meyers, BNA: PRO 964/15 1948 Memoranda received from members of the public—Accra and district.

89. BNA: PRO 964/15 1948 Memoranda received from members of the public—Accra and district.

90. BNA: PRO 964/15 1948 Memoranda received from members of the public—Accra and district; G. N. Alema BNA: PRO 964/15 1948 Memoranda received from members of the public—Accra and district.

91. G. N. Alema BNA: PRO 964/15 1948 Memoranda received from members of the public—Accra and district.

92. L. Val Vannis on behalf of the Freedom Defence Society, 30 April 1948, BNA: PRO 964/15 1948 Memoranda received from members of the public—Accra and district.

93. Eugene C. Kingspride Ugboma, *African Morning Post*, 21 April 1948, BNA: PRO 964/15 1948 Memoranda received from members of the public—Accra and district.

94. Gbese Mantse Nii Ayitey Adjin III BNA: PRO 964/15 1948 Memoranda received from members of the public—Accra and district.

95. BNA: PRO 964/15 1948 Memoranda received from members of the public—Accra and district.

96. BNA: PRO 964/15 1948 Memoranda received from members of the public—Accra and district.

97. The Gold Coast Merchants' Association BNA: PRO 964/15 1948 Memoranda received from members of the public—Accra and district.

98. BNA: PRO 964/15 1948 Memoranda received from members of the public—Accra and district.

99. "The Insatiable Pool," Ashanti Pioneer, 24 September 1947 BNA: PRO 964/5 1948 Gold Coast Commission of Enquiry—Press and Public Relations.

100. Verity, "AWAM Should Go: How Long Will the Government Live Under Its Charm?," *Spectator Daily*, 22 December 1947 BNA: PRO 964/5 1948 Gold Coast Commission of Enquiry—Press and Public Relations.

101. "One More River to Cross," *Ashanti Pioneer*, 1 August 1947 BNA: PRO 964/5 1948 Gold Coast Commission of Enquiry—Press and Public Relations; Leo Silberman, "The Evolution of Entrepreneurship in the Process of Economic Development," *The Annals of the American Academy of Political and Social Science* 305 (May 1956): 35; Report of the Commission of Enquiry into the Conduct and Management of the Supplies and Customs Departments (Martindale Commission), Accra, 1947; G. N. Alema BNA: PRO 964/15 1948 Memoranda received from members of the public—Accra and district.

102. Quoted in Bauer, *West African Trade*, 82, 83, 248. Cited in Winder, "The Lebanese in West Africa," *Comparative Studies in Society and History* 4, no. 3 (April 1962): 315, ft. 77; Report of the Commission of Enquiry into Representations Made by Mr. WE Conway, Esq, ADW Allen Esq., AG Leventis Esq., and AG Leventis & Co Ltd. Repudiating Allegations Made in the Report of the Commission of Enquiry into the Conduct and Mismanagement of the Supplies and Customs Dept (Sachs Commission), Accra, 1948.

103. "Past Performance," *Spectator Daily*, 18 June 1947, BNA: PRO 964/5 1948 Gold Coast Commission of Enquiry—Press and Public Relations.

104. "One More River to Cross," *Ashanti Pioneer*, 1 August 1947 BNA: PRO 964/5 1948 Gold Coast Commission of Enquiry—Press and Public Relations; John Gilpin, *Daily Echo*, 12 November 1947 BNA: PRO 964/5 1948 Gold Coast Commission of Enquiry—Press and Public Relations.

105. "Half-Hearted Measures," *Daily Echo*, 17 October 1947 BNA: PRO 964/5 1948 Gold Coast Commission of Enquiry—Press and Public Relations.

106. Nii Kwabena Bonne III Osu Alata Mantse and Oyokohene, 30 April 1948 BNA: PRO 964/15 1948 Memoranda received from members of the public—Accra and district.

107. John Gilpin, *Daily Echo*, 12 November 1947 BNA: PRO 964/5 1948 Gold Coast Commission of Enquiry—Press and Public Relations; Verity, "AWAM Should Go: How Long Will the Government Live Under Its Charm?," *Spectator Daily*, 22 December 1947 BNA: PRO 964/5 1948 Gold Coast Commission of Enquiry—Press and Public Relations.

108. Nii Kwabena Bonne III Osu Alata Mantse and Oyokohene, 30 April 1948 BNA: PRO 964/15 1948 Memoranda received from members of the public—Accra and district.

109. Nii Kwabena Bonne III Osu Alata Mantse and Oyokohene, 30 April 1948 BNA: PRO 964/15 1948 Memoranda received from members of the public—Accra and district.

110. Madam Eugenia Kai Sasraku and Madam Dora Afuah Quarshie, representatives of the women retail traders at Makola Market, conveyed by Ako Adjei BNA: PRO 964/15 1948 Memoranda received from members of the public—Accra and district.

111. Nii Kwabena Bonne III Osu Alata Mantse and Oyokohene, 30 April 1948 BNA: PRO 964/15 1948 Memoranda received from members of the public—Accra and district.

112. Nii Kwabena Bonne III Osu Alata Mantse and Oyokohene, 30 April 1948 BNA: PRO 964/15 1948 Memoranda received from members of the public—Accra and district.

113. Nii Kwabena Bonne III Osu Alata Mantse and Oyokohene, 30 April 1948 BNA: PRO 964/15 1948 Memoranda received from members of the public—Accra and district.

114. Nii Kwabena Bonne III Osu Alata Mantse and Oyokohene, 30 April 1948 BNA: PRO 964/15 1948 Memoranda received from members of the public—Accra and district.

115. "Anti-Inflation Campaign," Star of West Africa, 21 February 1948 BNA: PRO 964/5 1948 Gold Coast Commission of Enquiry—Press and Public Relations.

116. La Manche Nii Adjei Onano BNA: PRO 964/2 1948 Gold Coast Commission of Enquiry—Causes of the Disturbance.

117. "Mass Meet Calls Off Boycott," *Spectator Daily*, March 3, 1948, 1; BNA: PRO 964/5 1948 Gold Coast Commission of Enquiry—Press and Public Relations.

118. Madam Eugenia Kai Sasraku and Madam Dora Afuah Quarshie, representatives of the women retail traders at Makola Market, conveyed by Ako Adjei BNA: PRO 964/15 1948 Memoranda received from members of the public—Accra and district.

119. "After Boycott: Gambolling Crowd Shout at, Denounce UAC Staff," *Spectator Daily*, March 1, 1948, 1; BNA: PRO 964/5 1948 Gold Coast Commission of Enquiry—Press and Public Relations.

120. "After Boycott: Gambolling Crowd Shout at, Denounce UAC Staff," *Spectator Daily*, March 1, 1948, 1; BNA: PRO 964/5 1948 Gold Coast Commission of Enquiry—Press and Public Relations.

121. "After Boycott: Gambolling Crowd Shout at, Denounce UAC Staff," *Spectator Daily*, March 1, 1948, 1; BNA: PRO 964/5 1948 Gold Coast Commission of Enquiry—Press and Public Relations.

122. "Nii Bonne Denounces Looting," *Spectator Daily*, March 3, 1948, 3; BNA: PRO 964/5 1948 Gold Coast Commission of Enquiry—Press and Public Relations.

123. "Memorandum by Dr. J.B. Danquah on his Apprehension, Removal, and Detention, and Reply to the Reasons so Far Assigned by Government for Such Action," I. His Background BNA: PRO 964/2 1948 Gold Coast Commission of Enquiry—Causes of the Disturbance.

124. J. K. Appiah, Pensioner, Korle Woko, 27April, 1948 BNA: PRO 964/15 1948 Memoranda received from members of the public—Accra and district; "Memorandum by Dr. J. B. Danquah on his Apprehension, Removal, and Detention, and Reply to the Reasons so Far Assigned by Government for Such Action," I. His Background BNA: PRO 964/2 1948 Gold Coast Commission of Enquiry—Causes of the Disturbance.

125. BNA: PRO 964/1 1948 Commission of Enquiry—Composition of the Committee and Administrative Arrangements.

126. BNA: PRO 964/5 1948 Gold Coast Commission of Enquiry—Press and Public Relations; Gold Coast is Slipping Away, I. Enoch, *West African Monitor*, 2 March 1948; BNA: PRO 964/5 1948 Gold Coast Commission of Enquiry—Press and Public Relations.

127. Gold Coast is Slipping Away, I. Enoch, *West African Monitor*, 2 March 1948 BNA: PRO 964/5 1948 Gold Coast Commission of Enquiry—Press and Public Relations.

128. BNA: PRO 964/22 1948 Commission of Enquiry—Correspondence with Accra Town Council.

129. BNA: PRO 964/1 1948 Commission of Enquiry—Composition of the Committee and Administrative Arrangements.

130. BNA: PRO 964/32 1948 Gold Coast Commission of Enquiry – Report and Statement by HMG on the Report.

131. *Statement by His Majesty's Government on the Report of the Commission of Enquiry into Disturbances in the Gold Coast, 1948* (London: His Majesty's Stationery Office), 1948: 3 BNA: PRO 964/32 1948 Gold Coast Commission of Enquiry—Report and Statement by HMG on the Report.

132. Bayart, "African in the World: A History of Extraversion," 217–267.

133. Mayne, *Slums*, 12.

134. Simone, "Straddling the Divides"; Meagher, "Crisis, Informalization, and the Urban Informal Sector in Sub-Saharan Africa," 259–284.

135. Keith Hart, "Informal Income Opportunities," 61.

136. Keith Hart, "Informal Income Opportunities," 68.

137. Examples of such studies in Ghana include, for example: Clark, *Onions Are My Husband*; Roberts, *Sharing the Same Bowl*; Pellow and Chazan, *Ghana*.

4. OF PIRATE DRIVERS AND HONKING HORNS

1. PRAAD: NAG (Accra) CSO 20/8/4 1940–47 By-laws for the regulations of Municipal bus service Accra, "Letter from PATC to CS," May 31, 1940.
2. This was certainly not unusual. Rather, the experiences of drivers and passengers in the Gold Coast were representative of a much broader process throughout the imperial world—British or otherwise. See, for example, Fair, *Pastimes and Politics*.
3. Jennifer Hart, *Ghana on the Go*.
4. While the archival documentation on these incidents does give us a great sense of the drama of these debates, compared with the relatively dry formality of regulatory and policy debates that form much of the colonial archival record, there are some things we do not and cannot know given what sources are available. Records do not show police interactions or testimony from drivers and passengers, for example, and we do not have systematic surveys of drivers and passengers that might disaggregate the ethnic makeup of the city's driving population. As I have written about elsewhere, we do know that driving was gendered male in striking ways (see J. Hart, *Ghana on the Go*, 95–120); however, the gender of drivers does not seem relevant to these debates. While men who began driving during this period do remember these contestations, their memories are imprecise. Unfortunately, this lack of detail might mean that we cannot answer all questions, but it does not invalidate the exercise of asking *some* questions.
5. Myers, *Verandahs of Power*, 13.
6. Mavhunga, "Which Mobility for (Which) Africa? Beyond Banal Mobilities," 73.
7. Quayson, *Oxford Street, Accra*, 23. See also Larkin, "Politics and Poetics of Infrastructure," 327–343.
8. Mavhunga, *Transient Workspaces*, 13.
9. Interviews were collected by the author during two periods of fieldwork in 2007 and again in 2009. Interview subjects were identified in collaboration with leadership from the Accra branch of the Ghana Private Road Transport Union, the largest drivers' union in the country. Interviews began in areas where we had the strongest personal connections but quickly shifted in response to driver recommendation, focusing on areas of the city with the oldest histories and traditions of driving work, including La, Teshie, Tema, Mamprobi, Salaga, Accra Post Office, Korlebu, and Bukom. Drivers ranged in age from 19 to 90, but the vast majority of interviews were conducted with drivers who began their work in the 1930s and 1940s. Interviews were often conducted in Ga, with the help of a translator, Apetsi Amenumey.
10. Myers, *Verandahs of Power*, 2.
11. Parker, *Making the Town*, 170.
12. Moses Danquah, "The Romance of Our Roads," *Daily Graphic*, August 6, 1955; PRAAD: Accra, *Minutes of the Gold Coast Legislative Council*, 16 January 1901. See also, Dickson, *A Historical Geography of Ghana*, 221. For comparative examples, see Gewald, "Missionaries, Hereros, and Motorcars," 257–285.
13. The National Archives (TNA): Public Records Office (PRO) DO 35/359/7 Development of Transport Services in the colonies, 1930–1932; Tsey, *From Head-Loading to the Iron Horse*.
14. PRAAD: NAG (Accra) CSO 14/2/150 1929–47 Road Policy; PRAAD: NAG (Accra) CSO 14/2/123 1932–33 Scheduling of Roads; PRAAD: NAG (Accra) CSO 14/2/157 1935–39 Accra-Sekondi Road; PRAAD: NAG (Accra) CSO 14/2/200 1939 Closing of roads in connection with control of transport and fuel supplies, "Letter from JB Danquah, General Secretary of the Gold Coast Youth Conference to the Colonial Secretary, 20th October 1939" and "Letter from Secretary of the Accra & Eastern Province Chamber of Commerce to the

Colonial Secretary, 21 October 1939"; PRAAD: NAG (Accra) CSO 14/2/150 1929–47 Road Policy. The British colonial government did, in fact, build a few major trunk roads in the early twentieth century—most famously, the Accra-Kumasi Road, which ran nearly parallel to the railway. However, when Africans began utilizing motor transport and road technologies to bypass the railways altogether, officials quickly halted road construction and began a campaign of systematic disrepair and sabotage of existing roads, with particular focus on the trunk roads that provided direct competition for the railway. This campaign continued well into the 1930s and early 1940s, aided (or exacerbated) by the financial pressures of the global depression and the World Wars I and II, which strained colonial finances and left little money for even the most basic infrastructural construction and repair.

15. Guldi, *Roads to Power*; Ross, *Fast Cars, Clean Bodies*.
16. Seiler, *Republic of Drivers*.
17. See, for example, Aguiar, *Tracking Modernity*.
18. PRAAD-NAG (Accra) CSO 15/1/65 1932–40 Registration Statistics of Motor Vehicles Abroad—forms for.
19. PRAAD-NAG (Accra) CSO 17/4/9 1945 Vehicle Census.
20. "The Gold Coast Times," *Gold Coast Times*, August 12, 1882, 2; *Gold Coast Times*, December 10, 1881, 2.
21. "Accessories," *Gold Coast Independent*, August 3, 1918, 2.
22. "Accessories," *Gold Coast Independent*, August 3, 1918, 2.
23. "Accessories," *Gold Coast Independent*, August 3, 1918, 2.
24. "Letters to the Editor," *Gold Coast Independent*, July 13, 1918, 4.
25. "The Accra Town Council and the Town Councils Ordinance 1894," *Gold Coast Independent*, July 27, 1918, 3.
26. Gewald, "Missionaries, Hereros, and Motorcars."
27. Dickson, *A Historical Geography of Ghana*, 221; Hill, *Migrant Cocoa Farmers of Southern Ghana*, 235 fn1.
28. Hill, *Migrant Cocoa Farmers of Southern Ghana*, 234.
29. PRAAD: NAG (Accra) CSO 17/1/33 1933 Rail and Road Competition—Economic Situation of the Railway.
30. Jennifer Hart, *Ghana on the Go*, 74–88.
31. Ibrahim Ato, Anum Sowah, Yii O. Yem, J. F. Ocantey, La Drivers' Union Group Interview, Accra, March 26, 2009, interview by author; Hart, *Ghana on the Go*, 104.
32. Abraham Tagoe, Teshie Linguist, Accra, August 5, 2009, interview by author; Anon Circle Odawna Driver, Accra, August 27, 2009; Hart, *Ghana on the Go*, 103–105.
33. "Topical Jottings by Screech-Owl. Our Bush Roads," *Gold Coast Independent*, June 15, 1918, 1.
34. "Current Events," *Gold Coast Independent*, August 19, 1922, 9.
35. Jennifer Hart, "Motor Transportation, Trade Unionism, and the Culture of Work in Colonial Ghana," 185–209.
36. Much of the demand for regulation from British officials was rooted in a concern about road safety and the danger and risk of motor transportation. See, for example, Packer, *Mobility without Mayhem*, 13; Masquelier, "Road Mythographies," 831; Klaeger, "Introduction: The Perils and Possibilities of African Roads," 359.
37. PRAAD: NAG (Accra) CSO 17/1/15 1934 *Motor Traffic Regulations, 1934*; PRAAD: NAG (Accra) CSO 15/7/94 1936–38 *Motor Traffic Regulation No. 2 of 1934—Ashanti, Amendment to*; PRAAD: NAG (Accra) CSO 15/7/97 1937 *Regulation 21 of the Motor Traffic Ordinance, 1934—Amendment to*; PRAAD: NAG (Accra) CSO 15/7/93 1936 *Regulation 26 (6) of the Motor Traffic Regulation No. 31 of 1934—Amendment of*.

38. PRAAD: NAG (Accra) CSO 17/1/39 1935–1938 *Ashanti Motor Transport Union*, "Petition from Motor Transport Union Ashanti (WW Taylor, Secretary) to the Chief Commissioner of Ashanti, November 29th, 1937"; PRAAD-NAG (Accra) CSO 17/1/24 1935–1937 Motor Traffic Ordinance and regulations 1934—petitions against; Jennifer Hart, "Motor Transportation, Trade Unionism, and the Culture of Work in Colonial Ghana."

39. Quayson, *Oxford Street, Accra*, 70.

40. Cooper, *Africa Since 1940*.

41. The National Archives (TNA): Public Records Office (PRO) CO 96/773/20 1942–1943 Municipal Affairs: Accra Town Council legislation; Kumasi Town Council legislation.

42. PRAAD: NAG (ACCRA) CSO 20/1/1 1930–31 Minutes of Meetings, Accra Town Council.

43. PRAAD: NAG (ACCRA) CSO 20/1/2 1931–32 Minutes of Meetings, Accra Town Council.

44. PRAAD: NAG (ACCRA) CSO 20/1/3 1932–36 Minutes of Meetings, Accra Town Council.

45. PRAAD: NAG (ACCRA) CSO 20/1/2 1931–32 Minutes of Meetings, Accra Town Council; PRAAD: NAG (ACCRA) CSO 20/1/3 1932–36 Minutes of Meetings, Accra Town Council.

46. PRAAD: NAG (ACCRA) CSO 20/1/3 1932–36 Minutes of Meetings, Accra Town Council.

47. PRAAD: NAG (ACCRA) CSO 20/1/3 1932–36 Minutes of Meetings, Accra Town Council.

48. Quarshie Gene (chairman), P. Ashai Ollennu ("vice" chairman), and Simon Djetey Abe (secretary), La Drivers' Union Officers Group, La, Accra, March 23, 2009, interview by author; Abraham Tagoe, Teshie Linguist, Accra, August 5, 2009, interview by author.

49. "Letters to the Editor," *Gold Coast Independent*, July 13, 1918, 4.

50. Pellow, *Landlords and LodgersAccra*, 27.

51. The National Archives (TNA): Public Records Office (PRO) CO 96/712/10 "Report on the Accra Town Council, 1932–1933," *Municipal Annual Reports*, 1932–1933; The National Archives (TNA): Public Records Office (PRO) CO 96/767/11 "Annual Report of the Accra Town Council for the Year 1938–1939," *Municipal Affairs: Annual Reports*, 1940–1946.

52. PRAAD: NAG (Accra) CSO 14/6/78 1931–39 Street Lighting, Accra.

53. PRAAD: NAG (Accra) CSO 14/1/270 1938–39 Lorry Parks, Accra.

54. PRAAD: NAG (ACCRA) CSO 20/1/2 1931–32 Minutes of Meetings, Accra Town Council.

55. PRAAD: NAG (ACCRA) CSO 20/1/2 1931–32 Minutes of Meetings, Accra Town Council.

56. PRAAD: NAG (ACCRA) CSO 20/1/3 1932–36 Minutes of Meetings, Accra Town Council.

57. PRAAD: NAG (ACCRA) CSO 20/1/3 1932–36 Minutes of Meetings, Accra Town Council.

58. PRAAD: NAG (ACCRA) CSO 20/1/3 1932–36 Minutes of Meetings, Accra Town Council.

59. PRAAD: NAG (ACCRA) CSO 20/1/3 1932–36 Minutes of Meetings, Accra Town Council.

60. PRAAD: NAG (ACCRA) CSO 20/1/3 1932–36 Minutes of Meetings, Accra Town Council.

61. Alan Ryan argues that "liberal imperialism, or liberal interventionism, is the doctrine that a state with the capacity to force liberal political institutions and social aspirations upon

nonliberal states and societies is justified in so doing." Ryan, "Liberal Imperialism," *The Making of Modern Liberalism*.

62. PRAAD: NAG (ACCRA) CSO 20/1/3 1932–36 Minutes of Meetings, Accra Town Council.
63. PRAAD: NAG (ACCRA) CSO 20/1/3 1932–36 Minutes of Meetings, Accra Town Council.
64. PRAAD: NAG (ACCRA) CSO 20/1/3 1932–36 Minutes of Meetings, Accra Town Council.
65. PRAAD: NAG (ACCRA) CSO 20/1/3 1932–36 Minutes of Meetings, Accra Town Council.
66. PRAAD: NAG (ACCRA) CSO 20/1/3 1932–36 Minutes of Meetings, Accra Town Council.
67. PRAAD: NAG (ACCRA) CSO 20/1/2 1931–32 Minutes of Meetings, Accra Town Council.
68. PRAAD: NAG (ACCRA) CSO 20/1/2 1931–32 Minutes of Meetings, Accra Town Council.
69. PRAAD: NAG (ACCRA) CSO 20/1/3 1932–36 Minutes of Meetings, Accra Town Council.
70. PRAAD: NAG (ACCRA) CSO 20/1/2 1931–32 Minutes of Meetings, Accra Town Council.
71. PRAAD: NAG (ACCRA) CSO 20/1/3 1932–36 Minutes of Meetings, Accra Town Council.
72. PRAAD: NAG (ACCRA) CSO 20/1/3 1932–36 Minutes of Meetings, Accra Town Council.
73. PRAAD: NAG (ACCRA) CSO 20/1/3 1932–36 Minutes of Meetings, Accra Town Council.
74. PRAAD: NAG (ACCRA) CSO 20/1/3 1932–36 Minutes of Meetings, Accra Town Council.
75. PRAAD: NAG (ACCRA) CSO 20/1/3 1932–36 Minutes of Meetings, Accra Town Council.
76. PRAAD: NAG (ACCRA) CSO 20/1/3 1932–36 Minutes of Meetings, Accra Town Council.
77. PRAAD: NAG (ACCRA) CSO 20/1/3 1932–36 Minutes of Meetings, Accra Town Council.
78. PRAAD: NAG (ACCRA) CSO 20/1/3 1932–36 Minutes of Meetings, Accra Town Council.
79. Andrews A. C. Quaye (Chairman), Kobla, Tawiah Adjetey, and Tetteh, Tema Union Group, Accra, August 13, 2009, interview by author. In the 1960s, Minister of Transportation and Communication Krobo Edusei announced that taxis were to be painted "yellow-yellow," which, in addition to the light on the top of the taxi, required drivers to paint the front and back portions of their vehicle bright yellow. Such policies not only brought Ghanaian taxi services more closely in line with international practices, but they also helped to differentiate taxis from the increasing numbers of private vehicles on urban roads. Rumors circulated that the policy was the result of an unfortunate encounter in which a mistaken passenger seeking a taxi flagged down the car of Krobo Edusei himself who was driving his own private car in Accra.
80. Felicia, New Town Market Woman, Accra, August 18, 2009, interview by author; Ame, Ayo, Mary Yemokae Laryea, Rita Akoko Laryea, Labadi Market Women Group, Accra, August 18, 2009, interview by author.
81. Felicia, trader. New Town, Accra. August 18, 2009, interview by author.
82. The AAccraTC's archives are not currently open to the public, making it impossible to track revenues in any detail over time. Available documentation from town council reports in the 1930s, however, give the following figures (which apparently covered the running costs and drew a small profit): 1931–1932 (£9,288.19.7d, with £742.11.4d profit); 1932–1933 (£8,619.16.6d, with £676.18.2d profit); 1937–1938 (£12,348.11.2d, with £3,990.17.5d profit); 1938–1939 (£12,056.4.6d, with £3,817.12.1d profit). By comparison, in 1938–1939, the ATC contributed £1,000 to the Public Works Department toward the cost of maintaining town roads during the year. Profits from the municipal bus service were the primary source of Town Council revenue during the period beyond the taxes collected from ratepayers.
83. Ochonu, *Colonial Meltdown*.
84. Mamdani, *Citizen and Subject*; Lawrance, *Locality, Mobility, and "Nation."*
85. Mamdani, *Citizen and Subject*, 16–27.
86. PRAAD: NAG (Accra) CSO 15/7/94 1936–1938 Motor Traffic Regulation No. 2 of 1934—Ashanti, amendment to (speed limit in Kumasi); PRAAD: NAG (Accra) CSO 15/7/108 1935–1938 Motor Traffic on Roads in Accra—control of.
87. PRAAD: NAG (ACCRA) CSO 20/1/3 1932–36 Minutes of Meetings, Accra Town Council.

88. PRAAD: NAG (Accra) CSO 15/7/16 1934 *Yaw Kumah, motor driver, petition praying for restoration of his driving license.*
89. PRAAD: NAG (Accra) "Minute 3," Inspector General of Police, 4 January 1936, CSO 15/7/91 1936 Noise from traffic in residential areas—measure for the mitigation of.
90. PRAAD: NAG (Accra) "Letter from the Conservator of Forests to the Director of Public Works," 1 July 1936, CSO 15/7/91 1936 Noise from traffic in residential areas—measure for the mitigation of.
91. PRAAD: NAG (Accra) CSO 15/7/91 1936 Noise from traffic in residential areas—measure for the mitigation of.
92. PRAAD: NAG (Accra) "Minute 3," Inspector General of Police, 4 January 1936, CSO 15/7/91 1936 Noise from traffic in residential areas—measure for the mitigation of.
93. PRAAD: NAG (Accra) "Letter from Commissioner Western Province to the Colonial Secretary," 14 August 1936, CSO 15/7/91 1936 Noise from traffic in residential areas—measure for the mitigation of.
94. PRAAD: NAG (Accra) CSO 15/7/91 1936 Noise from traffic in residential areas—measure for the mitigation of.
95. Ibrahim Ato, Anum Sowah, Yii O. Yem, J. F. Ocantey, La Drivers' Union Group Interview, Accra, March 26, 2009, interview by author; Quarshie Gene (chairman), P. Ashai Ollennu (vice chairman), and Simon Djetey Abe (secretary), La Drivers' Union Officers Group, La, Accra, March 23, 2009, interview by author.
96. Hart, *Ghana on the Go*, 78–79.
97. Feld, *Jazz Cosmopolitanism in Accra*, 159–198. This book details the history of the La Drivers' Union Por Por Group, a musical group formed by drivers who use horns and tire irons to perform in La and throughout Accra.
98. The Accra Municipal Omnibus Services by-laws of 1927 forbid other vehicles competing for passenger hire along Accra streets, which are covered by municipal buses. This restriction applied only to Accra, which had an Omnibus Authority, and was not a general authority of all town councils. PRAAD: NAG (Accra) CSO 17/1/172 1943–1944 bus services legislation regarding.
99. PRAAD: NAG (Accra) CSO 17/1/172 1943–1944 bus services legislation regarding.
100. Fair, *Pastimes and Politics*.
101. Nate Plageman, *Highlife Saturday Night: Popular Music and Social Change in Urban Ghana* (Bloomington: Indiana University Press, 2012); Stephanie Newell, *Literary Culture in Colonial Ghana: How to Play the Game of Life* (Bloomington: Indiana University Press, 2002); Catherine Cole, *Ghana's Concert Party Theatre* (Bloomington: Indiana University Press, 2001).
102. Robertson, *Sharing the Same Bowl*; Clark, *Onions Are My Husband*.
103. Felicia, New Town Market Woman, Accra, August 18, 2009, interview by author; Ame, Ayo, Mary Yemokae Laryea, Rita Akoko Laryea, Labadi Market Women Group, Accra, August 18, 2009, interview by author.
104. Ibrahim Ato, Anum Sowah, Yii O. Yem, J. F. Ocantey, La Drivers' Union Group Interview, Accra, March 26, 2009, interview by author; Quarshie Gene (chairman), P. Ashai Ollennu (vice chairman), and Simon Djetey Abe (secretary), La Drivers' Union Officers Group, La, Accra, March 23, 2009, interview by author.
105. 8-8-32; PRAAD: NAG (Accra) "Letter from President, Accra Town Council to Colonial Secretary," 16 August 1935, CSO 15/7/108 1935–38 Motor Traffic on roads in Accra—control of.
106. PRAAD: NAG (Accra) "Letter from President, Accra Town Council to Colonial Secretary," 16 August 1935, CSO 15/7/108 1935–38 Motor Traffic on roads in Accra—control of.
107. PRAAD: NAG (Accra) CSO 20/8/4 1940–47 By-laws for the regulations of municipal bus service Accra.

108. The bomb failed to detonate, and the governor remained safe. However, La residents claim that this event darkened the reputation of La in the eyes of colonial officials. The damage to La's reputation, they argued, is evidenced in the colonial renaming of La as "Labadi" (or La Bad). It is still unclear what elements of this story are true and what others remain apocryphal. It is, at least, unclear in archival records on motor transportation that such a reputation impacted motor traffic regulations geared toward La. To the contrary, the first African driver in the Gold Coast was said to have come from La, chosen to drive Governor Guggisberg. La also established a reputation as a center for driver training and La drivers were widely known to be excellent. However, the negative perception about the residents of the town seems to be widely held both within and outside of La.

109. Mavhunga describes this as a form of extraversion (see also Bayart, "Africa in the World," 219) that has long been a part of African life and through which Africans engage and exchange with a broader world: "This behavior of incoming things in local hands does not necessarily represent the far-reaching tentacles of globalization; in fact, it also involves Africans themselves initiating the movements—of technology, capital, commodities, and other cultural goods. They are not necessarily appropriating modernities external to them, but are involved in a process of exchange, emitting their own things in exchange for those of the outside world. The goods are not just coming to them; they are actively constructing transnational networks through their own mobilities in the world—or those of their goods. Far from being a peculiar feature of today's cyber-connected world, this *extraversion* has been a persistent feature of African life, whether within the continent itself or beyond it, for millennia. It is within this global engagement that Africa has provincialized or tamed not just the cell phone and, more recently, revolutionized its applications, but before it guns, bicycles, cars, and so on. This is not particular to Africans but to colonized subjects elsewhere as well." (Mavhunga, *Transient Workspaces*, 11–12).

110. Mavhunga, *Transient Workspace*, 10.
111. Mavhunga, *Transient Workspaces*.
112. Myers, *Verandahs of Power*, 14/.
113. Larkin, *Signal and Noise*, 7.

5. BUILDING HOMES IN THE "NEW ACCRA"

1. Harold Cooper, Assistant Colonial Secretary, Gold Coast, "Emergency in Africa: The Gold Coast Earthquake," *Times*, 11/7/39 CO 96/762/3 1939 Earthquakes.
2. John Cadbury, H. L. Galway, Picton H. Jones, Trenchard, "The Gold Coast Earthquake: Opening of Relief Fund," *Times*, 8 June 1939 CO 96/762/3 1939 Earthquakes.
3. Despatch from Governor Arnold Hodson to Secretary of State Malcolm MacDonald, 2 August 1939 CO 96/762/4 1939 Earthquake—restoration of Accra rehousing.
4. Despatch from Governor Arnold Hodson to SOS Malcolm MacDonald, 5 July 1939 CO 96/762/4 1939 Earthquake—restoration of Accra rehousing).
5. Quayson, *Oxford Street, Accra*, 64–71.
6. CO 99/8 1893–1894 Gold Coast Gazette.
7. CO 99/8 1893–1894 Gold Coast Gazette.
8. Balakrishnan, *Anticolonial Public*, 186.
9. Parker, *Making the Town*, 144–145.
10. Balakrishnan, *Anticolonial Public*, 90.
11. Sackeyfio-Lenoch, *Politics of Chieftaincy*, 43–44; Balakrishnan, *Anticolonial Public*, 97; Parker, *Making the Town*.

12. Balakrishnan, *Anticolonial Public*, 97.
13. Quayson, *Oxford Street, Accra*, 87–88; Sackeyfio-Lenoch, *Politics of Chieftaincy*, 126–128.
14. Balakrishnan, *Anticolonial Public*; Sackeyfio-Lenoch, *Politics of Chieftaincy*, 132–133.
15. See, for example, Sackeyfio-Lenoch, *Politics of Chieftaincy*, 57–61, 126–128, 135; Quayson, *Oxford Street, Accra*.
16. Balakrishnan, *Anticolonial Public*, 102–103.
17. Sackeyfio-Lenoch, *Politics of Chieftaincy*, 43–44.
18. Quayson, *Oxford Street, Accra*, 37–63.
19. Balakrishnan, *Anticolonial Public*, 102–103.
20. Sackeyfio-Lenoch, *Politics of Chieftaincy*, 43–44.
21. Samuel Quarcoopome, cited in Sackeyfio-Lenoch, *Politics of Chieftaincy*, 57–61.
22. Balakrishnan, *Anticolonial Public*, 113–115.
23. Bissell, *Urban Design, Chaos, and Colonial Power in Zanzibar*, 133.
24. Balakrishnan, *Anticolonial Public*, 192.
25. CO 99/8 1893–1894 Gold Coast Gazette.
26. "Accra Town Council vs. Various Rate Payers," 11/9/30, PRAAD: NAG (Accra) SCT 17/4/51 Civil Record Book 20/5/30-23/10/31; In doing so, Blankson was following the processes laid out in the Town Councils Ordinance. See: CO 99/8 1893–1894 Gold Coast Gazette.
27. PRAAD: NAG (Accra) CSO 20/1/2 1931–32 Minutes of Meetings, Accra Town Council; PRAAD: NAG (Accra) CSO 20/1/3 1932–36 Minutes of Meetings, Accra Town Council.
28. PRAAD: NAG (Accra) CSO 20/1/3 1932–36 Minutes of Meetings, Accra Town Council; PRAAD: NAG (Accra) CSO 20/1/1 1930–31 Minutes of Meetings, Accra Town Council.
29. Balakrishnan, *Anticolonial Public*, 171–172.
30. Balakrishnan, *Anticolonial Public*, 190.
31. Sarah Balakrishnan cites a 1910 letter from the Ga *mantse* in which he protests that "'Our people [are] homeless and wandering till out of despair they are obliged to seek shelter somewhere out of the town, probably in the villages.' The colonial secretary did not deny the motive. He noted: 'proceedings under [the Infectious Disease Ordinance] are simpler and quicker than the acquisition of the houses under the Public Lands Ordinance.'" (Balakrishnan, *Anticolonial Public*, 190).
32. PRAAD: NAG (Accra) CSO 20/1/3 1932–36 Minutes of Meetings, Accra Town Council.
33. PRAAD: NAG (Accra) CSO 20/1/3 1932–36 Minutes of Meetings, Accra Town Council.
34. PRAAD: NAG (Accra) CSO 20/1/3 1932–36 Minutes of Meetings, Accra Town Council.
35. R.D. Pearce, *The Turning Point in Africa: British Colonial Policy 1938–48* (London: Frank Cass), 1982: 4. Cited in Harris and Parnell, "Turning Point in Urban Policy for British Colonial Africa, 1939–1945," 127.
36. PRAAD: NAG (Accra) CSO 20/1/3 1932–36 Minutes of Meetings, Accra Town Council.
37. PRAAD: NAG (Accra) CSO 20/1/3 1932–36 Minutes of Meetings, Accra Town Council.
38. PRAAD: NAG (Accra) CSO 20/1/3 1932–36 Minutes of Meetings, Accra Town Council.
39. PRAAD: NAG (Accra) CSO 20/1/3 1932–36 Minutes of Meetings, Accra Town Council.
40. PRAAD: NAG (Accra) CSO 20/1/3 1932–36 Minutes of Meetings, Accra Town Council.
41. PRAAD: NAG (Accra) CSO 20/1/3 1932–36 Minutes of Meetings, Accra Town Council.
42. Balakrishnan, *Anticolonial Public*, 145–146.
43. Balakrishnan, *Anticolonial Public*, 146; Parker, *In My Time of Dying*, 191–209.
44. Balakrishnan, *Anticolonial Public*, 152–153.
45. Balakrishnan, *Anticolonial Public*, 152–153.
46. Bissell, *Urban Design, Chaos, and Colonial Power in Zanzibar*, 173–175.
47. Mayne, *Slums*, 132.
48. Mayne, *Slums*, 76–79.

49. Mayne, *Slums*, 74–75.
50. For similar language in a European context see: Mayne, *Slums*, 91–92.
51. E. Maxwell Fry, Town Planning Adviser to the Resident Minister for West Africa, "Accra Town Planning Scheme Report," October 1945 PRAAD: NAG (Accra) CSO 20/12/20 1944–47 Town Planning Schemes for Accra.
52. As Fry notes in his report: "Unofficial census increases in this labor population during the middle of the war or as follows: Sabon Zongo: population increased in 1942 by 3993 of which 3077 are all casual or full-time imported laborers. Adabraka: Increased by 2211 in 1942 by 782 on a population of 7849. Agbogbloshi: Increased in 1942 by 782 on a population of 1187. Christiansborg: Increased in 1942 by 3129 on a population of 8495. To a slight degree this local overcrowding in poor conditions was balanced by a small exodus from other localities far removed from sites at which work is obtainable. In addition to the above, villages outside the municipal boundary, over which no sanitary control is exercised, except for larvae breeding, can be enforced, have deteriorated greatly by untoward labor immigration. This is noticeable at Malam Futa which has increased in population by about 2000" (Fry, "Accra Town Planning Scheme Report," October 1945 PRAAD: NAG (ACCRA) CSO 20/12/20 1944–47 Town Planning Schemes for Accra).
53. Grier, "Cocoa Marketing in Colonial Ghana," 89–115; Rhodie, "Gold Coast Cocoa Hold-Up of 1930–31," 105–118; Austin, "Capitalists and Chiefs in the Cocoa Hold-ups in South Asante, 1927–1938," 63–95.
54. Parker, *Making the Town*; Dumett, "African Merchants of the Gold Coast, 1860–1905"; Murillo, *Market Encounters*.
55. McCaskie, *Asante Identities*.
56. PRAAD: NAG (Accra) CSO 20/1/3 1932–36 Minutes of Meetings, Accra Town Council.
57. PRAAD: NAG (Accra) CSO 20/1/3 1932–36 Minutes of Meetings, Accra Town Council.
58. PRAAD: NAG (Accra) CSO 20/1/3 1932–36 Minutes of Meetings, Accra Town Council.
59. PRAAD: NAG (Accra) CSO 20/1/3 1932–36 Minutes of Meetings, Accra Town Council.
60. PRAAD: NAG (Accra) CSO 20/1/3 1932–36 Minutes of Meetings, Accra Town Council.
61. Quayson, *Oxford Street, Accra*, 67–68.
62. Quayson, *Oxford Street, Accra*, 70–71.
63. Appendix to the Report from NR Junner, Director of the Geological Survey to the Director of Public Works, 19 March 1935 TNA: PRO CO 96/762/3 1939 Earthquakes.
64. Appendix to the Report from NR Junner, Director of the Geological Survey to the Director of Public Works, 19 March 1935 TNA: PRO CO 96/762/3 1939 Earthquakes.
65. Minute 18/9/39 TNA: PRO CO 96/762/3 1939 Earthquakes.
66. Harold Cooper, assistant colonial secretary, Gold Coast, "Emergency in Africa: The Gold Coast Earthquake," *Times*, 11/7/39 TNA: PRO CO 96/762/3 1939 Earthquakes.
67. "The Accra Earthquake of 22 June 1939 by N. B. Junner—Recommendations for Rebuilding Accra," PRAAD: NAG (Accra) CSO 20/12/9 1939–40 Rebuilding of Accra. This proposal was ultimately deemed "impracticable" due to cost.
68. Minute 2/8/39 TNA: PRO CO 96/762/4 1939 Earthquake—restoration of Accra rehousing.
69. "The Accra Earthquake of 22 June 1939 by N.R. Junner—recommendations for Rebuilding Accra," PRAAD: NAG (Accra) CSO 20/12/9 1939–40 Rebuilding of Accra.
70. Minute 31/7/39 TNA: PRO CO 96/762/4 1939 Earthquake—restoration of Accra rehousing.
71. Minute from GLM Ransom 3/8/39 TNA: PRO CO 96/762/4 1939 Earthquake—restoration of Accra rehousing.

72. Minute from GLM Ransom 3/8/39 TNA: PRO CO 96/762/4 1939 Earthquake—restoration of Accra rehousing.

73. G. Orde Browne, "Notes on Rebuilding Projects for Accra" TNA: PRO CO 96/762/4 1939 Earthquake—restoration of Accra rehousing.

74. Despatch from Governor Hodson to the Lord Lloyd of Dolobran, SOS, 14 September 1940 TNA: PRO CO 96/769/1 1940 Earthquake restoration of Accra—rehousing.

75. Despatch from Governor Hodson to The Lord Lloyd of Dolobran, SOS, 14 September 1940 TNA: PRO CO 96/769/1 1940 Earthquake restoration of Accra—rehousing. The Governor proposed to build one Grade I (only as an example), 20 Grade II (5 rooms) and 135 Grade III (3–4 rooms) houses with self-contained kitchens, washing accommodations, etc.

76. Despatch from SOS Malcolm Macdonald to Governor Hodson, 30 March 1940 TNA: PRO CO 96/769/1 1940 Earthquake restoration of Accra—rehousing.

77. Dispatch from Governor Hodson to SOS MacDonald 29 December 1939 TNA: PRO CO 96/769/1 1940 Earthquake restoration of Accra—rehousing.

78. Pearce, *Turning Point in Africa*, 4. Cited in Harris and Parnell, "Turning Point in Urban Policy for British Colonial Africa, 1939–1945," 127.

79. Minute from Eastwood, 29/1/40 TNA: PRO CO 96/769/1 1940 Earthquake restoration of Accra—rehousing.

80. Letter from Sir Alan Burns to Oliver Stanley (secretary of state for the colonies?), 18 April 1945, TNA: PRO CO 96/803/5 Town and Country Planning Legislation 1945–1948.

81. As Quayson notes, these standards did exist for European housing, even if they were high-cost. But African communities were primarily designed with small-size, low-cost houses with shared latrines, built in close proximity. (Quayson, *Oxford Street, Accra*, 70–71). Acquah noted similar inequalities in the 1950s. See Acquah, *Accra Survey*, 50–51, 62.

82. E. Maxwell Fry, Town Planning Adviser to the Resident Minister for West Africa, "Accra Town Planning Scheme Report," October 1945 PRAAD: NAG (Accra) CSO 20/12/20 1944–47 Town Planning Schemes for Accra.

83. Quayson, *Oxford Street, Accra*, 70–71.

84. Fry, "Town Planning in West Africa," 203–204.

85. E. Maxwell Fry, Town Planning Adviser to the Resident Minister for West Africa, "Accra Town Planning Scheme Report." October 1945 PRAAD: NAG (Accra) CSO 20/12/20 1944–47 Town Planning Schemes for Accra.

86. Fry, "European Importation," 83–86; Whyte, "Modernism, Modernization and Europeanization in West African Architecture, 1944–94."

87. Fry and Drew, *Tropical Architecture in the Humid Zone* (London, 1956), 20. Cited in Whyte, "Modernism, Modernization and Europeanization in West African Architecture, 1944–94."

88. Fry, "European Importation," 80–82. Cited in Whyte, "Modernism, Modernization and Europeanization in West African Architecture, 1944–94."

89. PRAAD: NAG (Accra) CSO 20/12/20 1944–47 Town Planning Schemes for Accra.

90. Harris and Parnell, "Turning Point in Urban Policy for British Colonial Africa, 1939–1945," 141.

91. Harris and Parnell, "Turning Point in Urban Policy for British Colonial Africa, 1939–1945," 142; Acquah, *Accra Survey*, 53–54.

92. Acquah, *Accra Survey*, 46.

93. Acquah, *Accra Survey*, 54–57; Quayson, *Oxford Street, Accra*, 79–81.

94. Minute 5/6/45 TNA: PRO CO 96/803/5 Town and Country Planning Legislation 1945–1948.

95. Minute 5/6/45 TNA: PRO CO 96/803/5 Town and Country Planning Legislation 1945–1948.
96. Fry, "Town Planning in West Africa," 199–200.
97. Fry, "Town Planning in West Africa," 199–202.
98. Liscombe, "Modernism in Late Imperial British West Africa," 197–200.
99. For a study of modernism and its role in the shaping of social order and form in cities, see Holston, *Modernist City*.
100. Liscombe, "Modernism in Late Imperial British West Africa," 206.
101. Harris and Parnell, "Turning Point in Urban Policy for British Colonial Africa, 1939–1945," 138–139.
102. Uduku, "Modernist Architecture and 'the Tropical' in West Africa," 397–398; Harris and Parnell, "Turning Point in Urban Policy for British Colonial Africa, 1939–1945," 138–139; Bissell, *Urban Design, Chaos, and Colonial Power in Zanzibar*, 205.
103. This debate about the compound house dates back to at least 1908 when a committee of the ATC, including African barristers Thomas Hutton Mills and A. B. Quartey-Papafio, recommended the acquisition of "congested areas" and the abolition of the compound house. They argued that these houses were located on land that would be better for building stores and businesses because they were close to the harbor. Early visions for a new plan for Accra embraced the idea that only rich Ga people would be able to build within the town, and poorer residents would have to live outside the town. These plans were never realized—and it was often the wealthier Ga residents who relocated, rather than the poor ones so criticized by colonial officials (Parker, *Making the Town*, 198–201).
104. Quoted in Iain Jackson and Rexford Assasie Oppong, "The Planning of Late Colonial Village Housing in the Tropics: Tema Manhean, Ghana," *Planning Perspectives* 29, no. 4 (2014): 487–488.
105. Liscombe, "Modernism in Late Imperial British West Africa," 195–196.
106. Fry, "Town Planning in West Africa," 203.
107. Liscombe, "Modernism in Late Imperial British West Africa," 188.
108. Uduku, "Modernist Architecture and 'the Tropical' in West Africa," 400. In doing so, Fry and Drew, along with other modernist architects, evinced a fundamental ethnocentrism. As Jennifer Robinson notes, "Modernity could be understood as imply the West's self-characterization of itself in opposition to 'others' and 'elsewheres' that are imagined to be not modern, an opposition that was strongly reinforced through the mundane practices of colonization" (Quoted in Bissell, *Urban Design, Chaos, and Colonial Power in Zanzibar*, 24–25).
109. Petros Phokaides, "Detropicalizing Africa: Architecture Planning and Climate in the 1950s and 1960s," *docomomo* 48 (2013/1): 78.
110. Liscombe, "Modernism in Late Imperial British West Africa," 204; Fry, "European Importation," 83–86, 84.
111. Quoted in Liscombe, "Modernism in Late Imperial British West Africa," 194.
112. Quoted in Liscombe, "Modernism in Late Imperial British West Africa," 204.
113. Liscombe, "Modernism in Late Imperial British West Africa," 194.
114. Fry, "Accra Town Planning Scheme Report."
115. Murillo, "Ideal Homes and the Gender Politics of Consumerism in Postcolonial Ghana, 1960–70," 563–564; Holston, *Modernist City*, 4. Holston highlights CIAM's "premise of social transformation: that modern architecture and planning are the means to create new forms of collective association, personal habit, and daily life" (31).
116. Phokaides, "Detropicalizing Africa," 77. As Phokaides notes, not all architects working during this period embraced the tropical style. Constantinos Doxiadis's "ekistics" sought to

capture "the science of human settlements," connected more to "scientific planning theory" than imperial ideologies. The modernist presumptions in both, however, were remarkably similar (79).

117. Jackson and Oppong, "Planning of Late Colonial Village Housing in the Tropics," 493; Phokaides, "Detropicalizing Africa," 79.

118. Liscombe, "Modernism in Late Imperial British West Africa," 196.

119. Bissell, *Urban Design, Chaos, and Colonial Power in Zanzibar*, 219.

120. Fry, "Accra Town Planning Scheme Report."

121. Bissell, *Urban Design, Chaos, and Colonial Power in Zanzibar*, 269–270.

122. Liscombe, "Modernism in Late Imperial British West Africa," 208.

123. Fry, "Accra Town Planning Scheme Report."

124. Margaret Peil, *Cities and Suburbs: Urban Life in West Africa* (New York: Africana Publishing, 1981), 135.

125. Uduku, "Modernist Architecture and 'the Tropical' in West Africa," 402.

126. Pellow, "Group and Grid: Zongos and the British," 80–93.

127. Fry, "Accra Town Planning Scheme Report."

128. Fry, "Accra Town Planning Scheme Report."

129. Fry, "Accra Town Planning Scheme Report."

130. Fry, "Accra Town Planning Scheme Report."

131. Fry, "Accra Town Planning Scheme Report."

132. Fry, "Accra Town Planning Scheme Report."

133. Letter from the President of the Accra Town Council to the Acting Colonial Secretary, 28 July 1944, PRAAD: NAG (Accra) CSO 20/12/20 1944–47 Town Planning Schemes for Accra.

134. Quoted in Quayson, *Oxford Street, Accra*, 82.

135. PRAAD: NAG (Accra) CSO 20/12/20 1944–47 Town Planning Schemes for Accra.

136. Letter from Sir Alan Burns to Oliver Stanley (secretary of state for the colonies?), 18 April 1945, TNA: PRO CO 96/803/5 Town and Country Planning Legislation 1945–1948.

137. Minute from the Acting Colonial Secretary, 14 November 1946, PRAAD: NAG (Accra) CSO 20/12/20 1944–47 Town Planning Schemes for Accra.

138. TNA: PRO CO 964/2 1948 Gold Coast Commission of Enquiry—Causes of the Disturbance.

139. TNA: PRO CO 964/2 1948 Gold Coast Commission of Enquiry—Causes of the Disturbance.

140. Gold Coast is Slipping Away, I. Enoch, *West African Monitor*, 2 March 1948 TNA: PRO CO 964/5 1948 Gold Coast Commission of Enquiry—Press and Public Relations.

141. Acquah, *Accra Survey*, 28.

142. Acquah, *Accra Survey*, 46.

143. Acquah, *Accra Survey*, 47.

144. Plageman, "Accra Is Changing Isn't It?," 138.

145. Plageman, "Accra Is Changing Isn't It?," 139, 148.

146. Plageman, "Accra Is Changing Isn't It?," 148.

147. Plageman, "Accra Is Changing Isn't It?," 153.

148. Murillo, "Modern Shopping Experience," 376–377.

149. Inkumsah, "Introduction," in Trevallion and Hood, *Accra: A Plan for the Town*.

150. Inkumsah, "Introduction," in Trevallion and Hood, *Accra: A Plan for the Town*.

151. Barrett, "Preface," in Trevallion and Hood, *Accra: A Plan for the Town*.

152. Barrett, "Preface," in Trevallion and Hood, *Accra: A Plan for the Town*.

153. Trevallion and Hood, *Accra: A Plan for the Town*, 4.

154. Trevallion and Hood, *Accra: A Plan for the Town*, 23–31.
155. Trevallion and Hood, *Accra: A Plan for the Town*, 87.
156. Acquah, *Accra Survey*, 54–57.
157. Acquah, *Accra Survey*, 54–57.
158. "Mr. Mensah Builds a House," *Colonial Film: Moving Images of the British Empire*, http://www.colonialfilm.org.uk/node/615; "Mr. Mensah Builds a House," Colonial Film Archive, YouTube, December 13, 2013. https://www.youtube.com/watch?v=e_FXmC1Niwk.
159. Bloom and Skinner, "Modernity and Danger," 121–153.
160. "Mr. Mensah Builds a House," *Colonial Film: Moving Images of the British Empire*, http://www.colonialfilm.org.uk/node/615; "Mr. Mensah Builds a House," Colonial Film Archive, YouTube, December 13, 2013. https://www.youtube.com/watch?v=e_FXmC1Niwk.
161. Plans for the Development of Accra, 28 May 1954, Notes of a meeting attended by A.F. Greenwood, Permanent Secretary, Ministry of Local Govt; AES Alcock, Town Planning Adviser; C. Williams, Commissioner of Lands; L. Britton, Acting Permanent Secretary, Ministry of Local Govt and Housing PRAAD: NAG (Accra) RG 5/1/195 1954–1955 Improvement of Accra Vol. 1.
162. Johnson Appiah, "Vote to Improve Accra Is Cut Down," extracted from *Daily Graphic* of Saturday, September 24, 1955, PRAAD: NAG (Accra) RG 5/1/196 1955–56 Improvement of Accra Vol. 2.
163. Plans for the Development of Accra, 28 May 1954, Notes of a meeting attended by A. F. Greenwood, Permanent Secretary, Ministry of Local Govt; AES Alcock, Town Planning Adviser; C. Williams, Commissioner of Lands; L. Britton, Acting Permanent Secretary, Ministry of Local Govt and Housing PRAAD: NAG (Accra) RG 5/1/195 1954–1955 Improvement of Accra Vol. 1. These priorities reflected only thirteen out of forty-six submitted proposals that had been forwarded by the Accra Municipal Council to the working party planning the Independence Day celebrations. They specifically focused on those projects they thought "could be completed by the end of 1956 and which would improve parts of Accra which might figure prominently in the celebrations." (PRAAD: NAG (Accra) RG 5/1/195 1954–1955 Improvement of Accra Vol. 1).
164. Johnson Appiah, "Vote to Improve Accra Is Cut Down," in *Daily Graphic* of Saturday, September 24, 1955, PRAAD: NAG (Accra) RG 5/1/196 1955–56 Improvement of Accra Vol. 2.
165. Acquah, *Accra Survey*, 31.
166. Acquah, *Accra Survey*, 28.
167. Acquah, *Accra Survey*, 28–29, 31.
168. Acquah, *Accra Survey*, 47.
169. Attoh Quarshie, interview with author, August 24, 2009; October 17, 2009.
170. PRAAD: NAG (Accra) RG 5/1/170 1957–1961 Towns Ordinance.
171. PRAAD: NAG (Accra) RG 5/1/170 1957–1961 Towns Ordinance.
172. PRAAD: NAG (Accra) RG 5/1/170 1957–1961 Towns Ordinance.
173. Bissell, *Urban Design, Chaos, and Colonial Power in Zanzibar*.
174. Quayson, *Oxford Street, Accra*, 85–86; Manful, "Afterword," 232.
175. Quayson, *Oxford Street, Accra*, 86.

CONCLUSION

1. John Spaull, "World's Biggest E-dump, or Vital Supplies for Ghana?," The Trust Project, May 10, 2015, https://www.scidev.net/global/multimedia/electronic-waste-dump-supplies-ghana/.
2. Paul Stacey, *State of Slum: Precarity and Informal Governance at the Margins in Accra* (London: Zed, 2021).

3. Nil Ayikwe Okin, "Agbogbloshie Scrap Dealers Ask for Alternative Space after Demolition Exercise," CNR Citi Newsroom, July 7, 2021, https://citinewsroom.com/2021/07/agbogbloshie-scrap-dealers-ask-for-alternative-space-after-demolition-exercise/.

4. The campaigned kicked off with a massive clean-up operation on April 22, 2021 in four constituencies (Ayawaso Central, North, East, and West-Wuogon) executed by various members of the security service and employees of the waste management service, Zoomlion, with which the city contracts for waste removal. Okin, "Agbogbloshie Scrap Dealers Ask for Alternative Space after Demolition Exercise," CNR Citi Newsroom, July 7, 2021, https://citinewsroom.com/2021/04/lets-make-accra-work-campaign-kickstarts-with-clean-up-exercise-in-four-constituencies/.

5. Daisy Palinwinde Jacobs, "We Didn't Know Relocation to Adjen Kotoku Included Us—Agbogbloshie Scrap Dealers," CNR Citi Newsroom, July 7, 2021, https://citinewsroom.com/2021/07/we-didnt-know-relocation-to-adjen-kotoku-included-us-agbogbloshie-scrap-dealers/.

6. Jacobs, "We Didn't Know Relocation to Adjen Kotoku Included Us—Agbogbloshie Scrap Dealers."

7. For articles addressing Agbogbloshie dating back to 2015, see: https://qamp.net/press/.

8. Church of Pentecost, "Agbogbloshie Redevelopment Scheme Ready," April 20, 2022, https://thecophq.org/agbogbloshie-redevelopment-scheme-ready/.

9. Church of Pentecost, "Agbogbloshie Redevelopment Scheme Ready."

10. Church of Pentecost, "Agbogbloshie Redevelopment Scheme Ready."

11. Church of Pentecost, "Agbogbloshie Redevelopment Scheme Ready."

12. Spaull, "World's Biggest E-dump, or Vital Supplies for Ghana?"

13. Muntaka Chasant, "Agbogbloshie Demolition: The End of an Era Or Injustice?" *Muntaka: A Journal of Emerging Issues*, https://www.muntaka.com/agbogbloshie-demolition/.

14. Kwame Asare Boadu, "Agbobloshie Redevelopment Scheme Ready," Graphic Online, https://www.graphic.com.gh/news/general-news/ghana-news-agbogbloshie-redevelopment-scheme-ready.html; https://thecophq.org/agbogbloshie-redevelopment-scheme-ready/.

15. Stoler, *Duress: Imperial Durabilities in Our Times* 3–6; see also Mitchell, *Rule of Experts*, 1.

16. Stoler, *Duress: Imperial Durabilities in Our Times*, 3–4.

17. Porter, *Unlearning the Colonial Culture of Planning*; Demissie, *Colonial Architecture and Urbanism in Africa*; Jacobs, *Edge of Empire*.

18. Porter, *Unlearning the Colonial Culture of Planning*, 2.

19. Adas, *Machines as the Measure of Men*; Hodge, *Triumph of the Expert*.

20. Henri Lefebvre, *The Production of Space* (Hoboken, NJ: Wiley-Blackwell, 1992); Porter, *Unlearning the Colonial Culture of Planning*; Parker, *Making the Town*; Hodge, *Triumph of the Expert*, 7–8.

21. McFarlane, "Governing the Contaminated City," 418; Srivastava, *Entangled Urbanism*, 4; Demissie, *Colonial Architecture and Urban Planning in Africa*, 3; Home and King, "Urbanism and Master Planning," 74–75.

22. McFarlane, "Governing the Contaminated City," 419.

23. Crinson "Imperial Modernism."

24. Gandy, "Planning, Anti-Planning and the Infrastructure Crisis Facing Metropolitan Lagos," 371–396.

25. Murray, *Urbanism of Exception*, 11–12; On nuisance, see Sharan, "In the City, Out of Place," 4906.

26. Murray, *Urbanism of Exception*, 11–12.

27. Perera, "Planners' City," 61; Myers and Muhair argue that "it often seemed that the real concern of the British was simply with having things under control. To use Mitchell's words,

having the place 'contained' meant translating it into a special language that could 'read like a book'" (Myers and Muhair, "Afterlife of the Lanchester Plan," 113). On containment see also, Porter, *Unlearning the Colonial Culture of Planning*, 75–76.

28. Home and King, "Urbanism and Master Planning: Configuring the Colonial City," 51; Porter, *Unlearning the Colonial Culture of Planning*, 70–71; G. A. Bremner, "Introduction: Architecture, Urbanism, and British Imperial Studies," in *Architecture and Urbanism in the British Empire*, ed. G. A. Bremner (Oxford: Oxford University Press, 2016); Ambe J. Njoh, *Planning Power: Town Planning and Social Control in Colonial Africa* (London: UCL Press, 2007).

29. Jacobs, *Edge of Empire*, 20.

30. Sharan, "In the City, Out of Place," 4096.

31. Perera argues that "from a knowledge standpoint, colonial cities were orientalized through their absorption into the metropolitan discourse of town planning. Bernard Cohen emphasizes that the British believed they could explore and conquer the epistemological space through translation. In regard to planning, too, colonial authorities and experts 'translated' urban conditions into knowledge by means of exported ordinances. They employed a combination of, in Cohen's terms, historiographic, observational, survey, enumerative, and investigative modalities. . . . Socially, this perception also promoted the view that there are physical solutions to urban ills and poverty. Within the town planning discourse, it was not poverty and its causes that were not acceptable, but the way the poor live in their environments and the problems they caused to (middle class) city life" (Perera, "Planners' City," 68).

32. For a study of a similar process in Sri Lanka, see Perera, "Planners' City," 69.

33. Perera, "The Planners' City," 64; Demissie, *Colonial Architecture and Urbanism in Africa*, 3–4; Myers and Muhair, "Afterlife of the Lanchester Plan," 102–103.

34. Home and King, "Urbanism and Masterplanning," 82; Jackson and Uduku, "Sub-Saharan Africa," 407; Hodge, *Triumph of the Expert*, 8–14.

35. Home, "Colonial Urban Planning in Anglophone Africa," 53–54.

36. Gandy, "Planning, Anti-Planning, and the Infrastructure Crisis Facing Metropolitan Lagos," 376–77.

37. Perera, "Planners' City," 58.

38. Lefebvre, *Production of Space*; Porter, *Unlearning the Colonial Culture of Planning*.

39. Home, "Colonial Urban Planning in Anglophone Africa," 62.

40. Home, "Colonial Urban Planning in Anglophone Africa," 62.

41. Easterling, *Extrastatecraft*, 73.

42. McFarlane, "Governing the Contaminated City," 417; Edwards, "Infrastructure and Modernity: Force, Time, and Social Organization in the History of Sociotechnical Systems," 186.

43. Hodge, *Triumph of the Expert*, 19–20; Silva, "Urban Planning in Sub-Saharan Africa: An Overview."

44. Hodge, *Triumph of the Expert*, 19–20. King argues that "modern planning in postcolonial states is a European product and that colonialism was the vehicle of transfer" (cited in Perera, "Planners' City," 59). Van Beusekom argues that we should trace the roots of "development" back to at least the interwar period when colonial states began consolidating investments in colonies and crafting new models and theories of "improvement" on a large scale (Monica van Beusekom, *Negotiating Development: African Farmers and Colonial Experts at the Office du Niger, 1920–1960*. Portsmouth, NH: Heinemann, 2002, xxii).

45. Scott, *Seeing Like a State*, 4–5.

46. Tilley, *Africa as a Living Laboratory*, 7–12.

47. Murray, *Urbanism of Exception*, ix–x, 1–2; Perera, "Planners' City," 69–70; Easterling, *Extrastatecraft*, 167.

48. McFarlane, "Governing the Contaminated City," 431–432; Srivastava, *Entangled Urbanism*, 88.

49. Murray, *Urbanism of Exception*, 23–24; Manful, "Afterword," 239.

50. Sharan, "In the City, Out of Place," 4910. Gandy also argues that technocratic conceptions of urban governance have also shaped a focus on "good governance" about NGOs and other international and local observers, which obscures important questions about "the reasons why rent-seeking, clientelist, and 'neo-patrimonial' states have emerged across much of sub-Saharan Africa." (Gandy, "Planning, Anti-planning and the Infrastructure Crisis Facing Metropolitan Lagos," 372–373).

51. David Woode, "Artful Accra: Ghana's 60th Marked by the Birth of an Ambitious Gallery," *Guardian*, March 1, 2017, https://www.theguardian.com/travel/2017/mar/01/accra-ghana-ano-art-gallery-opening-60-anniversary.

52. To see images of these project plans see Talkingdrums, "Construction Projects in Accra and the Rest of Ghana" (blog), https://talkingdrumsblog.wordpress.com/2015/01/02/largest-african-ethnic-groups-or-nationalities-in-america/.

53. Playing Accra Monopoly feels like you're jumping feet first into the development game in the city. Similar games have apparently been developed for cities elsewhere on the continent, including Lagos and Cairo with cooperative licensing from Monopoly's parent company, Hasbro.

54. *Congress for the New Urbanism*, "What is New Urbanism?" https://www.cnu.org/resources/what-new-urbanism (accessed August 4, 2023).

55. Michael Vanderbeek and Clara Irazabal, "New Urbanism as a New Modernist Movement: A Comparative Look at Modernism and New Urbanism," *TDSR* 19(1) (2007): 41–58; Sonia A. Hirt, "Premodern, Modern, Postmodern? Placing New Urbanism into a Historical Perspective," *Journal of Planning History* 8, no. 3 (August 2009): 248–273.

56. Abourahme, "Of Monsters and Boomerangs," 106–115.

57. Alexander Lobrano, "Ghana's Capital of Cool," *New York Times*, July 12, 2016, https://www.nytimes.com/2016/07/08/t-magazine/travel/accra-ghana-travel.html.

58. Manful describes this kind of architecture as "unformal," "all the buildings and structures that occur outside of state purview and formalized design and construction industries" and argues that we should think beyond the scholarly focus on urban poverty in defining these processes ("Afterword,"232).

59. Sharon Benzoni, "Accra, Ghana," The Rockefeller Foundation's Informal City Dialogues, accessed August 4, 2023, https://nextcity.org/informalcity/city/accra.

60. Osei-Boateng and Ampratwum, "The Informal Sector in Ghana," 4.

61. Schauert, *Staging Ghana*, 8.

62. Schauert, *Staging Ghana*, 8.

63. Srivastava, *Entangled Urbanism*, xviii–xix.

64. Easterling, *Extrastatecraft*, 17–18.

65. Murray, *Urbanism of Exception*, 7; Marr, "Worlding and Wilding"; Srivastava, *Entangled Urbanism*, xxxvi; Myers, *Rethinking Urbanism*, xx–xxi, 5; Home and King, "Urbanism and Master Planning," 55–56; Gandy, "Planning, Anti-Planning, and the Infrastructure Crisis Facing Metropolitan Lagos," 390.

66. Murray, *Urbanism of Exception*, x–xi. Manful similarly argues that we could "look for an even more fundamental challenge to the politics of architecture, one that included studies of the informal and unformal, not solely as a lens through which to talk about struggles between states, governments, elites, and the common person, but as architectures in their own right, on their own terms, worth studying, worth theorizing about" (Manful, "Afterword," 241).

67. Murray, *Urbanism of Exception*, x–xii; Gandy, "Planning, Anti-Planning, and the Infrastructure Crisis Facing Metropolitan Lagos," 390.

68. Jacobs, *Edge of Empire*, 4.

69. Jacobs, *Edge of Empire*, 4; Murray, *Urbanism of Exception*, 24–25.

70. Jacobs, *Edge of Empire*, 6; Srivastava, *Entangled Urbanism*, xxi; Gandy, "Planning, Anti-Planning, and the Infrastructure Crisis Facing Metropolitan Lagos," 390.

71. Enwezor, *Under Siege*, 2002: 6–7.

72. Keith Hart, "Informal Income Opportunities and Urban Employment in Ghana," 68.

73. Quayson, *Oxford Street, Accra*, 199.

74. Keith Hart, "Informal Income Opportunities and Urban Employment in Ghana," 68.

BIBLIOGRAPHY

ARCHIVES

The National Archives (UK): Public Records Office (TNA: PRO)
Public Records and Archives Administration Department: National Archives of Ghana (Accra) (PRAAD: NAG (Accra))

NEWSPAPERS

Gold Coast Aborigines
Gold Coast Chronicle
Gold Coast Leader
Gold Coast Nation

BOOKS AND ARTICLES

Abourahme, Nasser. "Of Monsters and Boomerangs: Colonial Returns in the Late Liberal City." *City* 22, no. 1 (2018): 106–115.
Acquah, Ione. *Accra Survey: A Social Survey of the Capital of Ghana, Formerly Called the Gold Coast, Undertaken for the West African Institute of Social and Economic Research, 1953–1956*. London: University of London Press, 1958.
Adas, Michael. *Machines as the Measure of Men: Science, Technology, and Ideologies of Western Dominance*. Ithaca, NY: Cornell University Press, 1989.
Aguiar, Marian. *Tracking Modernity: India's Railway and the Culture of Mobility*. Minneapolis: University of Minnesota Press, 2011.
Akyeampong, Emmanuel. "Bukom and the Social History of Boxing in Accra: Warfare and Citizenship in Precolonial Ga Society." *International Journal of African Historical Studies* 35, no. 1 (2002): 39–60.

Amoako-Gyampah, Akwasi Kwarteng. "Household Sanitary Inspection, Mosquito Control and Domestic Hygiene in the Gold Coast [Ghana] from the Late-Nineteenth to the Mid-Twentieth Century." *Social History of Medicine* 35, no. 1 (2021): 278–301.

———. "Inherently Diseased and Insanitary? The Health Status of the Gold Coast [Ghana] from the 18th to the late 19th Century." *Nordic Journal of African Studies* 27, no. 2 (2018): 1–25.

Anand, Nikhil. "Pressure: The PoliTechnics of Water Supply in Mumbai." *Cultural Anthropology* 26, no. 4 (2011): 542–564.

Appadurai, Arjun, ed. *The Social Life of Things: Commodities in Cultural Perspective.* Cambridge: Cambridge University Press.

Asante, Kofi Takyi. "Nested Patriotism: Revisiting Collaboration, Resistance, and Agency in Colonial Ghana." *International Journal of Politics, Culture, and Society* 33, no. 3 (2020): 347–364.

Austin, Gareth. "Capitalists and Chiefs in the Cocoa Hold-ups in South Asante, 1927–1938." *International Journal of African Historical Studies* 21, no. 1 (1988): 63–95.

Balakrishnan, Sarah. *Anticolonial Public: From Slavery to Independence in Southern Ghana, c. 1500–1957.* PhD diss., Harvard University, 2020.

———. "Building the Ancestral Public: Cemeteries and the Necropolitics of Property in Colonial Ghana." *Journal of Social History* (2022): 1–25.

Barber, Karin. *Africa's Hidden Histories: Everyday Literacy and Making the Self.* Bloomington: Indiana University Press, 2006.

Barbot, John. *A Description of the Coasts of North and South Guinea.* (Translated from French.) Churchill's Collection of Voyages and Travels, Vol. 5. London, 1732. In *Pageant of Ghana.* Oxford: Oxford University Press, 1958.

Bashford, Allison. *Imperial Hygiene: A Critical History of Colonialism, Nationalism, and Public Health* (New York: Palgrave Macmillan), 2003.

Bauer, P. T. *West African Trade: A Study of Competition, Oligopoly, and Monopoly in a Changing Society.* Cambridge: Cambridge University Press, 1954.

Bayart, Jean-Francois. "African in the World: A History of Extraversion." *African Affairs* 99, no. 395 (2000): 217–267.

Berry, Sara. "Hegemony on a Shoestring: Indirect Rule and Access to Agricultural Land." *Africa* 62, no. 3 (1992): 327–355.

Bigon, Liora, and Yossi Katz, eds. *Garden Cities and Colonial Planning: Transnationality and Urban Ideas in Africa and Palestine.* Manchester: Manchester University Press, 2014.

Bin-Kasim, Waseem-Ahmed. *Sanitary Segregation: Cleansing Accra and Nairobi, 1908–1963.* PhD diss., Washington University, 2019.

Bissell, William Cunningham. "Between Fixity and Fantasy: Assessing the Spatial Impact of Colonial Urban Dualism." *Journal of Urban History* 37 (2011): 208–229.

———. *Urban Design, Chaos, and Colonial Power in Zanzibar.* Bloomington: Indiana University Press, 2011.

Bloom, Peter J., and Kate Skinner. "Modernity and Danger: *The Boy Kumasenu* and the Work of the Gold Coast Film Unit." *Ghana Studies* 12 (2009): 121–153.

Bremner, G. A. "Introduction: Architecture, Urbanism, and British Imperial Studies." In *Architecture and Urbanism in the British Empire*. Edited by G. A. Bremner. Oxford: Oxford University Press, 2016.

Brooks, George. *EurAfricans in Western Africa: Commerce, Social Status, Gender, and Religious Observance from the Sixteenth to the Eighteenth Century*. Athens: Ohio University Press, 2014.

Burke, Timothy. *Lifebuoy Men, Lux Women: Commodification, Consumption, and Cleanliness in Modern Zimbabwe*. Durham, NC: Duke University Press, 1996.

Burton, Antoinette. "The Unfinished Business of Colonial Modernities," In *Gender, Sexuality and Colonial Modernities*. Edited by Antoinette Burton. New York: Routledge, 1999.

Casely-Hayford, J. E. *Gold Coast Native Institutions*. London, Sweet and Maxwell, 1903.

Clark, Gracia. *Onions Are My Husband: Survival and Accumulation By West African Market Women*. Chicago: University of Chicago Press, 1995.

Clifford, Lady, ed. *Our Days on the Gold Coast in Ashanti, in the Northern Territories, and the British Sphere of Occupation in Togoland*. London: J. Murray, 1919.

Coe, Cati. *Dilemmas of Culture in African Schools: Youth, Nationalism, and the Transformation of Knowledge*. Chicago: University of Chicago Press, 2005.

Cole, Catherine. *Ghana's Concert Party Theatre*. Bloomington: Indiana University Press, 2001.

Cole, Festus. "Sanitation, Disease, and Public Health in Sierra Leone, West Africa, 1895–1922: Case Failure of British Colonial Health Policy." *Journal of Imperial and Commonwealth History* 43, no. 2 (2015): 238–266.

Collingwood, E. M., *Imperial Bodies: The Physical Experience of the Raj, c. 1800–1947* (London: Polity), 2001.

Comaroff, Jean, and John L. Comaroff, *Theory from the South: or, how Euro-America is evolving toward Africa*. Boulder, Paradigm, 2012.

Cooper, Frederick. *Africa Since 1940: The Past of the Present*. Cambridge: Cambridge University Press, 2002.

———. *Colonialism in Question: Theory, Knowledge, History*. Los Angeles: University of California Press, 2005.

———. *On the African Waterfront: Urban Disorder and the Transformation of Work in Colonial Mombasa*. New York: ACLS Humanities E-book, 2014.

———. *Struggle for the City: Migrant Labor, Capital, and the State in Urban Africa*. New York: Sage, 1993.

Crinson, Mark. "Imperial Modernism," In *Architecture and Urbanism in the British Empire*. Edited by G. A. Bremner. Oxford: Oxford University Press, 2016.

Crowder, Michael. "Indirect Rule—French and British Style." *Africa* 34, no. 3 (July 1964): 197–205.

Curtin, Philip. "Medical Knowledge and Urban Planning in Tropical Africa." *American Historical Review* 90, no. 3 (1985): 594–613.

Dakubu, Mary Esther Kropp. *Korle Meets the Sea: A Sociolinguistic History of Accra.* Oxford: Oxford University Press, 1997.

Daston, Lorraine. *Rules: A Short History of What We Live By.* Princeton, NJ: Princeton University Press, 2022.

de Boeck, Filip. "Infrastructure: Commentary from Filip de Boeck," *Cultural Anthropology* 2012 (2012).

Demissie, Fassil. *Colonial Architecture and Urbanism in Africa: Intertwined and Contested Histories.* Routledge: New York, 2016.

Dickson, Kwamina. *A Historical Geography of Ghana.* Cambridge: Cambridge University Press, 1974.

Dumett, Raymond. "African Merchants of the Gold Coast, 1860–1905: Dynamics of Indigenous Entrepreneurship." *Comparative Studies in Society and History* 25, no. 4 (October 1983): 661–693.

———. "The Campaign against Malaria and the Expansion of Scientific Medical and Sanitary Services in British West Africa, 1898–1910." *African Historical Studies* 1, no. 2 (1968): 153–197.

Easterling, Keller. *Extrastatecraft: The Power of Infrastructure Space.* New York: Verso, 2014.

Echenberg, Myron. *Plague Ports: The Global Impact of Bubonic Plague, 1894–1901.* New York: New York University Press, 2007.

Edwards, Paul. "Infrastructure and Modernity: Force, Time, and Social Organization in the History of Sociotechnical Systems." In *Modernity and Technology.* Edited by Thomas J. Misa, Philip Brey, and Andrew Feenberg. Cambridge, MA: MIT Press, 2003: 185–225.

Enwezor, Okwui. *Under Siege: Four African Cities.* Ostfildern-Ruit: Hatje Cantz, 2002.

Fair, Laura. *Pastimes and Politics: Culture, Community, and Identity in Post-Abolition Urban Zanzibar, 1890–1945.* Athens: Ohio University Press, 2001.

———. *Reel Pleasures: Cinema Audiences and Entrepreneurs in Twentieth Century Urban Tanzania.* Athens: Ohio University Press, 2018.

Feld, Steven. *Jazz Cosmopolitanism in Accra: Five Musical Years in Ghana.* Durham, NC: Duke University Press, 2012.

Ferguson, James. *Expectations of Modernity: Myths and Meanings of Urban Life on the Zambian Copperbelt.* Los Angeles: University of California Press, 1999.

Field, Margaret. *Search for Security: An Ethno-Psychiatric Study of Rural Ghana.* Evanston, IL: Northwestern University Press, 1964.

Fielding-Ould, R. "Observations at Freetown, Accra, and Lagos," *Memorial Liverpool School of Medicine* 2, no. 53 (1900).

Fortescue, Dominic. "The Accra Crowd, the Asafo, and the Opposition to the Municipal Corporations Ordinance, 1924–25." *Canadian Journal of African Studies* 3 (1990): 348–375.

Fry, E. Maxwell. "European Importation," *Progressive Architecture*. December 1962, 83–86.

———. "Town Planning in West Africa." *African Affairs* 45, no. 181 (October 1946): 197–204.

Fyfe, Paul. *By Accident or Design: Writing the Victorian Metropolis*. Oxford: Oxford University Press, 2015.

Gandy, Matthew. "Planning, Anti-planning and the Infrastructure Crisis Facing Metropolitan Lagos." *Urban Studies* 43, no. 2 (February 2006): 371–396.

Gewald, Jan-Bart. "Missionaries, Hereros, and Motorcars: Mobility and the Impact of Motor Vehicles before 1940." *International Journal of African Historical Studies* 35, no. 2/3 (2002): 257–285.

Grace, Joshua. "Poop," *Somatosphere* (2017), http://somatosphere.net/2017/poop.html/.

Grier, Beverly. "Cocoa Marketing in Colonial Ghana: Capitalist Enterprise and the Emergence of a Rural African Bourgeoisie." *Ufahamu* 10, no. 1/2 (1980): 89–115.

Griffith, William Brandford. *Ordinances of the Gold Coast Colony in Force June, 1898*, Vol. 2. London: Stevens & Sons, 1898.

Guggisberg, Gordon. *The Keystone*. London: Waterlow & Sons, 1924.

Guldi, Jo. *Roads to Power: Britain Invents the Infrastructure State*. Cambridge, MA: Harvard University Press, 2012.

Gundona, Sylvester. *Coping with This Scourge: The State, Leprosy, and the Politics of Public Health in Colonial Ghana, 1900-Mid 1950s*. Austin: University of Texas, 2015.

Harris, Richard, and Susan Parnell. "The Turning Point in Urban Policy for British Colonial Africa, 1939–1945." In *Colonial Architecture and Urbanism in Africa: Intertwined and Contested Histories*. New York: Routledge, 2017.

Hart, Francis. *The Gold Coast: Its Wealth and Health*. London: Ereckson's, 1904.

Hart, Jennifer. *Ghana on the Go: African Mobility in the Age of Motor Transportation*. Bloomington: Indiana University Press, 2016.

———. "Motor Transportation, Trade Unionism, and the Culture of Work in Colonial Ghana." *International Review of Social History* 59 (2014): 185–209.

Hart, Keith. "Informal Income Opportunities and Urban Employment in Ghana." *Journal of Modern African Studies* 11, no. 1 (1973): 61–89.

Harvey, Penny, and Hannah Knox. *Roads: An Anthropology of Infrastructure and Expertise*. Ithaca, NY: Cornell University Press, 2015.

Hawthorn, Nathaniel, ed. *Journal of an African Cruiser* by an Officer of the U.S. Navy, London, 1845. In *Pageant of Ghana*, edited by Freda Wolfson. Oxford: Oxford University Press, 1958.

Headrick, Daniel. *Power over Peoples: Technology, Environments, and Western Imperialism, 1400 to the Present*. Princeton, NJ: Princeton University Press, 2012.

———. *The Tools of Empire: Technology and European Imperialism in the Nineteenth Century*. Oxford: Oxford University Press, 1981.

Hill, Polly. *The Migrant Cocoa Farmers of Southern Ghana*. Cambridge: Cambridge University Press, 1973.

Hirt, Sonia A. "Premodern, Modern, Postmodern? Placing New Urbanism into a Historical Perspective." *Journal of Planning History* 8, no. 3 (August 2009): 248–273.

Hodge, Joseph Morgan. *Triumph of the Expert: Agrarian Doctrines of Development and the Legacies of British Colonialism*. Athens: Ohio University Press, 2007.

Holston, James. *The Modernist City: An Anthropological Critique of Brasilia*. Chicago: University of Chicago Press, 1989.

Home, Robert. "Colonial Urban Planning in Anglophone Africa." In *Urban Planning in Sub-Saharan Africa: Colonial and Post-Colonial Planning Cultures*. Edited by Carlos Nunes Silva. New York: Routledge, 2015: 53–66.

Home, Robert, and Anthony D. King, "Urbanism and Master Planning: Configuring the Colonial City." In *Architecture and Urbanism in the British Empire*. Edited by G. A. Bremner. Oxford: Oxford University Press, 2016.

Horton, James Africanus B. *West African Countries and Peoples, British and Native: With the requirements necessary for establishing that self-government recommended by the committee of the House of Commons, 1865; and a vindication of the African race*. London: WJ, 1868.

Hunt, Nancy Rose. *Colonial Lexicon: Of Birth Ritual, Medicalization, and Mobility in the Congo*. Durham, NC: Duke University Press, 1999.

Huntley, Sir Henry. *Seven Years' Service of the Slave Coast of Western Africa*. 2 vols. London, 1850. In Freda Wolfson, *Pageant of Ghana*. Oxford: Oxford University Press, 1958.

Ipsen, Pernille. *Koko's Daughters: Danish Men Marrying Ga Women in an Atlantic Slave Trading Port in the Eighteenth Century*. PhD diss., Kobenhavns Universistet, 2008.

Jackson, Iain, and Ola Oduku, "Sub-Saharan Africa." In *Architecture and Urbanism in the British Empire*, edited by G. A. Bremner. Oxford: Oxford University Press, 2016: 393–422.

Jackson, Iain, and Rexford Assasie Oppong. "The Planning of Late Colonial Village Housing in the Tropics: Tema Manhean, Ghana." *Planning Perspectives* 29, no. 4 (2014): 475–499.

Jacobs, Jane. *Edge of Empire: Postcolonialism and the City*. New York: Routledge, 1996.

Kilson, Marion. *African Urban Kinsmen: The Ga of Central Accra*. London, St. Martin's, 1974.

———. *Kpele Lala: Ga Religious Songs and Symbols*. Cambridge, MA: Harvard University Press, 1971.

Klaeger, Gabriel. "Introduction: The Perils and Possibilities of African Roads" *Africa* 83, no. 3 (2013): 359–366.

Konadu, Kwasi. *Our Own Way in This Part of the World: Biography of an African Community, Culture, and Nation*. Durham, NC: Duke University Press, 2019.

Korieh, Chima J. "'May it Please Your Honor': Letters of Petition as Historical Evidence in an African Colonial Context." *History in Africa* 37 (2010): 83–106.

Larkin, Brian. "The Politics and Poetics of Infrastructure," *Annual Review of Anthropology* 42 (2013): 327–343.

———. *Signal and Noise: Media, Infrastructure, and Urban Culture in Nigeria*. Durham, NC: Duke University Press, 2008.

Lawrance, Benjamin. *Locality, Mobility, and "Nation": Periurban Colonialism in Togo's Eweland, 1900–1960*. Rochester, NY: University of Rochester Press, 2007.

Lawrance, Benjamin, Emily Lynn Osborn, and Richard Roberts, eds. *Intermediaries, Interpreters, and Clerks: African Employees in the Making of Colonial Africa*. Madison: University of Wisconsin Press, 2006.

Lefebvre, Henri. *Le Droit à la ville*. Paris: Anthropos, 1968.

———. *The Production of Space*. Hoboken, NJ: Wiley-Blackwell, 1992.

Li, Tania Murray. "Beyond 'The State' and Failed Schemes." *American Anthropologist* 107, no. 3 (September 2005): 383–394.

Liscombe, Rhodri Windsor. "Modernism in Late Imperial British West Africa: The Work of Maxwell Fry and Jane Drew, 1946–1956." *Journal of the Society of Architectural Historians* 65, no. 2 (June 2006): 210–228.

Livingston, Julie. *Improvising Medicine: An African Oncology Ward in an Emerging Cancer Epidemic*. Durham, NC: Duke University Press, 2012.

Lorang, Kwaku Larbi. *Writing Ghana, Imagining Africa: Nation and African Modernity*. Rochester, NY: University of Rochester Press, 2004.

Lugard, Frederick. *The Dual Mandate in British Tropical Africa*. London: William Blackwood and Sons, 1922.

Lupack, Alan. "Vortigern," *The Camelot Project: A Robbins Library Digital Project*. University of Rochester. Accessed October 9, 2020. https://d.lib.rochester.edu/camelot/theme/Vortigern" https://d.lib.rochester.edu/camelot/theme/Vortigern.

Lyons, Maryinez. *The Colonial Disease: A Social History of Sleeping Sickness in Northern Zaire, 1900–1940*. Cambridge: Cambridge University Press, 1992.

Mamdani, Mahmood. *Citizen and Subject: Contemporary Africa and the Legacy of Late Colonialism*. Princeton, NJ: Princeton University Press, 2018.

Manful, Kuukuwa. "Afterword: Theorizing the Politics of Unformal(ized) Architectures." In *Architecture and Politics in Africa: Making, Living, and Imagining Identities through Buildings*. Rochester, NY: James Currey, 2022.

Marr, Stephen. "Worlding and Wilding: Lagos and Detroit as Global Cities." *Race and Class* 57, no. 4 (2016): 3–21.

Masquelier, Adeline. "Road Mythographies: Space, Mobility, and the Historical Imagination in Postcolonial Niger." *American Ethnologist* 29, no. 4 (2002): 829–865.

Mavhunga, Clapperton. *Transient Workspaces: Technologies of Everyday Innovation in Zimbabwe*. Cambridge, MA: MIT Press, 2014.

———, ed. *What Do Science, Technology, and Innovation Mean from Africa?* Cambridge, MA: MIT Press, 2017.

———. "Which Mobility for (Which) Africa? Beyond Banal Mobilities." In *Mobility in History: Reviews and Reflections*, edited by Peter Norton, Gijs Mom, Liz Millward, and Mathieu Flonneau. Neuchâtel, Switzerland: Éditions Alphil-Presses universitaires suisses, 2011, 73–84.

Mayne, Alan. *Slums: The History of a Global Injustice*. London: Reaktion, 2017.

McCaskie, T. C. *Asante Identities: History and Modernity in an African Village 1850–1950*. Bloomington: Indiana University Press, 2000.

McClintock, Anne. *Imperial Leather: Race, Gender, and Sexuality in the Colonial Contest*. New York: Routledge, 1995.

McFarlane, Colin. "Governing the Contaminated City: Infrastructure and Sanitation in Colonial and Post-Colonial Bombay." *International Journal of Urban and Regional Research* 32, no. 2 (June 2008): 415–435.

Meagher, Kate. "Crisis, Informalization, and the Urban Informal Sector in Sub-Saharan Africa." *Development and Change* 26, no. 2 (1995): 259–284.

———. "Introduction: Special Issue on 'Informal Institutions and Development in Africa,' *Afrika Spectrum* 42, no. 3 (2007): 405–418.

Mika, Marissa. *Africanizing Oncology: Creativity, Crisis, and Cancer in Uganda*. Athens: Ohio University Press, 2022.

Mitchell, Timothy. *Colonizing Egypt*. Los Angeles: University of California Press, 1991.

———. *The Rule of Experts: Egypt, Techno-Politics, Modernity*. Los Angeles: University of California Press, 2002.

Murillo, Bianca. "Ideal Homes and the Gender Politics of Consumerism in Postcolonial Ghana, 1960–70." *Gender & History* 21, no. 3 (November 2009): 560–575.

———. *Market Encounters: Consumer Cultures in Twentieth-Century Ghana*. Athens: Ohio University Press, 2017.

———. "The Modern Shopping Experience: Kingsway Department Store and Consumer Politics in Ghana." *Africa* 82, no. 3 (2012): 368–392.

Murray, Martin. *The Urbanism of Exception: The Dynamics of Global City Building in the Twenty-First Century*. Cambridge: Cambridge University Press, 2017.

Murunga, Godwin Rapando. "Review of *Verandas of Power: Colonialism and Space in Urban Africa*." *African Sociological Review* 8, no. 1 (2004): 208–211.

Myers, Garth. *Rethinking Urbanism: Lessons from Postcolonialism and the Global South*. Bristol: Bristol University Press, 2020.

———. *Verandahs of Power: Colonialism and Space in Urban Africa*. Syracuse, NY: Syracuse University Press, 2003.

Myers, Garth Andrew, and Makame Ali Muhair, "The Afterlife of the Lanchester Plan: Zanzibar as the Garden City of Tomorrow." In *Garden Cities and Colonial Planning: Transnationality and Urban Ideas in Africa and Palestine*, edited by Liora Bigon and Yossi Katz. Manchester: Manchester University Press, 2014: 99–120.

Newell, Stephanie. *Histories of Dirt: Media and Urban Life in Colonial Ghana*. Durham, NC: Duke University Press, 2020.

———. *Literary Culture in Colonial Ghana: How to Play the Game of Life*. Bloomington: Indiana University Press, 2002.

———. "Newspapers, New Spaces, New Writers: The First World War and Print Culture in Colonial Ghana." *Research in African Literatures* 40, no. 2 (Summer 2009): 1–15.

Njoh, Ambe J. *Planning Power: Town Planning and Social Control in Colonial Africa.* London: UCL Press, 2007.
Ochonu, Moses. *Colonial Meltdown: Northern Nigeria in the Great Depression.* Athens: Ohio University Press, 2009.
Odotei, Irene. "External Influences on Ga Society and Culture." *Research Review NS* 7, no. 1–2 (1991): 61–71.
Oliver, Paul. "Vernacular Know-How," *Material Culture* 18, no. 3 (Fall 1986): 113–126.
Osei-Boateng, Clara, and Edward Ampratwum. "The Informal Sector in Ghana," *Friedrich Ebert Stiftung Ghana Office.* October 2011. https://library.fes.de/pdf-files/bueros/ghana/10496.pdf.
Osei-Tutu, John Kwadwo. *The Asafoi (Socio-Military Groups) in the History and Politics of Accra (Ghana) from the 17th to the 20th Century.* African Studies Series No. 3 Trondheim: Norwegian University of Science and Technology, 2000.
Osseo-Asare, Abena Dove. *Atomic Junction: Nuclear Power in Africa after Independence.* Cambridge: Cambridge University Press, 2019.
———. *Bitter Roots: The Search for Healing Plants in Africa.* Chicago: University of Chicago Press, 2014.
Packer, Jeremy. *Mobility without Mayhem: Safety, Cars, and Citizenship.* Durham, NC: Duke University Press, 2008.
Parker, John. *In My Time of Dying: A History of Death and the Dead in West Africa.* Princeton, NJ: Princeton University Press, 2021.
———. *Making the Town: Ga State and Society in Early Colonial Accra.* Portsmouth, NH: Heinemann, 2000.
Patterson, K. David. *Health in Colonial Ghana: Disease, Medicine, and Socio-Economic Change, 1900–1955.* Waltham, MA: Crossroads, 1981.
———. "Health in Urban Ghana: The Case of Accra 1900–1940." *Social Science and Medicine* 13, no. 4 (December 1979): 251–268.
Pearce, R. D. *The Turning Point in Africa: British Colonial Policy 1938–48.* London: Frank Cass, 1982.
Peil, Margaret. *Cities and Suburbs: Urban Life in West Africa.* New York: Africana, 1981.
Pellow, Deborah. "Group and Grid: Zongos and the British." *Architext* 7 (2019): 80–93.
———. *Landlords and Lodgers: Socio-Spatial Organization in an Accra Community.* Chicago: University of Chicago Press, 2002.
———. *Women in Accra: Options for Autonomy.* Algonac, MI: Reference, 1977.
Pellow, Deborah, and Naomi Chazan, *Ghana: Coping with Uncertainty.* Boulder, CO: Westview Press, 1986.
Pels, Peter. "The Anthropology of Colonialism: Culture, History, and the Emergence of Western Governmentality." *Annual Review of Anthropology* 26 (1997): 163–183.
Perera, Nihal. "The Planners' City: The Construction of a Town Planning Perception of Colombo." *Environment and Planning A* 40 (2008): 57–73.

Peter, Marris, "The Meaning of Slums and Patterns of Change." *International Journal of Urban and Regional Research* 3, no. 1–3 (1979): 419–441.

Phokaides, Petros. "Detropicalizing Africa: Architecture Planning and Climate in the 1950s and 1960s." *docomomo* 48 (2013/1): 76–82.

Plageman, Nate. "'Accra Is Changing Isn't It?': Urban Infrastructure, Independence, and Nation in the Gold Coast's *Daily Graphic.*" *International Journal of African Historical Studies* 43, no. 1 (2010): 137–159.

———. "Colonial Ambition, Common Sense Thinking, and the Making of Takoradi Harbor, Gold Coast." *History in Africa* 40 (2013): 317–352.

———. *Highlife Saturday Night: Popular Music and Social Change in Urban Ghana.* Bloomington: Indiana University Press, 2012.

Porter, Libby. *Unlearning the Colonial Cultures of Planning.* Burlington, VT: Ashgate, 2010.

Quayson, Ato. *Oxford Street, Accra: City Life and the Itineraries of Transnationalism.* Durham, NC: Duke University Press, 2014.

Rankin, John. *Healing the African Body: British Medicine in West Africa, 1800–1860.* Columbia: University of Missouri Press, 2015.

Ray, Carina. *Crossing the Color Line: Race, Sex, and the Contested Politics of Colonialism in Ghana.* Athens: Ohio University Press, 2015.

Rhodie, Sam. "The Gold Coast Cocoa Hold-Up of 1930–31." *Transactions of the Historical Society of Ghana* 9 (1968): 105–118.

Roberts, Jonathan. "Korle and the Mosquito: Histories and Memories of the Anti-Malaria Campaign in Accra, 1942–5." *Journal of African History* 51 (2010): 343–365.

———. "Medical Exchange on the Gold Coast during the Seventeenth and Eighteenth Centuries." *Canadian Journal of African Studies* 45, no. 3 (2011): 480–523.

———. *Sharing the Burden of Sickness: A History of Healing and Medicine in Accra.* Bloomington: Indiana University Press, 2021.

———. "The Black Death in the Gold Coast: African and British Responses to the Bubonic Plague Epidemic of 1908." *Gateway Journal* 3 (2003): 1–51.

Robertson, Claire. *Sharing the Same Bowl: A Socioeconomic History of Women and Class in Accra, Ghana.* Ann Arbor: University of Michigan Press, 1984.

Roitman, Janet. *Fiscal Disobedience: An Anthropology of Economic Regulation in Central Africa.* Princeton, NJ: Princeton University Press, 2005.

Ross, Kristin. *Fast Cars, Clean Bodies: Decolonization and the Reordering of French Culture.* Cambridge, MA: MIT Press, 1996.

Ryan, Alan. "Liberal Imperialism." *The Making of Modern Liberalism.* Princeton, NJ: Princeton University Press, 2012.

Sackeyfio-Lenoch, Naaborko. *The Politics of Chieftaincy: Authority and Property in Colonial Ghana, 1920–1950.* Rochester, NY: University of Rochester Press, 2014.

Satia, Priya. *Time's Monsters: How History Makes History.* Cambridge, MA: Belknap Press, 2020.

Schauert, Paul. *Staging Ghana: Artistry and Nationalism in State Dance Ensembles.* Bloomington: Indiana University Press, 2015.

Scott, James. *Seeing Like a State: How Certain Schemes to Improve the Human Condition Have Failed.* New Haven, CT: Yale University Press, 1999.
Seiler, Cotton. *Republic of Drivers: A Cultural History of Automobility in America.* Chicago: University of Chicago Press, 2008.
Sharan, Awadhendra. "In the City, Out of Place: Environment and Modernity, Delhi 1860s to 1960s." *Economic and Political Weekly*, 41, no. 47 (November–December 2006): 4905–4911.
Silva, Carlos Nunes. "Urban Planning in Sub-Saharan Africa: An Overview." In *Urban Planning in Sub-Saharan Africa: Colonial and Post-Colonial Planning Cultures*, edited by Carlos Nunes Silva. New York: Routledge, 2015: 8–40.
Simone, Abdoumaliq. "Straddling the Divides: Remaking Associational Life in the Informal African City." *International Journal of Urban and Regional Research* 25, no. 1 (2001): 102–117.
Simpson, W. J. *A Treatise on Plague: Dealing with the Historical, Epidemiological, Clinical, Therapeutic and Preventive Aspects of the Disease* (Cambridge: Cambridge University Press), 1905.
Srivastava, Sanjay. *Entangled Urbanism: Slum, Gated Community, and Shopping Mall in Delhi and Gurgaon.* Oxford: Oxford University Press, 2014.
Stacey, Paul. *State of Slum: Precarity and Informal Governance at the Margins in Accra.* London: Zed, 2021.
Stanley, Henry Morton. *Coomassie and Magdala: The Story of Two British Campaigns in Africa.* London: Low, 1874.
Stoler, Ann L. *Along the Archival Grain: Epistemic Anxieties and Colonial Common Sense.* Princeton, NJ: Princeton University Press, 2009.
———. "Colonial Archives and the Arts of Governance." *Archival Science* 2 (2002): 87–109.
———. *Duress: Imperial Durabilities in Our Times.* Durham, NC: Duke University Press, 2016.
———. "Tense and Tender Ties: The Politics of Comparison in North American History and (Post)Colonial Studies." *Journal of American History* 88, no. 3 (December 2001): 829–865.
Tallie, T. J. *Queering Colonial Natal: Indigeneity and the Violence of Belonging in South Africa.* Minneapolis: University of Minnesota Press, 2019.
Tilley, Helen. *Africa as a Living Laboratory: Empire, Development, and the Problem of Scientific Knowledge, 1870–1950.* Chicago: University of Chicago Press, 2010.
———. *Ordering Africa: Anthropology, European Imperialism, and the Politics of Knowledge.* Manchester: Manchester University Press, 2007.
Trevallion, B. A. W., and Alan G. Hood. *Accra: A Plan for the Town.* Accra: Government Printer, 1958.
Tsey, Komla. *From Head-Loading to the Iron Horse: Railway Building in Colonial Ghana and the Origins of Tropical Development.* Bamenda, Cameroon: Langaa RPCIG, 2012.
Uduku, Ola. "Modernist Architecture and 'the Tropical' in West Africa: The Tropical Architecture Movement in West Africa, 1948–1970." *Habitat International* 30, no. 3 (September 2006): 396–411.

van Beusekom, Monica. *Negotiating Development: African Farmers and Colonial Experts at the Office du Niger, 1920–1960*. Portsmouth, NH: Heinemann, 2002.

Vanderbeek, Michael, and Clara Irazabal, "New Urbanism as a New Modernist Movement: A Comparative Look at Modernism and New Urbanism." *TDSR* 19, no. 1 (2007): 41–58.

Vaughan, Megan. *Curing Their Ills: Colonial Power and African Illness*. Stanford: Stanford University Press, 1991.

Walkowitz, Judith. *City of Dreadful Delight: Narratives of Sexual Danger in Late-Victorian London*. Chicago: University of Chicago Press, 2013.

White, Luise. *The Comforts of Home: Prostitution in Colonial Nairobi*. Chicago: University of Chicago Press, 1990.

———. *Speaking with Vampires: Rumor and History in Colonial Africa*. Los Angeles: University of California Press, 2000.

Whyte, William. "Modernism, Modernization and Europeanization in West African Architecture, 1944–94." In *Europeanization in the Twentieth Century*, edited by M. Conway, K. K. Patel. Palgrave Macmillan Transnational History Series. London: Palgrave Macmillan, 2010.

Winder, R. Bayly. "The Lebanese in West Africa," *Comparative Studies in Society and History* 4, no. 3 (April 1962): 315, ft. 77.

Wright, Gwendolyn. "Tradition in the Service of Modernity: Architecture and Urbanism in French Colonial Policy, 1900–1930." In *Tensions of Empire: Colonial Cultures in a Bourgeois World*, edited by Cooper and Stoler. Los Angeles: University of California Press, 1997: 291–316.

INDEX

Ababio, Kojo, 93, 107, 180
Aborigines Rights Protection Society (ARPS), 37, 42, 98, 117, 118, 136
Abossey Okai, 47, 160, 207
Accra Metropolitan Assembly (AMA), 225
Accra Town Council, 2, 3, 10–12, 15, 16, 18, 25, 26, 28–31, 33, 34–36, 42, 49, 53–56, 57, 59, 61, 64–66, 68, 72, 75, 79, 83, 86, 95, 96, 99, 100, 106, 110, 111, 112, 115, 123–127, 131, 136, 138, 139, 143, 148, 149, 150, 156–160, 164, 165, 168–172, 174, 184, 185, 206, 220
Adabraka, 47, 50, 52, 61, 96, 108, 157, 158, 161, 188, 191, 197, 199
Addy, Mark, 119
Agbogbloshie, 108, 188, 217–220
A.G. Leventis, 139, 141, 142
architect(s), 15, 20, 187, 196, 198–201, 204, 221, 225, 226; architecture, 13, 14, 24, 179, 190, 198, 201–205, 208, 220, 225; architectural, 192, 201–204, 208, 215, 227, 228; Architectural Association (AA), 201; Congress Internationale d'Architecture Moderne (CIAM), 202
asafo, 7, 117
asafoatse, 56, 116, 117
asafoatsemei, 40, 56, 116
Ashanti Confederacy Council, 141
Association of West African Merchants (AWAM), 138–140, 142
ATC. *See* Accra Town Council.

Bannerman, James, 5, 6
Basel Mission, 11
Basel Mission Church, 189
Basel Mission Society, 7, 130
Basel Mission Trading Company, 155
Big Six, 135, 136, 145

Cantonments, 197, 207, 226–229
capitalism, 12, 23, 160, 164, 231; colonial capitalism, 132, 143; expatriate capitalism, 221; extractive capitalism, 34; global capitalism, 20, 24, 28, 29, 145, 146; industrial capitalism, 14, 22, 224
Cemetery Bill (1888), 185
Chamberlain, Joseph, 14, 77, 78, 80, 82
Christiansburg, 47, 60, 66, 84, 90, 108, 116, 135, 148, 155, 157, 160, 188, 191, 197, 207, 225
classification, 10, 17, 21
cocoa, 59, 107, 115, 116, 136, 154, 155, 171; cocoa farmers, 154, 163; cocoa hold-ups, 138, 188; cocoa plantations, 6
Colonial Development and Welfare Fund, 46, 199
Colonial Office (CO), 14, 25, 75–77, 82, 84, 101, 102, 105, 108, 177, 191, 196, 199, 204, 206
compound (house), 20, 30, 33, 38, 84, 99, 101, 112, 119, 120, 122, 181, 183, 187, 198, 202
Convention People's Party (CPP), 214
cordon sanitaire, 94

cosmopolitan, 8, 9, 12, 15, 19, 25, 53, 90, 150, 164, 208, 214, 225, 227, 228
court(s), 9, 32, 50, 51, 54, 72, 86, 100, 101, 107, 110, 180–183, 209, 210; court proceedings, 7; power of the courts, 12, 15, 38, 69, 99, 107, 179, 186

Danquah, J.B., 136, 142
DeGraft Johnson, J.E., 50, 55, 60, 126, 156
Destruction of Mosquitoes Bill (1911), 99
development, 3, 6, 7, 10, 11, 14–16, 18, 21, 24, 25, 30, 31, 35–37, 42, 46, 47, 56, 62, 75, 77, 79, 80, 86, 104, 110, 111, 115, 118, 119, 124, 128, 136, 138, 144, 146, 151, 174, 178, 180, 187, 189, 190, 194, 195, 197, 200, 205–210, 212, 215, 218, 220, 223–225, 227–229, 231–233; colonial development, 16, 18, 24, 35, 36, 46, 75, 78, 98, 157, 204, 207, 220; development colonialism, 156, 173; development plan, 59, 119, 131, 216, 219; economic development, 9, 28, 44, 73, 78, 81, 119, 144, 199; housing development, 195–198, 200, 201, 212; infrastructural development, 3, 15, 17, 42, 46, 60, 61, 65, 95, 114, 115, 131, 133, 150, 156, 208, 212; road development, 61, 151, 166; underdevelopment, 62, 68, 233; urban development, 13, 15, 18, 24, 25, 29, 34, 36, 42, 44, 56, 61, 63, 66, 67, 130, 132, 134, 145, 146, 188, 189, 191, 195, 201, 207, 209, 216, 220, 222, 225, 228, 231
disease, 8, 29, 31, 34, 48, 58, 70–78, 80, 82–91, 93–95, 97, 99, 102–104, 108–111, 128, 156, 189, 190, 197; epidemic disease, 29, 34, 76, 77, 190; mosquito-born(e) disease, 96, 97, 99; swollen shoot disease, 136; tropical disease, 70, 72, 73, 77, 79, 80, 82, 96, 105
disorder, 13, 15, 18, 19, 21, 36, 95, 143, 186
Dowuona III, 116
Drew, Jane, 179, 196, 201–205. See also architect
driver(s), 17, 30, 49, 129, 131, 137, 148–150, 152–156, 163–168, 171–174, 233. See also lorry
Dual Mandate, 15

Easton, J. F., 79, 85, 97
engineer(s), 20, 46, 49, 60, 64, 67, 71, 107, 108, 157, 177, 193, 221; chief engineer, 201, 215; consulting engineer, 57; engineering, 3, 7, 13, 14, 20, 24, 36, 108, 161, 187, 196; engineering projects, 220; municipal engineer, 49, 61, 64, 157, 161, 184, 186, 206; social engineering, 133, 134, 221, 224
ethnocentrism, 13, 16, 18, 22
everyday life, 2, 12, 15, 21, 26, 30, 59, 70, 101, 150, 232
expatriate enterprise, 21, 35, 48, 112–114, 130, 132, 134, 145, 160, 221
expertise, 12, 16, 18, 20, 28, 155, 193, 199, 203
ex-servicemen, 135–137, 142, 143, 145

Fante Confederation, 136
Fry, Maxwell, 179, 187, 196, 197–206. See also architect

Ga Manche, 37, 40, 93, 94, 116, 118. See also Ababio, Kojo; Tackie Yaoboi
Ga Mashie, 4, 25
Ga Shifimo Kpee, 178, 214
G.B. Ollivant, 138, 142
germ theory, 72, 74, 83, 89, 94
Gold Coast Hospital, 86, 124
governance, 2, 10, 11, 14, 18, 19, 21, 24, 25, 33, 38, 41, 42, 46, 55, 56, 59, 67–69, 79, 95, 96, 106, 114, 117, 118, 132, 133, 145, 156, 214, 221, 223, 231; colonial governance, 2, 9, 10, 16, 18, 20, 22, 23, 28, 30, 33, 40, 41, 43, 44, 63, 66, 76, 77, 130, 132, 133, 137, 146, 164, 178, 186, 222; international governance, 12, 24, 224; regulation and governance, 223; urban governance, 2, 3, 10, 14, 16, 21, 25–29, 33, 35, 36, 44, 56, 67, 68, 114–116, 119, 123, 132, 136, 173, 178, 179, 186, 187, 189, 220–223, 232, 233
governor, 6, 11, 27, 34, 37–42, 44, 50, 57–61, 64, 76, 79, 82, 83, 94–96, 98, 103, 109, 113, 116, 134, 135, 139, 140, 143, 148, 154, 157, 158, 161, 164, 168, 172, 177–180, 191, 193, 196; Bryan, Major Herbert, 92, 93; Burns, Alan, 196; Clifford, Hugh, 48, 56, 76, 79, 98, 109; Guggisberg, Gordon, 42, 56, 59, 76, 110, 115, 116, 118, 119, 134, 156, 195; Hodgkin, Frederick Mitchell, 97; Hodson, Arnold, 177, 178, 191, 193–196; Maxwell, William Edward, 97; Nathan, Matthew, 94, 95, 97, 98, 106; Rodgers, John Pickersgill, 76; Thorburn, James Jamieson, 76

Horton, James Africanus, 13
hospital, 76, 80, 84–86, 88, 90, 96, 110, 219; Gold Coast Hospital, 124; Korle Bu Hospital, 49, 85, 124

INDEX

housing, 2, 3, 12, 19, 20, 23, 31, 96, 143, 144, 177, 178, 182, 184, 186–88, 191, 193, 196–200, 202, 203, 206, 209, 211, 212, 214, 217–219, 222, 223, 227; housing conditions, 95, 117, 187; housing development, 96, 195, 196–198, 200–201, 212, 227; housing estate, 196, 198, 199, 205–207; housing policy, 157; housing regulations, 156–178, 180, 185; housing scheme, 189, 206; housing shortages, 188, 207; rehousing, 177, 191, 195, 196, 197, 205, 206; temporary housing, 94, 188, 191
Hutton Mills, Thomas, 103
hygiene, 34, 35, 72, 78, 80, 89, 95, 102, 110, 111, 202

indirect rule, 6, 10, 20, 34–36, 38, 41, 65, 68, 82, 109, 165, 170
industry, 12, 123, 149, 154–156, 163, 169, 172, 209
informalization, 3, 12, 17, 18, 21–26, 28, 29, 114, 145, 146, 149, 223, 230, 231, 232, 233; informal city, 25, 232; informal economy, 22, 23, 114, 146, 147, 216, 232, 233; informal sector, 232; informal settlements, 23, 228
infrastructure, 2, 3, 12, 14, 15, 16, 19, 21, 23, 24, 27, 30, 35, 36, 41, 42, 44, 46, 47, 53, 56–58, 60, 61, 68, 79, 107, 109–111, 114, 115, 119, 124, 126, 133, 134, 145, 150, 157–160, 181, 190, 194, 195, 198, 199, 205, 207, 212, 215, 220–224, 229–231, 233; health infrastructure, 84, 88; public infrastructure, 47, 56, 57, 157; sanitation infrastructure, 33, 36, 43, 50, 51, 58, 66, 68, 90, 94, 134; technological infrastructure, 150; transportation infrastructure, 46, 151, 156, 157, 160, 162, 173, 175, 177, 194, 208, 215, 222, 230; urban infrastructure, 34, 42, 51, 61, 95, 156, 217, 221
inspector(s), 15, 38, 67, 83, 100, 183, 188; building inspector, 55, 130, 185, 186, 188; health inspector, 32, 49, 83, 84; malaria inspector, 30; mosquito inspector, 99, 100, 110; nuisance inspector, 38, 39, 80, 81, 103, 114; sanitary inspector, 38, 41, 48, 50, 51, 53, 55, 67, 84, 99, 100, 101, 107, 130

Jamestown (Nleshi), 4, 6, 63, 107, 113, 124–126, 158, 176, 187, 188, 190, 205, 210, 225, 226
Joint Provincial Council, 141
Jones-Nelson, T., 119, 143

Kaneshie, 125, 191, 207
Kitson Mills, J., 49, 50, 53–55, 61, 62, 100, 121, 125–128, 133, 160, 162, 183, 184, 188, 189
Korle Bu, 47, 49, 85, 108, 124, 191
Korle Gonno, 56, 61, 62, 93, 94, 96, 107, 125, 126, 157, 190, 191, 207

Labadi, 47, 60, 66, 126, 131, 133, 148, 156, 160, 171, 187, 207
lagoon, 49, 66, 76, 104, 107–109; Klottey Lagoon, 108; Korle(bu) Lagoon, 48, 49, 58, 97, 100, 104, 107, 108, 217
latrine, 32–34 39, 40, 49–53, 57, 58, 69, 71, 84, 134, 197
Legislative Council, 1, 6, 40, 68, 79, 103, 116, 117, 136, 144, 166, 200, 206
lorry, 49, 53, 65, 119, 129, 131, 137, 144, 154, 155, 163–168, 171–174, 210; lorry age, 153; lorry park, 112, 130, 131, 154, 158, 161, 163, 164, 171, 172, 209; mammy lorry, 163–166, 171–173; pirate passenger lorry, 25, 30, 148–150, 173–175. *See also* driver(s)
Lugard, Lord Frederick, 10, 20

malaria, 29, 30, 70, 72, 73, 75–79 82, 84, 94, 96, 97, 101, 104, 105, 106, 108; antimalaria campaign, 89, 106; Inter-Allied Malaria Control Group, 108. *See also* inspector(s)
Manson, Patrick, 77–79, 89, 96, 105
market(s), 15, 17, 30, 35, 37, 50, 53, 57, 88, 95, 112, 115, 121–132, 134, 139–141, 143, 154, 155, 158, 159, 161–165, 169, 171, 172, 174, 191, 194, 199, 203, 205, 209, 212, 217, 219, 229, 230, 233; Adabraka Market, 50; black market, 139–141; London Market, 63, 126, 127; Makola Market, 140, 158; market trading, 22, 23, 115, 147, 216, 229; market women, 36, 56, 116, 118, 130, 145, 163, 171, 174, 219; Salaga Market, 56, 116, 124, 158; Selwyn Market, 56, 116, 124, 127, 132, 142, 209
Martindale Commission Report, 139, 140
Maxwell, John, 115
miasma, 72, 87, 89, 107
mobility, 2, 9, 10, 12, 17, 59, 62, 90, 134, 149–152, 156, 165, 166, 168–170, 174, 227; African mobility, 30, 149, 151, 152; automobility, 154; autonomy and mobility, 152; banal mobility, 150; mobility politics, 150; mobility practices, 149, 150, 158, 164, 165, 169, 171, 172; urban mobility, 15, 150, 156, 165, 173, 174

model colony, 158, 164, 228
modernity, 7, 10, 12, 13, 14–21, 41, 58, 63, 67, 83, 107, 131, 145, 152, 158–161, 172, 174, 178, 179, 185–187, 198, 199, 203, 205, 208, 212, 215, 221, 222, 225, 231–233; colonial modernity, 174; laboratories of modernity, 14, 16, 221; modern capital, 67, 207; modern citizens, 208; modernism, 200–203, 207, 208, 224, 227; modernist, 2, 12, 18, 22, 24, 179, 196, 201, 202, 204, 208, 214, 215; modernization, 16, 24, 59, 65, 173, 204, 209, 211, 215, 216, 224, 228; ordered modernity, 14, 21, 35, 114, 130–132, 134, 145; technological modernity, 151; urban modernity, 12, 21, 158
mosquito, 32, 65, 67, 70, 71, 95–101, 103–108, 156, 182; anopheles mosquito, 70, 104, 106; Destruction of Mosquitoes Bill (1911), 99; mosquito brigade(s), 100, 106; mosquito larva(e), 50, 64, 84, 100, 105; mosquito problems, 99, 104, 107, 108; mosquito vector, 76, 79, 94, 96, 97, 105, 107. See also inspection
Motor Traffic Ordinance, (1934), 156, 163
Municipal Bus Service, 59, 148, 158, 161, 163, 164, 168, 169, 170, 172

Nanka Bruce, F.V., 102, 124, 125, 136
Nii Ayikai II, 206
Nii Ayitey Adjin III, 138
Nii Kwabena Bonne III, 140
Nkrumah, Kwame, 31, 136, 207–209, 213–216, 225
Noi Ababio (Osu Manche), 180
nuisance, 2, 21, 32, 37–39, 49, 54, 68, 80, 81, 88, 92, 100, 103, 105, 112–114, 118, 119, 121, 123, 129, 166, 173, 222, 223. See also inspector(s)

Odamtten, Solomon, 50, 119, 120, 128, 129
Old Fadama, 217, 218, 220
Omnibus Authority Act (1927), 169
order, 2, 3, 8, 10, 12–14, 18–21, 28, 34, 41, 48, 111, 129, 131, 144, 148–150, 152, 153, 158, 166, 173, 182, 194, 204–206, 222; colonial order, 2, 29, 150, 173; disorder, 13, 15, 18, 19, 21, 36, 95, 186; economic order, 145, 232; infrastructural order, 30; law and order, 7; political order, 12; social order, 10, 16, 202; spatial order, 2, 15, 22, 120, 123, 130, 145, 146, 187, 202, 231; urban order, 8
ordinance(s), 1, 10, 19, 20, 21, 25, 26, 29, 31, 37–39, 53, 99, 116, 118, 123, 185, 221, 223, 224; Municipal Corporations Ordinance (1923–1924), 56, 114–117, 125; Municipal Ordinance (1896), 44; Public Lands Ordinance (1876), 37, 38, 41, 180, 181, 183; Town and Country Planning Ordinance (1945), 200, 206; Town Councils Ordinance (1894), 1, 2, 15, 38, 40, 41, 57, 131, 179, 180, 182; Towns Amendment Ordinance (1901), 98; Towns Ordinance (1892), 37–39, 54; Towns Ordinance (1908), 99; Water Works Ordinance (1936), 47, 48

pirate(s), 21, 129, 149; piracy, 25, 26, 149, 168, 173. See also lorry: pirate passenger lorry
plague (bubonic), 52, 73, 75, 77, 83, 88–93, 95–97, 103–105, 109, 190; epidemic plague, 96, 107, 109; plague prevention/mitigation, 89, 94, 96; Treatise on Plague, 89
planning, 2, 3, 11, 13, 14, 18, 20, 24, 25, 31, 33, 35, 42, 46, 58, 67, 89, 125, 178, 180, 184, 188–190, 200, 202, 204–206, 209, 210, 212, 215, 216, 220, 222, 223, 226, 227, 232; colonial planning, 16, 215, 228; modernist planning, 179; spatial planning, 125, 133; technological planning, 150; town planning, 14, 15, 20, 31, 60, 84, 96, 105, 111, 123, 161, 178, 187, 193, 195–197, 200–202, 206, 207, 210, 215, 216, 222; urban planning, 10, 19, 20, 34, 36, 79, 84, 93, 96, 175, 187, 208, 209, 215, 216, 220, 221, 225, 230
police, 1, 2, 12, 15, 48, 69, 72, 85, 100, 131, 135, 141, 160, 165, 166, 168, 172, 176; policing, 12, 26, 30, 68, 69, 131, 132, 145, 185, 186, 223
progress, 12, 13, 14, 28, 65, 67, 75, 79, 144, 196, 208, 222–224
public health, 3, 10, 14, 20, 22, 24, 34, 36, 37, 39, 48, 49, 52, 54, 58, 60, 64, 67, 69, 71–80, 82–86, 88, 89, 93–97, 99–102, 104–107, 109–111, 114, 119, 123, 129, 130, 133, 156, 157, 178, 183, 185, 187–190, 220, 221
Public Works Department, 46, 57, 59, 60, 64, 65, 95, 157, 197

quarantine, 76, 90, 91, 93, 94, 102, 103
Quartey, Henry, 218–220

Quartey-Papafio, Dr. Benjamin William, 79, 85, 93

rate(s), 1, 3, 39, 40, 44, 45, 49, 56, 57, 59, 70, 72, 74, 75, 115, 117, 119, 131, 133, 138, 160, 161, 170, 178, 180, 182, 183; Accra Ratepayers Association, 183; ratepayers, 1, 11, 27, 28, 34, 36, 38, 53, 56, 64, 116, 132, 133, 160, 161, 170, 171, 179, 180, 183
regulation, 2, 3, 9, 12–17, 19, 21, 23–26, 28–30, 33, 35, 37, 41, 42, 47, 51, 54, 68, 71–73, 82, 88, 105, 107, 109, 111, 114, 119, 120, 123, 130–134, 136, 140, 146, 149–151, 153, 155, 156, 163, 166, 167, 169, 172, 178, 180, 182–188, 197, 204, 215; building regulations, 184, 185, 188, 189, 190, 215; colonial regulation, 21, 26, 73, 182, 195; housing regulation, 180, 185; politics of regulation, 24, 29, 36, 214; power of regulation, 2, 221; reform and regulation, 221; regulation and authority, 7; regulation and categorization, 21, 114, 205; rules and regulations, 2, 145; sanitary regulation, 29, 33, 34, 41, 51, 52, 54, 69, 75, 78, 119; spatial regulation, 25, 34; systems of regulation, 7, 12; technocratic regulation, 31
Reindorf, C.E., 60, 102, 157, 183, 184
ridge, 85, 97, 158, 189, 197, 228
road(s), 15, 34, 40, 50, 57, 58, 59, 61–66, 86, 95, 129, 131, 132, 148–161, 163, 165, 166, 168, 171–174, 177, 194, 197, 200, 201, 203, 205, 209, 210, 212, 221, 223, 225, 228, 229; dangers of the road, 164; road conditions, 61, 149, 151, 152, 156, 166; road construction, 59, 60, 61, 65, 66, 151, 154, 157, 158, 162, 166, 212; road drainage, 59, 60, 157, 215
Ross, Ronald, 70, 76, 79, 96, 97, 105–107

Sabon Zongo, 160, 187–190, 205, 207, 211
sanitation, 2, 12, 15, 19, 20, 23, 29, 30, 32–38, 40–42, 44, 48, 54, 56–59, 65, 69–73, 76, 80, 86, 91, 93, 94, 95, 97, 100, 108, 111, 119, 129, 130, 156, 173, 178, 182, 183, 186, 188, 199, 212, 221, 222; colonial sanitation, 34; politics of sanitation, 29, 32, 36, 58, 61, 67; Sanitary Committee, 93; sanitary inspector, 38, 41, 48, 50, 51, 53, 55, 67, 84, 99, 100, 101, 107, 130; sanitary policy, 35, 37, 49; sanitary reform, 33, 42, 186; sanitary regulation, 29, 33, 35, 38, 41, 51, 52, 54, 75, 78, 119; sanitation infrastructure, 33, 36, 51, 58, 66, 68, 71, 90, 94, 134, 208, 209; sanitation syndrome, 80; tropical sanitation, 105; unsanitary, 21, 50, 69, 89, 95, 101, 183; urban sanitation, 29, 34, 36, 51, 62, 68, 96, 123, 134
Sarbah, John Mensah, 91
Sawyerr Akilagpa, 53, 60, 66, 88, 100, 101, 136, 157
segregation, 15, 32, 76, 94, 96, 98, 101, 103, 104, 105, 111; colonial segregation, 228; infrastructural segregation, 68; racial segregation, 76, 110; residential segregation, 30, 72, 73, 95, 97, 98, 187, 230; spatial segregation, 15
Selwyn-Clarke, P. S., 83, 107, 108, 111
sewer, 48, 134; sewage/sewerage, 34, 36, 49, 53, 58; sewage/sewerage system, 48, 49, 50, 56, 57, 58, 212
Simpson, William John Ritchie, 29, 30, 89–96, 102, 109, 189, 190
slum(s), 22, 146, 178, 186, 187, 189, 194, 198, 205, 206, 228, 229; slum clearance, 96, 111, 143, 177, 187, 189, 191, 196, 205, 212; slum deceits, 22
social work, 3, 14, 187, 220
space, 2, 11–13, 19, 22, 28, 29, 35, 37, 38, 43, 46, 58, 84, 93, 100, 119, 123, 124, 127, 129, 131–134, 145, 146, 150, 152, 158, 159, 165, 173, 177, 183, 204, 210, 213, 220, 221, 222, 224, 227, 231, 233; built space, 2, 9, 14, 185, 208; colonial space, 9, 12; commodification of space, 124, 131, 146, 159, 181; organization of space, 73; private space, 36, 38, 47, 59, 69, 81, 82, 99, 107, 182, 186; public space, 36, 38, 50, 99, 107, 129–134, 159, 227; sacred space, 109; urban space, 14, 15, 19, 29, 94, 96, 110, 111, 148, 151, 165, 168, 169, 170, 173, 182, 221, 223, 231
Stanley, Henry Morton, 13

Tackie Yaoboi, 116
technocrat(s), 3, 16, 21, 28, 73, 76, 83, 107, 111, 123, 156, 161, 202, 204, 207, 220, 221, 223, 225; technocratic, 2, 3, 10–12, 14, 16, 18–21, 24, 28, 29, 31, 59, 79, 82, 83, 88, 114, 119, 178, 187, 191, 220–224; technocratic colonialism, 12, 14, 15, 18, 23, 25, 28

technology, 3, 13, 14, 16–19, 25, 42, 59, 115, 150–152, 154, 174, 175, 215, 217, 221–223; colonial technology, 17, 58, 151, 154, 175, 220; imported technology, 17, 18, 27; indigenous technology, 17, 18, 104, 174, 223; infrastructural technology, 12, 150, 221, 233; modern technology, 18, 151, 174, 203, 216, 222, 231; science and technology, 13, 14, 23; technological, 3, 14, 16, 17, 20, 118, 150, 164, 169, 174, 220, 227; technological expertise, 155; technological failure, 16; technological future, 10; technological solutions, 15, 34; technology-in-use, 150; transport technology, 150, 151, 152, 154, 158
technopolitics, 17, 26, 28, 150; African technopolitics, 17; colonial technopolitics, 19, 28, 36; technopolitical contestation, 18, 149
Ten-Year Plan, 119, 134
Teshie, 4, 47, 155, 158
therapeutic pluralism, 74, 83, 109
Thompson, Kojo, 52, 53, 55, 60, 123, 127, 133, 157, 161, 184, 185, 189
Town and Country Planning Board, 196, 200
trade, 2, 4–8, 11, 17, 20, 29, 30, 38, 59, 73, 90, 91, 95, 104, 112–114, 116, 117, 127, 132, 136–141, 143, 144, 152, 163, 170, 171, 179, 188, 190, 199, 223; cocoa trade, 116; free trade, 139; global trade, 14, 134; legitimate trade, 8, 181; slave trade, 8, 188; trade regulations, 156; trade roads, 65; traders, 4–8, 14, 17, 27, 30, 38, 41, 70–72, 74, 80, 84, 115, 118, 124, 125, 127, 131, 132, 135, 138–140, 158, 164, 165, 169, 171, 172, 210, 212, 215, 219, 233; trade unions, 155; urban trade, 36, 165
Trevallion-Hood Plan, 208, 210, 214, 216
tropical medicine, 20, 29, 34, 70, 77–80, 84, 89, 102, 105, 106, 202; Liverpool School of Tropical Medicine, 70, 77, 78, 84, 102; London School of Tropical Medicine, 77, 79, 89
trotro, 216, 233. *See also* lorry

United Africa Company (UAC), 115, 127, 138, 141, 142, 162. *See also* trade
United Gold Coast Convention (UGCC), 135–137, 142, 143
United Trading Company (UTC), 115, 138. *See also* trade

urban, 9, 10, 17–19, 21, 22, 25, 31, 34, 36, 43, 48, 50, 56, 58, 91, 130, 143, 148, 151, 152, 154, 165, 166, 186, 202, 222, 231; urban culture, 8, 12, 20, 207; urban future, 9, 225, 232; urban growth, 8; urban imaginary, 11, 12, 19, 37, 227; urbanism, 12, 175, 222, 227, 228, 230–232; urbanity, 8, 12, 15, 19, 24, 26, 169, 171; urbanization, 8, 58, 156, 157, 165, 166, 179, 181, 187, 195–197, 207, 213, 231; urban life, 2, 3, 9, 10, 15, 17, 19, 21, 30, 31, 36, 43, 58, 76, 96, 97, 111, 114, 149, 150, 158, 175, 194, 205, 221, 227; urban milieu, 7; urban modernity, 12, 21, 208; urban order, 8; urban planning, 10, 15, 19, 20, 34, 36, 79, 84, 93, 96, 149, 168, 171, 174, 175, 187, 208–210, 215, 220, 221, 225, 227, 228, 230; urban politics, 11, 12, 18, 24, 119, 123, 213, 216, 221, 223, 225, 227, 228, 230, 233; urban poor, 22, 76, 78, 146, 187, 229, 233; urban residents, 11, 12, 15, 18, 19, 21, 28, 38, 40, 41, 44, 50, 54, 71–73, 81, 97, 119, 125, 129, 133, 145, 146, 149–151, 156, 164, 165, 168, 171, 173, 174, 186, 210, 222, 227–230, 232, 233; urban settlement, 2, 8, 19, 36, 222. *See also* space, development, transport, infrastructure, technology
Ussher Town (Kinka), 4, 6, 93, 95, 107, 116, 124, 143, 158, 187, 188, 190, 199, 203, 205, 207, 210, 225

vaccination, 80, 93, 94, 103, 104
Victoriaborg, 94, 97, 189, 197

waste, 43, 47–50, 53, 58, 59, 66, 104, 183, 191, 193, 218, 219; e-waste, 217, 218
water, 17, 20, 30, 34, 36–39, 43–48, 50, 57, 58, 69–71, 81, 91, 97, 99–101, 107, 108, 161, 177, 194, 199, 200, 212, 217, 219, 229; Accra Water Supply, 46; water drainage, 61, 63–66; water rates, 56; water shortage, 43, 46; water works, 40, 43, 46–48, 57, 58, 191
Watson Commission, 134, 135, 144
Webb, Sidney (Lord Passfield), 14, 108, 222
Weija, 190
white man's grave, 72, 74, 96
Wulomei, 7, 116

yellow fever, 73, 75, 77, 83, 96, 97, 101–104; Yellow Fever Commission, 102

JENNIFER HART is Professor of History at Virginia Tech. She is the author of *Ghana on the Go: African Mobility in the Age of Motor Transportation* (Indiana University Press, 2016) and project director for *Accra Wala* (www.accrawala.com).

For Indiana University Press

Brian Carroll, Rights Manager
Gary Dunham, Acquisitions Editor and Director
Anna Francis, Assistant Acquisitions Editor
Anna Garnai, Editorial Assistant
Emma Getz, Editorial Assistant
Brenna Hosman, Production Coordinator
Katie Huggins, Production Manager
Darja Malcolm-Clarke, Project Manager/Editor
Bethany Mowry, Acquisitions Editor
Dan Pyle, Online Publishing Manager
Stephen Williams, Marketing and Publicity Manager
Jennifer Witzke, Senior Artist and Book Designer

www.ingramcontent.com/pod-product-compliance
Lightning Source LLC
Chambersburg PA
CBHW021346300426
44114CB00012B/1100